Rethinking Gandhi and Nonviolent Relationality

This book presents a rethinking of the world legacy of Mahatma Gandhi in this era of global violence. Through interdisciplinary research, key Gandhian concepts are revisited by tracing their genealogies in multiple histories of world contact and by foregrounding their relevance to contemporary struggles to regain the 'humane' in the midst of global conflict.

The relevance of Gandhian notions of *ahimsa* and *satyagraha* is assessed in the context of contemporary events, when religious fundamentalisms of various kinds are competing with the arrogance and unilateralism of imperial capital to reduce the world to a state of international lawlessness. Covering a wide and comprehensive range of topics such as Gandhi's vegetarianism and medical practice, the book analyzes his successes and failures as a litigator in South Africa, his experiments with communal living and his concepts of non-violence and *satyagraha*.

The book combines historical, philosophical and textual readings of different aspects of the leader's life and works. It will be of interest to students and academics interested in peace and conflict studies, South Asian history, world history, postcolonial studies and studies on Gandhi.

Debjani Ganguly is Head of the Humanities Research Centre in the Research School of Humanities at the Australian National University. Author of *Caste, Colonialism and Countermodernity: Notes on a Postcolonial Hermeneutics of Caste* (also published by Routledge), she also co-edited *Edward Said: The Legacy of a Public Intellectual*.

John Docker is Adjunct Senior Fellow in the Humanities Research Centre, Australian National University. Recent publications include *Postmodernism and Popular Culture: A Cultural History*; *1492: The Poetics of Diaspora* and, with Ann Curthoys, *Is History Fiction?*

Routledge Studies in the Modern History of Asia

1 **The Police in Occupation Japan**
   Control, corruption and resistance to reform
   Christopher Aldous

2 **Chinese Workers**
   A new history
   Jackie Sheehan

3 **The Aftermath of Partition in South Asia**
   Tai Yong Tan and Gyanesh Kudaisya

4 **The Australia–Japan Political Alignment**
   1952 to the present
   Alan Rix

5 **Japan and Singapore in the World Economy**
   Japan's economic advance into Singapore, 1870–1965
   Shimizu Hiroshi and Hirakawa Hitoshi

6 **The Triads as Business**
   Yiu Kong Chu

7 **Contemporary Taiwanese Cultural Nationalism**
   A-chin Hsiau

8 **Religion and Nationalism in India**
   The case of the Punjab
   Harnik Deol

9 **Japanese Industrialisation**
   Historical and cultural perspectives
   Ian Inkster

10 **War and Nationalism in China 1925–45**
   Hans J. van de Ven

11 **Hong Kong in Transition**
   One country, two systems
   Edited by Robert Ash, Peter Ferdinand, Brian Hook and Robin Porter

12 **Japan's Postwar Economic Recovery and Anglo-Japanese Relations, 1948–62**
   Noriko Yokoi

13 **Japanese Army Stragglers and Memories of the War in Japan, 1950–75**
   Beatrice Trefalt

14 **Ending the Vietnam War**
   The Vietnamese Communists' perspective
   Ang Cheng Guan

15 **The Development of the Japanese Nursing Profession**
Adopting and adapting Western influences
Aya Takahashi

16 **Women's Suffrage in Asia**
Gender nationalism and democracy
Louise Edwards and Mina Roces

17 **The Anglo-Japanese Alliance, 1902–22**
Phillips Payson O'Brien

18 **The United States and Cambodia, 1870–1969**
From curiosity to confrontation
Kenton Clymer

19 **Capitalist Restructuring and the Pacific Rim**
Ravi Arvind Palat

20 **The United States and Cambodia, 1969–2000**
A troubled relationship
Kenton Clymer

21 **British Business in Post-Colonial Malaysia, 1957–70**
'Neo-colonialism' or 'Disengagement'?
Nicholas J. White

22 **The Rise and Decline of Thai Absolutism**
Kullada Kesboonchoo Mead

23 **Russian Views of Japan, 1792–1913**
An anthology of travel writing
David N. Wells

24 **The Internment of Western Civilians under the Japanese, 1941–45**
A patchwork of internment
Bernice Archer

25 **The British Empire and Tibet 1900–1922**
Wendy Palace

26 **Nationalism in Southeast Asia**
If the people are with us
Nicholas Tarling

27 **Women, Work and the Japanese Economic Miracle**
The case of the cotton textile industry, 1945–75
Helen Macnaughtan

28 **A Colonial Economy in Crisis**
Burma's rice cultivators and the world depression of the 1930s
Ian Brown

29 **A Vietnamese Royal Exile in Japan**
Prince Cuong De (1882–1951)
Tran My-Van

30 **Corruption and Good Governance in Asia**
Nicholas Tarling

31 **US–China Cold War Collaboration, 1971–89**
S. Mahmud Ali

32 **Rural Economic Development in Japan**
From the nineteenth century to the Pacific War
Penelope Francks

33 **Colonial Armies in Southeast Asia**
Edited by Karl Hack and Tobias Rettig

34 **Intra Asian Trade and the World Market**
A.J.H. Latham and Heita Kawakatsu

35 **Japanese–German Relations, 1895–1945**
War, diplomacy and public opinion
Edited by Christian W. Spang and Rolf-Harald Wippich

36 **Britain's Imperial Cornerstone in China**
The Chinese maritime customs service, 1854–1949
Donna Brunero

37 **Colonial Cambodia's 'Bad Frenchmen'**
The rise of French rule and the life of Thomas Caraman, 1840–87
Gregor Muller

38 **Japanese–American Civilian Prisoner Exchanges and Detention Camps, 1941–45**
Bruce Elleman

39 **Regionalism in Southeast Asia**
Nicholas Tarling

40 **Changing Visions of East Asia, 1943–93**
Transformations and continuities
R.B. Smith (Edited by Chad J. Mitcham)

41 **Christian Heretics in Late Imperial China**
Christian inculturation and state control, 1720–1850
Lars P. Laamann

42 **Beijing – A Concise History**
Stephen G. Haw

43 **The Impact of the Russo-Japanese War**
Edited by Rotem Kowner

44 **Business–Government Relations in Prewar Japan**
Peter von Staden

45 **India's Princely States**
People, princes and colonialism
Edited by Waltraud Ernst and Biswamoy Pati

46 **Rethinking Gandhi and Nonviolent Relationality**
Global perspectives
Edited by Debjani Ganguly and John Docker

Rethinking Gandhi and Nonviolent Relationality
Global perspectives

Edited by Debjani Ganguly
and John Docker

LONDON AND NEW YORK

First published 2007
by Routledge
2 Park Square, Milton Park, Abingdon, Oxfordshire OX14 4RN

Simultaneously published in the USA and Canada
by Routledge
711 Third Avenue, New York, NY 10017

First issued in paperback 2014

*Routledge is an imprint of the Taylor and Francis Group,
an informa business*

© 2007 Debjani Ganguly and John Docker, for selection and editorial
matter; individual contributors, their contribution

Typeset in Times New Roman by
Taylor & Francis Books

All rights reserved. No part of this book may be reprinted or reproduced
or utilised in any form or by any electronic, mechanical, or other means,
now known or hereafter invented, including photocopying and recording,
or in any information storage or retrieval system, without permission in
writing from the publishers.

British Library Cataloguing in Publication Data
A catalogue record for this book is available from the British Library

Library of Congress Cataloging in Publication Data
Rethinking Gandhi and nonviolent relationality : global perspectives /
edited by Debjani Ganguly and John Docker.
  p. cm. – (Routledge studies in the modern history of Asia ; 46)
  Based on presentations at a symposium on Gandhi held in late 2004 on
the premises of the Humanities Research Centre at the Australian
National University.
  Includes bibliographical references and index.
  1. Gandhi, Mahatma, 1869-1948–Teachings–Congresses. 2. Gandhi,
Mahatma, 1869-1948–Influence–Congresses. 3. Nonviolence–Congresses.
4. Civil disobedience–Congresses. I. Australian National University.
Humanities Research Centre.
    DS481.G3R39 2007
    303.6'1–dc22
                    2007018153

ISBN 978-0-415-43740-0 (hbk)
ISBN 978-1-138-01134-2 (pbk)
ISBN 978-0-203-93355-8 (ebk)

Contents

Notes on contributors ix
Acknowledgements xii

1 Global state of war and moral vernaculars of nonviolence: rethinking Gandhi in a new world order 1
DEBJANI GANGULY

Part I
Worlding the Gandhian everyday 15

2 *Ahimsa* and other animals: the genealogy of an immature politics 17
LEELA GANDHI

3 The quack whom we know: illness and nursing in Gandhi 38
SANDHYA SHETTY

4 Emptied of all but love: Gandhi's first public fast 66
TRIDIP SUHRUD

Part II
Of friendship, law and language: shaping Gandhian 'weakness' 81

5 Gandhi moves: intentional communities and friendship 83
THOMAS WEBER

6 Gandhi: the transformation of a South African lawyer, 1897–1898 100
CHARLES R. DISALVO

7 Only one word, properly altered: Gandhi and the question of the *veshya* 115
AJAY SKARIA

Part III
Carrying Gandhi over: global peace movements   139

8   Globalising Gandhi: translation, reinvention, application, transformation   141
SEAN SCALMER

9   Gandhiji in Burma, and Burma in Gandhiji   163
PENNY EDWARDS

10   Nonviolence and long hot summers: black women's welfare-rights struggles in 1960s' Baltimore   183
RHONDA Y. WILLIAMS

Part IV
Interlocuting with modernity: Gandhi at home and in the world   203

11   Josephus: traitor or Gandhian *avant la lettre*?   205
JOHN DOCKER

12   Homespun wisdom: Gandhi, technology and nationalism   223
ANJALI ROY

13   Vernacular cosmopolitanism: world historical readings of Gandhi and Ambedkar   245
DEBJANI GANGULY

Index   265

Contributors

Charles R. DiSalvo is Woodrow A. Potesta Professor of Law, College of Law, West Virginia University, Morgantown, West Virginia. He has published widely in the areas of nonviolence and law and is currently completing a manuscript called *Gandhi: The Transformation of a Lawyer in South Africa*.

John Docker is Adjunct Senior Research Fellow in the Humanities Research Centre, Australian National University. Since the publication of *1492: The Poetics of Diaspora* (Continuum, 2001), he has researched and written on monotheism and polytheism, and most recently, on genocide in relation to the Enlightenment and to colonialism. He has recently published *Is History Fiction?* (University of New South Wales Press, Sydney, and University of Michigan Press, Ann Arbor, 2005), a book he co-authored with historian Ann Curthoys.

Penny Edwards is Assistant Professor in South-East Asian History at University of California, Berkeley. Her current interests are trans-colonial and intra-Asian traffic in cultural and religious beliefs and ideas in/between colonial Cambodia and Burma. Her book *Cambodge: The Cultivation of a Nation, 1860–1945* is forthcoming with Hawai'i University Press, and she has also edited two volumes on Chinese diaspora in Southeast Asia and Australia. She is currently gathering materials for a biography of Suzanne Karpelès (1890–1968), a French Orientalist of Jewish descent who was instrumental in establishing the Buddhist Institute and other indigenous intellectual forums in colonial Cambodia before being ousted from Vichy Indochina and joining the Sri Aurobindo Ashram in Pondichèrry.

Leela Gandhi is Professor of English at the University of Chicago. Her publications include *Affective Communities: Anti-colonial Thought, Fin-de-siecle Radicalism, and the Politics of Friendship* (Duke University Press, 2006), *Postcolonial Theory: A Critical Introduction* (Allen & Unwin, 1998), *Measures of Home* (2000) and *England through Colonial Eyes* (Palgrave Macmillan, 2002). She is co-editor of the journal *Postcolonial*

Studies. She is also the great granddaughter of the Mahatma. Her grandfather, Devdas Gandhi, was the Mahatma's youngest son.

Debjani Ganguly is head of the Humanities Research Centre in the Research School of Humanities at the Australian National University. A literary and cultural historian by training, she has published in the areas of postcolonial studies, global Anglophone writing, theories of world literature, caste and dalit studies, cultural histories of mixed race, Gandhi and non-violence, and Indian literary criticism. Her recent publications are *Caste, Colonialism and Countermodernity: Notes on a Postcolonial Hermeneutics of Caste* (Routledge, 2005) and (as co-editor) *Edward Said: The Legacy of a Public Intellectual* (Melbourne University Press, 2007).

Anjali Roy is Professor of English in the Department of Humanities and Social Sciences, Indian Institute of Technology Kharagpur, India. She has published two books, *Three Great African Novelists: Achebe, Soyinka, Tutuola* (2001) and *Wole Soyinka: An Anthology of Recent Criticism* (2006) and several articles on postcolonial literatures, cultures and theory in reputed journals. She is currently finishing a book on the revival of the Punjabi performance tradition of bhangra in the global era, which will be published by Ashgate.

Sean Scalmer is Senior Lecturer in the Department of History at the University of Melbourne. He is the author of *Dissent Events: Protest, the Media and the Political Gimmick in Australia* (University of New South Wales Press, 2002). In 2006 he also had published a co-authored book, *Activism Wisdom: Practical Knowledge and Creative Tension in Social Movements* (Sydney: University of New South Wales Press), and an edited collection, *What If? Counterfactual Essays in Australian History* (Carlton: Melbourne University Publishing). He is currently writing a book on the global circulation of Gandhian non-violence.

Sandhya Shetty, an Associate Professor of English at New Hampshire, USA, received her BA from Nowrosjee Wadia College in Poona, India, MAs from the University of Poona and the University of Rochester, and her PhD from the University of Rochester. Her research and teaching interests are in colonial discourse, postcolonial cultural studies and theory, and the Victorian novel. She has published in such journals as *Genders, differences, LIT, Journal of Commonwealth Literature, Journal of Modern Literature* and *Diacritics*. Her most recent work is a book in progress on medicine and imperialism in late colonial India.

Ajay Skaria is an Associate Professor in Global Studies and History at the University of Minnesota. His earlier work has been on forest communities of western India. He is the author of *Hybrid Histories: Forests, Frontiers and Wildness in Western India* (Oxford University Press, 1999) and is currently working on some intellectual and political questions raised by Gandhi's work.

Tridip Suhrud teaches at the DAIICT, Gandhinagar and Gujarat Vidyapith Ahmedabad. He has translated and edited *Harilal Gandhi: A Life* (Orient Longman, 2006) and is the author of *Writing Life: Three Nineteenth Century Gujarati Thinkers*. His translation of Narayan Desai's four-part biography of Gandhi will be published as *My Life Is My Message* by Orient Longman. He edits *Gandhi Studies*, a new academic series with Ashis Nandy and Thomas Weber.

Thomas Weber is Reader in Politics and Head of Peace Studies, La Trobe University, Melbourne. He has spent considerable time in India at Gandhi's ashrams and has written extensively on Gandhi, Gandhian philosophy and the post-Gandhi Gandhian movements. His Gandhi-related books include: *Hugging the Trees: The Story of the Chipko Movement* (Penguin, 1989), *Conflict Resolution and Gandhian Ethics* (Gandhi Peace Foundation, 1991), *Gandhi's Peace Army: The Shanti Sena and Unarmed Peacekeeping* (Syracuse University Press, 1996), *On the Salt March: The Historiography of Gandhi's March to Dandi* (HarperCollins, 1997), *Gandhi as Disciple and Mentor* (Cambridge University Press, 2004) and *Gandhi, Gandhism and the Gandhians* (Roli, 2006).

Rhonda Y. Williams is an Associate Professor in the History Department, Case Western Reserve University. She received her PhD at University of Pennsylvania, Philadelphia, in May 1998. While a graduate student there, she received many honours including a Malcolm X Outstanding Service to the African American Community Award and the Paul Robson award for academic excellence and leadership. In 1993, she was co-organizer of the Welcome Nelson Mandela Committee at the rally 'The Continuing Struggle for Peace and Freedom', featuring Nelson Mandela, at the Philadelphia Civic Center, Philadelphia, PA. She also received a post-doctoral research fellowship from the American Association of University Women. She has published *The Politics of Public Housing: Black Women's Struggle Against Urban Inequality* (Oxford University Press, 2004).

Acknowledgements

We wish to thank the Humanities Research Centre at the Australian National University for hosting a conference on 'Gandhi, Nonviolence and Modernity' in September 2004. The conference was convened by us in September 2004 at the invitation of Dr Caroline Turner, Deputy Director of HRC. Many of the chapters in the book draw on papers presented at the conference. We also wish to acknowledge the support of Australia–India Council which funded scholars from India to participate in the conference. The Centre for Cross Cultural Research, ANU, also deserves our thanks for its support of the conference and this volume.

Our contributors have worked patiently and diligently on the chapters over these years and we wish to express our gratitude for their ready cooperation and support through the project. We would also like to thank our editor, Dorothea Schaefter, and the two anonymous readers of the manuscript for their perceptive comments and suggestions.

Finally we wish to acknowledge our many interlocutors over the years who have shown such interest in our engagement with nonviolent relationality and Gandhi in our global era. They are too many to be named here, but we do wish to especially thank Leela Gandhi, Tridip Suhrud, Anthony Burke, Frances Peters-Little, Dipesh Chakrabarty, Thomas Weber, Robin Jeffrey, McComas Taylor, John Maynard, Larissa Behrendt, Makarand Paranjape, Satendra Nandan, Brian Martin, Rhonda Williams, Ann Curthoys and Ned Curthoys

Debjani Ganguly and John Docker
The Australian National University, Canberra
30 March 2007

1 Global state of war and moral vernaculars of nonviolence
Rethinking Gandhi in a new world order

Debjani Ganguly

1

Every year 21 September is commemorated across the globe as the International Day of Peace. Ten days later, on 2 October, India ritually marks the day on which one of the greatest advocates of peace and non-violence in the modern world was born. He was Mohandas Karamchand Gandhi. Given the state of the world today, however, one can be forgiven for thinking that these commemorative days are both symbolically and substantively empty. As the renowned historian Eric Hobsbawm wrote in his magisterial account of the short twentieth century, *The Age of Extremes*, 'The years after 1989 saw more military operations in more parts of Europe, Asia and Africa than anyone could remember'.[1] The last decade and a half has witnessed civil wars in the former Yugoslavia, genocide in Rwanda, resurgence of Hindu fundamentalism in India, rise of the Taliban and Al Qaeda in Central and West Asia, globalization of Islamic fundamentalism, the carnage of September 11, aggressive US-led neoliberal military occupation in Iraq and a West-led global War on Terror that appears interminable at least from the vantage point of the present. If anything has been democratized at all across the globe, it is the culture of death.

What traction do peace and Gandhi have in these violent times when religious fundamentalisms of various kinds are competing with the arrogance and unilateralism of imperial capital to reduce the world to a state of international lawlessness? In what possible registers can Gandhian moral vernaculars – *ahimsa, satyagraha, sarvodaya* – address the ravages of our contemporary world? How do instances from Gandhi's life inspire one to deal with what Judith Butler very evocatively calls 'the dry grief of endless political rage' that characterizes our times?[2] Do the distinctions that Gandhi posited between 'legitimate actions' and 'law' in challenging colonial sovereignty become dangerous when deployed to read the violent insurgencies against the global imperial order, some of which have been given the name of 'terrorism'? Or do they once again bring home to us the violent dissonance between the tenets of international law and principles of human equity?

Such questions and many others constitute the imperative behind producing this book. Conceived, debated and written in the shadow of the US Occupation of Iraq in 2003, this book has its genesis in a symposium on Gandhi held in late 2004 on the premises of Australia's foremost custodian of humanist values, the Humanities Research Centre at the Australian National University (ANU) Also the home of the radical project on Indian history *Subaltern Studies* from 1981 to 1995, ANU has a history of active intellectual and ethical engagement with human rights and democracy across the world. In rethinking Gandhi's relevance for our fraught times, the symposium chose to approach Gandhi not purely as a 'Indian' figure, as if he belonged in modernity to only one history, but as a activist-thinker with an eager cosmopolitan interest in diverse world histories. This exercise in claiming Gandhi as a citizen of the world resulted in a series of imaginative and thought-provoking presentations that explored eccentric and idiosyncratic aspects of Gandhi, that glanced off Gandhi to speculate about other figures and histories and that traced the resonance of Gandhian ideas and *praxis* with concerns and dangers of the present. This volume builds on the work of the ANU Gandhi symposium and attempts to rethink his legacy in the new war-torn millennium.

In Sydney a few months ago, an American peace activist, Scott Parkin, was arrested by ASIO (Australian Security and Intelligence Organisation) and deported to the US for being a 'threat to national security'.[3] His crime: participating along with other anti-globalisation demonstrators in a *peaceful* protest against the Forbes Global CEO Conference outside the Sydney Opera House. Parkin also helped stage a street play called 'The Coalition of the Billing' outside the Sydney headquarters of Halliburton of Dick Cheney fame and one of the largest US contractors in Iraq today. In Houston, his hometown, Parkin had been at the forefront of a community awareness group that protested against oil companies profiting and profiteering from war. The protests were always peaceful and generally involved staging street plays lampooning mascots or key corporate figures of the oil industry. Before his arrival in Sydney, this activist who counts Mahatma Gandhi and Martin Luther King among his sources of inspiration, spent days travelling around Australia conducting workshops on nonviolent activism. Apart from irritating American authorities with his criticisms of the Iraq War, and being briefly arrested for civil disobedience in 2003 – actions which any healthy democracy ought to be able to accommodate – Scott Parkin has had no record of violence against the American nation-state. Yet, when he was arrested in Sydney and taken to a nearby police station, he was asked to make a case for why he was *not* a threat to *Australian* national security. His response was 'I am a nonviolent person, a peace activist, I organize peace events, I do talks'. The Australian law-enforcement agencies nevertheless cancelled his visa and he was asked to leave Australia immediately.

The fact that even so-called 'benign' democracies such as Australia treat peace activists as threats to national security is a sign of the violent and morally skewed times we live in. The speculation that Australian law-enforcing agencies may have taken this action against Parkin at the behest of the Bush administration makes it even worse. Taken together these developments conjure up a scenario of global politics where, on the one hand, power is concentrated in the hands of a few hyper-masculine bullies and, on the other, all modalities of protest – which actually range the spectrum from peaceful to the utterly carnage-ridden – are invariably tarred with the brush of 'terrorism'.

It is at such junctures that we need to insert once again voices such as Gandhi's to stem the shrill and raucous 'good vs evil' or 'us vs them' rhetoric of the dominant political players of the global order. We need to retrieve for the amnesiac violent global players the Gandhian insistence on the inviolability of soul-force in each and every one of us, the force that conserves the world against all attempts to annihilate it. We need to remind the world that Gandhi's idiosyncratic, almost Chaplinesque political style that evoked humour, encouraged dialogue, and remained fundamentally humane in face of the most formidable colonial/imperial machinery, provides an alternative language of political engagement. It is the language of nonviolent relationality in the public domain, of a moral internationalism based on the notion of compassion for and connectivity with strangers, the language of soul-force based on truth and love. As Gandhi reminded us in the early years of the twentieth century in his classic political tract *Hind Swaraj*, the resilience of this world owes more to human care than we are willing to admit:

> The fact that there are so many men still alive in the world shows that it is based not on the force of arms but on the force of truth or love. Therefore, the greatest and most unimpeachable evidence of the success of this force is to be found in the fact that, in spite of the wars of the world, it still lives on.[4]

More than twenty years ago, India's renowned social scientist, Ashis Nandy, wrote that Gandhi's transcultural androgynous protest against the excessive aggression of British colonialism held in trust a peculiar form of ethically potent 'weakness' to which 'a violent, culturally barren and politically bankrupt world may some day have to return'.[5] That 'some day' is our *here-and-now*. European colonialism may have been defeated, but new modalities of enslavement that speak the language of religion, money and arms continue to be invented. They are modalities in which more and more people around the world are complicit than ever before.

The present volume undertakes to name and investigate this very particular form of Gandhian 'weakness' that Nandy talks of. It is not the weakness of passivity or piety. Rather it constitutes a transcultural nonviolent ethics of the everyday that is eminently translatable across a range of political sites. It is an ethics of relationality across strangeness and difference as against an orientation that valorizes propinquity and sameness to mark human sociality. That is why the book argues and makes a case for a global cosmopolitan instead of an exclusively indigenous traditional base for the very foundations of Gandhi's *ahimsa* and *satyagraha*. Such a theoretical position marks Gandhi as a hybrid cosmopolitan figure who transformed Third World anti-colonial nationalist politics in the twentieth century in ways that neither indigenous nor westernized Indian nationalists could. To that extent, the book's historicizing of Gandhi's thought, practice and legacy is novel. It does not prioritise the narrative of Indian nation making or the narrative of the Indian diaspora in situating Gandhi. Each is seen as embedded in the other and both are read as being oriented towards the world. It is also because of the permeability and translatability of specifically Gandhian modalities of 'weakness' that this book makes no attempt to either deify Gandhi or hail him as an apostle of nonviolence who now irrevocably transcends the messiness of our complex humanity. Rather it explores precisely the sheer worldliness and embodied nature of Gandhi's valiant 'weakness' and the modes of its global dissemination.

II

It is no coincidence that the next three chapters of the book give us vignettes of Gandhi's anti-imperial, nonviolent energy refined and filtered through acts of relational embodiment – his experience of vegetarianism, his quirky experiments with alternative medicine and his renowned fasts. These constitute the first part of the book, entitled 'Worlding the Gandhian everyday: food, medicine and fasts'. Leela Gandhi's chapter, '*Ahimsa* and Other Animals: the Genealogy of an Immature Politics', with which this part begins, traces a complex etymology of Gandhian *ahimsa*. She argues that Gandhi's anti-imperial politics and polemic have transnational sources in his active involvement with *fin de siècle* vegetarianism which itself constituted part of late-Victorian animal-welfare movements. In order to do so, she revisits Gandhi's young adult days in England where he first encountered Henry Salt's book *Plea for Vegetarianism*. This encounter was life changing for Gandhi for it opened up for him a world of hospitality and friendship via animal-welfare activists whose anti-colonialism directly emerged from what Leela Gandhi calls their 'zoophilia'. She cites a public letter Gandhi wrote in 1894 in which he expressed his solidarity with the English vegetarians on the grounds that 'the vegetarian movement' would 'aid India politically ... inasmuch as the English vegetarians ... readily sympathise[d] with the Indian aspirations'. The author carefully extricates three strands from the intellectual-activist repertoire of late-Victorian animal welfarism that discursively wove themselves into the elementary grammar of Gandhian *ahimsa*. They included, a radical cosmopolitanism most often manifested in a 'culinary' form, a critique of imperial masculinity based on meat-eating or kreophagy and, finally, a resistance to modern forms of governmentality that erect all kinds of barriers to multiple forms of relationality – both human and animal. These strands were themselves in turn inflected by the utilitarianism of Bentham and Mill (whose anthropocentric condescension and embargo on sentiment they rejected), by Darwinian evolutionism that asserted the connectedness of all sentient life, and by socialist and anarchist energies of various stripes. In tracing such a complex genealogy of *ahimsa*, Leela Gandhi's chapter sets the tone for the rest of the book which attempts to re-world Gandhi by situating him along multiple matrices across the globe.

The chapter that follows this one, Sandhya Shetty's 'The Quack Whom We Know: Illness and Nursing in Gandhi', identifies Gandhian dietetics, especially his philosophical and political adherence to vegetarianism, as the key framework within which Gandhian 'quackery' in relation to the issue of medicine becomes intelligible. Gandhi's views on medicine were, in fact, unambiguously set against the grain of all received positions: nationalist or colonialist, *shastric* or Western, professional or lay. The basic premises of medicine articulated in terms of the health and well being of man as a self-evident *good* – by all standards an irreproachable ideal – appear as negative impulses within the unrelentingly humane yet acerbic framework of Gandhian vegetarianism. As Shetty puts it, Gandhi's 'self-conscious ascetic disregard for life unlimited' made him very critical of the fundamental presupposition of conventional medicine: 'an excessive desire for living'. She adds that Gandhi's critique of medicine exceeded the Fanonian one of medicine's complicity in the productivity of colonial pathology, for it was founded on a deeper and more universal notion of ethical self-cultivation. Thus, both illness and nursing were reconceived in the Gandhian scheme of things as imperatives to an ethical way of living, a *saving* and *refashioning* of the body and the spirit that were both responsive to and could *feel* suffering and violation. As with his views on other matters, neither his critique of the *upas* tree of modernity nor his critique of modern medicine was rooted in Indian tradition, at least not in any simple way. As Shetty shows, his position on medicine involved a profound break with Ayurveda's therapeutic and cultural practice and precept, specifically a rejection of, what appeared to him, as *vaids*' laxity and equivocation, in the name of 'life' or health, with regard to the general scriptural taboo on meats and wines. He himself appeared to have recognized the idiosyncratic and utterly marginal nature of his own position, labelling himself 'quack' and 'crank' in his *Autobiography*. A significant aspect of Shetty's analysis consists in its elaboration of a notion of 'unconditional hospitality', *à la* Derrida, in relation to Gandhi's vision of nursing. She undertakes this analysis in the context of Gandhi's nursing of rank outsiders – an unknown leper and Zulu soldiers. This is a notion of intimate bodily contact, albeit palliative, which even in a context of aggressive imperialism and racism does not distinguish between friend and stranger. As such it articulates a complex bioethics of *singular* proximity that exceeds all notions of self-boundedness within communities or nations. It is the 'weakness' of excessive propinquity and relationality that threatens the 'strong', ordered, disciplinary norms of human sociality. It is a form of love that empties the self inside out, an affective ascesis.

Tridip Suhrud's chapter, 'Emptied of All But Love: Gandhiji's First Public Fast', reads Gandhi's fasts as practices *par excellence* embodying such affective, love-imbued ascesis. Since his return from South Africa, Gandhi undertook twenty 'public' fasts between 1915 and 1948. Some were of fixed duration while others were 'fasts unto death'. Apart from his experiments with sensual/sexual abstinence in order to test his will to celibacy, no Gandhian practice invited more controversy among his political contemporaries than his acts of fasting at crucial political junctures. His adversaries invariably read them in terms of blackmail – such as Ambedkar when he was compelled to accede to the Poona Pact in 1932. Gandhi's fasting attracted admiration, exasperation and resentment in equal measures. By his own account, Gandhi fasted at times for penance, at times for self-purification, at other times for reaching out to his political or cultural adversaries where, by emptying himself of all but love, he sought to awaken the humanity in them. We know from his writings that his reasons for fasting were at times so personal and intimate that he did not wish to share them with even his closest companions. He believed that fasting and other self-practices which accompanied the act of fasting were deeply personal, were singularly expressive of his very own spiritual agonism and, hence, not available to all as a life practice. He often made public appeals to his companions and people of India not to undertake what he called 'sympathetic fasts' while he fasted. Suhrud's chapter captures an early version of this Gandhian practice by narrating for us the sequence of events that led to Gandhi undertaking his first public fast in March 1918. It followed a breakdown in the arbitration process between the mill-owners of Ahmedabad and the textile workers. Gandhi supported and bore witness to the pledge of the workers not to return to work till they were paid fair wages. Gradually, the workers' resistance began wearing down as their families began to suffer. Not surprisingly their anger turned to Gandhi and his fellow workers who were urging them on to recognize the sanctity of their pledge. The workers were especially critical of what they saw as Gandhi's indifference to their visceral suffering – literally starvation – which no soul stirring word or act of resistance could instantly counter. For someone whose notion of the spiritual encompassed an ethical refashioning of bodily practices – Gandhi had already become a celibate by then – this was a wake up call to find a way of *embodying* his solidarity with the hapless workers. Ever a great believer in practice over precept, he decided to actually *live* their suffering with them by undertaking a fast till the workers' pledge broke the backs of the mill-owners. The chapter's focus here is not so much on the strategic outcome of Gandhi's first act of public fasting as on the marking of a momentous act of love wherein self-abnegation entwines with an intense awareness of corporeal vulnerability to generate a vision of dependency, responsibility and relationality. Projected onto our very present, when countless people around the globe live in fear of either being blown up by terrorist bomb attacks or being afflicted by pandemics such as the avian flu, such a confluence of corporeal relationality (through mutual vulnerability) and abnegation of individual autonomy – Gandhi famously did not ascribe to the notion of the 'private' much to the consternation of his intimate circle of family and friends – could provide us an ethical opening towards comprehending and addressing to some extent the mind-numbing fear that has become the dominant affective register of our times.

III

The second part of this book, called 'Of Friendship, Law and Language: Shaping Gandhian 'Weakness', contains chapters that mark three key sites of sociality, professional relationality and discursivity respectively, that were crucial in shaping Gandhi's political and ethical orientation to the times he lived in. These include his friendships in various *ashrams*, his practice as a lawyer in colonial South Africa, and his English rendering of the *Hind Swaraj* and tensions involved in the translation thereof.

Thomas Weber's chapter, 'Gandhi Moves: Intentional Communities and Friendship', foregrounds the trope of friendship in accounting for Gandhi's successive setting up of various communities – called 'farms' and *ashrams* at different times – across South Africa and India. These communities served as sites of his nonviolent *praxis*. Gandhi was famously peripatetic and physically relocated himself several times during his lifetime. Weber argues that these relocations can be accounted for by the very close spiritual friendships he developed throughout his life. He makes the point that, while many commentators have talked of Gandhi's numerous friendships, they have not seen these as central to either Gandhi's various communal settlements or to his political formation. Weber also argues that a politically instrumentalist reading does not account for all of Gandhi's moves. Reading popular life and times books about Gandhi, we are introduced to a group of his most prominent political co-workers and get a strong sense of the circumstances of the setting up of Tolstoy Farm and the Satyagraha Ashram at Kochrab and Sabarmati. But the reasons for the setting up of Phoenix Settlement, the leaving of Sabarmati and the choice of Wardha as the next headquarters cannot be accounted for in terms of just political expediency or contingency. While the setting up of Tolstoy Farm can largely (but not completely) be understood by reading about the political Gandhi, only a more holistic reading of Gandhi's life through his spiritual and constructive work relationships, Weber suggests, gives us worthwhile clues to his comings and goings from the other ashrams. In South Africa his semi-move from his middle-class suburban home to a life of simplified rural, communal, manual labouring existence at Phoenix Settlement appears to be tied inextricably to his relationship with his then soul mate Henry Polak. In the same way, his later move to Tolstoy Farm can only be understood in terms of his relationship with Hermann Kallenbach, his next spiritual fellow traveller. To understand why Gandhi left his seemingly idyllic community on the banks of the Sabarmati, it is necessary to view his relationship with the almost unknown Maganlal Gandhi, his chief non-political lieutenant. Again, Jamnalal Bajaj headed up many of Gandhi's constructive work organisations from Wardha. Gandhi's relocation to Wardha can only be accounted for through an understanding of his deep relationship with Bajaj whom he considered as his adopted son. Weber argues that Gandhi's friendship with Polak, Kallenbach, Maganlal Gandhi and Bajaj had as much influence on his political activism as did his involvement with various religious thinkers such as his mentor Raychand, his vegetarian 'new age' circle in London, his Christian missionary friends in South Africa and the writings of Ruskin and Tolstoy.

Weber's foregrounding of the trope of friendship in analysing Gandhi's various temporary, community-based settlements is significant in yet another respect, though it does not form part of his exposition in the chapter under discussion. Gandhi used the notion of friendship to counter the distancing effect of 'third party mediation' in situations of political or cultural conflict. His suspicion of legal or contractual attempts made by imperial authorities to mediate Hindu–Muslim conflicts in India is well known.[6] In terms reminiscent of Gandhi's notion of nursing without prejudice towards either friends or strangers, Gandhi saw 'unconditional' friendship as a much more effective means of overcoming communal conflict. Why does Gandhi's legally trained self reject the neat abstractions of the juridical and choose the unpredictability and messiness of human affect in resolving conflict? Why is Gandhi's notion of nonviolent protest predicated on the paradox of disobedience to imperial law and a deep caring for the 'human' in the imperial ruler? Charles DiSalvo's chapter, 'Gandhi: the Transformation of a South African Lawyer, 1897–1898', attempts to provide some answers.

DiSalvo sets his narrative against the backdrop of Gandhi's transformation from a suit-and-tie attired London-trained barrister in South Africa armed with a belief in the law in 1893, to his departure to India in 1914 dressed as a native Indian and convinced of the power of civil disobedience. Gandhi's life at the bar had three stages to it. In the first period, Gandhi saw his legal practice largely as a profession from which he could earn money to subsidize his political work as an organizer for the Indian community in South Africa. In the second period, Gandhi shifted much of his hope for change from the political arena to the courtroom, where he hoped to vindicate Indian civil rights. During this period he both represented civilly disobedient Indians and brought test cases against anti-Indian legislation. In the third and final period, Gandhi experienced the ultimate corruption of the South African legal system, gave up his practice of the law and conducted campaigns of nonviolent disobedience to the law. DiSalvo distils these three stages into one crucial year in Gandhi's life, 1897–1898, and reads this period as the microcosm that foreshadows and explains Gandhi's transformation from business lawyer to civil rights attorney to civil disobedient. His chapter meticulously marks out the stages through which Gandhi slowly came to realize that, when most severely tested, the legal system could do no more than reflect the corrupt society of which it was a part. South Africa's courts, Gandhi eventually understood, were profoundly limited as instruments of social change. In the end, Gandhi was led by the circumstances of his time and place to reject the legal system and to adopt nonviolence as both a philosophy and a 'thirty-three percent' way of life.

Was it Gandhi's turning away from litigation as recourse to justice that made him reflect and write at such length on the notion of a political and ethical 'proper' that could by no means be contained within the tenets of parliamentary democracy? That made him call Parliament a 'prostitute' or *veshya* in his tract *Hind Swaraj*? A term that one of his English friends took umbrage at and which he resolved to change if he got an opportunity to revise his text for a second edition? And which he eventually did not alter? Ajay Skaria's chapter, 'Only One Word, Properly Altered: Gandhi and the Question of *Veshya*', ponders this conundrum by taking us through an intricate discursive journey through the rhetorical and translational twists and turns of both the Gujarati and English versions of this key Gandhian text. From this reading emerges multiple meanings of the term *swaraj* – literally self-rule leading to emancipation in all possible human ways of being and becoming, social, political, ethical. Skaria highlights the rhetorical unpacking that Gandhi engages in, in order to force the colonized Indian to confront his or her own deep complicity in the colonisation process. Under Gandhi's discursive rapier, the Manichean dualism of colonizer–colonised lies in tatters, as do familiar notions of fair and just governmentality that the ideology of anti-colonial nationalism invokes. Skaria's meticulous deconstruction of Gandhi's utterly complex and, to the average Indian, almost unachievable notion of authentic selfhood – hailed by the prefix *swa* – causes us deep ethical discomfort. Can such an ethically soldered notion of 'self' be part of this imperfect world? And yet it must be. For this maverick, folksy, frail, loin-clothed dynamo of a human being embodied it and demonstrated its power across many life-worlds.

IV

We talked earlier about the permeability and translatability of Gandhian life practices across various global sites. The third part of the book, 'Carrying Gandhi Over: Global Peace Movements', delineates three such sites – Britain, Burma and the US – that witnessed the carrying over and the transformation of specifically Gandhian modalities of nonviolence. Sean Scalmer's chapter, 'Globalising Gandhi: Translation, Reinvention, Application, Transformation', studies the impact of Gandhism on British pacifists from the 1920s to the

10 *Debjani Ganguly*

1960s and then opens out his analysis to address the nature of diffusion and globalization of Gandhian nonviolence. It bases its analysis on two questions. First, how and why did Gandhism circulate the way it did? Second, how was Gandhism transformed by the process of diffusion? There are three parts to Scalmer's attempts to answer them and they are linked by three tropes: translation, experimentation and tension. We already saw the discursively fraught nature of translation in our discussion of Ajay Skaria's comparative study of the Gujarati and English versions of *Hind Swaraj*. In his chapter, Scalmer notes the disquiet of British pacifists over the exact import of Gandhi's expositions. Gandhi's ideas were frequently misunderstood. They were objects of bitter disagreement, especially over the question of their relevance to the British environment. Often they suffered from mistranslations characterized by either 'Orientalist hyper-difference' or 'Western over-likeness'. Second, Scalmer marks the significance of active experimentation to the successful diffusion of Gandhism. It substituted political action for sterile debate and hammered out a British version of nonviolence attuned to the needs of local pacifists. Third, the diffusion of Gandhism through translation and experimentation produced new kinds of tensions. In particular, Gandhians in Britain had to frequently endure attacks by political activists schooled in different traditions, and unimpressed by the ethical claims of nonviolence. British pacifists struggled to create a broader movement under the banner of a committed Gandhism, often with very little success. The chapter concludes with some more general observations on the dynamics of diffusion, and on the relevance of *satyagraha* to contemporary political struggle.

'To be Indian', Amitav Ghosh once declared, is 'to carry the experiences of Indians everywhere ... it is a truly global experience.' Gandhi's life and legacy, as refracted through the multiple media of modernity, have certainly globalized the notion of both 'being Indian' and 'being Gandhi'. Conversely, as if in homage to the late John Small's call for a 'history of Southeast Asia in which ... the Hindu should stand at the rear', traces of Gandhi's presence in Burma's past are all too often erased from modern historical accounts. Drawing on Indian and Burmese written and oral accounts, and exploring the nuanced and dynamic currency in ideas and perceptions between Gandhi, Burmese nationalists and Indian diaspora, Penny Edwards' chapter, 'Gandhiji in Burma, and Burma in Gandhiji', aims both to localize moments of Gandhi's life on Burmese terrain, and to emphasize the ways in which personalities and philosophies travelled (and still travel) across the colonial and national geographies of South and Southeast Asia.

In March 1929, the year in which Gandhi was arrested for burning foreign cloth in India, he visited Burma for the third time. Talking to packed audiences at Rangoon, Mandalay, Moulmein and Toungoo, Gandhiji explained his understandings of *ahimsa* and *satyagraha* to Burmese monks and laity, exhorted Burmese women to abandon foreign fineries for home-spun and paper parasols, and urged Burma's Indian community to unite with the Burmese against British rule. Replying to a welcome address by the Rangoon Municipality, Gandhi said he would feel honoured if he were claimed as a Buddhist and declared that Buddhism was to Hinduism what Protestantism was to Roman Catholicism. To Burmese nationalist monks such as U Ottama, whose sojourns in India shaped his advocacy of *swaraj* and *swadeshi*, Gandhi's social activism offered a refreshing alternative to the predominantly British schooled (and clothed) secular leaders of Burma's nationalist movement. Edwards argues that Gandhi's Burma visits were more than mere chapters in his, and Burma's, history. His encounters with, and reactions to, Burmese women, also shed light on and influenced his thinking on gender. Edwards also demonstrates that Gandhi's doctrine of *swadeshi*, as interpreted by Burmese monks and others, had a lasting impact on the shape of nationalist – and national – dress in colonial and post-colonial Burma. Against this backdrop, her chapter concludes by considering the contemporary symbolic function of key objects and sites in the Gandhi–Burma relationship, notably the *kamauk* (conical hat) adopted by Gandhi, and the Mahatma Gandhi Memorial Hall in Rangoon.

A third site of the diffusion of Gandhian thought and *praxis* can be found in Rhonda Y. Williams' delineation of the Black Women's movement in the US in the 1960s. Her chapter entitled 'Nonviolence and Long Hot Summers: Black Women's Welfare-rights Struggles in 1960s' Baltimore' explores the politicization of poor black women in Baltimore during the period and the ways in which it was shaped by the intertwining of two registers of protest: Gandhian nonviolence mediated through its globalization by peace activists around the world, and the local register of Black Nationalism. Among the many loci of activism for these women in Baltimore, one that is central to Williams' analysis is that of public housing: black women devised divergent strategies about how better housing, better services and adequate income could be achieved in the heroic era of the Civil Rights Movement. They expressed belief in nonviolent but active protest as well as a desire to participate in government decision-making while simultaneously contesting its discriminatory and violent stance against its low-income citizens. Like Gandhi and black activists in the United States, they believed that nonviolence meant much more than just passive resistance. The interesting fact about this movement, however, was that many of these grassroots women activists had probably never even heard of Gandhi. As Williams says, they discussed the influence of grandmothers and mothers, civil rights leaders and grassroots radical activists on their political education. But there was not a single mention of Gandhi in the archives she examines. Instead, Gandhian ways of being political were refracted through the figures of civil rights activists, Bayard Rustin and Martin Luther King Jr. In other words, these impoverished black women participated in a mode of global activism that contained components of Gandhian philosophy mediated through black prophetic leaders and grassroots organizers. As poor black women strived for respectability, they sometimes used nonviolence and sometimes discarded it, depending on the perceived needs and effectiveness of their particular urban-based, racialized, gendered and working-class issues. Their struggles not only had impact in the moment, but also transformed and complicated academic notions of working-class politics in post-Depression and postindustrial cities.

V

If the chapters in the previous part invoked politically active sites of global diffusion, translation and transformation of Gandhian nonviolence, the chapters in the final part of the book, entitled 'Interlocuting with Modernity: Gandhi at Home and in the World', contemplate the relevance of Gandhi to some of the key projects of modernity – nationalism, democracy and cosmopolitanism. Each of these is sought to be addressed through specific problematics in the three final chapters: Zionism, technologism and casteism. John Docker's 'Josephus: Traitor or Gandhian *Avant la Lettre*?' discusses the import of nonviolent thought and practice in the context of debates on Zionism and Jewish identity. It begins by taking us back to the ancient Jewish historical figure Josephus who is famous as the author of the historical tract called 'The Jewish War'. Josephus' treatise is a detailed evocation of the Jewish rebellion against the Roman Empire, the rebellion beginning in 66 CE and ending in a mass suicide at Masada, the fortress falling in 73 CE, three years after the fall of Jerusalem. Yet a cloud of infamy has always historically hung over Josephus' name and reputation. As commander of the Jewish forces defeated by the Romans at the siege of the town of Jotapata, Josephus refused to commit suicide along with his companions; he then went over to the Roman side, exhorting the rebels within Jerusalem to surrender. In modern times, the story of the heroic resistance at Masada has become a revered memory in the Zionist movement. Josephus, however, continues to be regarded as a traitor to his people. Docker's chapter undertakes a Gandhian reading of 'The Jewish War'. It raises questions about the wisdom of the rebellion of 66, about nationalism and violence, about Masada and suicide, and draws attention to Josephus' musings on nonviolence as part of Jewish tradition. It argues that such a Gandhian reading of 'The Jewish War' has clear relevance for the contemporary Middle East and the modern American empire.

The final two chapters of the book, Anjali Roy's 'Homespun Wisdom: Gandhi, Technology and Nationalism' and Debjani Ganguly's 'Vernacular Cosmopolitanism: World Historical Readings of Gandhi and Ambedkar', bring Gandhi back to India via the world by attempting to situate him in an interlocutary mode with two aspects of Indian nation-making and modernity that have, in more conventional accounts, featured adversarially in relation to the Mahatma. These include technological developmentalism and Ambedkarism. Ganguly's chapter recasts the tense relationship between

Gandhi and the dalit leader, Ambedkar, in terms of a dialogic exchange between two idioms of non-European cosmopolitanism respectively – *nonviolence* as Hinduized life practice, and *development* as a non-hierarchical, Buddhist orientation to life. It also argues that the sharp differences between them notwithstanding, both of these nationalist leaders were engaged in projects of global democratization in the era of the decline of high European colonialism. Roy in her chapter juxtaposes *Hind Swaraj* with the Sarker Committee Report (1948) that heralded the establishment of the Indian Institutes of Technology (IITs), referred to in Nehruvian terms as the 'temples of modern India'. She traces not merely the predictable disjunctions between the two texts, but also the ways in which the ghost of *Hind Swaraj*, in its relentless critique of technologism, industrialization and urbanization, haunts the periodic reviews of the 'success' of these Institutes. She also notes the irony of IITs' recent adoption of the idea of 'appropriate technologies' without their awareness of the term's genealogy in Gandhian thought. This term connotes the yoking together of technology, people and values to address needs of the underprivileged, an idea dear to Gandhi's heart. Gandhi's opposition to technology, Roy suggests, was not as total as many readings have made it out to be. It is just that he was intensely aware of its dehumanizing potential in its marriage with industrial capitalism and instrumental rationality, and saw it as his call to warn India and the world about it. Roy's chapter gives us fascinating vignettes of modernizing India's studied indifference to Gandhi, even as the latter persists as a ghostly presence in all development talk.

VI

This book, which begins with Gandhi in the world and appears to end with Gandhi in India, reflects in some ways the Rushdian quip on the Mahatama's political journey, that Gandhi 'gave up cosmopolitanism to gain a country'.[7] In these final words I stall the momentum of such a reading by quickly recouping the second half of Rushdie's statement, that 'in his strange afterlife' Gandhi has become a 'citizen of the world'. Unlike Rushdie, however, I do not read these terms to mean that Gandhi is up for grabs in the global supermarket and iconicized out of all recognition – as a recent advertisement for Apple Computers with a picture of Gandhi spinning above the caption, 'Think Different', exemplifies. On the contrary, the spirit of this book is oriented towards the utter necessity of claiming Gandhi once again as a 'citizen of the world' by invoking, in as much detail as one can, a world that is in real danger of being held hostage by unspeakable forms of global violence that show no signs of letting up. Gandhi showed that the only answer to collective grief over loss of whole communities and lifeworlds need not be a cry for war. It could well be a toothless smile masking an iron will to disarm the violator with compassion and love.

Notes

1. Eric Hobsbawm, *The Age of Extremes: The Short Twentieth Century*, London: Abacus Books, 1994, p. 560.
2. Judith Butler, *Precarious Life: The Powers of Mourning and Violence*, London: Verso, 2004, p. xix.
3. *The Sydney Morning Herald*, 'Rough Justice', weekend edition, September 17–18, 2005.
4. Gandhi, *Hind Swaraj*, ed. Anthony J. Parel, New York: Cambridge University Press, 1997 (1910), p. 89.
5. Ashis Nandy, *Intimate Enemy*, New Delhi: Oxford University Press, 1983, p. 111
6. See Uday Singh Mehta, *Liberalism and Empire*, University of Chicago Press, 1999, p. 41.
7. Salman Rushdie, *Step Across This Line*, London: Vintage, 2002, p. 185.

Bibliography

Butler, Judith, *Precarious Life: The Powers of Mourning and Violence*, London: Verso, 2004.
Gandhi, M.K, *Hind Swaraj*, ed. Anthony J. Parel, New York: Cambridge University Press, 1997 (1910).
Hobsbawm, Eric, *The Age of Extremes: The Short Twentieth Century*, London: Abacus Books, 1994.
Nandy, Ashis, *Intimate Enemy*, New Delhi: Oxford University Press, 1983.
Mehta, Uday Singh, *Liberalism and Empire*, University of Chicago Press, 1999.
Rushdie, Salman, *Step Across This Line*, London: Vintage, 2002.
The Sydney Morning Herald, 'Rough Justice', weekend edition, September 17–18, 2005.

Part I

Worlding the Gandhian everyday

Food, medicine and fasts

Part 1

2 *Ahimsa* and other animals
The genealogy of an immature politics
Leela Gandhi

Homesickness: preamble

It is lunchtime late in the century before last and the young Indian man, whom we must imagine standing hungrily on Farringdon Street, is not charmed by London. At least not today, Monday, October 22, 1888, a grey day announcing the irrevocable onset of winter. In time, true to that psychic distortion which makes us homesick for those places in which we were foreign, he will come to miss London bitterly. For the moment, however, his homesickness is rather more conventional: an acute state of corporeal disaggregation, a maladjustment of the body ill at ease among sofas, carpets, cornices, porticoes, vestibules, flower-beds, pavements, morning suits, bread, porridge and potatoes. Mostly bread, porridge and potatoes. For, to put it plainly, he is distraught about food, its lack and its unrecognisability. No stranger to meat eating and its guilty pleasures, his sojourn has only been authorised by the elders of his community under condition of a vow to abjure the triple temptations of liquor, meat and sex, and so to suffer a staple diet of, 'oatmeal porridge ... bread, butter ... meat and potatoes *ad libitum*'.[1]

Recently, though, the Anglo-Indian landlady of his new West Kensington digs, and author celebre of many plates of porridge, has mentioned the curious mushrooming of vegetarian restaurants in the city; one of which he finds today: the Central at 16 Saint Bride Street, the sight of which, as he writes later, 'filled me with the same joy that a child feels on getting a thing after its own heart'.[2] He notices for sale under a glass window near the door a copy of Henry Salt's *Plea for Vegetarianism*. Buying the book for one shilling he walks into the dining room where, choosing the six-penny dinner for three courses, he sits down with his book and begins to read, greedily.[3] Some time in the next three years the author, Henry Salt, will meet this young man at a vegetarian convention who, in an unreliable version of this encounter, will say with the obstinate sing-song of Kathiawar in his vowels, 'My name is Gandhi. You have, of course, never heard of it'.[4] In a more authentic testimony Salt claims to 'remember the now famous Mr Gandhi, who co-operated with us much more willingly than he has since done with the Indian government'.[5]

In his compelling and histrionic autobiography, *My Experiments with Truth*, Mohandas Karamchand Gandhi rates his encounter with Salt's ouevre as a life-changing experience. And, indeed, over the remaining three odd years of his legal studies in London, Gandhi's involvement with *fin de siècle* vegetarianism increased exponentially. He devoured, as he puts it, 'all books available on vegetarianism',[6] supplementing his urgent private dietetic studies with organisational and evangelical activism against kreophagy, or meat eating. It is with this early phase of Gandhi's 'formation' that this chapter concerns itself; seeking in his enmeshment with late-Victorian radicalism raw materials for the transnational or non-indigenous sources of his anti-imperial polemic. For, I will argue, the culture of *fin de siècle* animal welfare (of which vegetarianism was but one subsidiary) exerted profound influence on Gandhi's politics and ethico-ideological lexicon; giving substance to his critique of imperialism; shaping the complex etymology of Gandhian *ahimsa*.

From his earliest writings on the subject, Gandhi is quick to recognise the *zoophilia* of his English companions as a variety of *xenophilia*: that openness to outsiders, aliens, strangers, foreigners, ratified in the enduring Epicurean challenge to the Aristotelian circumscription of community; consolidated in its transmission as a flight from self-identical, self-confirming sociality. But what, then, of the aetiology of risk integral to this project? The structural demand that, in this case, Indian-loving be accompanied by a readiness for self-estrangement? A willingness, *à la* E. M. Forster, to 'run counter to the claims of the State' for the sake of an ally or friend?[7] It is worth referring here to a public letter of April 24, 1894, circulated by Gandhi from Pretoria to Indians in England, and subsequently reprinted in *The Vegetarian*. Writing now in the more commanding prose borne of increased political agonism, Gandhi informs his Indian readers that collaboration with English vegetarians is a duty, on the grounds, among others, that, 'The vegetarian movement will aid India politically ... inasmuch as the English vegetarians ... readily sympathise with the Indian aspirations (that is my personal experience)'.[8] Here we have it in rudimentary form: secreted within the culture of English vegetarianism a variety of hospitality whose logical fulfilment may at any time 'constitute a felony *contra patriam*',[9] defying the imperial state in order to honour the 'aspirations' of dispossessed (and hungry) Indian visitors. These sympathies are clearly confirmed, from the other side, in a letter from Salt to the Mahatma in 1931, affirming his sympathies with the anti-colonial movement in India while reiterating the view that imperialism was one of the many perverse manifestations of kreophagy: ' ... I feel as strongly as ever that food-reform, like Socialism, has an essential part to play in the liberation of man-kind. I cannot see how there be any real and full recognition of Kinship, as long as men continue either to cheat, or to eat, their fellow-beings!'[10] How, then, we might begin by asking, did Henry Salt *et al.* manifest – if at all – their dietetic and affective anti-colonialism to the callow Indian youth in their midst? Three points bear elaboration.

First, and briefly, Gandhi would have immediately observed in the culture of *fin de siècle zoophilia* a radical cosmopolitanism valorising and promoting difference against the cultural monochrome of Empire. Conveyed in various registers, this modality was frequently exemplified in the then unusual form of culinary cosmopolitanism. So, in an 1898 interview to *The Vegetarian*, the redoubtable Annie Beasant extols 'Dal and rice' as her favourite cuisine. And, to similar effect, a food review from 1887 of a new vegetarian eating house at Charing Cross lavishes praise upon the ecumenical board which includes, 'Macaroni and Indian sauce', the enticingly named 'Home-Rule Potatoes', and 'Japanese bean-curd'.[11]

Second, in this milieu of gastronomic experimentation Gandhi would also have encountered associated and powerful propaganda against the physiognomic basis of imperial argument-viz., that equation of vegetarianism with colonial enfeeblement – to which, as we know from his autobiography, he was unusually susceptible. So, for example, testifying vehemently in favour of the strength-giving properties of vegetarian diet, many contemporary publications feature a telling notice for 'Briggs Muscle-forming Indian Food', endorsed by a picture of a ferocious be-turbaned Indian with alarming pectoral development. Substituting, in these ways, the series beef/Europe/imperial strength with the contrasting if hopelessly contingent series vegetarianism/native races/anti-colonial vigour, contemporary vegetarians also deployed a far more interesting ideological tactic wherein the discourse equating beef with imperial virility was hoisted upon its own petard, such that colonialism was re-diagnosed precisely as the lamentable affliction of kreophagous virility, and one whose repudiation demanded, in its turn, a radical reformation of masculinity itself. As Salt opines in his *Killing for Sport*:

> Under the fostering wing of Imperialism, brute force is developed more and more into a political science ... The Englishman, both as soldier and colonist, is a typical sportsman; he seizes on his prey wherever he finds it with the hunter's privilege. He is lost in amazement when men speak of the rights of inferior races, just as the Englishman at home is lost in amazement when we speak of the rights of the lower orders. Here, as yonder, he is kindly, blatant, good-humoured, aggressive, selfish, and fundamentally *savage*.[12]

And thus, we may surmise, *fin de siècle* animal welfare demonstrates its discursive claim upon that association of unharmfulness and anticolonialism, compassion and anti-imperialism, fundamental to the elementary grammar of Gandhian *ahimsa*. But, in Gandhi's characteristically idiosyncratic idiom, this trope, meaning 'nonviolence', of course, is also (and bafflingly) elaborated as a rhetoric of revolutionary obstinacy, a refusal of government, a character signifying the courage of contradiction. Itemised, variously, in his *oeuvre* as 'passive resistance', 'boycott', 'non-cooperation', 'civil-disobedience', it is invoked again towards the end of his eventful life as a synonym for 'anarchy': bearing the promise of his last, unfulfilled dream of India as an ungoverned society. What possible connection can there be between this eccentric rendition of *ahimsa* and the more straightforward embargo on human violence toward the 'lower animals' that we find in the inchoate thoughts of the early Gandhi?

Third, it is my contention that Gandhian *ahimsa* obtains at least some of its semantic density from late-Victorian *zoophilia's* self-postulation precisely as a resistance to governmentality; poised on the estimate that if modern power was a pathological form of non-relationality, achieving its most pernicious dimension in the sequestering logic of imperialism, then its refutation had to proceed from the rehearsal of unmediated or immediate and extreme forms of relationality between beings with 'vastly different phenomenologies and ontologies': viz., across genders, races, classes and, paradigmatically, across the species barrier. We have testimony to this zigzag association between *fin de siècle* animal welfare's 'creed of kinship', on the one hand, and its allergy to governmentality, on the other, in a letter of 1888 from Oscar Wilde to Violet Fane:

> ... vegetarianism ... is very curious ... [in] its connection with modern socialism, atheism, nihilism, anarchy ... It is strange that the most violent republicans I know are all vegetarians: brussel sprouts seem to make people bloodthirsty, and those who live on lentils and artichokes are always calling for the gore of the aristocracy and for the severed head of kings ... in the political sphere a diet of green beans seems dangerous.[13]

If typically flippant in its seriousness, Wilde's assessment points to an unacknowledged strain in contemporary animal welfare, crucial, I submit, to the affectivity and anticonstitutionalism of Gandhian *ahimsa* and, congruently, to his anti-imperialism. It is to the elaboration of this strain as explanatory context for the seemingly ragged genealogy of *ahimsa* that I will direct my attention in the arguments to follow.

Utilitarianism, animal rights and colonialism

To argue the case for the socialist-anarchist anti-colonialism of Gandhi's friends, then, we need to examine the peculiar political/ideological pressures that shaped their emergence at the fringes of late-Victorian culture. Significant in this regard is the way in which they defined themselves against an earlier and dominant tradition of animal welfare well in place by the beginning of the nineteenth century. The years 1800, 1802, 1809 and 1810 each witnessed efforts to introduce into the English Parliament legislation for the prevention of cruelty to animals. These efforts finally bore fruit in 1822 when a historic bill, introduced by Sir Richard Martin, member for

Galway, into the Commons, succeeded in extending protection to 'Horses, Mares, Geldings, Mules, Donkeys, Cows, Heifers, Bull Calves, Oxen, Sheep, and other Livestock'. These stirrings of Parliamentary reform to improve the condition of animals in the early decades of the nineteenth century also inspired efforts to create an effective vigilante organisation committed to animal protection and to the promotion of legislation toward this end. And in 1824 the Society for Prevention of Cruelty to Animals (SPCA), was launched, with the project of bringing about in the sphere of 'morals' the changes that Martin had introduced within the law.

Few early reformers directly called themselves 'utilitarian', but the Victorian milieu of organised and official benevolence to which they laid claim was, to borrow some words from F. R. Leavis, 'in a general sense utilitarian'.[14] Indeed, so comprehensively did utilitarian philosophy capture in its inception the ethical foundations of animal welfare that even today philosophers of contemporary animal liberation like Peter Singer continue to insist that utilitarianism alone enables that appeal to the equal consideration of interests that gives the animal world any chance for justice in the face of anthropocentric dominion. It is not incidental, in this regard, that the first serious mention of rights for animals comes directly from the pen of Jeremy Bentham as footnote to a larger discussion about ethics, occurring toward the end of his monumental *An Introduction to the Principles of Morals and Legislation*. As he writes:

> The day *may* come when the rest of animal creation may acquire those rights which never could have been witholden from them but by the hand of tyranny ... The French have already discovered that the blackness of the skin is no reason why a human being should be abandoned without redress to the caprice of a tormentor. It may come one day to be recognised, that the number of legs, the villosity of the skin, or the termination of the *os sacrum*, are reasons equally insufficient for abandoning a sensitive being to the same fate ... the question is not, Can they *reason*? Nor, Can they *talk*? But, Can they *suffer*?[15]

While many early animal reformers claimed direct inspiration from and acquaintance with Jeremy Bentham, not everyone was as impressed by the indiscriminate democratisation apparently endorsed by the utilitarian discourse of rights. The self-fashioned 'Platonist', Thomas Taylor, for one, wrote an impassioned critique of the political costs likely to attend the profligate expenditure of privileges upon inferior beings. He protests in his 1792 tract, *A Vindication of the Rights of Brutes*:

> We may therefore reasonably hope, that this amazing rage for liberty will continually increase; that mankind will shortly abolish all government as an intolerable yoke; and that they will as universally join in vindicating the rights of brutes, as in asserting the prerogatives of man.[16]

But, I submit, in Taylor's critique we are in face of a supreme misunderstanding. For, in Benthamite hands, far from conspiring to an overthrowing of government, the language of rights is principally if not exclusively concerned with a vertiginous amplification of government activity. And, if available to reading as a subsidiary history of nineteenth-century benevolence, the story of utilitarian inspired animal rights also contains in microcosm the secret history of modern governmentality. This is the crux on which the ensuing discussion turns, and to understand it better we must return once more to Bentham's famous and influential defence of animal rights. Here, in the text framing his footnote, we find, in the main, arguments for increasing both the scope and scale of the law: that *summum bonum* of utilitarian theology. What, then, is the burden of Bentham's argument?

The question of our relation to other humans and to other animals, he opines, is properly speaking the subject of private ethics.[17] But the maximisation of maximum happiness requires the policing of individual desires in such a way that morals, to quote Halevy on Bentham, 'assume a commanding governmental nature'.[18] From the perspective of utility, Bentham insists, 'private ethics and the art of legislation go hand in hand. The end they have or ought to have is of the same nature'.[19] However, if ethics and legislation, so defined, are of the same epistemic family, what is there to prevent their active collaboration such that 'legislatio' might become 'a special branch of morals'?[20] Nothing, is the answer, since for Bentham the ethical subject is intrinsically the consenting object of legislation, and conscience, concomitantly, is that critical rupture in the fabric of the otherwise integral self through which the law can enter, without breaking, to work with and upon the innermost recesses of the empathetic individual. It is this process, whereby utilitarianism transforms the 'man of feeling' into the ideal citizen, that Foucault has in mind in his famous exculpation of Bentham as the genius behind 'what might be called in general the disciplinary society'.[21] Where once, Foucault famously argues, the offending individual experienced power as a singular force exerted ritually, violently, as constraint, from the outside, the utilitarian intervention achieved the opposite: reducing the costs of government and capitalising on the unmanageable increase of human population through an inspired dispersal of power within 'the cumulative multiplicity of man'.[22] We will return to Foucault later in this discussion to understand better the precise techniques by which utilitarian governmentality is held in place so as to identify correctly the principles upon which its undoing might proceed. For the moment, however, I simply wish to argue that the distinctly utilitarian inspiration for early animal welfare – in Parliament and through the activities of the RSPCA – makes itself visible in and as a sustaining will to governmentality; and one authorised to enforce the habits of conscientious obedience upon all those with underdeveloped or untutored ethical natures, for example women, children, the working poor, the inferior races.

Most historians of early animal reform agree that closer examination of that project reveals, first, a constitutive class-bias and, second, a relentless subjection of the working classes to increased scrutiny from the law; subtly widening the sphere of their amerciable transgressions such that the task of policing the poor gradually overwhelms the commitment ostensibly to protect animals.[23] These features are picked up and canvassed in arguments against animal protection as early as 1800 by William Windham, parliamentarian and Burkean champion of 'old' English ways. In response to William Pultney's proposed bill, in that year, to prevent bull baiting, Windham contends that the sentiments of animal welfare are doubly tainted: by a deplorable prejudice against the sports of the poor while maintaining a myopic disregard for the equally bloodthirsty sports of the rich, and by a mean spirit of legislative intrusiveness. 'This petty, meddling, legislative spirit', he maintains, 'cannot be productive of good: it serves only to multiply the laws, which are already too numerous, and to furnish mankind with additional means of vexing and harassing one another.'[24]

And, indeed, true to Windham's predictions, early animal welfare substantially increased the intrusion of the law into the lives of the poor in a bid to render them capable of self-regulative obedience. Notably, it is precisely in praise of this increased government interference that John Stuart Mill underwrites, in his 1848 *Principles of Political Economy*, the achievements of early animal welfare. In his words:

> The reasons for legal intervention in favour of children, apply no less strongly in the case of these unfortunate slaves and victims of the most brutal part of mankind, the lower animals. It is by the grossest misunderstanding of the principles of liberty, that the infliction of exemplary punishment on ruffianism practised towards these defenceless creatures has been treated as a meddling by government with things beyond its province; an interference with domestic life. The domestic life of domestic tyrants is one of the things which it is most imperative on the law to interfere with ... .[25]

Claimed as a means to justify the regulation of the working classes, indirectly, through the rhetoric of animal welfare, Mill's defence of government interference also points the way, directly, to the colonial imperatives of utilitarian philosophy. For, his advocacy of untrammelled legal intervention is framed by utilitarianism's abiding 'romance' with the law, and one articulated within the defining paradigms of what Asa Briggs has so appositely defined as an 'age of improvement'.[26] In this milieu, preoccupied with enumerating indices for progress, utilitarianism offered yet another benchmark; taking the view that nothing marked the distinction between savagery and civilisation more acutely than the difference (and distance) between natural or non-governmental society, on the one hand, and political or governmental society, on the other. And receiving this gift of government from within a discourse of 'improvement', political men, we might add, were also entitled if not obliged to spread the gospel of governmentality in and as a civilising mission. So it is that Mill rewrites colonialism as the attempt forcibly to civilise or governmentalise the East. In the case of 'those backward states of society in which the race itself may be concerned as in its nonage', he infamously observes, 'the early difficulties in the way of spontaneous progress are so great, that there is seldom any choice of means for overcoming them; and a ruler full of the spirit of improvement is warranted in the use of any expedients that will attain an end, perhaps otherwise unattainable'.[27]

The younger Mill's justification of colonialism as the principled rectification of inadequately governmental societies directly echoes similar arguments proffered by his father, James Mill, an administrator for the executive government of the East India Company, in his infamous *The History of British India*. We might also, *en passant*, acknowledge here Eric Stokes' convincing demonstration, in the company of a few other scholars, of the intimate philosophical contribution of utilitarianism to the formulation of colonial government in India. What bearing then, to gather this discussion into the larger themes of our argument, does this utilitarian compact with colonialism have upon the history of *fin de siècle* animal welfare? To reiterate: it is my – somewhat abbreviated – claim here that through a series of accidents the history of late-nineteenth-century animal welfare gets caught up in the utilitarian project of producing a disciplinary society; one whose force is felt at home, by the indigenous working classes, and abroad, by the colonised races. This enmeshment of animal welfare and governmentality or disciplinarity is, I propose, challenged in two ways by the *fin de siècle* dissidents whom Gandhi meets in London between 1888 and 1891. The first, and easier to apprehend, consists in their efforts to detach the project of animal welfare from the surrounding utilitarian agenda by making it perversely and directly co-extensive with the liberation both of the domestic working classes and of the foreign colonised races; namely, by rendering animal welfare into an associated form of socialism and anti-colonialism. Second, in a less obvious but possibly more profound manoeuvre, *fin de siècle* animal liberationists undo the symbolic logic of class and race oppressive (or colonial) governmentality by recasting human–animal relations as an enlightened model of anarchic, disobedient, cooperative and paradigmatically non-governmental sociality, which Gandhi, in time to come, would call *ahimsa*. Both these procedures are inextricable and interdependent, and their story will be told as such over the next two sections.

Undoing governmentality: cyborgs and socialists

To proceed with my proposed reading of *fin de siècle* animal welfare we need briefly to recall Foucault's now canonical analysis of the precise techniques of utilitarian disciplinarity, most palpably manifest, as he claims, in the model of Bentham's Panopiticon or ideal prison. This model, Foucault asserts, is of course designed principally to keep inmates in a condition of constant, exposed visibility (subjected to 'eternal vigilance') such that, in time, the perpetual, impassive and impersonal gaze from the central watchtower translates itself into the guilty and unforgiving eye of self-regulatory conscience. But the law of visibility enshrined in the structure of the Panopticon also relies heavily upon, and complements, its harsh architecture of separation. The technique of 'disciplinary partitioning' constructed through the isolating cell walls renders each individual singularly visible to the supervisor and insodoing simultaneously 'prevent[s] him from coming into contact with his companions'.[28] What, then, is the logic of panoptical separation? How is the project of power *qua* disciplinarity served, its catechisms of obedience rehearsed, through these concrete cell-dividers controlling the relations of men?

Within the Benthamite model, Foucault explains, it is understood that the inmate can only interiorise the disciplinary eye of power comprehensively if he is compelled into a state of extreme, pathological individuation: quarantined from the horizontal conjunction of collectivities; from their affective distractions and tendency to foment (in collaboration, through conversation) the logic of counter-discourse, countermanding the singularity of any law. This inextricability of disciplinarity and the logic of separation, made physically manifest in the Panopticon, recurs at a discursive level throughout Bentham's writings. The work of the early Bentham, especially, conveys the clear conviction that unmediated relationality, the horizontal arrangement of the 'face to face' relation, or what he calls 'conversation', is constitutively antithetical to the vertical axis of power along which are arranged the motions of obedience, the disciplinary rotations of governmentality. Formulating this schema in terms of the distinction between 'natural and 'political' society in his *A Fragment on Government*, Bentham notes the following:

> When a number of persons ... are supposed to be in the habit of paying obedience to a person, or an assemblage of persons ... such persons altogether ... are said to be in a state of *political* society ... [but] When a number of persons are supposed to be in the habit of *conversing* with each other, at the same time that they are not in any such habit as mentioned above, they are said to be in a state of *natural* society.[29]

That is to say, the condition of horizontal, direct or immediate relationality, that is, relationality *sans* obedience, equals a state of pre-political, non-governmental and anarchic sociality. So too, governmentality becomes, in effect, shorthand for the improved culture of mediated relationality: the superintending third term in a pyramidal structure continually interrupting the even groundwork of dialogic communication, compelling conversants to address each other, henceforth, only through the intercessory language of law. In other words, the privileges of govermentality require the sacrifice of direct conversational pleasure. *Vice versa*, the unmediated 'face to face' relation must eschew (or undo) the civilising conveniences of disciplinarity.

It is relevant to our argument that Bentham's allergy to immediate relationality is accompanied by a corresponding nausea for untrammelled 'feeling', 'sentiment', 'emotion'; the glue, that is, of affective affiliation. 'Among principles adverse to utility', he writes in *An Introduction*, 'that which at this day seems to have the most influence ... is what may be called the principle of sympathy.'[30] Elsewhere in the text he condemns the 'caprice' of sympathy or sentiment as intolerably 'anarchical'.[31] So too, as is well known, J. S. Mill testifies in his *Autobiography* to utilitarianism's informing suspicion of feeling. In his words

> the cultivation of feeling (except the feelings of public and private duty) was not much in esteem among us, and had very little place in the thoughts of most of us, myself in particular ... we did not expect the regeneration of mankind from any direct action on ... sentiments.[32]

If addressed, in the main, to the problematic of human sociality, utilitarianism's credo on behalf of separation and against the claims of sentiment also spread by contagion, showing its symptoms, in the period under review, within all available circuits of interaction: between human and divine orders and, so too, between human and animal worlds. Accordingly, most spokesmen of early animal reform render feeling or excessive sympathy between the species at best irrelevant and at worst detrimental to the cause of animal liberation. They are likewise determined that an equal consideration of animal interests does not, in any circumstances, imply an equivalence between human and animal interests.[33] Typically, Bentham is assiduously unsentimental in his defence of animal rights and insistent upon the hierarchy and unbridgeable gap separating human and animal sensibility, always privileging the capacities and claims of the former over those of the latter:

> 'If the being eaten were all, there is very good reason why we should be suffered to eat such of them as we like to eat: we are the better for it and they are never the worse ... If the being killed were all, there is very good reason why we should be suffered to kill such as molest us; we should be worse for their living, and they are never the worse for being dead.[34]

This insuperable barrier between benevolence and affinity, legislation and affect, takes an interesting turn in John Kipling's 1891 study *Beast and Man in India*. Citing as examples of Indian pre-political anarchy both the cruelty of Indians to their animals and the unpalatable consubstantiality of Indian animals and humans, Kipling's book catalogues, variously, the grotesque admixture of human and animal in Hindu iconography, the unwholesome proximity of *mahouts* with their elephants, the bizarre bed-sharing of tigers and their tamers.[35] But, of course, it is precisely this mode of affective consubstantiality that *fin de siècle* animal welfare invokes; as a means of transforming the very heart of human cruelty, but, also, as a symbolic means of dismantling the overriding principles of disciplinary partitioning. Donna Haraway is apposite here. In terms strikingly close to the concerns of our discussion, she poses throughout her corpus the struggle of colonial and anti-colonial energies as a contestation between two types of identity: the one accruing from a culture of self-contained, self-reflexive, humanism, the other, conversely, from the permeable boundaries and mixed spaces of a 'cyborg economy' or 'primate order'. Colonialism, she maintains, expresses a cloistered subjectivity: 'individuation, separation, the birth of the self, the tragedy of autonomy ... alienation, that is, war tempered by imaginary respite in the bosom of the other'. And anti-colonialism, in contrast, may well find its radical feet upon the uneven territory of self-dissolving coalition, affinity, relationality; namely, in the anarchic, 'interdigitations of human, machine, non-human, animal or alien, and their mutants in relation to the intimacies of bodily exchange and mental communication'.[36] Our historical subjects, arguably, anticipate Haraway's cyborg economy, entering into symbolic conflict with utilitarian governmentality in two ways: first, through a defiant discourse of *zoophilia* or love for animals, and, second, through the argument that the practice of such inter-species love itself paves the way to an enlightened affective socialism susceptible, in its turn, and with some help from Charles Darwin, to the themes of anarchist anticolonialism.

In the main, the ideological fissures in nineteenth-century animal welfare, with which we are concerned here, first manifest themselves in the antipathy of *fin de siècle* radicals toward the anthropocentric condescension that they see at work in the efforts of early reformers, specifically, their assiduous policing of the boundaries of humanity. Eschewing the condescending language of utilitarian benevolence, *zoophilic* radicals opt instead for the credo of 'sentiment', drawing, *ad nauseam*, upon Schopenhauer's *On the Basis of Morality* for arguments in favour of the annexation of feeling or compassion as 'the sole source of disinterested action and the only moral incentive'; as also for the philosopher's ratification of feeling as a salve for 'the barbarism of the West'.[37]

If more or less unanimous in the affective thrust of their radicalism, most representatives of the group under consideration are, nonetheless, at pains to variegate the many applications of 'love', and the means for its cultivation. Henry Salt, for instance, discloses an affective *askesis* in the art of poetry, finding in its renunciation of epistemic certainties (in favour of the inchoate language of the heart) techniques for dissolving the disciplinary partitions that mar human rationality. Much like Salt, the anti-vivisectionist Frances Power Cobbe also places poets at the vanguard of the sentimental revolution, honouring them, especially, as beacons for animal welfare in her curious anthology of animal verse, *The Friend of Man; and his Friends – the Poets*. Celebrating those poets capable of conjuring the irreducible particularity of animal–human sociability, Cobbe defends affect, in her turn, as the ability to register the conjunctural singularity of all relationship. Posing her arguments against the maximising and universalising protocols of utilitarian ethics, which she describes as the 'coldest of philosophies', she defends *zoophilia* as an aggressively minoritising perspective: ineluctably partisan, defiantly immediate.[38] Where, she argues, the undiscriminating eye of benevolence or philanthropy makes no distinction between one dog and another, treating all as grist to the mill (or, indeed, Bentham) of utility, the committed *zoophile* is incapable of 'polydoggery'; that 'thing against which all feeling revolts'.[39] Relentlessly particularising the animals of her acquaintance in *False Beasts and True*, Cobbe lovingly details the unique criminality of one as against the signatory intensity of another; elsewhere valorising the 'divine law of love' as a force against the utilitarian calculus of pleasure and pain.[40]

If eccentric to say the least in her passionate *zoophilia*, Cobbe's intensities are entirely overshadowed by those of her fellow anti-vivisectionist rival and ally, the occultist Anna Kingsford. What appears in the prose of others as protestations on behalf of 'sympathy' or 'feeling' becomes in Kingsford's practice a form of acute psychic excess, elaborating itself in visionary dreams of agonising self-identification with tortured animals. A strong advocate of the theory of spontaneous hydrophobia, Kingsford often defends the view that dogs become rabid in reactive fear of vivisection and human persecution.[41] Thus, commending dog-love as a natural vaccine against rabies, Kingsford's career also chronicles an incremental and corresponding mistrust of the human race which finds expression, once again, in her vivid dream life through anarchic fantasies of violence against leading vivisectionists: 'Yesterday' she records, 'November 11, at 11 at night, I knew that my will had smitten another vivisector! ... for months I have been compassing the death of Paul Bert, and have but just succeeded ... *I* have killed Paul Bert as I killed Claude Bernard; as I will kill Louis Pasteur, and after him the whole tribe of vivisectors'.[42]

To summarise, then, the trope of 'love' in *fin de siècle* animal welfare symbolically resists the credo of separation and the embargo on 'sentiment', underscoring utilitarian governmentality. Additionally, it prepares the route to contemporary utopian socialism through an internal logic wherein 'love' becomes a synonym for ascetic 'sacrifice' and the simplification of life, or dissolution, in other words, of the disparity between rich and poor, the owing and the labouring classes. 'Love is sacrifice', thunders Henry Light in his *Common-Sense Vegetarianism*, 'the perfected article finally breaks the bonds that would restrict its exercise to but one person, one family, one country, one race, or even one person. Love is noble, not selfish.'[43] It is the imperatives of *zoophilia* as sacrifice or affective self-denial that inform condemnations of the sports and fashions of the rich as variously 'indulgent', 'luxurious', 'greedy' and 'superfluous'. And where once cruelty to animals bespoke the brutality and profligacy of the labouring poor, it now becomes a signifier, quite simply, of conspicuous consumption; that indelible trail of blood in the milliner's workshop, the glover's boutique, the aristocrat's hunting fields, the coloniser's touristic pursuit of exotic big-game. Such condemnations of recreational class-indulgence are matched by the contiguous discourse of vegetarianism which takes as its target the culinary excesses of kreophagy. In this vast literature, perhaps the most coherent and influential case for vegetarianism as the key to the simplification of life comes from the puritanical Count Leo Tolstoy. His *The First Step* condemns meat-eating on two counts: first, as self-indulgent gluttony, that condition where 'killing ... is called forth only by greediness and the desire for tasty food'; and, second, as the cause of an industry that relies, for the satisfaction of a few palates, upon the exploitation and dehumanisation of a whole underclass of slaughterers, butchers, drovers, cooks.

Thus paving the way for socialist class-critique, the discourse of *zoophilia* also gains immeasurably from the claims of Darwinian evolutionism. Darwin's hypotheses, especially his insistence upon the interconnectedness of sentient life, enables the *fin de siècle* politics of love, that we have been canvassing, to transform itself into a cosmopolitan 'creed of kinship'. This credo, as I will suggest, briefly, in the next concluding section, is instrumental in translating the ethics of human–animal sociality, once again by degrees, into a subtle form of anarchist anticolonialism.

Charles Darwin and anti-colonial anarchism

On 27 December 1831 Charles Darwin sailed out aboard the *Beagle* on a voyage he would describe in time to come as 'by far the most important event in my life and ... whole career'.[44] This opportunity, we might note in passing, was entirely framed by colonial imperatives. The *Beagle's* cartographic investigations along the South American coast were intended to furnish the Admiralty with information to assist in future military and commercial operations, as also to 'enable Britain to establish a stronger foothold in these areas, so recently released from their commitment to trade only with Spain and Portugal'.[45] Ever susceptible to such designs and aspirations, Darwin's own commitment to British expansionism is revealed in a glowing encomium to Empire recorded toward the end of the *Journal of Researches* devoted to his amateur naturalist and anthropological musings. 'It is impossible', he writes, 'for an Englishman to behold these distant colonies, without a high pride and satisfaction. To hoist the British flag, seems to draw with it as a certain consequence, wealth, prosperity, civilisation ....'[46]

In large part, Darwin's patriotic fervour and singular failure of sympathy with the 'native' races he encounters is fashioned by the distinctly utilitarian view that lacking recognisable forms of governmentality, mediation and obedience they also lack civilisation, progress and improvement. As he observes of the tribes in Tierra Del Fuego:

> The perfect equality among the individuals composing these tribes, must for a long time retard their civilisation. As we see those animals, whose instinct compels them to live in society and obey a chief, are most capable of improvement, so is it with the races of mankind. Whether we look at it as a cause or a consequence, the more civilised always have the most artificial governments ....[47]

Yet, and inadvertently, the evolutionary train of thought to which he succumbs during the voyage of the *Beagle* comes eventually to contravene the principles of governmentality – certainly as they have been identified in the preceding discussion.

Darwin's accidental and indirect countermand to governmentality is, arguably, provoked by a little bird, specifically, the American ostrich or 'Rhea', replaced in southern parts of the continent by a different but closely allied species. The peculiar geographical distribution of the Rhea sets Darwin firmly on the course of contemporary evolutionary speculation, particularly in its challenge to earlier naturalist assumptions about the immutability of species. As is well known, from the beginning of the nineteenth century most evolutionary thinkers were agreed that far from being fixed within bounded taxonomic categories species became mutable through principles of lineal descent, changing constitution in the slow transition from extinct to extant forms. To this advance in nineteenth-century evolutionism Darwin acknowledges his debt in *The Origin of Species*. But Darwin's *Origin*, of course, poses an even more radical challenge to earlier theorists of species' immutability. Dispensing with the current notion of separate lineages, wherein mutation only occurs vertically in a linear series linking one species in the dead past to one in the living present, Darwin proffers two modifications. First, he claims, species also branch horizontally in time such that any given species might leave a variety of seemingly disparate descendants all intimately related to each other through shared ancestors. Second, dramatically extending the former observation, he asserts the single origin of all extant species. It is this notion of a shared community of descent which fuels Darwin's contention that, therefore, all sentient life is knitted together in an 'inextricable web of affinities'.[48] As he writes, with rising excitement, in a notebook entry of 1837:

> If we choose to let conjecture run wild, then animals, our fellow brethren in pain, diseases, death, suffering and famine – our slaves in the most laborious works, our companions in our amusements – they may partake [of] our origins in one common ancestor – we may be all netted together.[49]

It is not hard to imagine why Darwin's hypotheses would be of revolutionary significance to late-Victorian advocates of unmediated human–animal relationality. In particular, and with reference to our larger discussion, his postulation of sentient life as an inextricable web is eagerly absorbed within *fin de siècle* animal welfare as a theorem for radical cosmopolitanism; authorising intimacy with apparent strangers and facilitating, for our purposes, the anti-colonial hospitality of which Mohan Gandhi becomes a direct beneficiary. Thus, refusing to concede propinquity or 'similarity' as a prerequisite for community, Salt's *The Creed of Kinship* invokes Darwin to transform *zoophilia*, with its claims on behalf of inter-species relationality, into a rehearsal ground for *xenophilia*, with its unpartisan favour toward foreign guest-friends. Condemning imperial patriotism and nationalism, in these terms, he canvasses the subtle pleasures of imaginative identification with strangers and outsiders:

> in a happier age than any the world has seen it will be possible, and indeed necessary, that each individual, while not less conscious than now of the claims of neighbourhood, shall also be moved by a wider regard for the well-being of others – of those who are at present looked upon as 'outsiders' – and by a determination that they shall not be sacrificed to any interests or supposed interests of his own.[50]

Salt's sentiments are ubiquitous in the literature of *fin de siècle* animal welfare and no writer of note fails to see in Darwinian evolutionism a means of recasting the political as a demand for the claims of strangeness over propinquity, alterity over similarity, or, as Howard Moore puts it in his, *The Universal Kinship*, as a struggle between 'altruistic' and 'provincial' ethics.[51] And in each case, Darwin is invoked to confer a new status upon animal welfare, corroborating the view that human–animal sociality holds the key, *à la* Haraway, to a more generally egalitarian world, liberated from inequities of class, gender, race, and so on. But if Darwin's metaphor of a 'web of affinities' finds tacit political expression in these ways, it is his attending theory of ecological cooperation that achieves, once again despite his intentions, direct revolutionary articulation.

If nature, represented variously in *Origin* as a branched 'tree' or 'coral', confirms the kinship of sentient life, it also, Darwin argues, demonstrates in the apparently harsh economy of its selective procedures the necessity of co-operative co-adaptation between successful species, augmenting the subtle relation of life forms with a demand for their interactive sociality. Changes in one organism directly produce contingent effects in all other organisms with which it interacts in the prevailing ecosystem, thus creating complex genetic material wherein, say, the evolving structure of woodpeckers, will depend, in large part, on successful relations established between previous generations of woodpecker and coeval tree, bird and insect forms.

In due course, Darwin's view of nature as 'a tangled bank' demonstrating the complex interdependence of palpably different organisms, falls into the hands of the anarchist Peter Kropotkin, settled in England from 1886, and a close ally of the Salt circle.[52] Reformulating anarchism as the law of immediate and co-operative sociality or 'mutual aid', Kropotkin gains from Darwin a case for the irrefutable amity at work in the animal world. As he observes, apropos of evolutionary thought, in his *Mutual Aid*,

> we maintain that under *any* circumstances sociability is the greatest advantage in the struggle for life. Those species which willingly or unwillingly abandon it are doomed to decay; while those animals which know best how to combine, have the greatest chances of survival ... .[53]

Such animal sociability, however, is entirely 'natural', in Bentham's sense of the term, flourishing without the intrusive mediations of governmentality and the law. Indeed, Kropotkin avers, the jealous State with its vertical organisation has historically resisted the horizontal circuits of voluntary association; ever curtailing the affective intensities between people. 'In proportion as the obligations towards the State grew in numbers', he observes, 'the citizens were evidently relieved from their obligations towards each other.'[54]

Kropotkin is not by any means the only conduit for anarchism into late-Victorian England.[55] But his intervention at this scene is crucial for the concerns of the present discussion, explicating, through a specifically Darwinian model of human-animal sociality, the terms of conflict and contestation between the discourse of immediate love/relationality/affect, extolled by *fin de siècle* animal welfare, on the one hand, and that on behalf of separation and against the claims of feeling underpinning the grim protocols of Benthamite or utilitarian governmentality, on the other. A crucial node in the complex historical processes which gave to *fin de siècle* animal welfare a distinctly anarchist provenance, Kropotkin's ideas are amplified and echoed throughout the literature associated with this movement. Leo Tolstoy's influential writings on vegetarianism are typically shaped by a profound mistrust of ruling institutions; Elisee Reclus, friend of Kroptkin, early theorist of 'mutual aid', and author, with Ernest Crossby, of *The Meat Fetish*, consistently combines vegetarian *apologia* with a demand for the end of all government; and Edward Carpenter, the homosexual activist, vegetarian and anti-vivisectionist, seamlessly connects his own belief in a Darwinian creed of kinship with entreaties for non-governmental sociality.[56]

So, to bring this discussion to a close: a complex ideological mixture of affective socialism and post-Darwinian evolutionary anarchism sustains the anti-colonial hospitality, *à la* Derrida, that *fin de siècle* animal welfare offers to Gandhi between 1888 and 1891. But what is visible in the first instance as hospitality becomes over time a form of ideological parity, wherein, much in the manner of his early interlocutors, Gandhi distils in the affective language of *ahimsa* the prose of anarchist refusal: demanding that the British Quit India and that independent India, in its turn, quit governmentality. Is this a case of influence? Most certainly. In very large part the business of my argument has been to claim that mature Gandhian politics owes at least part of its inheritance to the tentative murmurings of a few radicals on the margins of late-Victorian culture. But, equally, in a gesture – let's call it 'postcolonial' – that Salt would doubtless condone, it has also been my purpose to offer a Gandhian reading of *fin de siècle* animal welfare; to assert under the comprehensive sign of *ahimsa* the integrity and organicity of its various and seemingly disparate obsessions: zoophilia, anti-colonialism, affect, the simplification of life, class-critique, socialism, cosmopolitanism, kinship and anarchism. Let us end, then, in honour of anticolonial collaboration, with a somewhat clumsy poem that Salt wrote about Gandhi toward the end of his own life. It is called 'India in 1930':

> An India governed, under alien law,
> By royal proclamation,
> By force, by pomp of arms, that fain would awe
> Her newly-awakened nation;
> While he who sways the heart of Hindustan,
> To more than Kingship risen,
> Is one old, powerless, unresisting man,
> Whose palace is – a prison!

Notes

1 M. K. Gandhi, *Collected Works of Mahatma Gandhi* (Delhi: Ministry of Information and Broadcasting, 1976), henceforth abbreviated as *CWMG*, vol. 1, 79.
2 Ibid., 41.
3 Ibid. In a later reminiscence Gandhi recounts that he chose porridge for the first course and a pie for the second: 'I saw the "Central" restaurant, and went there and had some porridge for the first time. I did not at first enjoy it, but I liked the pie I had for the second course', *CWMG*, vol. 1, 49.
4 Stephen Winsten, *Salt and his Circle* (London, 1951), 118.
5 George Hendrick, *Henry Salt: Humanitarian Reformer and Man of Letters* (University of Illinois Press: Urbana, Chicago, London, 1977), 111–12.
6 Gandhi, *Collected Works: An Autobiography*, 41.
7 E. M. Forster, *Two Cheers for Democracy* (Edward Arnold, London, 1951), 66
8 *CWMG*, vol. 1, 125.
9 Marios Constantinou, 'Spectral *Philia* and the Imaginary Institution of Needs', *The South Atlantic Quarterly*, 97: 1, Winter 1998, 156.
10 H. S. Salt to Gandhi, October 8, 1932, Gandhi National Museum and Library, New Delhi.
11 *The Vegetarian Messenger*, 1 (1887): 3–4.
12 Henry Salt, *Killing for Sport: Essays by Various Writers* (G. Bell and Sons Ltd: London, 1919), 150.
13 E. Mason (ed.), *Oscar Wilde on Vegetarianism* (London, 1991).
14 F. R. Leavis, *Mill on Bentham and Coleridge* (Cambridge University Press: Cambridge, 1950), 13.
15 Jeremy Bentham, *An Introduction to the Principles of Morals and Legislation*, eds J. H. Burns and H. L. A. Hart (Clarendon Press: Oxford, 1996), 282–83.
16 Thomas Taylor, *Vindication of the Rights of Brutes*, ed. Louise Shultz Boas, Gainsville (Scholars Facsimilies and Reprints: Florida, 1960), vii.

17 Bentham, *Introduction to the Principles of Morals*, 282.
18 Elie Halevy, *The Growth of Philosophical Radicalism* (Faber & Faber: London, 1928), 27.
19 Bentham, *Introduction to the Principles of Morals*, 285.
20 Halevy, *The Growth of Philosophical Radicalism*, 27.
21 Michel Foucault, *Discipline and Punish: the Birth of the Prison*, trans. Alan Sheridan (Penguin: Harmondsworth, 1987), 209.
22 Ibid., 221.
23 See, for example, Keith Thomas, *Man and the Natural World: A History of the Modern Sensibility* (Pantheon Books: New York, 1983), 186–88 and Harriet Ritvo, *The Animal Estate: The English and Other Creatures in the Victorian Age* (Harvard University Press: Cambridge, Massachusetts, London, 1987), 133–36.
24 *Debates*, vol. xxxv, 204.
25 John Stuart Mill, *Principles of Political Economy with some of their Applications to Social Philosophy*, ed. W. I. Ashley (Augustus M. Kelley: New York, 1965), 958–59.
26 Cited in Asa Briggs, *the Age of Improvement: 1783–1867* (Longman: London, 1959), 2.
27 J. S. Mill, *Utilitarianism, On Liberty, Essay on Bentham*, ed. Mary Warnock (Collins: Glasgow, 1962), 135–36.
28 Foucault, *Discipline and Punish*, 199, 200.
29 Bentham, *Fragment*, 40.
30 Bentham, *An Introduction to the Principles of Morals*, 21.
31 See ibid., 16.
32 John Stuart Mill, *Autobiography* (Kessinger Publishing, [1924] 2003), 67.
33 Peter Singer, *Animal Liberation* (Pimlico: London, 2nd edn, 1975), x, opens with an excoriating critique of 'feeling' as irrelevant and deleterious to animal welfare. Retelling the story of a student encounter that he and his wife have with a hypocritical ham-eating English animal lover, Singer launches into the following fulminations:

> ... we were not especially 'interested in' animals. Neither of us had been inordinately fond of dogs, cats, or horses in the way that many people are. We didn't 'love' animals. We simply wanted them treated as the independent beings that they are, and not as a means to human ends – as the pig whose flesh was now in our hostesses sandwiches had been treated ... The assumption that in order to be interested in such matters one must be an 'animal-lover' is itself an indication of the absence of the slightest inkling that the moral standards that we apply among human beings might extend to other animals.

Singer offers his most coherent defence of the 'separation' between animals and humans, once again in a startlingly utilitarian idiom in his ficto-critical reflection upon J. M. Coetzee's, *The Lives of Animals* (Princeton University Press: Princeton, 1999), 85–91.
34 Bentham, *Introduction to the Principles of Morals*, 282
35 See John Kipling (1891), *Beast and Man in India* (Macmillan and Co., Ltd., London: 1904)
36 Haraway, *Simians, Cyborgs, and Women*, 177, 378. Similar sentiments are repeated in Haraway's paen to human–dog relationality in, *The Companion Species Manifesto*, 2–3:

> We are training each other in acts of communication we barely understand. We are, constitutively, companion species. We make each other up, in the flesh. Significantly other to each other, in specific difference, we signify in the flesh a nasty developmental infection called love.

37 Arthur Broderick Bullock, *'The Basis of Morality': Schopenhauer's View of Ethics* (Swan Sonnenschein and Co.: London, 1903), 4, 2, 5.
38 Frances Power Cobbe, *Darwinism in Morals and Other Essays* (Williams & Norgate: London, 1872), 6.
39 Frances Power Cobbe, *False Beasts and True: Essays on Natural and Unnatural History* (Ward, Lock and Tyler: London, 1900), p?
40 See Frances Power Cobbe, *The Divine Law of Love and its Application to the Lower Animals* (Pewtress and Co.: London, 1895).
41 See Anna Kingsford, *Pasteur: His Method and its Results, a Lecture* (North London Anti-Vivisection Society: London, 1886), 11.
42 Edward Maitland, *Anna Kingsford: Her Life, Letters, Diary and Work* (John M. Watkins: London, 1913), 2 vols, vol ii, 268.
43 Henry Light, *Common-Sense Vegetarianism* (Manchester: Manchester Vegetarian Society, 1929), 96.
44 Charles Darwin, *Voyage of the Beagle: Charles Darwin's Journal of Researches*, ed. and abrid. Janet Browne and Michael Neeve (Penguin: Harmondsworth, 1989), 2.
45 Ibid., 9.
46 Ibid., 376.
47 Ibid., 183-84.
48 Ibid., 578.
49 Cited in James J. Sheehan and Morton Sosna, *The Boundaries of Humanity: Humans, Animals and Machines* (University of Californial Press: Berkeley, Los Angeles, Oxford, 1991), p. ?
50 Henry Salt, *The Creed of Kinship* (Constable and Co. Ltd.: London, 1935), 8.
51 See J. Howard Moore, *The Universal Kinship* (George Bell & Sons: London, 1906).
52 Haraway, in *The Companion Species Manifesto*, 9, draws attention to the anarchism, or mistrust of sequestering categories, implicit in the web of affinities postulated by Darwin:

> And like the productions of a decadent gardener who can't keep good distinctions between natures and cultures straight, the shape of my kin networks looks more like a trellis or an esplanade than a tree. You can't tell up from down, and everything seems to go sidewise. Such snake-like, sidewinding traffic is one of my themes. My garden is full of snakes, full of trellises, full of indirection. Instructed by evolutionary population biologists and bioanthropologists, I know that multidirectional gene flow – multidirectional flows of bodies and values – is and has always been the name of the game of life on earth. It is certainly the way into the kennel.

53 Peter Kropotkin, *Mutual Aid: A Factor of Evolution* (William Heinemann: London, 1910), 57.
54 Ibid., 226-27
55 The scene of *fin de siècle* English anarchism is comprehensively described in Hermia Oliver, *The International Anarchist Movement in Late-Victorian London* (Croom Helm and St. Martin's Press: London, Canberra and New York, 1983).
56 Edward Carpenter, *Prisons, Police and Punishment: An Inquiry into the Causes and Treatment of Crime and Criminals* (A. C. Fifield: London, 1905), 104, 113.

Bibliography

Bentham, Jeremy, *An Introduction to the Principles of Morals and Legislation*, eds J. H. Burns and H. L. A. Hart, Oxford: Clarendon Press, 1996.

Briggs, Asa, *The Age of Improvement: 1783–1867*, London: Longman, 1959.
Bullock, Arthur Broderick, *'The Basis of Morality': Schopenhauer's View of Ethics*, London: Swan Sonnenschein and Co., 1903.
Carpenter, Edward, *Prisons, Police and Punishment: An Inquiry into the Causes and Treatment of Crime and Criminals*, London: A. C. Fifield, 1905.
Cobbe, Frances Power, *Darwinism in Morals and Other Essays*, London Williams & Norgate, 1872.
—— *The Divine Law of Love and its Application to the Lower Animals*, London: Pewtress and Co., 1895
—— *False Beasts and True: Essays on Natural and Unnatural History* London: Ward, Lock and Tyler, 1900.
Constantinou, Marios, 'Spectral *Philia* and the Imaginary Institution of Needs', *The South Atlantic Quarterly*, 97: 1, Winter 1998.
Darwin, Charles, *Voyage of the Beagle: Charles Darwin's Journal of Researches*, ed. and abrid. Janet Browne and Michael Neeve, Harmondsworth: Penguin, 1989.
Forster, E. M., *Two Cheers for Democracy*, London: Edward Arnold, 1951.
Foucault, Michel, *Discipline and Punish: The Birth of the Prison*, trans. Alan Sheridan, Harmondsworth: Penguin, 1987.
Gandhi, M. K, *Collected Works of Mahatma Gandhi*, vol. 1, Delhi: Ministry of Information and Broadcasting, 1976.
Halevy, Elie, *The Growth of Philosophical Radicalism*, London: Faber & Faber, 1928.
Haraway, Donna, *Simians, Cyborgs, and Women*, New York: Routledge, 1991.
—— *The Companion Species Manifesto*, Chicago: Prickly Paradigm, 2003.
Hendrick, George, *Henry Salt: Humanitarian Reformer and Man of Letters*, Urbana, Chicago, London: University of Illinois Press, 1977.
Kingsford, Anna, *Pasteur: His Method and its Results, a Lecture*, London: North London Anti-Vivisection Society 1886.
Kipling, John (1891) *Beast and Man in India*, London: Macmillan and Co., Ltd, 1904.
Kropotkin, Peter, *Mutual Aid: A Factor of Evolution*, London: William Heinemann, 1910.
Leavis F. R., *Mill on Bentham and Coleridge*, Cambridge: Cambridge University Press, 1950.
Light, Henry, *Common-Sense Vegetarianism*, Manchester: Vegetarian Society, 1929.
Maitland, Edward, *Anna Kingsford: Her Life, Letters, Diary and Work*, 2 vols, London: John M. Watkins, 1913.
Mason E. (ed.), *Oscar Wilde on Vegetarianism*, London, 1991.
Mill, J. S., *Utilitarianism, On Liberty, Essay on Bentham*, ed. Mary Warnock, Glasgow: Collins, 1962.
—— *Principles of Political Economy with some of their Applications to Social Philosophy*, ed. W. I. Ashley, New York: Augustus M. Kelley, 1965.
Moore, J. Howard, *The Universal Kinship*, London: George Bell & Sons, 1906.
Oliver, Hermia, *The International Anarchist Movement in Late-Victorian London*, London, Canberra and New York: Croom Helm and St. Martin's Press, 1983.
Ritvo, Harriet, *The Animal Estate: The English and Other Creatures in the Victorian Age*, Cambridge, Massachusetts, London: Harvard University Press, 1987.
Salt, Henry, *Killing for Sport: Essays by Various Writers*, London: G. Bell and Sons Ltd, 1919.
—— *The Creed of Kinship*, London: Constable and Co. Ltd., 1935.

Sheehan, James J. and Morton Sosna, *The Boundaries of Humanity: Humans, Animals and Machines*, Berkeley, Los Angeles, Oxford: University of California Press, 1991.
Singer, Peter, *Animal Liberation*, London: Pimlico, 2nd edn, 1975.
Taylor, Thomas, *Vindication of the Rights of Brutes*, ed. Louise Shultz Boas, Gainsville, Florida: Scholars Facsimilies and Reprints, 1960.
Thomas, Keith, *Man and the Natural World: A History of the Modern Sensibility*, New York: Pantheon Books, 1983.
Winsten, Stephen, *Salt and his Circle*, London, 1951.

3 The quack whom we know
Illness and nursing in Gandhi

Sandhya Shetty

No other thinker from within the ranks of decolonization has presented as robust and radical a critique of medicine as has Mohandas Karamchand Gandhi. Gandhi's well-known opposition to medicine appears in capsule form in *Hind Swaraj*, his 'cranky' 1910 polemic against modern civilization.[1] A rich thematics of illness and therapeutics can, however, be traced elsewhere in his *oeuvre*. And yet, barring a few important exceptions, Gandhian scholars have not given this broader text of his critique of medicine the analytic centrality it deserves.[2] Within the framework of postcolonial theory as well, the specifics of Gandhi's critique of medicine in modernity have not generated wide interpretive interest. One has only to recall postcolonial critics' engagement with Frantz Fanon's diagnoses of colonialism's productivity in the realm of pathology, and western medicine's perverse implication in that process, to recognize the relative critical neglect of Gandhi's position on comparable matters.[3] Arguably, Gandhi's claims about medicine's chronic incompatibility with the ethical and political well being of humanity are at once more far-reaching and more radical than Fanon's compelling yet ultimately ambivalent critique of *colonial* medicine.[4] Unlike Fanon's, Gandhi's indictment stems from more than just his discontent with medicine's misappropriation as a mode of colonial power. Shaped by a bioethical commitment to self-liberating forms of *ascesis*, a far more deeply rooted antagonism frames the latter's critical stance on the professional practice of medicine.[5] Gandhi's zest for ethical self-cultivation grounded in the body transforms illness as well as therapeutics into lay ascetic domains. In this context, internalized presuppositions about human life and well being, manifest in the expert interventions of institutionalized medicine, find their limit in a self-conscious ascetic disregard for life unlimited.

A fundamental aspect of Gandhi's critique of medicine is his clear if startling antipathy for the most humane and seemingly irreproachable of medicine's axioms: the decree that 'Life' and its preservation at all cost stands as a self-evident good.[6] His own well-publicized experiments in amateur curing and intimate caring, elaborated in such texts as *My Experiments*[7] and *Key to Health*,[8] shape an anti-medical economy of health that struggles to break free from the absolutism of this imperative to preserve life at all cost. Not surprisingly, the cancellation of 'Life' as the *telos* of therapeutic practice calls into question a range of institutionalized medicine's fundamental assumptions about the body, illness, and cure. Most central and provocative of all is Gandhi's re-valuation of illness. In the several episodes of illness and nursing detailed in the autobiography and elsewhere, illness is not, as one would expect, ranged on the other side of life, of remedy, and of health. Despite the risks and anxieties associated with it, Gandhi attempts consistently to recast illness as a non-emergency event, requiring palliative care giving or amateur nursing rather than medical expertise or pharmacological intervention in the interests of urgent recovery. Sequestered from the busy incursions of professional doctors, illness in Gandhi's curative practice comes to be transformed into a matter of slow ethical self-fashioning for patient and caretaker alike. As ethical responses to illness, Gandhi's passion for nursing, and his dietetic asceticism displace conventional medicine's structuring presuppositions about the value of life, the goals of therapy, and about its own relation to the political and the moral.

A focus on Gandhi's anti-medical therapeutic practice, best illustrated by his passion for nursing and his dietetic philosophy, reveals what this essay takes to be the key element in understanding these two crucial components of his critique of medicine: his delight, or dare I say, love of the ill and of illness. This practically manifest love of illness, including the lay nurse's excitement at the prospect of intimacy with diseased bodies, is largely absent from the abstract *Hind Swaraj* provides of his complex position. But a careful look at other texts clearly suggests how much Gandhi's enthusiastic appropriation of illness for ethics and away from medicine lies at the core of an alternative therapeutic practice centred on asceticism. Directly linked to his principled rejection of the premise that life must be preserved at all costs, the ethical centrality of Gandhi's love of illness and the ill calls for fresh examinations of his critique of medicine, especially the famed dietetic asceticism and the understudied nursing hospitality that constitute the key components of his 'quackery'.[9]

Gandhi's antipathy for what he deemed the ethically dubious presuppositions of conventional medical practice, namely, 'the love of life' or, what he also identified as 'an excessive desire for living', shapes a proportionately ascetic, bold, and even risky conception of health, illness, and cure. It is this risky, even reckless, disregard of the imperative to preserve life at all cost – an imperative to be found in both western as well as *ayurvedic* medical practice – that earned for Gandhi his reputation as crank and quack. Interestingly, no one was as keen on designating his peculiar brand of therapeutics 'quackery' as was, in this case, the quack himself. Self-consciously opposed to a secularized understanding of illness and to the vaunted expertise of a drug-based medical science, Gandhi assigned himself the labels 'quack' and 'crank' in satisfied recognition of the utterly idiosyncratic, fringe nature of the perspective and practice he came to fashion in relation to illness.[10] Designed to clear the ground for a radically new understanding of illness and cure, this ascetic brand of quackery, not medicine, Gandhi imagined, would save both body and spirit, by making possible a new body-based practice of the ethical self responsive to violence and suffering.

Contrary to conventional medicine of every stripe, Gandhi's quackery is identifiable first and foremost as radically anti-pharmacological and anti-oral. Re-orienting the entire problem of the ethico-politics of medicine as a problem of overcoming the mouth, that is, overcoming the natural oral-alimentary violence of life or existence, Gandhi posited his special brand of dietetics as conventional therapeutics' great other. While in both European and Indic traditions, food/eating (and of course sexuality) has historically functioned as a field for tests of self-control, medicine/illness, especially in emergencies, has less usually been viewed as an occasion for heroic routines of self-denial.[11] In fact, within most medical traditions, what *ayurveda* terms '*apad-dharma*' would dictate 'emergency' conduct responsive to the goals of easing suffering and preserving life at all cost. As we shall see, in the next two sections, the rejection of the moral legitimacy of *apad-dharma* defines Gandhi's dietetic quackery as a delighted, unhurried experimentation with illness and cure that transforms the very temporality of therapeutic intervention. As the illness and nursing incidents Gandhi recalls in *My Experiments* suggest, the slow *andante* movement of self and other testing focused on the sickbed opens up a gap in the time of modern living. Within this other temporality, Gandhian dietetic quackery allows bodily suffering ample time to run its course toward, just short of, or away from death. What matters most here is the savour of recovery within the ethical limits set on consumption by eagerly self-imposed dietary restrictions. This everyday dietary discipline cuts across sickness and health, attenuating the structuring binary of modern discourses that produces the divide between 'the normal' and 'the pathological'. Courting the risk of death in illness, Gandhi's quack-doctoring or dietetic asceticism rehabilitates instead the question of the ethical versus the unethical way to eat, to live, to be ill, to recover, or, possibly, even to die.

Besides the non-dramatic yet self-conscious practice of food asceticism, nursing hospitality at home and on the battlefield constitutes another key item in the battery of experiments with which Gandhian quackery sought to perfect 'the art of using illness'.[12] In many of the scenes of illness Gandhi narrates in his autobiography and elsewhere, nursing and food asceticism are therapeutic practices that presuppose one another. If, however, we bracket for the moment the much-discussed issue of dietary practice, nursing comes more clearly into view as a distinct second line of inquiry. Most significantly, nursing highlights the physical proximity between bodies and the potential for intimate and tactile caring that can transform the scene of the other's bodily suffering into a sphere of 'hospitality'. Partially identifiable within non-secular parameters as an *imitatio Christi* of sorts, it is my contention that Gandhian nursing speaks to a broader spectrum of ethico-political issues that the idioms of humanitarianism, Christian healing, or good samaritanship, resonant as they were for Gandhi, can only insufficiently grasp. Gandhi's peculiar brand of nursing hospitality therefore challenges us to find a more nuanced and context-sensitive mode of translating its therapeutic, ethical, and political force.

The final section of this essay takes up this challenge, exploring two episodes that dramatize the charge of Gandhi's nursing hospitality. The first involves the arrival of an unnamed leper at Gandhi's door – an incident I explicate at some length in relation to what Jacques Derrida terms 'the Law of unconditional hospitality' in his own explorations of that theme.[13] While this incident occurs in an everyday context, the second episode I discuss occurs in the context of explicit nationalist and racist violence during the Zulu Rebellion. More often than not, as Gandhi's autobiographical narrative reveals, his intimate nursing of nameless and diseased strangers was embedded in public contexts of political and social hostility. Of these military events the Zulu Rebellion of 1906 and the Boer War of 1899 are the most notable.[14]

The interpretive significance of these wartime contexts is heightened if we recall that in *My Experiments* a vaguely awkward locution yokes Gandhi's avowal of his love for nursing to his avowal of a passion for the British Constitution and loyalty to the Empire: 'Like loyalty, an aptitude for nursing was also deeply rooted in my nature' (152). Here, the specific terms in which he elaborates his 'aptitude for nursing' tightens the screw weakly holding together Gandhi's 'two passions' in the same thought: 'I was fond of nursing people, *whether friends or strangers*'.[15] This seemingly casual disregard for the stipulated border between friend and stranger is significant, however, for (despite the implication of an analogy) it actually intensifies the mutual tension between political loyalty, founded on the citizen/foreigner distinction and Gandhi's nursing hospitality, apparently dismissive of the distinction.

In addition to this bald summary statement of his 'two passions', the rich textual and historical detail in which several memorable instances of nursing activity are delineated confirms the conceptually crucial (dis)junction between the roving passion for nursing friends and strangers alike on the one hand and the more discriminating, not to mention abstract, passion that underwrites political loyalty on the other. If we keep in mind this odd textual, conceptual, and even ethical convergence of incommensurable passions (both, of course, deeply rooted impulses to sacrifice self), then the physical and ethical effects of proximity desired by Gandhi's nursing hospitality can become more precisely and broadly comprehensible. Placed in relation to his thinking on political loyalty, the rights and duties of the citizen, racism, western war, and western medicine, Gandhi's unconditional nursing of lepers, indentured labourers, Zulus, and other strangers unfolds a space beyond aversion, beyond self-interest, and beyond (self) identity.

As we shall see in the incident of the leper, the hospitable nurse (as practising lawyer in Gandhi's case) actively seeks opportunities to nurse – takes time off so to speak – thus rendering his therapeutic practice conceptually at odds with the time and understanding of modern medicine and nursing as professional enterprises. Moving beyond the logic of exchange between human beings, Gandhian nursing of the other is also for nothing. In effect, it unveils the social, economic, and temporal commonsense of modernization that naturalizes speed, efficiency, and profit as givens. Outside the logic of exchange and fashioned in the interests of an intimate physical-therapeutic mode of human *relation*, Gandhian nursing is also beyond the modern premise of individual *autonomy* as a basis for collective being or community. It is, above all, his nursing hospitality's active inattention to rational self-interest on the individual and national level that speaks, as Alter contends, to the potential effects that intimate, local encounters between singular bodies/selves can produce on a national and imperial scale.[16] Gandhi's love of nursing afflicted *strangers*, as witnessed in his care of lepers or victims of the plague and war, neither presupposes nor desires kinship, friendship, or the totalizing abstraction of national identity/community. Essentially a close face-to-face encounter with a singular other, it involves rather a kind of 'love' that requires the nursing self be drawn out of its secure domicile.[17] In following 'the Law of unconditional hospitality', that is, in requiring no identification papers as it were, nursing as represented in the Gandhian text incorporates the bodies of foes *and* allies, friends *and* strangers alike, bringing them 'in close touch' with the nurse's own body/self.

The third section three unpacks and elaborates a bioethics of proximity implicit in the highly condensed narratives of Gandhi's practice of nursing (subaltern) strangers, of both foreign and Indian origin. Analytically, these strangers are distinct by virtue of their location or provenance. They emerge from and remain outside even the redefined spaces of Gandhian domesticity (the ashram) and the circles of friendship regulated, as Ajay Skaria has pointed out, by the idea of *mitrata* or neighborliness with equals.[18] My focus is exclusively on these shadowy subaltern objects of Gandhi's nursing, who arrive unexpectedly and briefly from 'the outside' and are taken in and absorbed into the nurse's hospitable care in an ascetic act that draws the other close at the same time that it moves the self out of itself toward the other. The political stakes of such a bioethics of proximity are best exemplified by Gandhi's volunteer ambulance work amidst wounded Zulus during the so-called Zulu Rebellion, which I discuss at some length. The unexpected close contact between nurse and nursed on this occasion both illuminates and interrogates the self-isolating discourses of colonial racism and nationalism that Gandhi personally encountered in South Africa and against which he conceptualized the notion and practice of *satyagraha*. I argue that Gandhi's quackery constitutes an integral part of the nexus of ethical, religious, and political forces at play in that crucial development responsive to the unjust Bill to institute Pass Laws governing the movement and status of Indians in South Africa at the turn of the nineteenth century.

While Gandhi's nursing of ill strangers broaches the possibility of new ethical relations of proximity, interestingly, none of this intimate and sometimes perilous care giving necessarily entails that the nurse-ascetic be motivated by a secular, humanitarian desire to preserve life for the sake of life.[19] When, for instance, an acquaintance, Parchure Shastri, a Sanskrit scholar afflicted with leprosy, wrote to Gandhi, expressing his wish to commit suicide and so put an end to all his misery, Gandhi took no serious issue with this desire. More than the prospect of mere death, it was the mode of dying or self-sacrifice proposed that appears to have bothered Gandhi. Therefore rather than attempt to dissuade Parchure, Gandhi strongly urged the incurably ill scholar to consider the most ethical mode of bringing about voluntary death, his own quack anti-alimentary suggestion being that he fast to death. In enjoining the afflicted scholar to die well, that is, to choose another mode of shaping his suicide, Gandhi was advocating a position on how to live well through renunciation in a manner that echoes Jain soteriology or 'prescriptions for how to bring one's life to an end'.[20] James Laidlaw identifies these prescriptions in a way that helps make sense of Gandhi's 'quack' practice in an Indic context:

> Such a death (*samadhi maran*) [death by fasting] is valid for both renouncers and lay Jains, but it is insistently distinguished both in teaching and practice from 'religious suicide'. In the final stages of a fatal illness, or, in the case of the very old, at the natural end of life, people sometimes vow to accept no more food or water and thus end their life in a fast. ... Thus those taking this fast do not bring about their death, instead they accept it in an act of disciplined restraint.[21]

Gandhi's advice to Parchure thus stands as a dramatically clear summation of his therapeutic approach to illness as, one, an occasion for zestful ascetic labour (on the part of nurse and patient alike) consistent with ethical principles of nonviolent existence, and, two, as an occasion for teaching oneself how to die well even when in the throes of extreme physical and mental suffering.[22]

Both aspects of this approach set Gandhian quackery in determined opposition to the modern profession of medicine. Gandhi's insistent attempt to realign therapeutic strategies with ethical principles centred on diet and fasting finds its clearest expression in his narration of his self-treatment as well as of his nursing of various family members in the teeth of lay and expert medical opposition. These episodes bear a slightly different valence and emphasis from those in which we witness Gandhi's passion for nursing strangers. While in all instances the nurse-ascetic remains unmotivated by 'the desire for living', it is Gandhi's nursing of his own immediate family that illuminates most clearly the ideals of '*aparigraha*' (non-possession) and '*samabhava*' (equability) that form the ethical substrate of Gandhian quackery's anti-alimentary impulse.[23] The sections that follow highlight the fact that nursing, or for that matter any aspect of illness, as represented in the Gandhian text cannot be conceptualized simply in terms of the humanitarian desire to cure disease or save lives in the ordinary sense; for these benevolent desires, the familiar *teloi* of pharmacologically oriented medicine, presuppose and foster the unrestrained forms of oral consumption and bodily incorporation that constitute the real *bête noire* of Gandhian quackery.[24]

Eating and illness: the consuming violence of life on life

In one of the most striking accusations *Hind Swaraj* levels against the medical profession, doctors are likened to parasites.[25] Gandhi's brief but specific attribution of parasitism to the medical profession calls for further explication because it compresses much that is of fundamental importance to his critique. Sought after repeatedly to attend to overloaded modern bodies, doctors, Gandhi argues, do not cure their patients in any meaningful sense as much as they batten on them; as guests at the bedside, their mode of cure ensures that they never have cause to leave but can continue to grow thick on their indisposed hosts. The medical profession thus stands accused of expeditiously returning its hosts/patients to their original 'immoral' habits of consumption rather than ushering in an alternative regimen of bodily conduct that might minimize the damage inflicted by unlimited consumption.

Striking and typical in Gandhi's casting of the medical profession as parasitical is an implicit allusion to the base metaphor of eating or consuming. As parasites, medical men are nothing if not eaters; impostors in the sickroom, their vaunted 'high medical skill' is in effect only an endorsement of a modern regime governed by orality, consumption, ingestion. In other words, modern medicine in Gandhi's view ensures the full, unhealthy functioning of, what David Krell in another context refers to as, 'the systems of the mouth', that is, of eating and nourishment.[26] This accusation against medicine is, of course, entirely consistent with *Hind Swaraj's* overall conception of the affliction of modern civilization as pre-eminently a distemper of the oral-alimentary tract: overeating, indigestion. In fact in *Hind Swaraj*, the entire argument against modernity comes to be staked, despite its large 'civilizational tenor', on the example of this seemingly minor complaint. Of course indigestion as an ailment is more than any other to be located at the charged crossroads of soul and body where the ascription of agency can be relatively less vexed than in the case of, say, epidemic diseases such as consumption or the plague. As such, it serves Gandhi's exposition of the ethical life well. For a man engaged in a critique of over-consumption and of the excess of capitalist economies, the disease with appropriate metaphoric power to condemn such excess had paradoxically to be a literal consequence as well of, what he saw as, soul-depressing orality. While it is impossible to determine whether Gandhi finds the alimentary or the spiritual more gripping in his insistent linking of the two, what is clear is that when we encounter the ailment identified as 'the indigestion of enslavement' in Gandhi's diagnosis of colonizer and colonized alike, we are to read it as more than a quirky metaphoric turn. Functioning at multiple levels, this conceptual coinage signals the impossibility of disentangling the literal from the metaphoric, the bodily from the spiritual and the pathological from the political.

But there is another point to be made here with regard to the turn to digestive disturbances as fitting corporeal metaphors for patients' and modern physicians' moral derelictions. The highly metaphoric circulation of gastrointestinal disturbances throughout the text also flags Gandhi's concern with the literal alimentary violence or violence of consumption that sustains life itself. I am fully persuaded that this aspect of Gandhi's critique of medicine is richly accounted for by the influence of the English vegetarians[27] and perhaps less directly reinforced by feminine strains of Christian ascetic practice that scholars[28] have studied. At the same time it is important to recognize that Gandhi's preoccupation with the ethical problem of *all* eating and consumption and his perception of the natural violence of existence *as* a problem of nourishment identifies his dietetic minimalism with certain traditional Indic epistemologies. As scholars have shown in the case of *ayurvedic* medicine and Jain asceticism, concepts of nonviolence were absolutely central to Indic epistemologies and the rituals and ethics derived from them.[29] In these contexts, eating and not eating become acts that implicate one in the natural violence of existence itself. Located within this way of thinking, the problem of indigestion seemingly belaboured in *Hind Swaraj* appears less trivial than at first sight.

The parasite as biological fact is the perfectly apt base metaphor that broadly signifies the food chain (or chain of being) that identifies living on earth itself as inescapably a violent matter: life against life. The puzzling characterization of doctors as parasitical also becomes less gratuitous when placed in this context where it appears as a highly apposite metonym for an egregious medical profession. To this inescapably violent aspect of living, grotesquely mirrored by a (self) indulgent, parasitical medical profession, Gandhi opposed his own unique brand of dietetic asceticism. Anti-medical in inspiration, aspects of this dietetic experiment such as fasting and vegetarianism are uniquely designed to minimize precisely that alimentary excess and violence of life against life that eating represents. Gandhi's obsessive minimalism with regard to food – his insistence in various writings that in quality and quantity it be regarded and consumed as one would medicine – becomes intelligible in the peculiar light of this interrogation of the 'alimentary violence' that *both* food and medicine inevitable participate in.[30] I have lingered on *Hind Swaraj's* under-examined perception of medicine as parasitical because the charge is so clearly linked to what I see as absolutely fundamental to Gandhi's therapeutic vision, namely, the circumvention of 'the systems of the mouth'. In this context, it is unsurprising that dietary abstinences understood as counterweights to the parasitic regime of orality stand out as the centrepiece of Gandhian quackery as it attempted to minimize the demands of the mouth in both sickness and in health.

And, of course, illness is that which most threatens the daily maintenance of dietetic asceticism that the apprentice *satyagrahi* finds perfectly sustainable and defensible in health. If in *Hind Swaraj* illness or disease is moralistically read as an embodied effect of immoral habits, in *My Experiments* we witness a series of concrete ethical engagements with the ill body that engenders another view of it. Here in illness episode after illness episode narrated by Gandhi the semiotic of illness is scrambled, and its standard meaning signifying 'bodily crisis' demanding rapid and efficient medical interventions in the interests of restoring health and ensuring the continuation of life is displaced. For Gandhi it is precisely the efficiency and speed of drug-based conventional medicine that negate the overriding imperative of patiently experimental ethical living, ideally indifferent to the influential binary distinction between the normal and the pathological, identified as a key development in the construction of modern discourses on life. In entailing the abrupt cessation of that meticulous, daily monitoring of *himsa* (violence), effected by careless consumption, illness conceived as emergency militates against dietetics as slow ethics.

Dietetic asceticism then critically marks the point at which the ethical conduct of quotidian life is habitually deferred/sidetracked by an unnecessary and avoidable sense of crisis presided over by professional doctoring in the interests of material well-being and self-preservation. As a response to this sanctioned flight of medicine from the everyday domain of conviction, Gandhian quackery is invested in a fundamental realignment of the matter of illness with ethical living – something that can only occur as a result of radical distancing from institutions and expert discourses on health and life. So much so, Gandhi's therapeutic practices begin to lose their 'medical' lineaments altogether becoming instead a matter of simply applying the ready to hand earth, sun, and water based 'household remedies', compiled in *Key to Health* for example, and which interfere minimally with everyday habit and conduct.[31] As alluded to above, food is likened to medicine in the context of health: food should be taken as one would medicine. In the context of illness then food (in 'normal' medicinal proportions) is always already medicine. But fasting is best. Whatever the case, central to all these scenarios is the absence or near absence of eating as the best medicine even when (or especially when) life itself is endangered.

Again, Gandhi's dietetic quackery – here producing an anti-medical blurring of the lines between illness and health – might be understood from within the Hindu tradition. Scholars have pointed out that medicine in the Indic context is always understood as a practice that breaks into conviction, vows, determination, ritual abstinence, that is, into the entire domain of everyday self-regulation and, in Brahminical terms, purity.[32] This deferral of the ritualism and principled conduct of quotidian life by medical emergency/urgency in fact constitutes the crisis. In other words, within medicine the crisis is constituted not by the suffering entailed by disease *per se* but by the fact that the doctor by virtue of his knowledge (*veda*) of the continuation of life (*ayush*) imposes, as Zimmerman claims, on religious and ethical principles. More than any other discipline, then, medicine within the Hindu tradition of vegetarian nonviolence presents a contradiction of the imperative to be nonviolent. What I am suggesting here is that Gandhian quackery recognizes with some distaste and, vigorously, opposes the fact Zimmerman observes in *ayurvedic* medical treatises: 'the doctor makes use of [ ] natural violence for therapeutic ends'.[33] The Gandhian quack-nurse, on the other hand, attempts to reverse this trend, making use of nonviolent dietetics for therapeutic ends.

Not even in the treatment of epidemic disease does the imperative to resist the radical violence inflicted by medical aid, under the guise of beneficence, lose its urgency. The plague itself appears in the form of an opportunity to reverse, by means of the introduction and continuation of ascetic body practices, violent and excessive processes of consumption/incorporation and thus to break the hold of medicine on the body. The asceticism of the nurse in a hazardous context of public emergency is deliberately accentuated in *My Experiments'* narration of Gandhi's nursing work amidst plague victims in Johannesburg. The lesson that emerges in Gandhi's account of the plague is the necessity of the nurse's defiance of the principles of *apad-dharma* in relation to both the sick and the nursing body. Acceptance of *apad-dharma* would have enabled the nurse to expand the limits of permissible conduct with regard to everyday bodily practices in the interests of sustaining life. On this particular occasion of collective public distress experienced by the lowliest members of colonial South African society, recourse to *apad-dharma*, recognized by Hindu *shastric* literature, would have legitimated administering brandy to the plague sufferers and to the nursing assistants as a prophylactic. But we see Gandhi and his co-workers refuse the brandy of *apad-dharma* offered by the municipality nurse, who functions as a metonym for modern medicine in Gandhi's hidden parable. What is more, the volunteer nurses under Gandhi reduce their diet as well during the outbreak of the deadly pneumonic plague: 'I had long made it a rule to go on a light diet during epidemics.'[34] Nursing as here narrated becomes one more self-incitement to bodily asceticism which in turn minimizes the alimentary violence of consumption Gandhi saw inevitably preceding as well as following in the train of medical intervention.

In its efforts to restore the conjunction of the ethical and the somatic, the religious and the medical, Gandhian dietetics then rests at bottom on a radical redefinition of what, under the modern episteme, biologists and rational science have appropriated as their exclusive domain: the discourse on life, when it begins, how it should be maintained, what constitutes the pathological and how it should be rendered 'normal'. Inserting himself at precisely the point where illness severely tests assumptions about the value of life for its own sake, Gandhi moves the problematic of therapeutics beyond the economy of both 'natural' parasitical self-interest and the absolutism of 'mere' remedy/cure. Illness as the taken for granted scene wherein all parties – patient, doctor/nurse, and family – are motivated by a 'healthy' and 'natural' instinct for bodily preservation is thoroughly defamiliarized. This clearing of the conceptual and medicinal clutter in the space of illness allows an alternative range of ethical effects to be somatically grasped. De-linking the ill body from this clutter, Gandhi reinserts it into a larger theatre of ordinary living where it becomes one opportunity, among others, to re-sculpt bit by bit the 'normal' world of violence and immorality in favour of a radically different notion of life and health (as *ahimsa*). Gandhi's quack-doctoring, as narrated in the autobiography, implies that ethical biotherapies do not 'return' the ill body to 'normality', but rather rend that veil and move it toward the (im)possible ideal of humanly achievable nonviolence. Displacing the modern normal/pathological binary and relocating itself within an alternative 'household' economy of unhurried caregiving, Gandhi's quack treatment aspires toward *ahimsa*, offering therapies for nothing – not for money, not only *for* cure and never *for* the sake of *life* itself as defined by convention or science.

Against life unlimited: the risky art of using illness

The myriad instances of nursing care that Gandhi records in *My Experiments* confirm the startling fact that Gandhi's critique of conventional medicine and his alternative therapeutics begins from an ideal opposition to life itself. A close examination of this narration however reveals a meticulous delineation of the ambiguous and hazardous terrain of the experimenter's ethical dilemmas and the surprising decisions and undecidable effects that radiate from it. The deliberate detachment of nursing care from a return to 'normality' and a concern with life produces the ailing body as a risky ground for the kind of ethical experimentation Gandhi undertook. Despite Gandhi's relentless adherence to principle, the therapeutic experiments he performed on himself, Kasturba and Manilal (and on the plague-stricken indentured labourers in South Africa discussed above) nevertheless appear as agonistic struggles on perilous terrain where decision wavers, success is not easily reproducible, and results never guaranteed. Even more than the impossible ideal of disregard for life (or self-sacrifice) that stands as the ethical high water mark then, it is the spectacle of what it means to conduct one's life within sight of this ideal that matters most in these nursing episodes.[35] Speaking of his nature cure experiment on his son Ramdas and others, he writes frankly, 'The reference here, therefore, to these experiments is not meant to demonstrate their success. I cannot claim complete success for any experiment. My object is only to show that he who would go in for novel experiments must begin with himself.'[36]

That the conflict between therapeutic goals and practical ethics is always tense and never resolved once and for all is well illustrated in Gandhi's narration of the incident involving Manilal's typhoid fever.[37] As Gandhi tells it, we become privy to the full range of effort, anxiety, and doubt attendant on one who would be enthusiastic rather than merely stoic about illness. It is precisely Gandhi's active appropriation of illness (via dietetics) into the field of ethical self-testing that allows him to prolong the struggle, court risk, and recast the meaning of life and death as conventionally understood. Gandhian nursing's positioning of vegetarianism against the imperative to preserve human life at all cost is seen in its most tense and disturbing form on the occasion of Manilal's serious bout with 'typhoid, combined with pneumonia and signs of delirium'. Gandhi writes:

> Rightly or wrongly it is part of my religious conviction that man may not eat meat, eggs, and the like. There should be a limit even to the means of keeping ourselves alive. *Even for life itself we may not do certain things.* Religion, as I understand it, does not permit me to use meat or eggs for me or mine even on occasions like this [e*specially* on occasions like this we may interpolate], and I must therefore take the risk that you say is likely.[38]

At the threshold of life itself potentially passing over into death, Gandhi records the most strenuous of ethical struggles between his quackery (here specifically his vegetarianism) on the one hand and 'life' on the other. At this critical liminal site, we see health and life startlingly fail to appear as goals to be snatched for their own sake. Life without limits (even for a young boy of ten it would seem) becomes instead the dire antagonist of 'truth' while death is contiguous with health. In this risky business of nursing, vegetarianism then becomes conceivable as a nonviolent and therefore ethical mode of dying as much as it is, in times of health, an anti-parasitic remedy against violent living.

Therapeutically acceptable as a mode of dying, vegetarianism challenges the *apad-dharma* permissible to indigenous medical practitioners, such as *vaids*, who consequently come in for as scathing a critique in Gandhi's narrative as do western allopathic doctors. What is casually adverted to in *Hind Swaraj* as the morally problematic response of *vaidyas* in matters of illness and principle is in *My Experiments* fully critiqued by Gandhi's insistence on the place of scruples in therapeutics. In episode after episode, we see his absolute rejection of what he perceived to be the *vaids'* laxity and equivocation, in the name of 'life' or health, with regard to religious principles and general scriptural taboo on meats and wines. As Wendy Doniger[39] too has pointed out, *Manusmriti* and Indian medical *shastras* gave Gandhi no help because of their own sophistry and ambivalence about taboos against meat eating. Hence Gandhi's disavowal: 'I held my vegetarianism independently of religious texts.'[40] On the occasion of treating Kasturbai's illness with his 'household remedies', a *swamiji*'s advice regarding the 'religious harmlessness of taking meat' *as medicine* drew from Gandhi the terse response: 'I knew the verses from the *Manusmriti,* I did not need them for my conviction.'[41] In these and other experiments with (self) cure we see, again and again, the ill body's positioning as an ultimate test case for principled vegetarianism, construed as a disciplining of the self's freedom and inclination to 'eat all you can'.

Gandhi's refusal to accept either western practice or indigenous law as binding on his conduct in relation to illness stems from his conviction that it would make, in his phrase, 'medical morals' a contingent rather than an absolute matter. Self-discipline as a contingent matter makes illness too much the scene of a narrow cure, that is, a scene evacuated of any *agon* or open, unguaranteed struggle. The immediate recourse to medicine entails a short cut to bodily health that reduces and renders the sublimity of pathology– its potential for creative self-transformation – into a mere inert matter of bodily suffering. Krell's citation of Novalis's question is deeply resonant in this context of Gandhi's enthusiastic positioning of illness at the crossroads of ethics and pathology: 'Does not the best everywhere begin with illness?'[42] In other words, rational medicine, Western or *ayurvedic*, presupposes a 'will to health' that turns a potentially polymorphous experience of illness into dull un-used matter/material. Pre-empting struggle, it misses an opportunity for thinking or, better still, risking the self in response to the nonhuman other who demands to be accounted for in the register of a good life.

It is important to underline the notion of 'risk' in Gandhi's bold recasting of acceptable therapeutics as nothing other than the best, that is, the most ethical mode of being or dying offered to the sick self or other. But the reference to risk also reveals the morally unguaranteed and ambiguous terrain upon which Gandhi appears to have been aware he was treading when he undertook his experiments with illness and cure as a mode of ethical self-fashioning. To begin ethical self-fashioning with experiments on the body is surely to begin from the most enigmatic and uncertain realm, one quite alien to the certitudes of morality, reason, and transcendence. But it is this corporeal realm of uncertainty that best provides the experimenter with the ultimate opportunity for self-examination – the kind that can only come from the palpable gap between the impossible shaping ideals of asceticism and the inadequate practical grasp of them. Statements and questions such as 'I began to get anxious', 'I was haunted ... ' or 'What would people say?' nicely illustrate Gandhi's didactic yet open, self-doubting mode in writing up his medical experiments. Although he remembers ten-year-old Manilal's illness, for example, with a clear view to drawing out for pedagogical use the lessons inherent in it, it is also the case, as noted by Roy,[43] that Gandhi's relentless scruples produce their own complex, even morally ambiguous, results that enter a murky and hazardous ethical terrain: 'What right had the parents to inflict their fads on their children?' The lessons to be drawn prove both difficult and indefinite. While on this occasion disaster was avoided, at other times, the older autobiographer implies, his application of household remedies to wounds, fevers, jaundice, and dyspepsia was not always successful. Gandhi's detailing of his risky nursing of family members can, therefore, hardly be said to equate with the quacksalvering of more confident quacks. In fact, beset by doubts and anxiety, he is candid in his acknowledgment that 'experience has shown that these experiments involve obvious risks' and could not be recommended to others as a programme since there were no warranties attached.[44]

Finally, it is not only conventional therapeutics but also politics that lay in a tense interruptive relation with the asceticism of Gandhi's quackery. Despite the seeming distance of these household scenes of cure from worldly matters, the project of ethical self-fashioning to which they are integrally linked is unquestionably grounded in the historical moment. Whether in the form of family responsibilities, legal work, public service or political agitation, the world constantly impinges upon and defers the 'leisurely' everyday art of using illness that Gandhi's narration sketches. Scholars such as Joseph Alter and Susanne and Rudolph Lloyd[45] have forcefully argued for the ways in which Gandhi's 'private' experiments with truth articulate with the broader political problems of the day. Gandhi's own recollection of his dietetic dilemma during the agitation against the Rowlatt Bills however underlines the utterly different spatio-temporal location of the art of using illness, allowing for a rather surprising reading of this alleged articulation of the 'local', intimate art of using illness and the defining 'global', public issues of the day.

In an account of his painful recovery from a severe attack of dysentery (a near-death experience), Gandhi reveals how his absorption in using his illness as a means of testing his vow to abstain from milk was interrupted, perhaps even judged, by the contingencies of political action in the moment of decolonization. On this occasion, looking to continue to live without milk, Gandhi had turned to doctors and *vaidyas* for recommendations: 'The *vaidyas* read verses to me from Charaka to show that religious scruples about diet have no place in therapeutics. So they could not be expected to help me to continue to live without milk.'[46] The relentless adherence to his vow would very nearly have cost him his life but for the agitation against the Rowlatt Bills. The desire to launch and lead political action or *satyagraha* against these oppressive colonial laws pressured Gandhi to recover as quickly as possible. And yet his continuing search (against the advice of doctors, friends, and political associates) for an ethical mode of recovering his physical strength remained fruitless. Gandhi's narration of this as an aporetic moment dramatizes the convergence of opposing bioethical and political imperatives with equal force on his suffering body. The temporal coincidence of the two unveils a fascinating view of the asymptotic relations between the ascetic ideals of quackery (which forbade nourishing the weakened body with cow's milk extracted via a cruel method) and the contingencies of political action (which becomes synonymous with a *desire to live* strongly and actively): 'The will to live proved stronger than the devotion to truth, and for once the votary of truth compromised his sacred ideal by his eagerness to take up the Satyagraha fight. The memory of this action even now rankles. ... But I cannot free myself from the subtlest of temptations, the desire to serve, which still holds me.'[47] His choice to take up 'the Satyagraha fight' against the colonial state ends up deferring his experiment in dietetic *Ahimsa* (he agreed to take goat's milk at this time), abruptly cutting short his ethical self-testing in favour of a speedier recovery and life. In effect, Gandhi's love of bodily illness is here relativized by larger disturbances in and obligations to the body politic. Although Gandhi's concept of *swaraj* insists on the continuity between the two, the demands of the politics of decolonization remain discontinuous with his ascetic ideals (especially with the ideal of disregard for life). The desire for political *swaraj* compels him to miss the high water mark of personal *swaraj* in this single, Gandhi insists, but revealing case.

The leper at the door: nursing hospitality and the bioethics of proximity

I have concentrated thus far on acts of nursing and illness involving Gandhi and his immediate family, acts narrated predominantly from an anti-alimentary and anti-pharmacological standpoint. These cases involving the relentless testing of 'his wife, children, and self' do not, however, exhaust the full range of meanings evoked by the Gandhian narrative of nursing care. Extending beyond family and even community, this nursing care also embraced many named (Lutavan, Parchure Shastri) and nameless sufferers (the Zulus). With the exception of Parchure Shastri, for the most part these subaltern objects of Gandhi's nursing care remain outside not only the given networks of kin, race, and nation but also the radically experimental communal spaces of the ashrams Gandhi himself devised in South Africa and India. Although each nursing encounter with the afflicted bodies of strangers bears a slightly different valence or lesson, this section tracks the thematic main line of hospitality that criss-crosses a number of them.

In my view, Gandhi's narration of his eager and unconditional reception of variously ill or diseased strangers points to an ethical affinity between his nursing and the rich thematics of hospitality developed with reference to the work of Emmanuel Levinas (1969) in Derrida's *Of Hospitality* (2000). Derrida's meditations on hospitality in this text provide a clarifying idiom that can render the conceptual and ethico-political challenge of Gandhi's intimate nursing performances most closely, if not entirely perfectly. The particular etymological history of the term 'hospitality' reveals a tissue of usages and meanings that resonates deeply with the unique profile of Gandhi's nursing love that emerges from his own and others' reports. The social meaning of hospitality involving the generous offer of food, shelter, company, and care (*hospes, hospit*) to a guest (*ghosti*) links up etymologically with its medical meanings, that is, with treatment, hospice from Old French *ospital*. Furthermore, the medieval *hospitale* referred to a religious order dedicated to the care of sick and needy pilgrims, providing palliative care and so on. As we can see from this bit of etymological tracking, the notion of hospitality nicely captures the layered meanings that appear folded into Gandhi's narrated acts of nursing outsiders or guests. Like so many of his other biomoral performances that Alter has brilliantly commented upon, nursing as hospitality, too, might be understood as at once social, medical, religio-ethical, and political.

Let us turn to the incident in Gandhi's life that most succinctly and powerfully encapsulates the thematic of hospitality toward the other/afflicted stranger. This particular incident occurred during Gandhi's early years working as a lawyer in South Africa. As told in *My Experiments*, legal work, despite its satisfactory progress, was beginning to prove inadequate to Gandhi's need for 'some concrete act of service'.[48] During precisely this season of discontent, in other words, at a highly opportune moment, a leper is said to have arrived at his door. Gandhi's recounting of this incident in *Experiments* possesses all the spareness and clipped brevity of a simple parable, the figure of the leper disappearing from narrative view as rapidly as he had appeared in the telling.

> My profession progressed satisfactorily, but that was far from satisfying me. The question of further simplifying my life and of doing some concrete act of service to my fellowmen had been constantly agitating me, when a leper came to my door. I had not the heart to dismiss him with a meal. So I offered him shelter, dressed his wounds, and began to look after him. But I could not ... afford, I lacked the will to keep him always with me. So I sent him to the Government Hospital for indentured labourers. But I was still ill at ease. I longed for some humanitarian work of a permanent nature.[49]

What most remarkably characterizes this scene of the nursing 'I' is an impossible desire 'to keep [the ill leper] always with me' – a longing for endless closeness or proximity with an abject-ed other. Represented thus as a self already positioned in an ethical relation (that is as open to his 'fellowmen'), Gandhi is called upon suddenly to make a choice, that is, to respond to a concrete appeal for help in the form of the (un) expected leper at the door. Both the appeal and the response are incarnated in the intimate care (summarily detailed in a single sentence) provided to the outsider's afflicted body. But interestingly at this early stage of Gandhi's nursing experiments in fashioning an ethical self via nursing, there is a sense of the impossibility of keeping up the tactile service of the other forever. Yet, once the leper is sent away back into the space of colonial medical administration (the Government Hospital), the nurse is ill at ease and driven by the desire for more–for 'some humanitarian work of a permanent nature'.[50] The reason for this desire without end, the narrative suggests, is that Gandhi's embrace of the necessity for self-sacrifice or 'humanitarian work' (let us stay with his phrasing) is at this juncture more of an ideal than an achieved act; he lacks 'the will to keep him [the leper or diseased other who makes an appeal for attention] always with me'. In other words, Gandhi's choice to submit himself to the leper's appeal for nursing hospitality is a choice to throw away the self in the service of the other and such a choice always and of necessity fails to achieve the (im)possible: complete self-denial or sacrifice.

Without providing much here by way of detail or atmosphere, this pared down telling of a tale of nursing hospitality offered to a nameless leper possesses an uncanny force somewhat in excess of its narrative presentation and rhetorical poverty. The seemingly *ex nihilo* appearance of a wandering leper on the threshold of Gandhi's establishment, conveyed in the simple dehistoricizing accents of a parable, has an enormous affective impact on the reader as much as it seems to have done on Gandhi. Indeed the highly condensed retelling creates a certain miraculous aura around this figure of abjection and utter destitution. The *unheimliche* figure of the leper arrives at the door unexpectedly and yet as if he had been expected or even sent. On a later occasion in 1939 and on another continent, when another leper, Parchure Shastri, made a sudden appearance at the ashram in Sevagram, Gandhi quite explicitly cast the unanticipated coming of this named leprosy-afflicted figure as a sign that he was sent from God.[51] Here it is almost as if the apparition of the leper who comes in from the outside uncannily materializes a prior knowledge that has already been intuited by the would-be nurse: the ethical necessity of being there for the other rather than for his own self-interest, professional or domestic. 'The question of ... doing some concrete act of service to my fellowmen had been constantly agitating me, when a leper came to my door', Gandhi writes. The arrival of the unknown stranger and the intimacy with which Gandhi responds to the appeal of his diseased body satisfies for once the would-be nurse's discontented hankerings after 'humanitarian work', a phrase that barely captures, if at all, the particular tactile satisfactions that Gandhian nursing here and elsewhere entail: 'I ... dressed his wounds ... '[52] The discourse of the parable dissolves quickly enough into historicity as the paragraph comes to a close, dispelling the aura as the near miraculous figure of the leper is identified as an indentured Indian labourer and absorbed into the multitude of 'suffering Indians, most of them indentured Tamil, Telugu or North India men'.[53] No more is said of the diseased subaltern stranger who, in appearing to fulfil the would-be nurse's desire for rendering concrete acts of *seva*, stands at the narrative origin of Gandhi's hospitable acts. We, however, cannot turn away from this scene without noting that as a guest-stranger, the leper makes the appeal for the hospitality that 'saves' from autonomy and malaise the host-nurse, who has been waiting ill-at-ease, longing to come into 'close touch' with the unaccounted foreign body. What is significant about this seeming reversal in the direction of aid is the suggestion of a mutual permeability of selves and bodies that bridges distance and (in)difference. In taking the leper in, the nurse ethically chooses to submit *as if* he had no choice but to turn *the one-for-himself* into a *one-for-the-other*. Saving saves (one's self).

One other central point remains to be made here. We might guess that the un-accommodated status of the leper, subsequently identified as an indentured labourer, was the effect of an inhospitable combination of stigmatizing disease, colonial racism, and oppressive labour conditions in South Africa. But what remains remarkable about Gandhi's account of him is that we are given no account of him. At first sight, the namelessness of the leper-guest identified solely by his affliction and his status as a foreign commodity in the South African labour-market seems to hint at narcissistic self-absorption on his nurse's part. But another reading of this self-absorption is available if we locate the diseased stranger's unbidden arrival and welcome at the door within the problematic of hospitality. Within this problematic the dynamics of *self-absorption* is both unstable and complicated. As the passage reveals, Gandhi's self-absorption has to do with a certain ethical agitation that stems from a lack – a lack of commitment to that which the successful professional lawyer here senses to be inescapable, something he *must* do/ become: a self absorbed by the other. Put this way, arguably, the longing 'to keep' the nameless leper-guest 'with him always' suggests a radically different concept of 'humanitarian work' (Gandhi's own phrase). This longing or desire for opportunities to nurse afflicted strangers – to live for the other or throw one's life away for the stranger – is readable as a commitment to create new, yet-to-be codified relations of proximity that might lie beyond the contractual space defining 'subjects in law' in the language of rights, duties, and debts. This nursing hospitality stands in opposition to not just the abstractions of legal work. It speaks not just to the rationalized parasitism and co-option of modern medicine by imperial and colonial nationalisms and the wars they lead to. Gandhi's nursing hospitality casts into relief and interrogates the communal spaces and relations articulated under political and civil jurisdiction as well. It hints of an an-archic space prior to or beside the governing friend/foe distinctions that structure modern liberal discourses of kinship and political community.

In this context, the namelessness of the leper can be better understood as a welcome sign as it were. The anonymity of the leper-guest in the narration signals Gandhian nursing's disinterest in demanding that the object of hospitality 'state' or 'guarantee his identity' even as a merely customary preliminary to the acknowledgment of his right to hospitality as a 'subject in law'.[54] Nameless, the leper in this *ur*-scene, as it were, of Gandhian nursing is not construed as 'a subject in law', but as a suffering body that constitutes the always unanticipated but always irresistible demand for an 'unquestioning welcome', for a hospitality that is 'rendered or given to the other before they [sic] are identified as a subject nameable by their family name,' a name that 'places' them within civil discourse.[55] Nursing hospitality exceeds the bounds of modern civil and political society, incarnating an anarchic act or rather a relation that *is* public – brought into being often in the direct line of enemy *and* friendly fire – yet not articulated within the homogeneous time-space of modern civility. From the perspective of Gandhian nursing and unlike it, medicine is synchronized with modernity and subsumed into its time-space. Within this dispensation, only certain sufferers, and some strangers – those able to account for themselves as 'subjects in law' – are entitled to equal consideration in matters concerning the preservation of bodily health and life.[56] Medicine follows, in the words of Derrida, 'the laws of conditional hospitality', laws synchronic with modern civility; within the purview of such civility, the afflicted must be nameable, that is, recognized by these laws before his 'right' to hospitality can be assured. Nothing makes this more brutally evident than medical work in times of colonial war.

Gandhi's volunteer ambulance work during the Boer War and, most particularly, during the 1906 Zulu Rebellion constitutes a significant turning point in the unfolding of his bioethical critique of modern medicine. Not the least of the lessons learnt on this occasion was, quite simply, that doctors work within borders.[57] Against this colonial collaboration of medicine and nationalist identification (or more broadly loyalty to one's kin, race, or state), Gandhi's own (dis)loyal nursing of the nameless wounded Zulu, both friends and foes, emerges as another order of being and relating. Conscientiously offered *as a citizen* of Natal, his nursing hospitality in effect carves out an enclave of bioethical responsibility that remains critically out of sync with the state, its war, and its medicine, even interrogating implicitly 'citizenship' itself. Following, again, in Derrida's terms the 'Law of unconditional hospitality', Gandhi's nursing of wounded Zulus opens to view an ethical, therapeutic, and political space beyond the reason of medical humanitarianism and the 'laws of conditional hospitality' governing colonial civility.[58]

Satyagraha in South Africa (1928) and *My Experiments* both offer glimpses of the Zulu Rebellion of 1906 from the perspective of Gandhi's position in the Natal Volunteer Ambulance Corps. Following Gandhi's own representation, this well-known event of South African history has been inextricably aligned with the formulation of his central ethicopolitical strategy of *satyagraha* (variously translated as 'passive resistance' or 'Truth Force') directed against political injustice and violence. The inauguration of this radically new concept and practice of *satyagraha* has also been integrally linked to Gandhi's famous epiphanic experience on the *veldt*, an experience that underlined the necessity of *brahmacharya* or sexual celibacy to his ongoing project of ethical self-fashioning. What has less frequently been noted is that this central event is also dramatically tied to Gandhi's nursing activities among wounded Zulus and more generally to his philosophical opposition to medicine. Although scholars have more or less followed Gandhi's lead and centred their discussion on the relationship between sexual celibacy and ethico-political action, Alter's perceptive study must once again be cited here as an exception. Alter quite astutely recognizes the ethical imperative to celibacy (that Gandhi is so voluble about) was heavily mediated by a 'medical' context. Gandhi's cleaning of the wounds suffered by 'enemy' Zulus must be read then as more than simply an incidental backdrop, or even as more than merely a precipitating event. Giving the medical dimension of this event interpretive priority allows two relevant aspects of Gandhi's nursing to come into clearer view: its ascetic disregard for the self as well as the bi-directional relations of embodied proximity realized by that disregard. As a crucial realization of the ascetic ideal, celibacy but also nursing, we must emphasize, is linked in essential ways to the formulation of *satyagraha*.

Both texts in which Gandhi discusses the Zulu Rebellion elaborate at some length his concurrent elaboration of the *satyagrahi*'s need for sexual asceticism. It is my sense that this elaboration curtails discussion of the full range of bio-ethical and political valences that attach to his nursing of the enemy/guest. In *My Experiments* certainly a conceptual caesura appears to mark and separate the details of Gandhi's report on nursing Zulus on the one hand and his thinking on 'much else', that is, on sexual celibacy and *satyagraha* on the other.[59] Yet despite this gap the filiation between nursing and sexual asceticism, two forms of *ascesis* requiring self-suffering and self-discipline respectively, is noteworthy. But nursing provides Gandhi with something unique: an intimation of relations of proximity between bodies (and selves) that, nevertheless, remain *outside* those domains of domesticity and sexuality that Gandhi was emphatic in renouncing. As such an intimate yet nonsexual relation, Gandhi's nursing hospitality in permitting (even demanding) loving care expressed through touch emerges as a form of ethical self-fashioning on par with, or possibly even one up on, the isolating physical distances demanded by celibacy. Yet the point is not made frequently enough that the justly famous focus on sexual celibacy on the one hand and the formulation of *satyagraha* as a new mode of political action on the other exist in a triangular relationship with Gandhian nursing hospitality.

It is also worthwhile recalling that Gandhi initially came to fashion *satyagraha* as the most ethical way of nonviolently countering the hatred of Indians in South Africa and the stigmata of their foreignness officially emblematized by the proposed Pass Laws. As such, this mode of political action, keeping Skaria's (2002) account in mind, was an attempt to create new forms of neighbourliness that would bridge the distance between the master consumers of power and those unbidden guests, namely indentured and other labourers, arriving from outside to sit at the table of Empire in South Africa.[60] Conceptually, nursing hospitality as the experience of opening one's body and self to the inescapable appeal of the suffering outsider neatly aligns with Gandhi's formulation of *satyagraha* as a mode of political agitation against the inhospitable treatment of Indians in South Africa. The pass that every Indian would by law be required to bear constitutes in this context the ultimate stigmata of the stranger or guest as 'enemy' (*ghosti*) who must, according to the colonial laws of conditional hospitality, be disabled from ever passing for or too close to the self.[61]

To return to the occasion of the Zulu Rebellion, the nursing hospitality Gandhi offers in the face-to-face encounter with the 'enemy' is consistent with the disciplinary self-formation of the ethical subject that we have noted as central to Gandhian quackery as a whole. With respect to his unanticipated duties in the ambulance corps, he writes, 'I was delighted ... to hear that our main work was to be the nursing of the wounded Zulus. The Medical Officer in charge welcomed us. He said the white people were not willing nurses for the wounded Zulus, that their wounds were festering.'[62] These Zulu suspects' wounds and sores were the consequence of floggings. Among the wounded were 'friendlies' too, caught in the crossfire despite the badges designed to distinguish them from 'enemy Zulus'. Whether enemy or friend, they are in Gandhi's account nameless outsiders subjected to the laws of conditional hospitality, applied especially mercilessly in wartime. Worse, Gandhi writes in *My Experiments*: 'this was no war but a manhunt'.[63] As with the leper at his door, the suffering Zulu as other/stranger/foe appears unbidden as a guest, requiring – even demanding in terms of a Levinasian ethics of hospitality or responsibility – the sacrifice of (in this case the nursing) self. As a stretcher-bearer, Gandhi's delight in shouldering, literally and metaphorically, wounded Zulu bodies contrasts markedly with the Europeans' refusal to respond to the appeal issued by their festering sores, irrespective of their friendly or hostile status. From the security of his thriving professional position and as a 'loyal citizen' of Natal, albeit highly problematically positioned as such a 'subject in law' within a colonial economy of racialization, Gandhi instead ventures out to 'delight' in the privations of nursing the subaltern body: 'But I swallowed the bitter draught, especially as the work of my Corps consisted only in nursing the wounded Zulus.'[64] In the hoary traditions of western nursing history, when one nurses as a loyal citizen of one of the warring parties, as does Gandhi here, nursing the enemy with delight surely suggests a certain form of hospitality that moves the nurse 'beyond war' or political loyalty. In other words, nursing the subaltern enemy or other is in ethical terms a response that negotiates with the contrary demands of war and Gandhian medicine. The intimate, tactile relations, materialized in the nurse's dressing of the enemy's festering, stinking sores, constitute an embodied ascetic response that, significantly, underlines the abdications and aberrations of modern medicine in times of war and more generally of modern living. Gandhi's nursing hospitality as sketched above reveals the degree to which familiar questions of war and nonviolence are intertwined with both his critique of medicine and his ascetic counter practice of 'quackery'.

The conjunction of medicine and war is illuminating from another perspective as well. It provides a framework within which to understand more precisely the peculiar attraction of nursing for Gandhi and what it was that he sought to perfect through his caring for the diseased and wounded body, frequently in situations of public state-legitimated violence. Like the encounter with the leper, Gandhi's nursing activity during the Zulu Rebellion – a central autobiographical event – exemplifies a mode of being for the other that in effect creates new relations of proximity via acceptance of responsibility for the ill or afflicted body. Furthermore, the impossible ethical ideal of complete and utter self-sacrifice called for by such responsibility to the other's body returns us to that which so centrally drives Gandhi's critique of medicine and his alternative therapeutics in the first place: suspicion of the spontaneous and limitless 'love of life'. In an interview printed in *Harijan*, Gandhi makes a crucial point about the contradiction between war and medicine on this very question of 'life'. A close examination of his observations to an English journalist on this occasion clarifies the distinct appeal that nursing in times of war held for Gandhi.

> I have spoken against Western medicine, which I have called the concentrated essence of black magic. ... You do not know that I had very nearly taken the medical line, when, in order to respect the wishes of my dead father, I took up law. But, in South Africa, I again thought of medicine. ... But the West attaches an exaggerated importance to prolonging man's earthly existence. Until the man's last moment on earth, you go on drugging him even by injecting. That, I think, is inconsistent with the recklessness with which they [sic] shed their lives in war. Though I am opposed to war, there is no doubt that war induces reckless courage. Well, without ever having to engage in a war, I want to learn from you (Englishmen) *the art of throwing away my life for a noble cause*. But I do not want that excessive desire of living that Western medicine seems to encourage in man even at the cost of tenderness for subhuman life. ... [65]

Two final points need to be emphasized here. The first is that war as an inducement to complete self-disregard in response to the demand of a transcendent cause or authority – loyalty to the State – provides a morally desirable ideal for the ascetic nurse while the field of medicine, afflicted by the reckless desire to preserve life, is rejected. Gandhi's piece on Florence Nightingale in *Indian Opinion* makes a similar point.[66] Second, de-linked from war, violence, and the destructive friend/foe axis, the art of throwing away life for a noble cause (associated with soldiers on the battlefield) reveals a surprising affinity with nursing hospitality driven by the ethical ideal of the self-for-the-other. In their suggestion that Gandhi's alternative therapeutic practice found more to emulate in western war than in western medicine, these unexpected equations between soldier/war and nurse/bioethics are provocative indeed. They are also perhaps the most under-noted aspect of his epiphanic experience during the Zulu War. As Gandhi's narration of this experience reveals, nursing in times of war embodies precisely that which Gandhian quackery as a whole finds most desirable: a negation of the excessive desire for living freely, that is, living without limit or responsibility for the other, namely, for the entire range of human and 'sub-human life'.

But Gandhi's nursing as wartime self-sacrifice does not completely ignore the state's self-legtimizing call for *himsa* (violence) nor, it must be stressed, does it passively submit to that call. *As loyal citizen* (and despite his vexed status as a colonial citizen, Gandhi was always careful to present himself as such during all of England's wars prior to World War II), the figure of the nurse ascetic presents himself as answerable (as having proper duties) to even the most oppressive state. Hence, we have Gandhi's repeated *voluntary* involvement in ambulance work during several wars and, by implication, his acquiescence to 'the laws of conditional hospitality' that order modern civility and war. This goes some way toward explaining the dissonance produced by Gandhi's likening of his passion for loyalty to the imperial state to his passion for nursing, discussed at the outset. This acquiescence to the demand for good citizenship, however, does not fully account for the specificities characterizing his fondness for nursing friend and stranger alike although it does mark the inevitable high tension between the laws of conditional hospitality, shaping the citizen's rights and conduct, and the 'Law of unconditional hospitality'.[67] The tense co-existence of these two passions, one inclusive the other exclusive, within a single project of ethical self-fashioning allows us to posit the complicated ethico-political location of nursing in between a just and unjust loyalty. Responding as would/should a citizen to the state's call for loyalty, Gandhi dutifully chooses to offer himself up to a higher authority, that is, to become self-detached for-the-other – 'for a noble cause'. But he chooses to respond to the state's appeal for the participation of citizens by locating his response within the domain of humanitarian or medical work entailing face-to-face encounters with bodies suffering the violence of war. As the details of his narration suggest, in this volunteer domain Gandhi as an ascetic self-for-the-other (that is as one already imprinted by the call of the other to bear the burden of responsibility) is *unexpectedly* called upon to nurse the festering sores of wounded Zulus: the enemy or absolute other.[68] And he makes a choice to answer this call (in contrast with the loyal Europeans who refuse the choice). In thus throwing itself open to the suffering *stranger/foe*, the nursing self responds to a transcendent 'law of unconditional hospitality' anterior to the 'laws of conditional hospitality' formulated by the state and deemed just by conventional medicine. In this, Gandhi's nursing hospitality approaches a realm of justice quite different from, although presupposed by, the civil justice realized by the laws of conditional hospitality. To offer nursing hospitality to the enemy (and to the friend) in wartime is therefore to remain simultaneously in an obliging yet tense and critical relationship to the state's demand for (an unjust) loyalty. A truthful and just act that brings the nurse into close contact with 'the enemy's' suffering body (a throwing away of the self in response to 'a noble cause', here hospitality/responsibility/justice), this 'soldierly' nursing of Zulus within the protocols of conventional war negotiates a complex bioethical status for Gandhian quackery as not (conventional) medicine, not-quite war.

Conclusion

What has often been referred to as Gandhi's biomoral politics[69] is also, I have tried to show, a profound destabilization of medicine's metaphysics that brings to crisis (renders thoroughly ill one might say) the signifying certitude of those privileged set of terms – 'medicine,' 'health,' and 'life' – that have underwritten and elevated 'pure' therapeutics or the will to instant cure as an unquestionable and uncontaminated good in itself. The self-evident singularity and goodness of 'Life', the central concept around which all of the biological sciences, religion, morality, and of course medicine turn, is undone in the Gandhian text as it clears the ground for a new understanding of and reaction to the self-alienating experience of illness and cure.

The most startling aspect of such a radical re-valuation is the re-inflection of illness as a mundane amateur theatre of ethical self-cultivation. Far from being a self-absorbing process, Gandhi imagined this self-cultivation as in fact a mode of turning the self inside out to face and touch and be touched by the ill and suffering other in the spirit of *seva*. Only when we understand Gandhian asceticism as a set of deliberately imposed and carefully observed limits on the self, designed to transform this self into one for the other, can we understand the full force, meaning, and inimitability of Gandhi's acts of amateur curing and intimate caring. Having brought us to a sense of the receptivity or hospitality of self to other, these acts invite us to think further about how in turning the body and pathology into indispensable sites of a liberating *ascesis*, Gandhi reconfigures therapeutics as a mundane and patient search for biopositive ethical and political enhancement.

Notes

1 M.K.Gandhi, *Hind Swaraj and Other Writings*, ed. Anthony Parel, Cambridge: Cambridge University Press, 1997, pp. 34–38, 62–71.
2 Notable exceptions are J. Alter, *Gandhi's Body: Sex, Diet, and the Politics of Nationalism*, Philadelphia: University of Pennsylvania Press, 2000; Ashis Nandy and Shiv Vishwanathan, 'Modern Medicine and It Nonmodern Critics: A Study in Discourse' in *The Savage Freud and Other Essays on Possible and Retrievable Selves*, Princeton University Press, Princeton, 1995, pp. 145–95; and Gandhi, 1997.

3 Any interest in the subject of medicine in the context of decolonization inevitably recalls us beyond the South Asian context to the work of Frantz Fanon who in the decades after Gandhi's death found himself compelled as a professional doctor to meditate on the disturbing proximity of violence and modern medicine in the context of revolutionary Algeria. My essay 'Fanon and Colonial Medicine' (unpublished) is a lengthier consideration of the alternative pathways traveled by these two men, both of who felt keenly the troubling co-implication of what were to them the virtually conjunct categories of biomedical therapy and political enslavement.
4 See Frantz Fanon, 'Medicine and Colonialism' in *A Dying Colonialism,* trans. Haakon Chevalier, New York: Grove Press, 1965, pp. 121–45.
5 Asceticism has been widely understood in terms of a dualist, self-denying, even pathological practice and ideal. My understanding of asceticism is, however, indebted to more recent rethinkings of the phenomenon, influenced by Michel Foucault. James Laidlaw in *Riches and Renunciation: Religion, Economy, and Society among the Jains,* Oxford: Clarendon Press,1995 and Tyler Roberts in *Contesting Spirit: Nietzsche, Affirmation, Religion,* Philadelphia: Princeton University Press, 1998, provide excellent clarifying discussions of asceticism in relation to Indic and Christian religious traditions.
6 As we will see shortly there is no more ambiguous term in Gandhi's writing than 'life'. Like other obviously idiosyncratically inflected terms – '*satyagraha*', 'swaraj', 'religion' – 'life' cannot be taken to have a stable signification as it is undone and re-done to keep up with the open, dynamic and contingent nature of Gandhi's experimental therapeutic practices. This suspension of metaphorical, literal and conventional significations of familiar terms (Alter too notes) contributes to the shifting nature of the Gandhian text. Key concepts are denied a simple 'presence' undercutting immediate impressions of the spareness of Gandhi's prose (Alter, 2000, p. 165).
7 Gandhi, *Autobiography: The Story of My Experiments with Truth,* trans. Mahadev Desai, New York: Dover Publications, 1983.
8 Gandhi, *Key to Health,* Ahmedabad: Navjivan, 1948
9 Gandhi, 1983, p. 272
10 Gandhi, 1983, pp. 292, 408.
11 Caroline Walker Bynum, *Holy Feast and Holy Fast: The Religious Significance of Food to Medieval Women,* Berkeley: University of California Press, 1987, Laidlaw, 1995.
12 I adapt for use the phrasing David Farrell Krell, *Infectious Nietzsche,* Indiana University Press, Bloomington, 1996, devises in his discussion of German romantic approaches to illness.
13 Jacques Derrida, *Of Hospitality,* trans. Rachel Bowlby, Stanford University Press, Stanford, 2000, pp. 75–83.
14 Gandhi, 1983, pp. 188–89, 278–83
15 Gandhi, 1983, 152, emphasis added.
16 Alter, 2000, pp. 6–7, 19–20, 23–27.
17 Here I am echoing the language of a Levinasian ethics of responsibility that we will have occasion to further elaborate. Derrida's readings are also immensely useful in thinking through the question of hospitality in relation to dwelling and domicile. See Derrida/Anne Dufourmantelle (2000, p. 55–56).
18 Ajay Skaria, 'Gandhi's Politics: Liberalism and the Question of the Ashram', *South Atlantic*
Quarterly, vol. 101, no. 4, 2002, pp. 979–81.
19 Parchure did not commit suicide, but turned up unexpectedly at Sevagram where Gandhi, after great deliberation, took him in and nursed him for two years. See Narayan Desai, *Bliss Was It To Be Young – With Gandhi: Childhood*

Reminiscences, trans, Bhal Malji, ed. Mark Shepard, Bharatiya Vidya Bhavan, Mumbai, 1988.
20 Laidlaw, 1995, p. 4.
21 Laidlaw, 1995, p. 239.
22 Laidlaw provides an illuminating discussion of Jain self-emaciation as a deliberate, enthusiastically self-imposed austerity with regard to Raychandbhai, the successful Jain gem merchant who Gandhi has identified as a key influence on his own thinking on asceticism and detachment (ibid., 233–39).
23 Gandhi,1983, p. 233.
24 Alter, 2000, pp. 13–14; Parama Roy, 'Meat-Eating, Masculinity, and Renunciation in India: A Gandhian Grammar of Diet', *Gender and History*, vol. 14, no.1, p. 2002.
25 Gandhi, 1997, p. 62.
26 Krell, 1996, pp.177–95.
27 Gandhi, 1983; Alter, 2000; Roy, 2002.
28 Bynum, 1987.
29 Francis Zimmerman, *The Jungle and the Aroma of Meats: An Ecological Theme in Hindu Medicine*, Berkeley: University of California Press, 1987; Laidlaw, 1995.
30 M.K.Gandhi, *Key to Health*, 1948, p. 13; *From Yervada Mandir*, trans. Valji Govindji Desai, Ahmedabad: Navijivan, 1932, p. 11; *The Teaching of the Gita*, ed. Anand T. Hingorani, Mumbai: Bharatiya Vidya Bhavan, 1998, pp. 76–77.
31 Alter's is the best exposition of the content of Gandhi's remedies as well as interpretation of their ethico-political value/effects.
32 Zimmerman, 1987, p. 2.
33 Gandhi, 1987, p. 2.
34 Gandhi, 1983, p. 260.
35 Laidlaw, 1995, makes a similar claim in his brilliant study of Jain worldly asceticism.
36 Gandhi, 1983, p. 273.
37 Gandhi, 1983, p. 219.
38 Ibid., emphasis added.
39 Wendy Doniger, 1999, pp. 95–97.
40 Gandhi, 1983, p. 290.
41 Gandhi, 1983, p. 290
42 Krell, 1997, p. 201.
43 Roy, 2002.
44 Gandhi, 1983, pp. 240, 272–73.
45 Alter, 2000, pp. 23–25; Susanne and Lloyd Rudolph, 1983, pp.16–17.
46 Gandhi, 1983, p. 240
47 Ibid., pp. 410–11.
48 Ibid., 1983, p.177.
49 Ibid., p. 177.
50 Ibid., p. 177.
51 Dongre, 2003, pp. 5–7.
52 Gandhi, p. 177.
53 Gandhi, p. 177.
54 Derrida, 2000, p. 24.
55 Derrida, 2000, p. 29.
56 The best discussion of such co-option comes from Fanon whose essay 'Medicine and Colonialism' agonizes over the nature of that conjunction, especially in the face of French *colon* doctors who actively or silently participated in the torture of Algerians implicated in the revolutionary struggle.

57 I echo John Archer's adaptation (of the name of the familiar organization, Doctors without Borders) in his response to my talk, 'Medicine and Imperialism' at The Center for the Humanities, Faculty Fellows Lecture, January 2001.
58 In light of this discussion, Gandhi's statement that even Brig. Dyer had a right to be cared for becomes comprehensible beyond the piety of forgiveness and generosity.
59 Gandhi, 1983, p. 281.
60 Gandhi, *Satyagraha in South Africa.*, trans. Valji Govindji Desai, Ahmedabad: Navjivan, 1928.
61 Gandhi, 1928.
62 Gandhi, 1983, p. 279.
63 Gandhi, 1983, 281.
64 Ibid.
65 Gandhi, 1997, emphasis added.
66 *Collected Works of Mahatma Gandhi*, vol. 4, Delhi: Publication Division, Ministry of Information and Broadcasting, Government of India, 1958–94, pp. 405–7.
67 Derrida, 2000, p. 77.
68 Jeffry Bloechl, *Liturgy of the Neighbor: Emmanuel Levinas and the Religion of Responsibility*, Pittsburgh: Duquesne Universwsity Press, 2000, pp. 42–47.
69 Alter, 2000.

Bibliography

Alter, Joseph, *Gandhi's Body: Sex, Diet, and the Politics of Nationalism*, Philadelphia: University of Pennsylvania Press, 2000.
Bloechl, Jeffry, *Liturgy of the Neighbor: Emmanuel Levinas and the Religion of Responsibility*, Pittsburgh: Duquesne UP, 2000.
Bynum, Caroline Walker, *Holy Feast and Holy Fast: The Religious Significance of Food to Medieval Women*, Berkeley: University of California Press, 1987.
Canguilhem, Georges, *The Normal and the Pathological*, Cambridge: Harvard University Press, 1991.
Derrida, Jacques, *Of Hospitality*, trans. Rachel Bowlby, Stanford: Stanford University Press, 2000.
Desai, Narayan, *Bliss Was It To Be Young – With Gandhi: Childhood Reminiscences*, trans. Bhal Malji, ed. Mark Shepard, Mumbai: Bharatiya Vidya Bhavan, 1988.
Dongre, Vijay Kumar, 'Bapu's Concern for Leprosy', in *Here's the Key: A Complete Health Education Magazine*, vol. 2, Noida, Delhi: Leprosy Mission Trust, 2003.
Doniger, Wendy O'Flaherty, 'Reflections' in *The Lives of Animals* by J.M. Coetzee, ed. Amy Gutzman, Princeton: Princeton University Press, 1999.
Fanon, Frantz, 'Medicine and Colonialism' in *A Dying Colonialism*, trans. Haakon Chevalier, New York: Grove Press, 1965.
Gandhi, M.K., *Collected Works of Mahatma Gandhi*, Vol. 4, Delhi: Publication Division, Ministry of Information and Broadcasting, Government of India, 1958–94.
—— *Autobiography: The Story of My Experiments with Truth*, trans. Mahadev Desai, New York: Dover Publications, 1983.
—— *From Yervada Mandir*, trans. Valji Govindji Desai, Ahmedabad: Navijivan, 1932.
—— *Hind Swaraj and Other Writings*, ed. Anthony Parel, Cambridge: Cambridge University Press, 1997.
—— *Key to Health*, Ahmedabad: Navjivan, 1948.

―― *Satyagraha in South Africa.*, trans. Valji Govindji Desai, Ahmedabad: Navjivan, 1928.
―― *The Teaching of the Gita*, ed. Anand T. Hingorani, Mumbai: Bharatiya Vidya Bhavan, 1998.
Krell, David Farrell, *Infectious Nietzche*, Bloomington: Indiana University Press, 1996.
Laidlaw, James, *Riches and Renunciation: Religion, Economy, and Society among the Jains*, Oxford: Clarendon Press, 1995.
Nandy, Ashis and Shiv Vishwanathan, 'Modern Medicine and It Nonmodern Critics: A Study in Discourse' in *The Savage Freud and Other Essays on Possible and Retrievable Selves*, Princeton University Press, Princeton, 1995.
Roberts, Tyler, *Contesting Spirit: Nietzsche, Affirmation, Religion*, Princeton: Princeton University Press, 1998.
Roy, Parama, 'Meat-Eating, Masculinity, and Renunciation in India: A Gandhian Grammar of Diet', *Gender and History*, vol. 14, no.1, 2002.
Rudolph, Susanne H. and Lloyd, I, *Gandhi: The Traditional Roots of Charisma*, Chicago: University of Chicago Press, 1967.
Skaria, Ajay, 'Gandhi's Politics: Liberalism and the Question of the Ashram', *South Atlantic Quarterly*, vol. 101, no. 4, 2002.
Zimmerman, Francis, *The Jungle and the Aroma of Meats: An Ecological Theme in Hindu Medicine*, Berkeley: University of California Press, 1987.

4 Emptied of all but love
Gandhiji's first public fast

Tridip Suhrud

From 15 to the 18 March 1918 Gandhiji observed a fast. This was his first public fast after returning to India from South Africa in 1915.[1] Twenty-two days before he announced his decision to fast, Gandhiji along with Anasuyaben Sarabhai and Shankarlal Banker had been leading the strike of the workers of the Ahmedabad textile mills. The issue, which divided the mill-hands and the mill-owners, was payment of increased wages. The textile mills had been paying a 'plague bonus' to the workers since August 1917. The mill-owners had unilaterally decided to stop the payment of the additional bonus.

While Gandhiji was still occupied with the Commission of Inquiry in Champaran, he had gone to Bombay on 2 February 1918 in connection with the Kheda situation. Sheth Ambalal Sarabhai had requested Gandhi to intervene in the textile mills dispute. Gandhiji accepted the request on the condition that both parties accept arbitration. The workers and the mill-owners accepted the principle of arbitration and appointed three arbitrators each. Seth Ambalal Sarabhai, Sheth Jagabhai Dalpatbhai and Sheth Chandulal were appointed as arbitrators by the mill-owners, while Gandhiji, Vallabhbhai Patel and Shankarlal Banker represented the workers. The Collector of Ahmedabad, Mr Chatfield, was appointed the Umpire.

Gandhiji and Vallabhbhai had to leave for Kheda to conduct an enquiry into the problem of the assessment of land revenue. While they were involved in the struggle for the postponement of land revenue recovery in Kheda, the situation in Ahmedabad turned critical. The workers in the weaving departments of some mills struck work. The mill-owners declared that since the workers had resorted to strike after the appointment of the arbitrators, the arbitration stood cancelled *ipso facto*. They decided to declare a lockout in the mills. Gandhiji expressed regret on behalf of the workers and agreed to rectify the mistake, but the mill-owners remained adamant. The lockout commenced on 22 February. The mill-owners offered a 20 per cent increase in the wages. The workers were dissatisfied, accepted discharge and the lockout commenced. The workers had decided that they would not accept an increase less than 35 per cent, which was considered just and within the means of the mill-owners.

The workers took a pledge in a public meeting with God as their witness. The workers resolved: 1) not to resume work until a 35 per cent increase on the July wages is secured; 2) during the period of the lockout not to cause any disturbance, not to indulge in beating or assaulting, not to commit robbery, not to damage employers' property, not to use abusive language, but to remain peaceful.[2] This pledge was reminiscent of the pledge taken on 11 September 1906 in a meeting held at the Empire Theatre in Johannesburg. The meeting was called to resolve not to submit to the ordinance demanding compulsory registration of the Asiatics in the Transvaal. At this meeting Sheth Haji Habib made an impassioned speech in favour of a resolution calling all Asiatics not to submit to the new provisions and suffer all penalties for non-submission. Sheth Habib was so deeply moved that he called upon all Indians to pass this resolution with God as their witness. He went on to declare in the name of God that he would not submit to the law and called upon everyone to do likewise.

As the crowd cheered Sheth Haji Habib, Gandhiji was 'at once startled and put on my guard'.[3] He says:

> Only then did I fully realize my own responsibility and the responsibility of the community. The community had passed many a resolution before and amended such resolutions in the light of further reflection or fresh experience ... Amendments in resolutions and failures to observe resolutions on the part of the persons agreeing thereto are ordinary experiences of public life all over the world. But no one ever imports the name of God into such resolutions.[4]

Gandhiji was aware that in abstract there should be no distinction between resolution adopted as a deliberate choice and an oath taken in the name of a God. He was also aware that the world saw a resolution and an oath as poles asunder. A man deviating from a resolution is not ashamed of his conduct but a man who violates an oath not only falls in his own esteem but is also looked upon as a sinner in the society. Gandhiji was deeply aware of the resonance that a vow with the God as witness had for himself and his people. Before sailing for England he had also taken three vows. He believed that constant awareness of these vows had given him the strength to resist many a temptation and saved him from moral decline. He was proud of his success in observing the vows and understood the inner meaning of the act of administering and accepting an oath.[5]

As Gandhiji rose to explain the significance of Sheth Habib's call, his perplexity and anxiety had given place to enthusiasm. He told the meeting

> to pledge ourselves or to take an oath in the name of God or with him as witness is not something to be trifled with. If having taken such an oath we violate our pledge we are guilty before God and man. Personally I hold that a man, who deliberately and intelligently takes a pledge and

then breaks it, forfeits his manhood ... a man who lightly pledges his word and then breaks it becomes a man of straw and fits himself for punishment here as well as here-after.[6]

Gandhiji then invoked the inner voice. Pledge or an oath had to be taken, he said, on rare occasions. A man who takes a pledge lightly was sure to stumble. For him the pledge was located within the conscience. It could not be administered from the outside, nor could it be taken with a view to produce an effect. He said, 'Everyone must only search his own heart, and if the inner voice assures him that he has the requisite strength to carry him through, then only should he pledge himself and then only will his pledge bear fruit.'[7] He explained the nature of his personal responsibility and said that once having taken a pledge there was only one course open to someone like him, to die but not to submit to the law. He called upon each one to take the pledge only with the consent of the inner voice, independent of others, and once having taken such a pledge they must remain true to it even unto death. This was the 'Advent of Satyagraha'.

It was Gandhiji who administered the oath to ten thousand mill-hands of Ahmedabad in a public meeting held under a Babul tree, which came to be known as the *Ek Tek* tree. From the day the mill-owners announced the lockout, the workers went on a strike. Anasuyaben Sarabhai, Shankarlal Banker and Chhaganlal Gandhi were given the responsibility of visiting the living quarters of the workers daily to assess their needs, to advise them on their conduct during the struggle and to help them in their difficulties. Daily mass meeting were held, which were addressed by Gandhiji and others and where instructive leaflets written by Gandhiji but issued under the name of Anasuyaben were distributed. During the course of the strike seventeen such leaflets were issued. In each of these Gandhiji reminded the workers about their pledge and their responsibility in upholding the pledge. Gandhiji told the workers that they held the key to the situation as no wealth can be created without workers. This was possible he told them only if they cultivated truthfulness, courage and sense of justice, and harboured no animosity towards the employer.[8]

In this leaflet as in all subsequent ones Gandhiji wrote about the necessity of undergoing suffering in order to secure justice. Gandhiji dealt with the idea of justice in a leaflet issued on 3 March 3 1918.[9] In this he returned to the theme central to the *Hind Swaraj*. He differentiated between pure, or Eastern or ancient, justice and Satanic, or Western or modern, justice. Pure justice was that which was inspired by fellow feeling and compassion. This system was governed by sharing of joys and sorrows and was based on mutual regard, discipline, courtesy and affection. He argued that a totally different way of life prevailed in the modern West. The modern West had no place for feelings or mercy in public activities: 'each thus thinks of himself and is not bound to think of the other'.[10] He cautioned against introducing this 'despicable' justice in India. Workers ought not to raise a demand just because they had the strength to do so. If the employers' decided to oppose just demands of the workers it would amount to raising an army of elephants against the ants. He was confident that 'the Jain and Vaishnava employers in the capital city of this worthy land of Gujarat would never consider it a victory to bear down on the workers or deliberately to give them less than their due. We are sure this wind from the West will pass as quickly as it has come.'[11]

Gandhiji also tried to awaken the conscience of the mill-owners. Throughout the strike Ambalal Sarabhai and Gandhiji maintained a deep and affectionate relationship. Gandhiji wrote to him on 1 March and cautioned him about the serious consequences that a victory of the mill-owners would have. He wrote:

> What about your efforts, though? If you succeed, the poor, already suppressed, will be suppressed still more, will be more abject than ever and the impression will have been confirmed that money can subdue everyone. If, despite your efforts, the workers succeed in securing the increase, you, and others with you, will regard the result as your failure. Can I possibly wish you success in so far as the first result is concerned? Is it your desire that the arrogance of money should increase? Or that the workers be reduced to utter submission? Would you be so unkindly disposed to them as to see no success for you in their getting what they are entitled to, maybe even a few pice more? Do you not see that in your failure lies your success, that your success is fraught with danger for you? How if Ravana had succeeded? Do you not see that your success will have serious consequences for the whole society? Your efforts are of the nature of duragraha. My success everyone will accept as success. My failure, too, will not harm anyone; it will only prove that the workers were not prepared to go farther than they did. An effort like mine is satyagraha. Kindly look deep into your heart, listen to the still small voice within and obey it, I pray you. Will you dine with me?[12]

He shared with the workers the experience of the satyagraha in South Africa. He narrated instances from the lives of Harbat Singh, Sheth Ahmad Muhammad Kachhalia and Valliamma who suffered for the sake of truth. He repeatedly assured the workers that if they remained nonviolent, observed their pledge steadfastly they were bound to succeed in the struggle for truth, 'both the sides need not be followers of truth. Even if one side alone follows it, satyagraha will finally succeed'.[13]

While the lockout continued the employers also issued their own pamphlets, which Gandhiji decried as having been written in anger, as misleading and exaggerated. The employers announced that they were ready to pay an increase of 20 per cent in the wages and promised to take back workers who returned to work. They also announced rewards for a worker who brought with him five or more workers. Gandhiji could sense that the workers were tempted to accept the conditions of mill-owners. He reminded the workers that they could not resume work without compromising their pledge, their honour and their manliness. He said: 'If you weigh a pledge against a sum of hundreds of thousands, the pledge will be seen to be of greater consequence.'[14] He told them that the only way for them to rise higher was to abide by their pledge. He reminded the mill-owners that a religiously minded person never sought happiness in breaking the pledge of others. He told them that the employers' welfare could not be secured by keeping workers who could not keep an oath. He warned the workers not to use force or coercion against those 'black legs' who wished to return to work. Use of force was tantamount to breaking the pledge. It was not sufficient in struggle for truth merely to have just demands; the rightness of action was equally important. As the lockout was prolonged, the hardships of the workers also intensified. Sympathisers of the workers offered to raise collections to sustain the strike. Gandhiji refused such good intentioned help as he believed that those who sought to maintain themselves in such funds had no right to succeed. A pledge had to be maintained with self-respect and honour. 'Those who want food without working for it do not, it may be said, understand what a pledge means.'[15]

Twenty-two days had passed. The mill-owners remained obstinate; their agents were trying to sow seeds of doubts in the mind of the workers. Anasuyaben, Shankarlal Banker and Chhaganlal Gandhi were visiting them regularly. One day Chaganlal Gandhi was confronted with the following words, while he was trying to persuade the workers of Jugaldas Chawl to attend the daily mass meeting: 'What is it to Anasuyaben and Gandhiji? They come and go in their car, they eat sumptuous food, but we are suffering death-agonies; attending meetings does not prevent starvation.'[16] These words reached Gandhiji. The next day when he reached for the meeting what did he see there?

To quote him: 'One morning instead of an eager and enthusiastic crowd of 5 to 10 thousand men with determination written on their faces, I met a body of 2000 men with despair written on their faces.'[17] In the *Autobiography* he has described his moment of illumination:

> One morning – it was at the mill-hands' meeting – while I was still groping and unable to see my way clearly, the light came to me. Unbidden and all by themselves the words came to my lips: 'Unless the strikers rally,' I declared to the meeting, 'and continue the strike till a settlement is reached, or till they leave the mills altogether, I will not touch any food.'[18]

Mahadevbhai who was present at the meeting reports:

> Tears flowed from the eyes of everyone present in the meeting ... standing up one by one they said, 'We shall never fail in our pledge,

come what may, even though the heavens fall. We shall not weaken. We shall go to the houses of those who are vacillating and talk to them and will not allow them to weaken. Kindly give up this terrible resolve.'[19]

As the news spread crowds gathered at the Sabarmati Ashram to plead with Gandhiji to give up his oath to fast. Workers came to assure him that they would not falter even if the strike were to continue for months. Anasuyaben had also declared at the meeting that she too would fast along with Gandhiji. One worker came with a big knife and threatened to commit suicide; Anasuyaben relented and agreed to take food. A workers' meeting was called in the evening. Gandhiji assured the workers that he was not angry at the criticism made by the residents of the Jugaldas Chawl. He said, 'I, and others as well who want to serve India, have much to learn from it.'[20] Gandhiji then went on to explain to the workers the reason for his fast. Workers had taken an oath relying on his advice and now they were ready to break their oath. He said:

> In this age the oath has lost its value. Men break their oath at any time and for any reason and I am grieved to have been instrumental in thus lowering the value of an oath. There is nothing else that will bind a man as effectively as an oath does. The meaning of an oath is that we decide to do a particular thing with God in whom we believe as our witness. People who are on a higher plane can perhaps do without oaths, but we who are on a lower one cannot. We who fall a thousand times cannot raise ourselves without oaths.[21]

He said that fasting was the only way available to him if he wanted the workers to do their duty. He was no God who could provide demonstration of an oath and value of labour by other means. His fast was not to be construed as a threat that he had held out to the workers in order to induce them to abide by the pledge. Pledge could not be upheld by threat or inducement as pledge was founded on love. He told the workers: 'Nobody can be induced or coerced to keep his oath. Love is the only inducement that can be offered. You must understand that he alone, who loves his religion, loves his honour and country, will refuse to give up his resolve.'[22]

The mill-owners and other citizens of Ahmedabad also tried to persuade Gandhiji to give up his fast. Professor Anandshankar Dhruv, who was finally appointed the sole arbitrator of the dispute, argued with Gandhiji that an act like fast could only temporarily alter the outward behaviour of an opponent and could not bring about a change of heart. Gandhiji failed to convince this philosopher that the fast was not offered against the employers but it was intended to teach the workers the significance of a vow in public and private life.

Ambalal Sarabhai spent hours at the Ashram trying to persuade Gandhiji to give up his fast. Some mill-owners suggested that they were willing to give the workers 35 per cent increase this time for *his sake*. Gandhiji turned down the offer; he told them: 'Do not give 35 per cent out of pity for me, but do so to respect workers' pledge and to give them justice.'[23] On the third evening of the fast he shared the mill-owners' offer and his denial with the workers. He said: 'I thought that ten thousand men debasing themselves would be like a curse from on high. It is extremely humiliating to me that they offer you 35 per cent for my sake.'[24] Sheth Ambalal renewed his efforts to get Gandhiji to break his fast. He wanted Gandhiji to keep away from the owner–worker dispute in the future. He feared that Gandhiji's continued support would make the workers defiant and undisciplined and would lower the prestige of the mill-owners further. This exorbitant demand was unacceptable to Gandhiji; he had in fact involved himself in the dispute at the request of Ambalal Sarabhai. Gandhiji was extremely conscious that his fast was indeed putting pressure on the mill-owners to accept the demand of the workers. As a satyagrahi Gandhiji could not fast against them or coerce them in any way; he could only plead with them to do what was right. He tried his utmost to convey to the mill-owners that his fast was on account of a lapse on part of the workers. He wrote to Ambalal:

> Be guided by your sense of justice rather than your desire to see that I break my fast. The latter gives me immense pleasure and, therefore, need not cause pain to anyone. The workers will profit more from what they get as a matter of justice—they will enjoy the benefit longer.[25]

Gandhiji began considering a compromise, as in spite of his intentions the fast weighed heavily on the mill-owners and did not allow them to act freely. This was the 'grave defect'[26] of his fast. A compromise formula was arrived at, one which honoured the pledge of the workers, the decision of the mill-owners and accepted the principle of arbitration. Accordingly, the workers called off the strike, the mill-owners agreed to pay them an increase of 35 per cent on the first day, 20 per cent on the second day and 27.5 per cent from the third day till the arbitrator's award was declared. Both parties agreed that the increase of the interim period was only temporary and final wages would be decided after the sole arbitrator Prof. Anandshankar Dhruv gave his award.[27]

On 18 March 1918 Gandhiji announced the terms of settlement to thousands of jubilant workers. Speaking from under the Babul tree he told the workers:

> The settlement which I place before you merely upholds the workers' pledge. There is nothing more in it ... I thought over the pledges of both. My fast stood in the way. I could not tell them: "I will break my fast only if you concede my demand." I felt that this would have been cowardice on my part. I, therefore, agreed that for the present both may maintain their pledges, and what the arbitrator decides should finally prevail.[28]

Even amidst jubilation Gandhiji did not resist himself from pointing out defects of the workers. He warned them that they should henceforth not take an oath. He said:

> He who has no experience, and has attempted nothing big, has no right to take an oath. After twenty years' experience, I have come to the conclusion that I am qualified to take a pledge. I see that you are not yet so qualified ... You have yet to learn how and when to take a pledge.[29]

On the same day in a public meeting organised in the compound of the Sarabhai house Gandhiji said to the mill-owners:

> I must apologize to the employers. I have pained them very much. My vow [to fast] was aimed at you, but everything in this world has two sides. Thus, the vow had an effect on the employers as well, I apologize to them humbly for this, I am as much their servant as the workers. All I ask is that both should utilize my services to the full.[30]

On 27 March 1918 Gandhiji issued a public statement giving an explanation regarding the struggle and his fast. He gave a detailed account of the dispute and the events of the twenty-two day lockout. He shared his pain with the country at the lapse of part of the workers. He reminded the countrymen that inability to keep a pledge was not peculiar to the mill-workers of Ahmedabad. It was a failing common to all countrymen. He wrote:

> I believe in God as I believe that I am writing this letter. I believe in the necessity of the performance of one's promise at all costs. I knew that the men before us were God-fearing men, but that the long-drawn-out lockout or strike was putting an undue strain upon them. I had the knowledge before me during my extensive travels in India, hundreds of people were found who as readily broke a promise as they made them. I knew, too, that the best of us have but a vague and indistinct belief in soul-force and in God. I felt that it was a sacred moment for me, my faith was on the anvil, and I had no hesitation to rising and declaring to the men that a breach of their vow so solemnly taken was unendurable by me and that I would not take any food until they had the 35 per cent increase given or until they had fallen. A meeting that was up to now unlike the former meetings, totally unresponsive, woke up as if by magic ... It was a privilege to witness the demonstration of the efficacy of truth and love. Every one immediately realized that the protecting power of God was as much with us today as it used to be in the days of yore. I am not sorry for the vow but with the belief that I have, I would have been unworthy of the trust undertaken by me, if I had done anything less.[31]

He said that his fast was not unblemished as it did affect the mill-owners. But the damage of ten thousand men breaking their pledge taken with God as their witness far outweighed the danger of the fast being misunderstood. Gandhiji observed that the ability of people to remain firm in their convictions and to consider an oath as unbreakable and inviolable was necessary for people to become a nation. Thus for Gandhiji the nation was predicated upon the moral character of the people. People who did not have faith in God, did not have the capacity to undergo suffering for the sake of truth could not constitute themselves as a nation. Nation for him thus became a moral category. The fast at one level was intended to awaken the morality that lay dormant in his countrymen.

It was this 'great idea' that he wished to share with the countrymen through the fast. On 17 March 1918 he spoke to the Ashramites, who were his closest associates and people he had the greatest faith in. The occasion was one of the most sacred rituals of the Ashram life – the Morning Prayer. Like many other occasions he opened his heart to the Ashramites. The prayer discourse he said 'is indeed the best occasion for me to unburden my soul to you'.[32] The decision to fast, he said, was a grave one but behind it stood a great idea. The fast was a means of conveying this beautiful idea; an opportunity he could not miss. This beautiful idea was the truth that he had gleaned from the ancient culture of India, which, even if mastered by a few he felt, would give them the mastery over the world. The fast according to him was not just aimed at the mill-hands of Ahmedabad, nor did it desire to teach them merely the value of an oath. The fast for him laid the ground for a civilisational dialogue with the people of India. This dialogue with the people of India was conducted through a dialogue with two of her finest leaders.

One of them was Tilak Maharaj, on whom, according to Gandhiji, 'millions are crazy, for whom millions of our countrymen would lay down their lives'.[33] The other leader was Pandit Madan Mohan Malaviya, a man Gandhiji described as possessing 'the holiest character'.[34] The fast, Gandhiji said, was an attempt to converse with these two great leaders and through them with the country. Tilak Maharaj had written on the inner meaning of the *Gita*. But, despite this he had not understood India and her people. Gandhiji said: 'But I have always felt that he has not understood the age-old spirit of India, has not understood her soul and that is the reason why the nation has come to this pass.'[35] At the root of this failure was Tilak's desire that India should be like Europe. Gandhiji said that Tilak Maharaj had undergone six years of internment to 'to display a courage of the European variety'.[36] He likened Tilak Maharaj's internment to the great men of Russia who were wasting their whole lives in Siberia. Gandhiji was saddened that our greatest treasure was expended to no purpose. Gandhiji felt that if Tilak Maharaj's imprisonment had spiritual promptings and spiritual motives its results would have been far different.

It was this absence of spiritual motive that Gandhiji wanted to convey to Tilak Maharaj. Gandhiji had written and spoken about this to him with the greatest of respect. But it was not something that could be captured in some words, though Gandhiji was certain that with his sharp intellect Tilak Maharaj had understood Gandhiji's criticism. Gandhiji wanted to convey the true meaning of the soul of India and of spiritual suffering to him. Gandhiji said:

> This is, however, no matter to be explained orally or in writing. To give him first-hand experience of it, I must furnish a living example. Indirectly, I have spoken to him often enough but, should I get an opportunity of providing a direct demonstration, I should not miss it, and here is one.[37]

Pandit Malaviya was of holy character, was learned and well informed on points of *dharma*. But, he too had failed to understand the spiritual basis of India. Gandhiji said of him, 'he has not, it seems to me, properly understood the soul of India in all its grandeur'.[38] Gandhiji felt that Pandit Malaviya, with whom he was tied with bonds of affection and had for that reason frequent quarrels with him, might get very angry with Ganhdi and consider him swollen-headed for having said so. But Gandhiji felt that it had to be said. The fast was an opportunity to convince Pandit Malaviya regarding the truth of India. 'I have this opportunity to provide him, too, with a direct demonstration. I owe it to both to show now what India's soul is.'[39]

Through his suffering Gandhiji wanted to awaken India to her soul. His decision to fast was not only to uphold the faith in God and prevent annihilation of dharma but to test whether Indians still responded to a call to their soul. Gandhiji told the Ashramites that his vow to fast had an instant and electrifying impact on the mill-hands whose faith had faltered. He said:

> They awoke to the reality of their soul, a new consciousness stirred in them and they got strength to stand by their pledge. I was instantly persuaded that dharma had not vanished from India, that people do respond to an appeal to their soul. If Tilak Maharaj and Malaviyaji would but see this, great things could be done in India.[40]

If the pledge were broken, Gandhiji said, it would have spelled the ruin of India. It was by suffering himself that Gandhiji wished to save the nation of certain ruin. Having awakened the soul of India Gandhiji did not experience any pain of hunger or suffering. On earlier occasions he had felt torn between the cravings of his body and warnings of his mind. But this fast was different. He said: 'I am at present overflowing with joy ... My mind is filled with profound peace. I feel like pouring forth my soul to you all but I am beside myself with joy.'[41]

But just a day later this sense of overflowing joy and profound peace gave way to a sense of gloom. The 'taint' of his vow had forced him to accept a compromise that ought to have been quite unacceptable to him. Despite his best efforts he felt he had failed to convince the world that his fast was not aimed at the mill-owners. He told the Ashramites before the compromise was announced that, 'It is my vow of fasting which is to blame. The vow is open to criticism from many points of view.'[42] He was overpowered by a sense of shame, as he knew that if he had insisted that the demands of the workers be met in full, the mill-owners would have met them. This would have been unbecoming of a satyagrahi. He was forced to swallow something most repulsive by way of the compromise. He said, 'How could I, who would not take even *amrit* except at the proper hour, swallow such a thing?'[43]

He spoke about the teachings of the sacred books, which taught him that where injustice prevailed, an upright man just could not live. That was the reason why sacred men withdrew from the world of 'crooks' to the Himalaya or the Vindhya mountains and mortified their bodies. Some did return having purified themselves, so that even in the midst of world's hypocrisy they could follow their own dictates. He considered himself a mere pigmy compared to these illuminated souls. He had a fair measure of his strength but the world esteemed it much higher than it ought to be. He spoke words of pain and despondency. Such words rarely came to Gandhiji:

> Every day I discover so much of hypocrisy in the world that many times I feel I just cannot go on being here ... if one day you did not find me in your midst, you should not be surprised. If this feeling comes over me, I will go where you will never be able to seek me out. In that hour, do not feel bewildered, but go on with the tasks on hand as if I were with you all the time.[44]

Thus ended Gandhiji's first attempt to awaken the soul of the country and give her a measure of the soul-force. The fast was a dialogic exercise. It was a moral dialogue that was attempted at many levels. At one level it was aimed at the mill-hands of Ahmedabad. He sought to teach them the value of an oath and suffering that had the power to alter an unjust situation. The strike and the fast was also a conversation with the employers. It was an exercise in conflict resolution and an attempt to affirm 'pure justice'. It was an attempt to awaken the employers and the moneyed people of the country to their *dharma*. Their *dharma* was not just to give fair wages but it was also to recognise that they had to allow the dissenting workers to perform their *dharma*. This they could do by understanding the true meaning of the workers' pledge.

The most important conversation was about the nature of India's civilisation. In the *Hind Swaraj* Gandhi had described India as a civilisation that elevated the moral being and as based on a belief in God. He called her the source of religions. The Western civilisation tended to propagate immorality and was godless. India, he felt, had lost the ability to listen to the call of its conscience and therefore tried to imitate Western morality, which was based on bodily welfare and use of brute-force. The only way to *swaraj* according to Gandhiji was that India had to awaken to the reality of her soul and learn once again to have faith in the power of spiritual suffering and soul-force. The fast was a demonstration of what poet Tulsidas has said: 'Of religion, pity, or love, is the root, as egotism of the body. Therefore, we should not abandon pity so long as we are alive.'

Notes

1 Gandhiji had fasted thrice before this public fast after coming back to India. On 1 June 1915 he fasted for a day on account of a lie told by some Ashram children (see Dalal, C.B., *Gandhiji Ni Dinwari*, p. 14). In September 1915 the first untouchable family consisting of Dudabhai, Danibehn and Laxmi came to live at the Satyagraha Ashram, Kochrab. This caused consternation among the Ashramites. Many, including Kasturba and Santokbehn Maganlal Gandhji, opposed their induction. Some Ashramites gave up food. Gandhiji was deeply perturbed at the orthodoxy of the Ashramites and fasted on 11 and 12 September 1915 (see, ibid., pp. 16–17). The third private fast was of three days. Manilal Gandhi had sent some money from his private funds to Harilal Gandhi who was in Calcutta. The receipt sent by Harilal fell in Gandhiji's hands and he decided to fast for three days for this act of transgression. The fast was conducted in May or June of 1916 (see Dalal, Chandulal and Dalal, Bhagubhai, *Harilal Gandhi: A Biography*, translated from original Gujarati by Tridip Suhrud, Orient Longman, forthcoming).
2 Desai, Mahadev, *A Righteous Struggle*, translated from original Gujarati by Somnath P. Dave (Navajivan: Ahmedabad 1951, 1968), p. 41.
3 Gandhi, M. K., *Satyagraha in South Africa*, translated from original Gujarati by Valji Govindji Desai, (Navajivan: Ahmedabad 1928, 1950, 2003), p. 96.
4 Ibid.
5 Eric Erickson has observed: 'That Gandhi left England with his vow intact was a matter of enormous importance, not only in his own eyes, but later also for his ethical stature among his people.' Erickson, Eric H., *Gandhi's Truth on the Origins of Militant Nonviolence* (Faber and Faber: London), 1970, p. 152.
6 Gandhi, M.K., *Satyagraha in South Africa*, p. 97.
7 Ibid., p. 98.
8 *CWMG*, Vol. 16, pp. 289–90, 'Ahmedabad Mill-Hands' Strike, Leaflet No. 2, February 27, 1918'. All references to the *CWMG* are from the electronic version.
9 Ibid., pp. 302–4, 'Ahmedabad Mill-Hands' Strike, Leaflet No. 6, March 3, 1918'.
10 Desai, Mahadev, *A Righteous Struggle*, p. 49.
11 *CWMG*, Vol. 16, p. 304, 'Ahmedabad Mill-Hands' Strike, Leaflet No. 6, March 3, 1918.'
12 Ibid., p. 300, ' Letter to Ambalal Sarabhai, March 1, 1918'. Ambalal Sarabhai and Gandhiji shared a deep personal regard and affection for each other. It was Ambalal Sarabhai who had given Rs. 13,000 to Gandhiji as expenses towards the Ashram at a time when the Ashram was facing its most serious monetary crisis. All monetary help to the Ashram had stopped when Dudabhai and his family came to live at the Ashram. Gandhiji was considering a move to the 'untouchable quarters'. See Gandhi, M.K., *An Autobiography or The Story of*

My Experiments with Truth, translated from the Gujarati by Mahadev Desai (Navajivan: Ahmedabad, 1927, 1999), p. 332.
13 *CWMG*, Vol. 16, p. 307, 'Ahmedabad Mill-Hands' Strike, Leaflet No. 7, March 4, 1918'.
14 Ibid., p. 327, 'Ahmedabad Mill-Hands' Strike, Leaflet No. 12, March 12, 1918'.
15 Ibid., p. 333, 'Ahmedabad Mill-Hands' Strike, Leaflet No. 14, March 15, 1918'. He told the sympathisers: 'What is the meaning of satyagraha if you help the workers with money to carry it on or if, this time, they have joined it in the hope that you will support them with such help? What will be the value of such satyagraha? The essence of satyagraha lies in cheerful submission to the suffering that may follow it. The more a satyagrahi suffers, the more thoroughly he is tested.' See ibid., p. 332, ' Reply to Sympathisers, *Before* March 15, 1918'.
16 Desai, Mahadev, *A Righteous Struggle*, pp. 25–26.
17 *CWMG*, Vol. 16, pp. 363–64, ' Letter to the Press, *The Leader*, 3.4.1918'.
18 Gandhi, M.K., *An Autobiography*, p. 359. This idea of the inner voice commanding him to undertake a fast is often repeated in his narratives about the act of fasting. He often used the metaphor of darkness, groping and illumination to describe the definitive moment when the inner voice commanded him to fast.
19 Desai, Mahadev, *A Righteous Struggle*, pp. 26–27.
20 *CWMG*, Vol. 16, ' Speech to Ahmedabad Mill-Hands, March 15, 1918'.
21 Ibid.
22 Ibid., p. 336.
23 Desai, Mahadev, *A Righteous Struggle*, p. 32.
24 *CWMG*, Vol. 16, p. 343, 'Speech to Ahmedabad Mill-Hands, March 17, 1918'.
25 Ibid., pp. 342–43, ' Letter to Ambalal Sarabhai, March 17, 1918'.
26 Gandhi, M.K., *An Autobiography*, p. 360.
27 Prof. Anandshankar Dhruv gave his award on 10.8.1918 in which he accepted that the demand of 35 per cent increase was just and asked the mill-owners to give that increase. The arbitration proceedings were delayed because of the hesitation on the part of the mill-owners to share certain facts and provide certain explanations to the arbitrator. Under these circumstances Prof. Dhruv observed: 'I cannot come to a decision regarding a really *just* solution to the dispute. But it being desirable that the workmen should get the arbitrator's award without further delay, I have had to arrive at *practical justice*' (Desai, Mahadev, *A Righteous Struggle*, p. 93, emphasis in the original).
28 *CWMG*, Vol. 16, p. 346, ' Speech to Ahmedabad Mill-Hands, March 18, 1918'.
29 Ibid., pp. 346–47.
30 Ibid., p. 347, ' Speech to Ahmedabad Mill-Hands, March 18, 1918'.
31 Ibid., p. 364, ' Letter to the Press, The Leader, 3. 4. 1918'.
32 Ibid., p. 339, ' Prayer Discourse in Ashram, March 17, 1918'.
33 Ibid.
34 Ibid., p. 340.
35 Ibid.
36 Ibid.
37 Ibid.
38 Ibid.
39 Ibid., p. 341.
40 Ibid., p. 341.
41 Ibid.
42 Ibid., p. 344, ' Address to Ashram Inmates, March 18, 1918'.
43 Ibid., p. 345.
44 Ibid.

Bibliography

Dalal, Chandulal Bhagubhai, *Harilal Gandhi: A Biography*, translated from original Gujarati by Tridip Suhrud, Delhi: Orient Longman, 2006.

Desai, Mahadev, *A Righteous Struggle*, translated from original Gujarati by Somnath P. Dave, Ahmedabad: Navajivan, 1951, 1968.

Erickson, Eric H., *Gandhi's Truth on the Origins of Militant Nonviolence*, London: Faber and Faber, 1970.

Gandhi, M. K., *Satyagraha in South Africa*, translated from original Gujarati by Valji Govindji Desai, Ahmedabad: Navajivan: 1928, 1950, 2003.

—— 'Letter to the Press, *The Leader*, 3. 4. 1918', CWMG, Vol. 16.

—— 'Prayer Discourse in Ashram, March 17, 1918'. CWMG, Vol. 16. Gandhi, M.K, 'Address to Ashram Inmates, March 18, 1918'. CWMG, Vol. 16.

—— 'Speech to Ahmedabad Mill-Hands, March 18, 1918'. *CWMG*, Vol. 16.

—— *An Autobiography or the Story of My Experiments with Truth*, translated from the Gujarati by Mahadev Desai, Ahmedabad: Navajivan,1927, 1999.

—— *Complete Works of Mahatma Gandhi*, Vol. 16, pp. 289–90, 'Ahmedabad Mill-Hands' Strike, Leaflet No. 2, February 27, 1918. All references to the *CWMG* are from the electronic version.

Part II
Of friendship, law and language
Shaping Gandhian 'weakness'

5 Gandhi moves
Intentional communities and friendship
Thomas Weber

In 1982–83 I spent some months at Gandhi's Sabarmati Ashram when I was doing research on Gandhi's celebrated Salt March. I often wondered how Gandhi could have left this utopia, especially given that it would have been even more of a utopia in 1930, when it was still surrounded by fields and orchards. The explanation that Gandhi sacrificed his home at the altar of nationalist struggle was never completely satisfying. As time went by I realised that I was also not satisfied with the reasons given for Gandhi founding his first intentional community, Phoenix settlement: that he read Ruskin's *Unto This Last* on a train trip and this changed his life. Most changes of such magnitude have a context. They are not stand-alone events that happen on the way to Damascus. The founding of Tolstoy farm seemed a little more straightforward, but the reasons why he ended up in Sevagram were also a little overly simple – it was the geographical centre of India and that he wanted to go and live in a village. Wardha is out of the way with a very unpleasant climate and he did not end up in a village for some years. There was obviously more to these stories.

The political Gandhi and the whole Gandhi

Our knowledge of the life of Mahatma Gandhi, when it does not come from Attenborough's landmark film, is generally provided by popular biographies. The biographies, especially the best-known ones, such as those by Fischer (1962) and Nanda (1958), tend to be political biographies. Gandhi is the main player in India's freedom struggle, the eventual 'father of the nation'. His fight for the rights of Indians in South Africa and his struggle for India's independence are generally the main focus of the story. The central narrative of the India phase of his life focuses on the three main political campaigns that he led: the 1921–22 Non-Cooperation Movement, the 1930–33 Civil Disobedience Movement and the 1942–43 Quit India Movement. The lengthy periods between these campaigns spent on self-discovery or anti-untouchability and other social work are often seen as lulls in Gandhi's life. This, however, gives a very limited view of the Mahatma and different biographies of Gandhi could be written. How about a spiritual or constructive work biography with the political campaigns being mere extensions of these more fundamental projects which are far from being periods of marking time? A different picture of Gandhi would emerge, and certainly not a less accurate picture. Gandhi's own autobiography, *The Story of my Experiments with Truth* (1940), is not a political autobiography.

Narayan Desai, one of the few remaining Gandhians who knew the Mahatma intimately (his father was Mahadev Desai, Gandhi's chief personal secretary, and he grew up in Gandhi's ashrams), who was a leading figure in the post-Gandhi Gandhian movement and who is the most recent Gandhi biographer, notes that Gandhi gave three great gifts to humanity and that *satyagraha*, Gandhi's nonviolent activism, representing the political Gandhi, is only one of them.[1] This, however, is the one that English-language books about Gandhi focus on. With this focus, Gandhi's co-workers, the ones who take on starring roles in the biographies, are Jawaharlal Nehru and Sardar Vallabhbhai Patel. The political Gandhi, however, is a very incomplete representation of the person. I argue that a more holistic analysis of the Mahatma life and work would include comprehensive reference to other important co-workers.

Gandhi held before himself, and attempted to place before the masses, a picture of an ideal society that was to be the goal of collective endeavour, as the approach towards Truth was to be the goal for the individual. This vision was summed up in the word '*Ramrajya*', the 'Kingdom of God', where there were equal rights for princes and paupers, where even the lowliest person could get swift justice without elaborate and costly procedures, where inequalities that allowed some to roll in riches while the masses did not have enough to eat were abolished, and where sovereignty of the people was based on pure moral authority rather than coercive power. Political independence for the country may have been a step towards *Ramrajya*, but was certainly no guarantee of it.

Gandhi firmly believed that all forms of exploitation and oppression rested to a large degree on the acquiescence of the victims. With this in mind he noted that 'exploitation of the poor can be extinguished not by effecting the destruction of a few millionaires, but by removing the ignorance of the poor and teaching them to non-cooperate with the exploiters'.[2] It was again partly for the educative purpose of pointing this out to the oppressed that he instituted what he called the 'constructive programme'. Although this program was tied to India's independence struggle, it was not merely a tactical adjunct to assist in achieving that seemingly larger and more important goal. The constructive programme involved future leaders in the struggle and put them in contact with the masses (working not just *for* the people, but *with* them). Its goal was to help bring about the society Gandhi envisaged in a future free India, and indeed a future just world. In fact, Gandhi claimed that the wholesale fulfilment of the constructive programme '*is* complete independence' because if the nation was involved in the very process of rebuilding itself in the image of its dreams 'from the very bottom upwards', it would by definition be free.[3]

In situations of social conflict and mass *satyagraha* campaigns, Gandhi made it a point to couple constructive work with civil disobedience, sometimes seeming to say that constructive work was an aid to the civil disobedience campaign and at other times putting the formula around the other way. In fact civil disobedience 'without the constructive programme', said Gandhi, would be 'like a paralysed hand attempting to lift a spoon'.[4] Perhaps, it can even be said that large oppositional *satyagraha* campaigns cannot be fully nonviolent if they are not accompanied by some form of positive constructive programme. *Sarvodaya* (the welfare of all), the aim of the constructive programme, in Desai's scheme, is the second of Gandhi's great gifts.

For Gandhi this constructive work offered replacement for what the nationalists were opposing. He was firmly convinced that unless fundamental changes were made to governing structures both socially and politically, civil disobedience, if it succeeded in overthrowing a set of oppressors, would merely exchange one group of leaders with another similar group. Contrasting himself with the 'born politician' Sardar Patel, Gandhi claimed that 'I was born for the constructive programme. It is part of my soul. Politics is a kind of botheration for me.'[5] Further, during one of his major political campaigns, Gandhi remarked that 'the work of social reform or self-purification ... is a hundred times dearer to me than what is called purely political work'. During another, following pressure to launch civil disobedience, Mahadev Desai records Gandhi as having said that 'in placing civil disobedience before constructive work I was wrong ... I feared that I should estrange co-workers and so carried on with imperfect *Ahimsa* [nonviolence]'.[6] Gandhi was well aware that political freedom was easier to achieve than economic, social and moral freedom in part because they are 'less exciting and not spectacular'.[7] Political biographies also seem to be more exciting and spectacular than those focussing on the social and moral aspects of Gandhi's life. The main co-workers he had in his constructive work, who, like Jamnalal Bajaj, were at least as important to him as his political co-workers, tend to disappear from the record.

If we look at Gandhi's relationship with his second cousin Maganlal Gandhi and his spiritual heir Vinoba Bhave we realise that there is even more to the Mahatma, something obvious to Desai but that most biographies make far too little of. Desai points out that there was a third gift from Gandhi: his eleven vows, a set of rules which established the code of conduct for his ashram inmates and which were the key to understanding Gandhi's religious quest.

Gandhi firmly believed that life could not be compartmentalised, that actions and the reasons on which they were based, whether they were political, economic, social or spiritual, were all interrelated, and that these actions had a direct bearing upon the achievement of life's ultimate aim. Gandhi himself named this aim as 'moksha', a liberation of the self, and claimed that his life, including his 'ventures in the political field are directed to this same end'.[8] Again, although the spiritual Gandhi does not fit too comfortably in primarily political biographies except to set the Mahatma up as the conscience of humanity, without understanding Gandhi's spiritual quest, we do not understand Gandhi. As he is secularised on the political stage we are left with no easy way of coming to terms with a more whole Gandhi.

For Gandhi the vow was a powerful tool in the spiritual quest because vows enable acts to become possible through extraordinary self-denial. Through his eleven ashram vows, Gandhi turned personal virtues into public values. The vows were to adhere to truth, nonviolence, celibacy, non-possession, non-stealing, control of the palate, fearlessness, equal respect for all religions, bread labour (the dignity of manual work), the removal of untouchability (as an institution and from one's own heart), and *swadeshi* (the favouring of locally produced goods, neighbourliness).

Gandhi spent a lifetime struggling with these vows. And how could he have done otherwise? They constituted the road map of his spiritual quest. His political activities were only an adjunct to this quest. For Gandhi, applying a set of techniques may have meant that nonviolent political activism was more likely to achieve its immediate political goals. However, living within the rules required for a successful *satyagraha* campaign, as Gandhi understood it, also constituted the type of life that was ethically and spiritually ennobling.

Gandhi and his ashrams

It is in the context of my argument that we need to consider Gandhi's life and work in more holistic terms that I now propose to look at Gandhi's various ashram settlements. I suggest that his many moves can be attributed to his friendships with key associates such as Henry Polak, Hermann Kallenbach, Maganlal Gandhi and Jamnalal Bajaj.

Polak and Phoenix

It was the relatively short full-tilt soulmate relationship between Gandhi and the youthful reporter Henry Polak, in March–April 1904 that led to the formation of Phoenix Settlement in South Africa and changed the course of Gandhi's life.[9] Inspired by his creative-critical relationship with 'chhotabhai' (younger brother) Henry, Gandhi started his simple life experiments. The relationship made Gandhi receptive to Ruskin's message in *Unto This Last*, a book given to him by Polak. Ruskin and Polak's influence helped set the tone for the constructive programme and Gandhi's economic philosophy, and, in the more immediate term, the founding of Phoenix Settlement.

The 22 year-old Polak had a glimpse of the 35-year-old Gandhi at Ziegler's vegetarian restaurant. Although he saw nothing remarkable about the black turbaned lawyer, his desire to meet him and discuss the Indian question was increased on the discovery that Gandhi was a fellow Tolstoyan and a vegetarian. A few days later the opportunity came. Miss Ada Bissicks, the proprietor of another vegetarian restaurant that Gandhi frequented (and partially financed), informed Polak that Gandhi would be attending an 'At Home' at her house the following evening and invited him to come as well. 'So we met, and the meeting changed the current of both our lives', recalled Polak.[10] It was clear from the start that the meeting would not be merely one of journalist and subject. The 'real card of introduction' was the fact that Polak was the only other person Gandhi had met who had read a certain book on nature cure for disease. Gandhi invited Polak to his office so that the latter could peruse the shelf full of Tolstoy's books that Gandhi kept there. A lengthy conversation in Gandhi's chambers followed. It soon became apparent to Gandhi that Polak was a lover of justice who harboured no racial prejudice and that besides vegetarianism and nature cure the two of them had many other things in common including a pull towards a more simple life, an interest in the Hindu texts and the writings of Tolstoy and Ruskin. Green notes that 'theirs was a New Age union, cemented in the presence of the New Age icons in Gandhi's office'.[11] Soon they were sharing quarters.

After discovering the financial plight of the newspaper *Indian Opinion* (which he was financing) in September 1904, Gandhi undertook a hurried trip to Durban (from where the paper was being published) to set things right. For the journey, Polak lent Gandhi Ruskin's *Unto This Last* which he had just finished reading. Gandhi couldn't put it down. The book resonated with some of Gandhi's own deep convictions. It caused him a sleepless night. Then and there he made a resolution to 'change' his life in 'accordance with the ideals of the book'. Gandhi claimed that the book 'brought about an instantaneous and practical transformation' in his life.[12]

In an important and early biography of Gandhi, written in three sections by those who knew him at the relevant time, the small biographical sketch of Polak, who covered Gandhi's early life until he left South Africa, informs us that, 'In 1904 he launched Gandhi on the "simple-life" practice which he maintained till his death.' We are further informed that, 'From 1904–14 he was Gandhi's closest colleague and confidant, and his lieutenant in his long Passive Resistance struggle in South Africa. He was a pioneer of Gandhi's movement to end indentured-labour emigration from India.'[13] Elsewhere, Polak notes that in giving Gandhi Ruskin's *Unto This Last* he had helped generate a 'deep and fundamental change' in Gandhi's thinking that had been 'developing quietly for some time'.[14] Of course self-claims do not always stand up to more objective scrutiny. After all who would not want to be credited with, if it was not an entirely preposterous proposition, something of the order of launching the Mahatma on the life practice that became synonymous with his saintly persona? Nevertheless, in this case they should not be discounted too easily.

In the early, most creative time in their relationship, Polak and Gandhi lived in such close physical proximity that there is no available correspondence to shed further light on other forms of closeness. Diary extracts of the time when they were engaged in their most creative experimentation, had they existed, would have been most illuminating. However, some later letters, especially those between Gandhi and Millie, who became Henry's wife, do throw some light on their interactions. In their 'bachelor' days, before the return of his family to South Africa from India and the arrival of Millie, Henry and Gandhi used to eat salads and uncooked vegetables regularly at vegetarian restaurants. In some of their dietary experiments, Henry was ahead of Gandhi: for example when Polak decided to go on a cleansing and will-power affirming fast, Gandhi and the other friends tried to dissuade him lest it do him harm.

Until his first intense encounter with his new young English friend, Gandhi was still something of an armchair New Ager. Now living together they could put their shared ideals into practice. They read books on nature cure and healthy and ethical diets and followed the various mud and water therapies (steam baths, cold plunge and hip baths, enemas) they espoused, used their recipes and experimented with their diets. There was no one before Henry with whom Gandhi could do these things. Green perceptively notes that 'this rebellion against scientific medicine was profoundly important for its symbolic rejection of elements of Western culture of which most people were most proud'.[15] This rebellion was facilitated by Polak's wholehearted participation and even leadership.

Even though he was rarely able to stay there for longer than a few weeks at a time, often with very lengthy periods in between, the settlement at Phoenix was far more than a communal effort at producing a newspaper – it was crucial in the development of Gandhi's ideas and future domestic and political *modus operandi*. Probably at some time Gandhi would have come to the idea of setting up a self-sufficient rural community even if Polak had not given him a copy of Ruskin's book to read. After all, that book was just the final nudge in Gandhi's steady journey towards the idea. One could say that the journey gained further momentum between the meeting of Gandhi and Polak at Mrs Bissiks' home and Gandhi's trip to Durban to investigate the financial position of *Indian Opinion*. While the establishment of the settlement was important in itself, it was only the most visible symbol of changes that Gandhi was undergoing at this time. To understand these changes adequately, one must also understand the relationship between Gandhi and Polak.

Kallenbach and Tolstoy Farm

The second intentional community was Tolstoy Farm. It was to be run on the principles of simple living, bread labour and spiritual practice in keeping with what Gandhi and his next soul-mate, Hermann Kallenbach, saw as the teachings of their spiritual mentor Leo Tolstoy. Kallenbach not only allowed the setting up of the farm through his financial support (in fact,

Gandhi moves 89

legally, he was the owner of the property), but the bond of love between him and Gandhi and the experimental ferment of their relationship set the climate for the move to Tolstoy Farm and its communal living arrangements.[16]

Kallenbach was perhaps less challenging to Gandhi than Polak possibly because at the stage of their greatest closeness Gandhi was more sure of himself and Kallenbach resisted his ideas less than Polak.[17] When he came into contact with Gandhi, he threw in his lot with his mentor, turning his back on his former profligate life with the type of zeal displayed by late-in-life converts. When he was separated from Gandhi he readily fell back into his old ways, only to give them up once more when later in life he again spent time with the Mahatma. Regardless of his changes of direction and the power Gandhi held over him, he also had a big influence on Gandhi. Tolstoy Farm became the prototype Gandhian ashram and the forging of the institution as a spiritual laboratory, rather than merely as an experiment in communal living, was done together with Hermann Kallenbach. In fact Tolstoy Farm owes its very existence to Kallenbach. Gandhi's life may have been significantly different without Tolstoy Farm, and without Kallenbach there may have been no equivalent of Tolstoy Farm to help mould the Mahatma we know.

Sometime in 1903 Kallenbach met Gandhi. At the first meeting, Gandhi was 'startled by his love of luxury and extravagance'. However they discussed deep matters of religion such as those concerning the Buddha's renunciation. As was the case with Polak, he ate with the barrister Gandhi at vegetarian restaurants and eventually their acquaintance grew 'into very close friendship, so much so that, we thought alike, and he was convinced that he must carry out in his life the changes I was making in mine'.[18] But the influences were not all one way, and even if again in this important relationship Kallenbach was the junior partner (with the exception of Gokhale, this was usual with Gandhi's close relationships after about this time), his own progress was facilitated by the company of someone who agreed with him, supported him and made suggestions about possible further life changes.

Although in 1908 Kallenbach was not yet ready to live communally at Phoenix, in a letter to his brother, Kallenbach recounted how he had not eaten meat for two years, fish for one year, and 'for the last 18 months I have given up my sex life'.[19] From 1909 Gandhi and Kallenbach addressed each other as Upper House and Lower House respectively. Gandhi termed Kallenbach's letters 'charming love notes', and Kallenbach referred to Kasturba as Mother. After 1910 Gandhi signed his letters to Kallenbach 'with love'. Hunt asserts that the relationship was 'clearly homoerotic' while certainly not homosexual.[20]

Gandhi's struggle with the South African government over the unfair treatment of Indian indentured labourers lasted for eight years. He later admitted that he was unsure whether they could have managed this and whether the people could have borne the hardships had there been no

Tolstoy Farm.²¹ As the campaigners were becoming dispirited at the length of the struggle and as the more wealthy merchants drifted away leaving a greater number of poorer resisters, Gandhi realised that they needed to be properly trained in the resolve necessary to prosecute an effective *satyagraha* campaign and somehow that campaign had to be put on a sounder financial footing. For this a 'central place where a corporate sense of purpose might be instilled' became necessary.²² The struggle had shifted to the Transvaal after 1906 and this meant that Gandhi could not spend the time he may have wanted at Phoenix. Instead he had to operate from his Johannesburg headquarters. During the intensification of the *satyagraha* campaign in 1908–9, Gandhi cut back on his practice of law for lack of time, abandoned his Johannesburg home and moved in permanently with Kallenbach. In the following year, when it was time for the establishment of a settlement for the dependents of the *satyagrahis* who had been imprisoned, it was clear that it had to be near Johannesburg. These *satyagrahis* could do some valuable work to help defray the costs of the campaign and even earn something for a living. Gandhi had money and was also being funded by the Indian community in whose name he was leading the struggle. However, the legal position in the Transvaal was different to the one in Natal. Here Indians could only legally own land in certain urban locations, and, for Gandhi's plan to come to fruition, European ownership was required. Kallenbach came to the rescue and purchased land and in 'June 1910 we all moved to Tolstoy Farm. We lived the life of simple farmers, and had only one vegetarian kitchen for all settlers.'²³

In 1912 Gandhi and Kallenbach were heavily back into dietetic experimentation and Kallenbach suggested that they give up milk because they constantly discussed its harmful effects and unnaturalness after infancy. Both of them gave up milk there and then. Soon the two Tolstoyans began to live on a diet of fruit, nuts and olive oil, enabling them to abandon cooking almost entirely. The ingredients were the cheapest available because their 'ambition was to live the life of the poorest people'.²⁴

Gandhi and Kallenbach engaged at length in spiritual discussions and if either was convinced intellectually of a new truth, attempts to put it into practical application were made immediately. This is best illustrated when Gandhi convinced Kallenbach that it was wrong to 'kill snakes and other such animals'. Once the logic of the position was clear, it had to be pushed to its inevitable conclusion: if it was wrong to kill snakes, friendship with snakes should be cultivated. Kallenbach purchased books on snakes in order to be able to identify the species, taught the inmates of the farm the ability to distinguish the poisonous ones from those that protected field crops and even caught and tamed a large cobra which he hand fed. He and Gandhi had discussions on fear and love in respect to the relationship between snakes and humans.²⁵

Less than seven months after he had written the Gujarati document *Hind Swaraj* (for which Kallenbach had just helped Gandhi prepare an English translation), Tolstoy Farm provided Gandhi with a way to put his arguments in his political and spiritual manifesto into practice. Here was a real chance to experiment in a rural setting with the dignity of human labour in a community without doctors, lawyers or the oppressive hand of the state. He could, in fact, implement his ideas of communal harmony as the residents were from different races and linguistic groups as well as from different religions. It contained men, women and children with residents staying for varying periods of time. In Bhana's assessment, this provided Gandhi with a 'heterogeneous microcosm in which his leadership would prepare him for his role in the macrocosm of his battles in India later'.[26] Here the motivation in the first instance was not about running a printing press but to see the experience as training in a *satyagrahi* lifestyle through spiritual, mental and physical exercise. In short, it served as a training ground for spiritual matters that would also give the residents the strength needed for the political campaign that was unfolding in much the same way as later the Sabarmati Ashram would for the Salt Satyagraha.

In short, Tolstoy Farm not only formed the prototype for Gandhi's future ashrams, it also contributed to his political methods. According to Gandhi, the shared experiments in diet and physical labour yielded excellent spiritual results. These 'dangerous' experiments were only possible 'in a struggle of which self-purification was the very essence'.[27] And Gandhi and Kallenbach 'set the example of renunciation and discipline' that permeated Tolstoy Farm.[28] For Gandhi the political struggle was closely linked with the inner struggle, and Tolstoy Farm was a crucible of both.

Maganlal and the Sabarmati Ashram

There is some fairly often cited but poorly thought through rhetoric about why Gandhi left his first Indian purpose-built ashram at Sabarmati on the outskirts of Ahmedabad and why he eventually settled in the village of Sevagram near Wardha. Most books tell us that he left Sabarmati when he embarked on the historic Salt March in 1930 vowing not to return until he had achieved independence for India. Gandhi was not politically naive. He knew that he would not achieve independence in a month or a year. In fact it took another 17 years after the dramatic march to Dandi. He also knew that the campaign he was launching would result in serious sacrifices for many, and he certainly did not want his sacrifice to be any less than that of his followers. They would possibly be stripped of their lands and homes. Could he do any less than give up his? On the night before he set out for the seaside to make illegal salt, the Mahatma informed a crowd of 10,000 which had gathered on the sandy expanse of the Sabarmati river bank below the ashram that he would not return 'till Swaraj is established in India. ... We are as good as parting from the Ashram and from our homes. Only with complete victory can we return to this place.'[29]

However, at this stage property had not been confiscated and Gandhi could have vowed to make any number of other sacrifices that would cause less distress to those he was leaving behind. It seemed that he was emotionally ready to leave the ashram and this readiness is not understandable without understanding Gandhi's relationship with Maganlal Gandhi.[30] The 'spirit of the ashram' had departed with Maganlal's sudden death in 1928 and the decision to leave his home and ashram family became much less difficult for the Mahatma than it seems possible from reading the sections dealing with this in the English sources. Although Maganlal is generally reduced to the young person who helped to coin the term *satyagraha* as the winner of a competition in Gandhi's South African newspaper in 1907,[31] the relationship Gandhi had with him was one of the most important of his life. Maganlal was the embodiment of Gandhi's ideal of what an ashram inmate should be. But because Maganlal was integral to the Gandhi of the eleven vows rather than a fellow politician he disappeared from the (at least non-Gujarati) record almost completely.

After eight years in South Africa where he had moved from being a successful barrister to a champion of the rights of indentured Indians, Gandhi had sailed to his native India in early 1902 with the promise to return within a year if the community he had been working with again needed him. Eight months later he was on his way back. Although he left his wife and children behind, believing that the need for his work would take no more than a year, he was accompanied by some young members of his family including Maganlal.

While Maganlal was determined to work hard to help out his parents who had financially overcommitted themselves in arranging his marriage, the direction of his life had come from Gandhi, under whose guidance he claims to have 'put myself wholly'. His letters about his 'uncle' portray a 'starry-eyed admiration'.[32] When Gandhi was setting up his Phoenix Settlement in 1904, he invited friends and relatives to join and help him. Maganlal and others volunteered, but as Gandhi noted: 'The others went back to business. Maganlal Gandhi left his business for good to cast his lot with me, and by ability, sacrifice and devotion stands foremost among my original co-workers in my ethical experiments.'[33] And Gandhi was not wrong. As he moved to simplify his own life, Maganlal followed suit, giving up spicy food and, though young with his new wife at his side, taking a vow of celibacy. Even Gandhi's son Manilal did not choose to make that sacrifice. Soon Maganlal was looking after Gandhi's new Phoenix Settlement.

Back in India, while Gandhi was busy being the Mahatma, Maganlal took care of business. At the religious festival, the Kumbh Mela, in Haridwar in 1915, while Gandhi was constantly preoccupied with darshan-seekers, his trusty lieutenant had to fulfil his master's pledge to take care of the covering of excreta in the latrines.[34] When following a plague outbreak Gandhi decided to take his group of over 40 souls who shared a common kitchen from the crowded building at Kochrab, to a plot of land at Sabarmati, where 'there was no building ... and no tree' and house them under canvass, he admitted that 'the whole conception about the removal was mine, the execution was as usual left to Maganlal'.[35] Under Maganlal's leadership the prickly shrubs, rocks, sand and cacti were removed from the river bank and vegetables and neem trees were planted, and 'in a very short time the barren land became green with vegetables'.[36] Maganlal designed and supervised the construction of all the buildings, systematised the management of the ashram, introduced discipline and took control of ashram craft work. Maganlal Gandhi was not just another ashramite who happened to be in charge. It is not an exaggeration to say that the ashram at Sabarmati was Maganlal's creation and that to a large degree he was the 'soul' of the Ashram. Gandhi's later secretary and biographer, Sabarmati Ashram resident Pyarelal, records that the Mahatma was grooming Maganlal 'as his heir'.[37] Gandhi himself made this explicit in his letter to his wife when he requested her to be a mother to the one who had trained himself to carry on his work, and when there was the occasional unrest among the ashramites over Maganlal's leadership, Gandhi always backed his 'nephew'.[38]

News of Maganlal's sudden death from pneumonia in Patna on 23 April 1928 reached Gandhi on his weekly day of silence. Although ordering that daily work must not cease, Gandhi broke his silence 'to express his own grief and to console those around him'. At the time, Gandhi stated that 'Maganlal was the life of the Ashram, I am not it, it was his light that illuminated me. ... I could drink the cup of poison like Mirabai. ... But this separation from Maganlal is more unbearable. But I must harden my heart.'[39] Gandhi's secretary commented that Gandhi's 'loss at this moment is far greater than I can imagine'.[40]

The importance of Maganlal for Gandhi and the ashram at Sabarmati, although it tends to disappear from Gandhi biographies, cannot be overestimated. He planned every building, planted every tree, lived Gandhi's philosophy the way others could not and maintained ashram discipline. Kaka Kalelkar, a close associate of Gandhi's at the time, claimed that the light of idealism and sincerity that shone in the ashram was that of Maganlal and even that the richness of the living atmosphere of the community was due to Maganlal rather than to Gandhi himself.[41] Mark Thomson, the biographer of Gandhi's ashrams, notes that Maganlal's death 'was a crushing blow to Gandhi and seemed to hasten the decline of standards within the Ashram'.[42] In turn, these declining standards seem to have made it easier for the Mahatma to turn his back on his community. The absence of the soul of the ashram and Gandhi's 'noblest representative' was deeply felt in terms of the functioning of the community and in terms of Gandhi's connectedness with and commitment to it.

After Maganlal's death Gandhi spent most of the year in Maganlal's home, consoling Maganlal's wife Santok (and probably himself) and did not return to live in his own house for the remainder of his stay at the ashram. During the following year he was there only for short visits. In 1930 he was more or less a permanent resident up until the start of the Salt March in March. Thomson notes that at the time he was probably 'relieved to have an opportunity of dissociating himself from the Ashram. However, during the struggle the ashramites performed creditably, and renewed his faith in the worthiness of the Sabarmati experiment. But now he was unable to settle there without attracting the attention of a host of critics.'[43]

Maganlal Gandhi did not influence the Mahatma the way that his early colleagues Polak and Kallenbach did. He was, after all, much younger and a disciple. However, Gandhi relied on Maganlal and his death seems to have been a watershed event in Gandhi's life. It would probably be an exaggeration to say that Gandhi could leave the Ashram merely because Maganlal had died almost two years before. But it does seem that with the departure of his right-hand man at the ashram, the soul of the establishment had to a large extent departed. The ashram was now little more than a collection of buildings with all too frequently squabbling inmates. It seems that this made it far easier to leave, and the time had come to set up new headquarters in a place where the void left by Maganlal's passing was not felt too acutely.

Bajaj and Sevagram

When Gandhi left Ahmedabad he could have set up his headquarters anywhere in India. The Gandhi texts inform us that he chose Wardha because it was the geographical centre of the mother India, implying his own symbolic identification with the country, that the location made it easier for followers and fellow workers from all over the sub-continent to be able to reach him, and because it could provide the stepping stone to settling in an out of the way village. In terms of sacrifice Wardha is ideal, providing a thoroughly unpleasant environment for much of the year. The thought of settling in a village did not come to Gandhi till years after he had made Wardha the centre of his activities. And the symbolic explanation does not seem to be quite adequate to the task. The move is intricately tied up with Gandhi's relationship with Jamnalal Bajaj, a fellow spiritual seeker and leader of constructive work activities who in childhood had been taken from his parents and later adopted Gandhi as a father. It was because of Bajaj the 'son' who wanted his 'father' near him that Gandhi ended up in this geographical centre, Bajaj's home town.[44] The popular English Gandhi biographies make even less of Bajaj than they do of Maganlal.

After having left his ashram near Ahmedabad, before settling (as much as the Mahatma was ever able to settle anywhere) by the side of Segaon village, Gandhi lived for a while with some of his erstwhile ashramites in Wardha at the branch Satyagraha Ashram which had been set up by his disciple and future spiritual heir Vinoba Bhave. He then lived for a while with a group of followers at a large house with extensive orange orchards which had been donated to him by Jamnalal Bajaj. The property was named Maganwadi in memory of Maganlal Gandhi. Following rounds of imprisonment in the early 1930s, Gandhi was finally set free, homeless, in August 1934. Two months later he officially retired from Congress and spent a year touring India for the cause of the removal of 'untouchability'. Bajaj again, as he had often done in the past, started urging Gandhi to settle in Wardha (as Vallabhbhai Patel had been pushing for Bardoli in Gujarat) where he had dreams of setting up a fully fledged Gandhian centre. To placate Bajaj, Gandhi had committed himself to spending around one month a year there, staying with Vinoba, before attending the annual Congress session. He did this more or less regularly from 1925 onwards. However, from 1933 Wardha increasingly became Gandhi's base. In December 1934 Gandhi decided to set up the All India Village Industries Association (AIVIA) and, while considering where it should be located, Bajaj reiterated the offer he made to Gandhi 18 years before. Bajaj argued strongly for Wardha, pointing out that not only was it in a central position in India, but also that he would provide the land, building and furniture to get the project established.[45] When Gandhi accepted the offer, Bajaj placed Maganwadi, his spacious two-storied garden house on the outskirts of the town, with its 20 acres of orange orchards, at the Mahatma's disposal. Along with 15 to 20 followers, Gandhi moved into the building which also came to serve as the headquarters of the AIVIA. Gandhi noted that his moving to Wardha was done 'ignoring the Sardar's anger born out of his love', adding that Patel 'could have easily secured for me ten orchards against one here, but he could not find for me a Jamnalal there and, therefore, I let the ten orchards go'.[46]

At Wardha, as at Sabarmati a few years before, Gandhi became frustrated with the demands made on him, not least by the squabbling, eccentric and dependent people he managed to attract to himself. His nerves were affected and he wanted space, to be alone. The poverty and filth he saw around himself, perhaps exacerbated by the constant demands on his time for articles and interviews, forced him to realise that his political and literary activities were not going to achieve the social changes he so desired. He had been preaching his social message for a long time with precious few indications that he was being listened to. The answer was to live alone in a village, to be an example of the changes he wanted to see adopted by the masses, by doing scavenging work directly with the downtrodden. In this way he could get away from the constraints that had taken over his life, and live the simple life of service he craved.

Jamnalal Bajaj was born into a family of modest means in 1889 in a village in Jaipur state. He was adopted (almost kidnapped) by Marwari Seth Bachharaj Bajaj, a well-to-do Wardha businessman. The childless Seth had earlier adopted a son who died soon after his marriage, before the birth of any children. Now he, his wife and bereaved daughter-in-law returned to their home district seeking a child for adoption by the young widow so that the family line could continue.[47] When Jamnalal was 18, Bachharaj died and Jamnalal inherited the family fortune, which, with his acute business acumen, he managed to increase further, but without ever doing anything unfair or unethical. Unfortunately, no psycho-biography of Bajaj has been written, but the circumstances of his childhood provide a rich mine for the understanding of his relationship with Gandhi who he so badly needed to fulfil the role of father figure. While Gandhi was still in South Africa, Bajaj had heard of his work and was impressed. He visited Gandhi at Kochrab as soon as he could and by the end of 1915 he was completely under the Mahatma's spell. Quickly, Bajaj became one of his chief financial backers and soon the acquaintanceship grew into a deep affection on both sides. Bajaj insisted that his family wear khadi and attempted to reorganise his life along the lines of Gandhi's idea of trusteeship, where the wealthy person sees his money as being held in trust for the poor. When Gandhi set up his ashrams in Ahmedabad, Bajaj started visiting Gandhi regularly and sent his wife and their five children to stay at the Sabarmati Ashram from time to time. After the Nagpur Congress of 1920, where at Gandhi's urging he had served as chairman of the reception committee and where Gandhi assumed supreme leadership of the organisation, Bajaj consciously adopted Gandhi as his father by asking the Mahatma to adopt him as a son.[48]

In Wardha, Gandhi decided that he had to settle in a village and work alone because village co-workers should be cultivated from within the village itself rather than imposed upon it from the outside. As his English disciple Mirabehn had already made a start there, that village was to be Segaon as soon as he could convince Bajaj of the idea. In April 1936 Bajaj gave full authority to commence building operations.[49] Gandhi arrived in mid-June to take up residence, but very quickly, against his wishes, he had gathered a group of followers around himself. He wrote in some sadness that 'This has become a confused household instead of a hermitage it was expected to be. Such has been my fate! I must find my hermitage from within.'[50] As the number of cows increased, the need for extra grazing land and an additional well became apparent, Bajaj provided them. Later Bajaj was asked for his whole estate and he acceded to the request and handed it in its entirety to the enterprise and soon a complete ashram had again established itself around the Mahatma. This hot, sickness-inducing, snake-, scorpion- and tick-infested area became Gandhi's final ashram.

The 52-year-old Bajaj collapsed and died of a cerebral haemorrhage on 11 February 1942 after being Gandhi's closest associate in his constructive activities and after truly having served as a surrogate son. Mahadev Desai, in his summation of Bajaj's life work, noted that:

> Never since the death of Maganlal Gandhi in 1928 had any bereavement dealt such a staggering blow on Gandhiji as the sudden and premature death of Jamnalalji. Words fail me when I attempt to describe the feeling of desolation. For two days he bore up bravely consoling the bereaved

widow and the aged mother, but on the third day he broke down as he was saying: 'Childless people adopt sons. But Jamnalalji adopted me as father. He should have been an heir to my all, instead he has left me an heir to his all!'[51]

Whatever can be said about the success or otherwise of the Sevagram experiment, it served as a laboratory for the investigation of the plight of villages and for attempts at instituting a constructive programme aimed at helping to usher in a *sarvodaya* social order, and even for Gandhi's larger quest in trying to find his own self-realisation through identification with his fellow humans. Without the hold of Jamnalal Bajaj, his 'fifth son', on him, Gandhi would not have been in Wardha to initiate at least the more prosaic of these experiments, and, without the financial backing of Bajaj, neither Sevagram nor the many Gandhian hospitals, dairies or educational institutions would have come into existence.

Conclusion

Phoenix Settlement and Tolstoy Farm had been early experiments in communal living and stepping stones on the path to building a viable fully fledged ashram around the Mahatma. In South Africa, Gandhi wanted to finish the political struggle quickly so that he could return to the spiritual life of the commune. In India Maganlal built such a communal institution as a centre of political, social and spiritual experimentation. Here Gandhi could train his co-workers to be the nonviolent fighters in the cause of the freedom struggle and his constructive programme. Although his headquarters at Wardha may have started out as a continuation of the ashram at Sabarmati, gradually Gandhi wanted to leave institutions behind. At the time of his relocation to Sevagram, Gandhi was distancing himself from power politics and Bajaj became instrumental in assisting this move from a concentration on the first to the other two gifts. Without an understanding of more than the political Gandhi, some of his most important relationships become invisible to us, and without an understanding of these relationships we cannot fully understand Gandhi's inner journey or his various physical and spiritual relocations.

Notes

1 Desai, Narayan, *My Gandhi*, Ahmedabad: Navajivan, 1999, pp. 51–90.
2 Gandhi, M.K., *Harijan*, 28 July 1940.
3 Gandhi, M.K., *Constructive Program: Its Meaning and Place*, Ahmedabad: Navajivan, 1941, p. 3.
4 Ibid., p. 36.
5 'Speech at Malikanda', 21 February 1940.
6 *Harijan*, 21 July 1940.
7 Gandhi, 1941, p. 37.

8 Gandhi, M.K., *An Autobiography or the Story of my Experiments with Truth*, Ahmedabad: Navjivan, 1940: xiv.
9 See Weber, Thomas, *Gandhi as Disciple and Mentor*, Cambridge: Cambridge University Press, 2004, pp. 54–68.
10 Polak, H.S.L., H.N. Brailsord and Lord Pethick-Lawrence, *Mahatma Gandhi*, London: Odhams Press 1949, p. 231.
11 Green, Martin, *The Origins of Nonviolence: Tolstoy and Gandhi in their Historical Settings*, University Park: Pennsylvania State University Press, 1986, p. 153.
12 Gandhi, 1940, p. 220.
13 Polak et al., 1949, p. 9.
14 Polak, H.S.L., 'Some South African Reminiscences', in Chandrashanker Shukla (ed.), *Incidents in Gandhiji's Life*, Bombay: Vora, 1949, p. 238.
15 Green, Martin, *Gandhi: Voice of a New Age Revolution*, New York: Continuum, 1993, p. 154.
16 See Weber, 2004, pp. 69–83.
17 Green, 1986, p. 151.
18 Gandhi, 1940, p. 242.
19 Quoted in Sarid Isa and Bartolf, Christian, *Hermann Kallenbach: Mahatma Gandhi's Friend in South Africa*, Berlin: Gandhi Informations Zentrum and Bartolf, 1997, p. 16.
20 Hunt, 1995, p. 4.
21 Gandhi, M.K., *Satyagraha in South Africa*, Madras: S.Ganesan, 1928, p. 393.
22 Bhana, Surendra, 'The Tolstoy Farm: Gandhi's Experiment in "Cooperative Commonwealth"', *South African Historical Journal*, available at www.anc.org.za/andocs/history/people/gandhi/bana.htm 1975
23 Quoted in Sarid, 1997, p. 34.
24 Gandhi, 1940, pp. 242–43.
25 See Gandhi, 1928, pp. 382–85.
26 Bhana, 1975.
27 Gandhi, 1928, pp. 392–93.
28 Thomson, Mark, *Gandhi and His Ashrams*, Bombay: Popular Prakashan, 1993, p. 74.
29 Weber, Thomas, *On the Salt March: The Historiography of Gandhi's March to Dandi*, New Delhi: HarperCollins, 1997, 132.
30 See Weber, 2004, pp. 84–101..
31 Gandhi, 1940, p. 235.
32 Pyarelal, *Mahatma Gandhi, volume III: The Birth of Satyagraha: From Petitioning to Passive Resistance*, Ahmedabad: Navajivan, 1986, p. 431.
33 Gandhi, 1940, p. 222.
34 Gandhi, 1940, p. 286.
35 Gandhi, 1940, p. 316.
36 Narayan Desai, *The Fire and the Rose [Biography of Mahadevbhai]*, Ahmedabad: Navajivan, 1995, p. 85.
37 Nayar, Sushila, *Mahatma Gandhi, volume VI: Salt Satyagraha: The Watershed*, Ahmedabad: Navajivan, 1995, p. 96.
38 'Address to Ashram Inmates', 17 February 1919.
39 Nayar, 1995, p. 97.
40 Desai, 1995, p. 417.
41 Kalelkar, Kaka, 'Tapasvi Jivan', in Navajivan Trust (ed.), *Ashram No Pran*, Ahmedabad: Navajivan, 1993, p. 80.
42 Thomson, 1993, p. 117.
43 Thomson, 1993, p. 132.
44 See Weber, 2004, pp. 102–19.
45 Balvantsinha, *Under the Shelter of Bapu*, Ahmedabad: Navajivan 1962, p. 33.

46 'Letter to Kamalnayan Bajaj', 22 November 1945.
47 See Nanda, B.R., *Mahatma Gandhi: A Biography*, Oxford: Oxford University Press, 1990.
48 See 'Fiery Ordeal', *Harijan Sevak*, 22 February 1942.
49 Letter to Mirabehn, 21 April 1936.
50 Letter to Mirabehn, 20 July 1936.
51 *Harijan*, 22 February 1942.

Bibliography

Balvantsinha, *Under the Shelter of Bapu*, Ahmedabad: Navajivan, 1972.
Bhana Surendra, 'The Tolstoy Farm: Gandhi's Experiment in "Cooperative Commonwealth" ', *South African Historical Journal*, 1975, available at www.anc.org.za/andocs/history/people/gandhi/bana.htm
Desai, Narayan, *My Gandhi*, Ahmedabad: Navajivan, 1999.
—— *The Fire and the Rose [Biography of Mahadevbhai]*, Ahmedabad: Navajivan, 1995.
Fischer, Louis, *The Life of Mahatma Gandhi*, New York: Collier, 1962
Gandhi, M.K., *Satyagraha in South Africa*, Madras: S.Ganesan, 1928.
—— *An Autobiography Or The Story of My Experiments With Truth*, Ahmedabad: Navajivan, 1940.
—— *Constructive Programme: Its Meaning and Place*, Ahmedabad: Navajivan, 1941.
Green, Martin, *Gandhi: Voice of a New Age Revolution*, New York: Continuum, 1993.
Hunt, James D., 'The Kallenbach Papers and Tolstoy Farm', unpublished working paper presented to the Association for Asian Studies meeting in Washington, DC, 6-9 April, 1995.
Kalelkar, Kaka, 'Tapasvi Jivan', in Navajivan Trust (ed.), *Ashram No Pran*, Ahmedabad: Navajivan, 1993.
Nanda, B.R., *Mahatma Gandhi: A Biography*, Oxford: Oxford University Press, 1958.
—— *In Gandhiji's Footsteps: The Life and Times of Jamnalal Bajaj*, New Delhi: Oxford University Press, 1990.
Nayar, Sushila, *Mahatma Gandhi, volume VI: Salt Satyagraha: The Watershed*, Ahmedabad: Navajivan, 1995.
Polak, H.S.L., 'Some South African Reminiscences', in Chandrashanker Shukla (ed.), *Incidents in Gandhiji's Life*, Bombay: Vora, 1949.
Pyarelal, *Mahatma Gandhi, volume III: The Birth of Satyagraha: From Petitioning to Passive Resistance*, Ahmedabad: Navajivan, 1986.
Sarid, Isa, and Christian Bartolf, *Hermann Kallenbach: Mahatma Gandhi's Friend in South Africa*, Berlin: Gandhi Informations Zentrum, 1997.
Thomson, Mark, *Gandhi and His Ashrams*, Bombay: Popular Prakashan, 1993.
Weber, Thomas, *On the Salt March: The Historiography of Gandhi's March to Dandi*, New Delhi: HarperCollins, 1997.
—— *Gandhi as Disciple and Mentor*, Cambridge: Cambridge University Press, 2004.

6 Gandhi
The transformation of a South African lawyer 1897–1898

Charles R. DiSalvo

Mohandas Gandhi journeyed to South Africa in 1893 wearing the clothes of a London-trained barrister and armed with a belief in the legal system. He departed South Africa in 1914 wearing the dress of an ordinary Indian and convinced of the power of nonviolent disobedience to the law. What caused this transformation?

For the most part of the years 1893–1914, Gandhi practised law. Very little of the scholarship on Gandhi, however, examines the significance of Gandhi's professional legal experience in the development of his philosophy and practice of nonviolence.[1] The proposition I advance here is that the experiences Gandhi underwent during the time he practised law in South Africa transformed his vision of law as an engine of social change. I argue that this transformation, during which Gandhi lost faith in an ultimately corrupt legal system, constituted a key pre-condition for his eventual embrace of nonviolence. Gandhi's experience with the law in 1897 and 1898 in particular constitutes a microcosm that foreshadows and helps explain his transformation from business lawyer to civil rights attorney to civil disobedient.

The Natal colony and the attack on Indian interests

In 1893 Durban and the colony of which it was the commercial centre, Natal, had been under the control of the British from mid-century. The colony was prized in part for the fertility of its coasts where sugar and tea plantations prospered. These enterprises required enormous amounts of labour. When native Africans refused the colonists' entreaties to work the land, Natal addressed this need by importing tens of thousands of Indian indentured servants, many of whom remained in Natal after the expiration of their indentures. These workers formed an Indian community whose needs soon came to be served by large Indian mercantile and shipping interests. Litigation between these Indian concerns was not uncommon. Indeed, it was the opportunity to play a minor role in resolving a lawsuit between two such businesses that caused Gandhi to leave India for South Africa in 1893. The timing was good, for Gandhi's attempt to establish a practice in India had been less than a rousing success. He agreed to a one-year term of duty in South Africa for his new client, Dada Abdulla and Company.

Gandhi's dexterity in dealing with the European lawyers impressed Dada Abdulla and the other Indian businessmen. The success of these entrepreneurs was perceived as a threat by their European counterparts. Indeed, just as Gandhi was ready to return to India in 1894, the Natal legislature was beginning to embark on a series of steps designed to weaken the influence of Indian entrepreneurs. Faced with this development, a group of Indian merchants persuaded Gandhi to stay in South Africa to organize their resistance to the European assault on their rights. Gandhi refused their offer of payment, stating that 'public work' should be done without charge. To sustain himself, he settled for their pledge to refer their legal work to him. With a committed pool of clients, his practice as a business lawyer was instantly established in South Africa.

At the end of 1896, Gandhi was returning to South Africa from a trip to India, accompanied by several hundred Indians, most of whom were residents returning to Natal or the Transvaal.

Waiting for him at the docks was a roiling mob of some five thousand European colonists who wanted to lynch him. They were upset for three reasons:

- The press had incited them by inaccurately reporting statements Gandhi had made in India about the colonists.
- They believed, incorrectly, that Gandhi was aiding the importation of skilled Indian workers who would take their jobs.
- There was an exaggerated fear of plague from India.

Natal's Attorney General Harry Escombe's intervention saved Gandhi. Escombe spoke with eloquence and convinced the mob to go home. But it cost Escombe. He had to pledge that, if the demonstrators would leave the Indians alone, the government would act on the anti-Indian legislation that had been proposed earlier. Gandhi, who would later campaign for the Indian cause using the threat of nonviolence, watched the threat of violence purchase new law.[2] When the Natal Legislative Assembly convened, the task of paying Escombe's debt stood at the top of the agenda. The Assembly, however, needed no encouragement. Gandhi and the Indian community had many enemies and but a few friends in the legislature; most of Natal's legislators must have been grateful to the dockside mob for forcing them to address 'the Asiatic question', as Europeans called it, in dramatic terms. They promptly took up four pieces of anti-Indian legislation: the Quarantine Act, the Uncovenanted Indians Act, the Immigration Restriction Act and the Dealers Licenses Act. These measures were designed to block Indian immigration, make life uncomfortable for Indians already in the colony and extinguish the capacity of Indian entrepreneurs to compete with

Europeans. It was a forceful and comprehensive assault on Indian interests. These proposed legislations dictated the course of Gandhi's life for the next several years, causing him to dedicate much of his professional and political energy to countering them.

The Quarantine Act was actually an anti-Indian immigration bill dressed up as a health measure.[3] The Uncovenanted Indians Act would immunize police officers from the liability of arresting Indians wrongfully. The Immigration Restriction Act would restrict the flow of Indians into Natal.[4] These acts, however, were fairly mild measures in comparison to the Dealers' Licenses Act ('DLA'). This last Act posed a grave danger to the interests of Gandhi's clients. The Act required every wholesale and retail business in Natal to have a licence. Town councils were authorized to appoint Licensing Officers from whom applicants might seek licenses. The Act instructed Licensing Officers to deny permits to those who could not maintain their books in English and those who intended to operate their businesses in facilities that were either unsanitary, 'unfit for the intended trade', or 'not affording sufficient and suitable accommodations for salesmen, clerks, and servants, apart from the stores or rooms in which goods and wares may be kept ... '. Beyond these imprecisely drawn grounds upon which licenses had to be denied, however, there were no standards established in the Act to guide the decisions of Licensing Officers. Rather, the Act simply entrusted the Officer with the 'discretion to issue or refuse a wholesale or retail Licence ... '. Without even the subtlety of a wink and a nod, the councils would send out their Licensing Officers to accomplish the legislature's mission.[5]

The Act further strengthened the hands of Licensing Officers by prohibiting disappointed applicants from appealing to a court. The only appeal allowed was to the Town Council – the very body that appointed the Licensing Officer. There was no pretence here of an unbiased, objective process operated by an impartial judiciary. A scheme more lacking in due process and more openly the instrument of racial prejudice could scarcely be imagined. The Act, without explicitly stating its goal, was crudely but clearly designed to put Indians out of business. If it were allowed to go into force, the businesses of many of Gandhi's merchant clients, as well as many lower-level Indian entrepreneurs, would be destroyed.[6]

Petitioning for redress

Gandhi's reaction to this wave of anti-Indian legislation would mark the beginning of a distinct shift in his understanding of the relationship between law and political power. Up until this campaign against the legislation, Gandhi's efforts to resist anti-Indian discrimination had relied almost exclusively on petitioning – incessant, persistent, unrelenting petitioning. Gandhi believed that once the Indian petitions demonstrated the unfairness with which Indians were treated in South Africa either the colonial or the imperial governments would order the situation to be rectified. Despite the repeated failure of this tactic, Gandhi did not give it up easily, even as he himself began to see its futility.[7] It was a slow transformation that would result in his eventually moving the fight from legislative and executive chambers to courtrooms, from legislation to litigation, from politicians to judges. But in the first part of 1897, the petition was still Gandhi's preferred instrument of opposition and one with which the still somewhat timid lawyer felt at ease. So he set about storming the colonial and home governments with petitions.

The Colonial Office had the responsibility of approving or disapproving colonial legislation. Thus Gandhi directed his first petition to the Secretary of State for the Colonies, Joseph Chamberlain. The prospects of swaying him to disapprove the legislation Natal was about to enact were not good; Chamberlain, not wishing to alienate the colonists whom he foresaw federating into an independent union, was distinctly less friendly to the Indian cause than his predecessor, Lord Ripon.[8] The likely outcome of his effort seemed not to matter to Gandhi, however. He poured himself into the work, taking at least six weeks to produce a massive document that takes up fifty-four pages in *The Collected Works*, exclusive of an appendix that contains more than two dozen documents. Less than two weeks after completing the writing of the Chamberlain petition, Gandhi peppered each body of the Natal Parliament, the Legislative Assembly and the Legislative Council, with petitions.

It was not surprising that Gandhi's petitioning was of no effect. All four bills were passed with but a few changes and their texts promulgated in the government *Gazette*. Accordingly, Gandhi again petitioned Chamberlain. What Gandhi wrote, however, was an ordinary, tired and unimaginative piece of work. Perhaps Gandhi's approach was shaped by his understanding that there was little likelihood the Secretary would disallow the Acts on the basis of yet another Indian petition. Gandhi's lack of enthusiasm in drafting the petition could perhaps also be attributed to his gradual realization that petitioning itself was not the tool he once thought it was. When London turned a deaf ear to the Indians' plea and refused to exercise its disallowance power with respect to the four anti-Indian Acts, Gandhi took it as a sign that it was time for something different – litigation.

The turn to litigation

Gandhi's practice of law, to this point, had been fairly apolitical. His work was that of the business lawyer. He helped his commercial clients engage in property transactions, collect debts and sue on back rent. Those few cases with political overtones were exceptions, not the rule. In 1897, however, a convergence between Gandhi's professional and political work began to develop that would signal the start of a radical change in the nature of his practice. It is not clear that litigation was, at the start, a strategy intentionally chosen by Gandhi and the Natal Indian Congress (the merchants' political arm of which Gandhi was a moving force) or whether the strategy chose them. After the defeat of his petition by the legislature and his last plea to Indian and European figures that they urge London to disallow the anti-Indian bills, Gandhi seemed to lose focus. There is almost no evidence of political or legal activity by Gandhi from early July to late September 1897. In mid-September, however, Gandhi was called on to intervene in a case that had been developing north of Durban, in Dundee.

Seventy-five Indians, trying to enter Natal from the Transvaal, had been arrested for violating the Immigration Restriction Act ('IRA'). They were promptly jailed. Two local European attorneys, arguing that the men were Natal citizens, repeatedly, but unsuccessfully, pleaded for their release. When Gandhi arrived in Dundee to take up the Indians' cause, he was very quickly succeeded in securing the prisoners' freedom. According to *The Natal Mercury*, 'The legal circle here [was] much annoyed at the course adopted in refusing two attorneys what they allowed to the third (Mr. Gandhi).' This was a rare circumstance for Gandhi – succeeding in court where European lawyers had failed. But it was more than that. Pre-eminently, it was a heady victory of the law over racism. Might the courts be used to defend against, and even attack, the anti-Indian legislation?

The IRA proved to be ineffective and highly unpopular. The Uncovenanted Indians Act created a nuisance with which the Indians were resigned to live for the moment. The Quarantine Act would become an issue only when the danger of plague arose. The DLA, however, was ruthlessly being implemented to put existing Indian businesses out of commission and to prevent new ones from beginning. The Act's vesting of virtually unchecked discretion in licensing officers and its bar on appeals to the courts, made decisions that were nakedly race-based easy to formulate and to defend. A licence denial did not have to be specifically authorized by law. A licence *could* be denied on sanitary grounds or because the applicant could not keep books in English – bases specifically mentioned in the law. But the law did not restrict denials to these grounds alone. A licensing officer could deny a permit for any reason he chose. Nor did the Act require the officer to justify his decision. The Act required neither the officer nor the Town Council to provide the applicant with reasons. A denial could be based on any reason or on no reason.

It did not take a keen eye to spot the arbitrariness permitted by the Act. In late 1897 Indians, Chinese and Jews were denied applications simply because of who they were. None of these decisions, reported in a paper which Gandhi scrutinized daily, was made on a principled basis. But each found support in a DLA that provided to town councils what appeared to be total freedom from accountability.

Soon enough Gandhi found himself with a licence case. Moosa Hajee Adam operated a small fruit and vegetable stand. The stand was not a fixture, but removable. Moosa would set out fruits and vegetables on his stand during the day, transfer them indoors at day's end, and throw a canvass over the stall for the night. The city's licensing officer spotted Moosa operating this business, found he had no dealer's licence and cited him for violating the DLA. When Moosa appeared before Resident Magistrate Saunders, Gandhi was at Moosa's side equipped with a clever argument for his client's innocence. Gandhi claimed that the DLA did not displace Ordinance 3 of 1850 from which the city's right to require licences under the DLA flowed. Natal legislation of this era was notoriously poorly written[9] and in this case Gandhi was determined to take advantage of the Parliament's failure to coordinate the DLA with the Ordinance. While it was true that the DLA was written to apply to 'retail dealers', Gandhi argued, Ordinance 3 permitted the city to require licences only of those who operated retail 'shops'. Moosa's stand, on which he set up and dismantled his business every day, had no permanence to it, concluded Gandhi. It failed to qualify as a 'shop'.[10] Unconvinced, Magistrate Saunders found Moosa guilty and, accepting Gandhi's representation that this was a 'test case', levied a nominal fine of five shillings.

Moosa appealed to the Supreme Court. Gandhi rarely appeared before the Supreme Court on his own. Perhaps he was too timid. Perhaps he was sensitive to the criticism that as a political figure his arguments would not be given their full weight by the court. In this instance, Gandhi brought in an experienced European lawyer to argue the case for the Indian side. Kenneth Hathorn echoed Gandhi's argument:

> In this case the licence in question is described in Ordinance 3, of 1850, as a 'licence to keep a retail shop", and the entire question ... is "does the appellant keep a retail shop?'. ... The only way in which he could be required to have a licence was if he kept a retail shop, under Ordinance 3, of 1850.[11]

Hathorn's opponent, saddled with an indefensible position, satisfied himself with arguing that there was a distinction between the 'question whether he can take out a licence' and the question of 'whether he can carry on a business without a licence'.[12] The Court rejected the city's argument, unanimously ruled for Moosa and set aside the Magistrate's judgment.

To Maritzburg

This relatively easy win could only have encouraged Gandhi as well as his friend and fellow lawyer Frederick Laughton, who joined Gandhi in the fight against the Act. In fact, Laughton attempted to strike at the heart of the Act in early 1898 after his Indian client had been denied a licence by the licensing officer in Newcastle, a decision sustained by the Newcastle Town Council. Against conventional wisdom, which held that the Act allowed no appeals to the courts, Laughton headed to Maritzburg, the colonial capital, to lodge an appeal with the Supreme Court. Laughton was a particularly skilled lawyer. Amongst a bar that was at best mediocre, Laughton's ability to engage in sophisticated legal analysis easily distinguished him. Now, in *Vanda v. Newcastle,* his careful reading of the Act led him to develop the novel argument that while the Act clearly prohibited appeals from *licensing officers* to the courts, it just as plainly did not prohibit appeals from *town councils* to the courts.

Laughton's argument got strong support from the text of the Act. Section 5 read:

> ... a decision come to by a Licensing Officer as to the issue or refusal of a License, shall not be liable to review, reversal, or alteration, by any Court of Law or otherwise than is in the next section provided.

The next section of the Act stated:

> There shall be a right of appeal by the applicant, or any other person having an interest in the question, from the decision of the Licensing Officer to the Town Council. ... The Town Council ... may direct that the License, the subject of appeal, shall be issued or cancelled.

Nowhere did the Act address itself to appeals from the Town Council. The vacuum on that point, Laughton argued, was filled by previous legislation. Section 8 of Law 39, passed two years earlier by the Natal Parliament, vested the Supreme Court 'with jurisdiction to review the proceedings of all Inferior Courts of Justice or tribunals'. Laughton claimed that 'all' meant all – that it included town councils that were, in his view, judicial bodies for the purposes of the Act.

Justice Mason challenged Laughton: 'Surely it was playing with words to say that they were not to review the decisions of the Licensing Officer, but were to review the decision of the Court sustaining it'. Laughton, quick on his feet, responded:

> Supposing the Town Council had said, 'You are entitled to a license, but inasmuch as there is no appeal, we won't grant it.' Did their lordships mean to say that there was no appeal to that Court, in view of what was laid down in Section 8 of the Supreme Court Law. ... The Town Council of Newcastle had said 'We will get rid of Indians in this town.' and had the Court jurisdiction in such cases? Every Court of law was jealous in sustaining its jurisdiction, not in throwing it away'. The argument of Mr Watt, representing Newcastle, was simple, if incorrect: 'The law was not ambiguous, but was perfectly clear.'

Chief Justice Gallwey was convinced by Laughton's argument. Justice Mason, who had disagreed with Watt's point that the Act was clear, was not: 'How can it be maintained that this Court can review the decision of the Town Council on the granting or refusal of a license, and yet at the same time neither review, reverse, or alter the granting of the license itself?' Justice Finnemore agreed with Mason that the Act was clear enough to determine that the legislature's intent was to bar appeals of the sort contemplated by Laughton.[13] The Act, which was susceptible to two reasonable, yet opposed, interpretations, had yielded a split decision. It was a defeat for the Indian side, but not a final one. Two avenues of recourse were yet open. The decision could be appealed to the Judicial Committee of the Privy Council, the body in London responsible for hearing appeals from colonial courts. The Indians did, in fact, make such an appeal. Laughton and Gandhi knew that the Council took a long time to issue its decisions. In the meantime, they paid attention to a section of Mason's opinion that, surprisingly, suggested a second avenue of action:

> Where either a licensing officer or a Town Council proposes to exercise powers with regard to trade licences which it does not possess, the position of this Court would in all probability be very different. ...

Mason was as much as inviting the Indians to bring to the courts any procedural irregularities to which they were subjected. Gandhi could read. When he appeared four weeks later at an appeal hearing before the Durban Town Council, he was ready. Despite having received a satisfactory sanitation report, his client, Somnath Maharaj, had been denied a licence for property that he intended to rent from the Natal Indian Congress. (The involvement of the Congress, an institution controlled by Gandhi's merchant clients, signals that this case was part of a planned campaign of litigation against the Act.) Gandhi immediately attacked the process. He had asked to be provided with the reasons the licence application was denied and for a copy of the Officer's report to the Council. He had been refused on both counts. Gandhi pointed out that the Council was acting in the nature of a court and that,

> There was nothing in the law to provide that the ordinary rules of procedure were to be subverted. It was only common sense to presume that if the right to appeal was allowed the subject, the ordinary procedure that guarded the conduct of such appeals should be observed. If it was not to be so, it would simply mean that the law gave a right to a subject with the one hand and snatched it away with the other, and the right to appeal became a phantom.[14]

Gandhi went on to say that, unless he was provided with the reasons for the denial, 'how on earth' was he going to argue his case? Gandhi demanded that the Council rule on his request for a copy of the record in the case and the reasons for the refusal. Gandhi knew that a specific Council ruling would provide him with a clear and crisp appellate issue. To his legal strategy he added indignation:

[Maharaj] had been practically opposed by the whole machinery. Every obstacle was placed in his way – he had to anticipate reasons, come to the Council and spend a lot of money, and then perhaps be told that the Licensing Officer's decision was upheld. ... [Was this] an appeal under the British Constitution?[15]

The Council then adjourned the public portion of the hearing to huddle in private with the Licensing Officer. There the Officer provided the Council with his reasons for denying the application. When the Council emerged from this meeting, it attempted to skirt the issue of what information Gandhi was entitled to and go directly to a decision on the appeal itself. Councilman Brown moved that the Officer's denial of the license be affirmed. The motion was no sooner seconded than Gandhi interrupted to say, 'I have not been heard.' Gandhi then pressed his demand: 'I have not yet got the Council's decision whether I am entitled to a copy of the record.' The Mayor was forced to respond: 'The decision of the Council is against that.'

Gandhi now had his issue for appeal on the record.

With his appellate issue secured, Gandhi moved on to lay bare his opponents' motivations. In this case he had proved that Maharaj was solvent, that he could keep books in English, that he had run a business elsewhere for several years, and that he had been responsible enough to make a full settlement with his creditors before disposing of that business. The only faults that could be attributed to Maharaj were that he had not held a Durban licence before and,

That he had a brown skin. ... [I]f a man having a brown skin was not to have a licence, that ... savoured of a great deal of injustice. It was certainly un-British and un-English. There was nothing in the law to show that licences had to be refused on account of nationality. ...

Gandhi concluded:

In exercising the [licensing] power ... the Council would take away the bread from hundreds of respectable and deserving men, who had given their best services to the Colony. [Maharaj] had come to Natal at the wish of the Colony. He came under indenture and was told that he would better his prospects. He had given the best part of his life to the Colony for a miserable pittance, and then he was refused a livelihood because his skin was against him.[16]

Gandhi sat down. Gandhi's petition work had always been characterized by circumspection. One would strain to find a harsh word in any of his petitions. Starting with this case, litigation would change him. Gandhi's frankness left Daniel Taylor, one of the most racist public figures in Natal, unmoved. The councilman proposed that the appeal be dismissed. Maharaj's appeal was dismissed without a single vote in dissent. Laughton and Gandhi headed straight for Maritzburg, seeking a writ of mandamus.[17] Intent upon redeeming Mason's pledge, they had behind them the editorial support of *The Natal Advertiser* and an unusually friendly headline – 'Mr. Gandhi Eloquently Appeals' – in *The Natal Witness*.

When Laughton stood before the Court he rested the Indians' case on three points:

- The refusal of the Officer to give reasons violated his duty to judicially exercise his discretion.
- The refusal of the Council to permit the applicant to see the record violated the rules by which such hearings were to be conducted.[18]
- The appointment of a licensing officer who was also an employee of the city created an improper bias.

Laughton must have been surprised when Justice Wragg raised a different issue and made a key distinction: '[The Council had] a right to retire and to take their legal advisor with them, but what they did in this case was to hear evidence in private, and refuse all information to the appellant.' Wragg's comments were a strong indication of how the court would rule. Mason also interrupted to inquire whether it was 'not an abuse of terms to call what took place an appeal?' In his opinion deciding the case, Wragg stated that the court would not decide the question of whether the Officer's employment by the Council created an impermissible bias; he did advise the Council, however, that 'it would be better that some person who is more or less distinct, should be the Licensing Officer'. Wragg went on to base his vote to invalidate the Council's action on the Council's refusal to provide reasons and a copy of the record. In Wragg's view, the Council also acted improperly when it retired and took evidence from the Officer 'without giving the appellant a chance of hearing what that evidence was'. In the face of the provision in the DLA prohibiting appeals, Wragg then set forth Mason's earlier pledge in *Vanda* as a point of law: 'Where a very great irregularity takes place, this Court has the power to set aside the proceedings.' Justices Mason and Finnemore joined with Wragg to unanimously overrule the Council, with Mason pointedly calling the Town Council proceedings 'not only oppressive, but ... a disgrace to the Town Council'.[19]

The Court had been true to its word. While it would not invalidate the provision of the DLA barring court appeals, it would see to it that whatever proceedings were held before town councils offered appellants at least one characteristic of fair hearings – notice of the grounds for the denial. When Gandhi, armed with this decision, renewed his appeal of the licensing officer's decision against Somnath before the Town Council, the Council read aloud the record of the case. Gandhi then pushed the Council, inquiring whether any other reasons existed for the denial of the licence. By a 4 to 3 vote, the Council required the officer to state his reasons, which he articulated as follows: 'That the applicant had no claim whatever upon Durban, as the class of trade he was engaged in was sufficiently provided for in the town and borough.'[20] Gandhi knew this was a pretext. ' ... [T]he only reason the licence was withheld was because [my] client belonged to a class who were not much in favour in Durban, or for that matter in the Colony. The reason now submitted by the Licensing Officer was ... not sufficient to warrant the Council to reject the appeal. The man, being Indian, could not change his skin'.[21] Gandhi wanted the real basis for the decision on the record.

Councilman Farman, in an effort to avoid such unseemliness, first tried to adjourn the Council to the executive session where he could more freely argue with his colleagues about the basis of their decision. That attempt failed. Then he obtained the Mayor's permission to examine the applicant. Farman quickly demonstrated that Somnath was incapable of taking the oath because he could not speak English. Farman, his goal of avoiding an openly race-based decision now in sight, reminded the Council that the Act required 'that the applicant should be able to keep his books in the English language'.[22] The rebuttal to this point was in plain view of anyone who had read the Act. It did not require that the applicant *personally* keep his books in English, only that they *be kept* in English. A bookkeeper who knew English would do. Gandhi, however, was speechless. Before he could open his mouth, a motion to deny the licence was approved by unanimous vote. The case was lost.

The Council took up a second appeal that Gandhi presented, an appeal on behalf of Mahomed Majam & Co. It was only then that Gandhi offered the obvious response to Farman's point that an applicant could keep his books 'by means of an accountant'.[23] Gandhi, however, was too late. The Council ignored his point and promptly turned Majam & Co. down, too. In *Somnath*, the Supreme Court had forced town councils to offer disappointed Indian applicants some measure of due process when it required councils to state the reasons upon which denials rested. In the Majam appeal and in Gandhi's second appeal of the Somnath case, the Durban Town Council had complied with this mandate. It had stated reasons – and then dismissed the appeals. Gandhi got his due process – and nothing else.

This new regime would become unmistakably clear when Gandhi pursued yet another appeal some three months later on behalf of Dada Osman, a Natal Indian Congress activist. Gandhi asked the Council to provide him the reasons for the denial. Councilman Taylor moved that the officer not be required to state his reasons. This time it was Councilman Collins who countered with a motion that Gandhi be provided a copy of the reasons. Collins' motion carried. If Gandhi wanted his due process, a majority of the Council was prepared to give it to him.

The Town Clerk read aloud the licensing officer's statement:

> The Act of 1897, as I understand, was passed with a view of placing some check on the issue of trading licences to certain classes of people, generally regarded as undesirable, and, as I believe I am right in assuming that the applicant in question is one that would be included in that class, and, moreover, as he has never before had a licence in Durban, I have felt it to be my duty to refuse the licence.[24]

This statement was read after the Council had already conceded that sanitation was not an issue. Accordingly, Gandhi's strategy, in the face of this statement, was to show the absurdity of classifying Dada Osman as 'undesirable'. To do so, he called witnesses to speak to the applicant's capability as a businessman and to his upright character. A long-time European merchant in Durban vouched for the applicant's integrity and knowledge of English, while a prominent Indian businessman, Dada Osman's future landlord, testified as to the losses he would incur should the application be denied. Gandhi also called upon Dada Osman himself to speak. Osman informed the Council of his long history as a businessman in the colony, much of which had been spent in agreeable relationships with European businessmen. He was fluent in English, could write English and understood both single and double entry bookkeeping. Indeed, the Licensing Officer had already inspected and approved his bookkeeping.

Gandhi had put together an impeccable factual record. The only issue was 'desirability'. Gandhi argued first that the DLA spoke not one word with regard to the 'desirability' of persons applying for licences and, accordingly, judgments about an applicant's desirability constituted an improper basis for the decision on whether a licence should be issued. The licensing officer had based his decision on 'desirability', however, and Gandhi knew he must address that question squarely. Gandhi relied on the authority of no less a figure than Secretary Chamberlain, who had recently spoken out against colonial legislation that explicitly discriminated on the basis of race and colour, for an authoritative set of characteristics that defined 'undesirable': 'It was not because a man was of a different colour from themselves that he was necessarily an undesirable ... but it was because he was dirty, or immoral, or a pauper, or had some other objection which could be defined'. Gandhi argued that because the proof had demonstrated that Dada Osman was neither dirty, nor immoral, nor a pauper he was, by definition, not 'undesirable'. It was a sound argument. To it, Gandhi added a policy argument. The Officer himself had said that Dada Osman would conduct a sanitary business. If the Council now 'refused this licence, it would go forth among the Indian population of Durban that the desire of Council was not really that the Indians should conform to the sanitary requirements of the Council, but would as soon have them live in contravention of those orders'.[25] The only remaining possible reason for the denial, Gandhi concluded, was that Dada Osman was an Indian. In Gandhi's view this would be a clearly impermissible basis for the denial.

That was not the view of the Town Council. Councilman Collins was forthright: the Council would refuse the licence

> not because the applicant or the premises were unsuitable, but because the applicant was Indian. ... Parliament, representing the community of Natal, had come to the conclusion that it was undesirable that the Indians should increase their hold on the trade of Durban, and it was on that account that [the Council was] practically called upon to refuse the licenses which were not otherwise objectionable.

Collins seconded the motion of Daniel Taylor to confirm the decision of the Officer. The motion passed. Dada Osman would not get his licence.

There is no question Gandhi had put on a superb case. Even the press had to confess that Gandhi was 'to be complimented for the able defence ... he made of his client's application for a license. ... '.[26] By the testimony of his witnesses and the force of his arguments, he defeated every substantive objection to the application the Council could muster. None of this, however, was sufficient to win the day. The Supreme Court had proven itself to be the one governmental institution to which the Indians could turn with the expectation of receiving a fair hearing. Laughton had convinced the Chief Justice, if not the full court, that appeals to the judiciary from town-council decisions under the DLA should be allowed. Gandhi had obtained a ruling that held the authorities in check in terms of how a retail shop was defined. The two lawyers had succeeded in convincing the Court to force town councils to provide an important measure of due process to applicants. But in the end Gandhi and Laughton must have realized that the Court's reach was limited. While the Court had forced town councils to extend significant procedural rights to the Indians, Gandhi and Laughton never asked the Court to rule on the ultimate substantive question: would the law permit a town council to deny an applicant a licence solely because the applicant was Indian?[27]

Perhaps they were afraid of the answer.

Epilogue

Gandhi's recognition of the judiciary's limitations as a tool of social change marked an early but key turning point in his transformation from lawyer to civil disobedient. While the courts might address *procedural* irregularities, they could not be counted on to attack basic, underlying norms and the power establishment of which they themselves were a part. The courts would not turn on themselves. The law would not free Gandhi's people – at least not in the manner he expected it would in 1898.

After his frustrating experience with the courts in Natal, Gandhi's political activity drops precipitously. Finally, he quits South Africa for India but consents to return a year later to fight for Indian rights in the Transvaal. Again he uses the courts to defend Indian interests. Just as it took him repeated failures with petitioning before he gave that up, it takes him repeated failures with litigation before he gives that up. Despite a sporadic win here and there, his efforts are, in the end, unsuccessful. Gandhi eventually abandons his practice altogether. In the Transvaal he becomes a nonviolent civil disobedient.

Is this the end? Does he give up on the law entirely? Gandhi's frustration with the courts led him to abandon litigation as a tool for social change and contributed to his decision to embrace nonviolent civil disobedience. But let us be careful in reading this rejection of the courts. It is a rejection of litigation. It is not a rejection of law. His rejection of litigation is a stage in his developing understanding of the law as much deeper, more expansive and more filled with promise than litigation. In the remainder of his life, he comes to see and believe in the deep underlying structure of the law. It is to this that his nonviolent disobedience appeals. A civil disobedient who willingly subjects himself to the punishment of the system, as Gandhi did, believes in the grand structure of the law, in the rule of law.

He believes that undeserved suffering at the hands of the law can, in the end, change the law.

He believes that undeserved suffering touches the heart and mind of even the oppressor.

He believes that undeserved suffering is, in the end, redemptive.

Notes

1 Gandhi's early experiences at the bar are the focus of much of Burnett Britton's *Gandhi Arrives in South Africa*, Canton, Maine: Greenleaf Books, 1999.
2 South Africa was not alone at this time in constructing race-based systems of discrimination. See John Cell, *The Highest Stage of White Supremacy: The Origins of Segregation in South Africa and the American South*, Cambridge: Cambridge University Press, 1982.
3 See *Collected Works of Mahatma Gandhi,* Vol. 2, Ahmedabad: Government of India, 1976, p. 262.
4 Because Natal was not fully independent of Great Britain, the Crown could disallow legislation. The British had made it clear that legislation that was *overtly* racial would not be approved. Legislation had to be facially race-neutral. Natal's legislators played along. But for the Uncovenanted Indians Act, the acts did not specifically mention Indians. The openly discussed premise of the legislation, however, was that the acts would be enforced exclusively against Indians.
5 The Town Councils had advocated clamping down on the growth of Indian economic power even before the dockside incident. 'Petition to Chamberlain', *Collected Works of Mahatma Gandhi,* Vol. 3, 1960, p. 37.
6 *The Collected Works of Mahatma Gandhi*, 1960, pp. 40–41.
7 Indeed, after the conclusion of the litigation campaign described here Gandhi returns to petitioning. See 'Petition to Chamberlain', *Collected Works of Mahatma Gandhi*, Vol. 3, 1960, p. 26.

8 See Maureen Swan, *Gandhi: The South African Experience*, Johannesburg: Ravan Press, 1985.
9 Professor Spiller observes that 'the drafting of legislation in Natal was often of a low standard'. Peter Spiller, *A History of the District and Supreme Courts of Natal, 1846–1910*, Durban: Butterworth Publishers, 1986, p. 94.
10 There is some evidence that the argument was not original to Gandhi. More than 11 months earlier, Gandhi's former partner, Coakes, presented much the same argument. Coakes won the case at the Magistrate level; there was no appeal to the Supreme Court. 'Are They Retail Shops?', *The Natal Mercury*, 26 February, 1897; 'Not a Retail Shop', *The Natal Mercury*, 27 February, 1897.
11 XIX Natal Law Reports 1898, *Musa v. Dyer*, pp. 26–27.
12 XIX Natal Law Reports 1898, *Musa v. Dyer*, pp. 26–27.
13 XIX Natal Law Reports 28, *Vanda v. Newcastle*, 1898. All previous references are to this Report.
14 *Natal Advertiser*, 3 March 1898.
15 *Natal Advertiser*, 3 March 1898.
16 *Natal Advertiser*, 3 March 1898.
17 *Vanda v. Newcastle* would not permit a conventional appeal to the Supreme Court of a Town Council decision. Laughton and Gandhi postured the case as petition for a writ to avoid this problem. A petition for such a writ often seeks intermediate relief on a point of procedure.
18 See Government Notice No. 517 of 1897.
19 *Solnath v. Durban Corporation*, XIX Natal Law Reports, 1898, p. 70.
20 *The Natal Advertiser*, 7 June 1898.
21 *The Natal Advertiser*, 7 June 1898.
22 *The Natal Advertiser*, 7 June 1898.
23 *The Natal Mercury*, 7 June 1898.
24 *Collected Works of Mahatma Gandhi*, Vol. 3, 1960, p. 18.
25 *The Natal Advertiser*, 15 September 1898.
26 *The Natal Advertiser*, 15 September 1898
27 On 22 December 1898 Gandhi drafted a brief in which he sought a legal opinion regarding this very question, apparently from European lawyers. There is no record of any answer Gandhi may have received (*Collected Works of Mahatma Gandhi*, Vol. 3, p. 24, 1960).

Bibliography

Britton, Burnett, *Gandhi Arrives in South Africa*, Canton, Maine: Greenleaf Books, 1999.

Cell, John, *The Highest Stage of White Supremacy: The Origins of Segregation in South Africa and the American South*, Cambridge: Cambridge University Press, 1982.

Gandhi, M.K., *The Collected Works of Mahatma Gandhi*, Ahmedabad: Government of India, 1960–1976.

Spiller, Peter, *A History of the District and Supreme Courts of Natal, 1846–1910*, Durban: Butterworth Publishers Ltd., 1986.

Swan, Maureen, *Gandhi: The South African Experience*, Johannesburg: Ravan Press, 1985.

7 Only one word, properly altered
Gandhi and the question of the *veshya*

Ajay Skaria

In a foreword in 1919 to the first Indian edition in English of *Indian Home Rule* (as many early English translations of *Hind Swaraj* were titled), Gandhi wrote: 'if I had to revise it, there is only one word I would alter in accordance with a promise made to an English friend. She took exception to my use of the word "prostitute" in speaking of the Parliament. Her fine taste recoiled from the indelicacy of the expression.'[1]

As the 'only' suggests, Gandhi did not think of the change that he suggested as major – it was merely a matter of making the book a little less indelicate (*gramya* – also rural) so that it would not upset fine tastes (*komal dil* – sensitive minds). Effectively, he seemed to contemplate altering the word, but retaining the argument signalled by the word – the argument that more robust minds would already have muscled onto, brushing past the word.

But could this alteration (and surely any alteration less than a deletion would have been inadequate for a delicate taste such as that possessed by Annie Beasant, who Anthony Parel speculates was the 'English friend') be delimited in the sense specified in this 'only'?

Annie Besant quite possibly intended to point to the sexism of the term. And Gandhi, in proposing its alteration, quite possibly intended to get rid of the sexism. My argument, however, is that such matters cannot be contained within this realm of intentions. I would like to suggest that the effort to alter the word *veshya* is symptomatic of a trembling in the texture of *Hind Swaraj* itself. The term *veshya* ('prostitute') marks the moment when a certain tension within *Hind Swaraj* over the question of the 'proper' becomes especially fraught. It occurs in the fifth chapter, at a crucial turn in the development of the argument of *Hind Swaraj*. *Hind Swaraj* is staged as a dialogue between a nationalist reader who is willing to use violence to drive the British out of India, and an editor who, ventriloquizing Gandhi's explicit positions, argues that such violence would not bring about *swaraj* ('home rule'). The first four chapters are devoted to bringing out the precise question the book asks. For the reader, initially, *swaraj* is a self-evident term: it involves driving out the English and continuing with broadly the same structures of state that the English had put in place. By the fourth chapter, the editor has problematized this understanding, suggesting that 'this means that we want English rule, but don't want the English'.[2] With this rejection, *swaraj* is no longer a self-evident term in *Hind Swaraj*. Now the question can be seriously asked: what is *swaraj*?

The question provides the title of the fourth chapter, but only the reader presents his views of *swaraj* there, not the editor. And the chapter draws to a close with the reader asking about Gandhi's thoughts on *swaraj*. Gandhi refuses an immediate answer. 'There is still time ... I find it just as difficult to understand *swaraj* as you find it easy.'[3]

Leaving for another occasion a consideration of the time that occurs here and elsewhere in *Hind Swaraj*,[4] let us ask this more preliminary question: why is *swaraj* so difficult to understand for Gandhi?

This essay will suggest that what makes the question of *swaraj* so vertiginous in *Hind Swaraj* is that it is meticulously attentive to the prefix *swa*. Indeed, there is a proliferation of the prefix *swa* in his writing – for instance, *swadharma*, *swadeshi*, *swaadhyaya*, *swaroop*. But what is one's 'own'? To ask this question seriously is to insist that the 'own' is not transparent, it is to ask: what is 'proper' to the 'own'? Etymologically, this questioning nature of the own, which is what always transforms a thoughtful consideration of the own into a concern with the proper, is marked in both the *swa* and its European cognate *se* – both carry connotations of the proper.

In the word *swaraj*, furthermore, the *swa* is conjoined with *raj* – a term conventionally rendered as rule. *Hind Swaraj*: involved in this title is the question of proper nature of rule for India or Hind. And attending to this question is itself impossible without attention to the *ownmost or proper nature of the proper* – what it is (if indeed the proper 'is'), and what its rule would entail.

For Gandhi, I will argue, 'true civilization' (*kharu sudhaara*) involved a staying with the question of the proper. This insistence on thinking the proper produces Gandhi's attack on 'modern civilization' (*aadhunik sudhaara*) or, more precisely, 're-form'.[5] For the reader, because the *swa* is transparent, not worth hesitating over, *swaraj* is simply self-rule in the sense of the sovereignty over India of the Indian national community (even if the precise boundaries of that community remain to be decided). This sovereignty will simply replace the sovereignty of the British over India. This is why for the reader *swaraj* involves becoming like the English, why the reader is fundamentally sympathetic to re-form or 'modern civilization' – it will enable this sovereignty.

Gandhi in contrast, denies that the sovereignty involved in re-form is *swaraj*. For him, it cannot be *swaraj* since it is not attentive to the *swa*. Indeed, Gandhi thought only one thought about 'modern civilization' – that it erased and forgot the proper. For Gandhi, re-form or 'modern civilization' eschewed the finitude of the proper and claimed infinity and godliness for itself. Within its terms the question of the proper and thus of *swaraj* could not even be raised. Therefore the remark at the end of Chapter 4: 'There is still time. ... So for now I will try to persuade [*samjhav-va*] you only of this – that, when viewed truly, what you call *swaraj* is not *swaraj*.'⁶ Viewed truly, which is to say viewed in terms of the *swa* that it did not attend to, 'modern civilization' was not *swaraj*. Beginning with this, the next eight chapters develop Gandhi's arguments against 'modern civilization'.

This thought about 'modern civilization' and its unthought are the concerns of this essay.

I would like to suggest that while *Hind Swaraj* criticizes 'modern civilization' for not staying with the proper, and while it affirms a staying with the proper, it nevertheless remains profoundly fractured in its thinking of the proper, and of *swaraj*. The word *veshya* or prostitute, and the desire to alter it, are particularly forceful, even violent, symptoms of this fracture. The term occurs during the discussion of *swaraj*. When the reader describes the English Parliament as the 'mother of parliaments', as effectively the epitome of *swaraj*, as a model of the *swaraj* that Indians should seek, the editor says: 'That which you call the mother of parliaments, that parliament is a *vaanjani* [sterile woman] and a *veshya* [prostitute].'⁷

In this use of the term *veshya* to describe Parliament, and in the later desire to alter it, two heterogeneous and even antithetical ways of thinking the *swa* or the proper clash. One of these ways – the one that Gandhi most evidently affirms – is, in a sense, conservative: it is disturbed by the impropriety of the Parliament as *veshya* and seeks to re-establish a properly substantive order.

But there is also another, more thought-provoking, engagement with the *swa* going on here – one which, also unhinged by the impropriety of the Parliament as *veshya*, breaks with conservative critiques of 'modern civilization' or *sudhaar*, re-form, and responds with questions about how the proper is to be thought. It is the insistent force of thinking the proper this other way that makes *Hind Swaraj*'s unthought press in so urgently on us today. In this essay, I shall be considering two questions that this unthought raises.

First, it raises the question of how violence is to be thought. It is surely a striking feature of modern thought – or more precisely of the ontotheological tradition – that its concept of violence is that of abstraction from presence (and the even more impoverished statist one, derived from this concept, of violence as wrong measure). To the extent that the concept is inseparable from measure, violence is constitutive of the order of the concept. This is why the ontotheological tradition has always regarded measure itself as the primary violence. In its most explicit (and conservative) thinking of the *swa*, *Hind Swaraj* remains within this tradition. Here, the emphasis is on a constitutive *separateness* which is heterogeneous to measure and therefore on the other side of violence. Yet on closer scrutiny, we will see, this separateness turns out to be founded on its own measure and violence.

This closer scrutiny, I will argue, also yields *Hind Swaraj*'s unthought – another thinking where the *swa* is figured as a constitutive *separation* produced by a giving without measure, where the *swa* is a separation which does not allow oneself to be constituted as one, as present. Concomitantly, violence (and not just the violence of colonialism) here comes to be practised in the re-form (Gandhi's word *sudhaara*, which he translates as 'modern civilization' can also be used a verb) of that which can only be given without measure, the *swa*, into that which can be thought within the opposition of abstraction and presence.

Second, it would be very easy (and justified) to view Gandhi's questioning of Parliament as produced by a conservative suspicion of representative democracy. But I would like to suggest that this questioning also, in its unthought, pushes the stakes of democratic thinking to a point where the name democracy is itself no longer appropriate. Trying to think an equality and empowerment of the people, democratic thinking – whether it proceeds to emphasize the majority, minority or the part that has no part – proceeds, as the suffix 'cracy' suggests, within the thought of sovereignty.

Hind Swaraj, in contrast, insists on an equality and separation that cannot be subsumed under sovereignty. *What would be a democratic politics that remains heterogeneous to democratic sovereignty? Would it even still go under the name democracy?* – this is another question raised by Gandhi's insistence on the proper. *Swaraj*: this does not mean only the rule of the proper (in which case, the question could be simply one of what is the proper in the Indian context – the Indian equivalent of the *demos*, the native princes, an enlightened middle class?), it also asks questions about the proper of rule itself. Can this proper of rule be thought under the concept-suffix 'cracy'? What is the violence that this concept-suffix practices? What would be a politics (if we can still call it a politics) that breaks with this concept-suffix?[8]

Hind Swaraj reaches these questions because it breaks with the modern tradition of conceptualizing domination as the taking away of power and agency, and of conceptualizing resistance as the recovery of agency. Instead, it questions domination by insisting on a subaltern responsibility for subordination. Here, subordination – which in the terms of *Hind Swaraj* is the re-form of the *swa* by measure – is thought not as the loss of power but as the loss of the *swa*. A politics of resistance, such as that involved in *satyagraha*, attempts to redress this loss by staying in a constitutive separation, and by giving this separation also to the dominant. To trace this unthought of a subaltern responsibility for subordination – this is the most pressing concern of this essay.

It may not be out of place to also quickly make two prefatory remarks on my mode of proceeding, both in this essay and in my other writings on the question of Gandhi. First, out of a fidelity to the distinctive modality of responsibility that I pointed to above, the arguments I make here will proceed through a process of displacement. That is to say, I will be eliciting arguments from *Hind Swaraj* not to dismiss them, overcome them, or move beyond them, but *rather to set them aside*. That which is thus set aside, need it be said, is not nothing. Only that can be set aside which gives not only itself but more than itself, and is in this sense oriented towards what it is not, towards what is given from. It is against the finitude of that which thus sets itself aside that other arguments and positions can emerge. Conversely, it is only in emerging from this setting aside these other arguments and positions can practise their distinctive responsibility.

Second, the arguments that I shall be developing turn crucially on issues of translation. Gandhi wrote almost all his major essays first in Gujarati, and then either himself translated them into English (as in the case of *Hind Swaraj*) or had his close associates do the translation under his supervision. But in *Hind Swaraj* as in other writings, the texts in the two languages diverge significantly from each other: entire words and phrases are missing in the English translation, or carry quite different connotations. These divergences cannot be adequately explained as caused by bad translation, or by the texts being addressed to different audiences. Rather, as I hope to indicate, they are symptomatic of a certain trembling in Gandhi's text, where an unthought disrupts the conservative vocabulary which Gandhi's critique of 'modern civilization' inhabits. It is by focusing on the *gap* between the English and the Gujarati texts (rather than by any attempt to produce a correct translation), then, that the arguments here are developed.[9]

Not restraint but thekaana

Let me begin by considering, in order to set aside and apart, the conservative ordering of the *swa*. This ordering is signalled by the word *thekaana*. The editor says: 'I said *vaanjani* [sterile woman] because the Parliament has not till now, of its own, done a single good work. That it can do nothing if there is nobody putting pressure on it is its proper condition [*svabhaavik sthithi*: situation of its ownmost or most proper orientation].'[10] A paradoxical formulation, thus: to not have a proper condition is the proper condition of the Parliament. The reader protests: 'The word *vaanjani* does not yet apply to the Parliament. The Parliament is made of the people [*lokoni baneli*], so it must doubtless work under the pressure of the people. This is its very quality, the *ankush* [restraint] on it.'[11] But the editor insists: 'It is not possible to see a single instance till now of Parliament taking even one thing [*vastu*, 'matter'] to its *thekaaney* [finality].'[12]

In this exchange between the reader and the editor, there emerges a distinction between the reader's *ankush* and the editor's *thekaana*. The two come to name heterogeneous orderings of productivity and fertility.

Both these terms prove difficult for Gandhi to translate into English. There is simply no equivalent for the word *ankush* in the English sentence, which is truncated to only read: 'This is its quality.' But *ankush* or restraint is distinctive as a quality: it is a force. Not only that, it is for the reader a legitimate force, a force that is not a violence, a force that produces *swaraj* or self-rule. This legitimacy is signalled by the genitive *ni* (in the word *lokoni*, of the people), poised as it is between the two senses where people make the parliament (thus perhaps Gandhi's English translation, 'by the people'), and where a transformation of the people makes the parliament.

Furthermore, this affirmation of representative democracy is quite different from Gandhi's *swaraj*: the reader's *swaraj* is not organized around the *swa* or the *thekaana*. Thus, in the reader's conception, the parliament cannot have a *swa* or proper that is independent of the people. It achieves its goals only under the restraint of the people, who are, as the genitive *ni* suggests, the true figures of fertility. For the reader, that the parliament should be productive only under such restraint is its distinctive quality – the quality which makes it more like a productive mother than a sterile woman.

Concomitantly, here the fertility and productivity of the people (and ministers) is constituted by their ability to be sovereign, without restraint. Elsewhere in *Hind Swaraj*, the editor remarks of the English people they 'cannot stay at a *thekaana*' [*thekaaneysar besi shakta nathi*; 'are never steadfast']. But for the reader, it is precisely this refusal of a *thekaana* that constitutes the sovereignty of the people (and, by extension, of ministers and prime ministers). Indeed, as sovereign subjects, the English people can only assert the irrelevance of the question of proper itself. For the latter, as the sovereign who exercises restraint and knows no proper bounds, boundaries and finitudes are contingent and fluid.

We need little reminder that such a rendering of boundaries (which is also the founding gesture of modern cosmopolitanism) has often been powerfully enabling. Over and again, this insistence on a sovereign subject has allowed a questioning of the conservative insistence on a substantive proper, whether that proper take the form of gender, class, caste or civilizational hierarchies.

Perhaps this is also indicative of the stakes for the reader of insisting on restraint: by producing the parliament as a sovereign body that is nevertheless of the people (*loko-ni*), it institutionalizes that conception of democracy which takes democracy to be the sovereignty of the people. *Ankush* or restraint: condensed in this word is *an argument that the democratic state embodies a force measured so correctly that it is not a violence*, a force that because it represents the people need not be bound by any proper.[13]

For the reader, to reiterate, neither the people nor the parliament has a *swa* – the former because their nature is to act, and the latter because its nature is to be acted upon. Through restraint, both a masculine and a feminine fertility and productivity outside the proper are affirmed – the parliament as wife-mother, and the people or ministers as masters.

Against restraint, Gandhi develops the thought of *thekaaney*. Unlike *ankush*, this word is at least translated, though very unusually, as 'finality'. Etymologically, *thekaana* is related to *sthaan*, place. A *thekaana* is a place that is a dwelling, a home (including, of course, a place within some hierarchy or order). A *thekaana* is not externally assigned; it is a destination that is a thing's or being's own. Objects cannot have a *thekaana*; only that can come home which has a proper.

It needs to be said right away that the editor's insistence, in opposition to the reader, on things being governed and brought to their *thekaana* is symptomatic of a conservatism. Here, the proper is elided into a *thekaana* thought substantively; furthermore, this substantive *thekaana* is presumed to be already inherent in the *swa* of the things themselves. Hence the disquiet about Parliament – for the editor, it raises the spectre of the rule of empty representation, one that does not have any proper in itself, and that takes its content from whatever the electorate or ministers gives it. Hence also the description of the Parliament as a *veshya* – the figure who on the most evident argument of the editor has no *thekaana* and therefore no proper.

If I nevertheless propose to stay with this conservatism, this is for two reasons. First, as I shall suggest in the rest of this section, even this conservative attention to the proper raises questions about that which is occluded by the vision of representative democracy articulated through *ankush* or restraint. Second, as I shall argue from the next section onwards, while the most immediately apparent formulations of *Hind Swaraj* render the proper through an insistence on the substantivity and unicity of *thekaana*, *Hind Swaraj* also initiates also another thinking of democracy. With the figure of the *veshya*, an abyssal distance opens up between the proper and the *thekaana*, such that the *thekaana* itself is interrogated, and it becomes of the nature of the proper to not reside in the proper and yet be oriented towards it, to raise questions about the proper as the manner of being oriented towards it.

To return, with this anticipation of later arguments, to the editor's reserve about *ankush*. The editor questions, first, the productivity of Parliament: 'it has not till now, of its own, done a single good work. That it can do nothing if there is nobody putting pressure on it is its proper condition [*sthithi svabhaavik reetey*, 'natural condition'].'[14] To not do anything of its own – this is its ownmost condition. Furthermore, not doing anything of its own, it cannot take things (and a thing, we don't need to be told, is not an object) to their *thekaana*. The converse of this argument would be that for Parliament to do a good work on *its* own would be to take things to *their* own place. *Initiated here, in other words, is a thinking of a constitutive separateness.* To insist on an own *thekaana* – this is to insist that true productivity would result in a constitutive separateness, where that which gives a *thekaana* separates from that which is given a *thekaana*.

Such separateness presumes an irreducible multiplicity which cannot be encountered through number. In number, separateness is rendered through the multiplicity of abstract equivalence, of homogeneous and interchangeable units. It is of the nature of the *thekaana* that it can never be homogenized this way, that it can only separate from itself through and in a giving without measure, or a giving outside number. And yet, it is only through the multiplicity of number and equivalence that the basic categories of representative democracy (of which parliament is the institutional apex) such as the electorate, or majority and minority, can be constituted. The insistence on separateness, thus, signals also profound reserve about representative democracy.

Second, the editor questions the sovereignty that the people exercise through *ankush* or restraint. A first reservation about sovereignty is implicit in the argument above: the sovereign of restraint, instead of recognizing that things have their own *thekaana* and are therefore constitutively separate, asserts sovereignty over them and denies their separateness. A second reservation: because the sovereign has no *thekaana*, this sovereignty is not truly sovereignty. Drawing on his English translation: 'These people [the English] change their views frequently. It is said that they change them every seven years. These views swing like the pendulum of a clock and are never steadfast (*thekaaneysar*). The people would follow a powerful orator or a man who gives them parties, receptions, etc.' And again (drawing for now only the English translation):

> The Parliament is without a real master. Under the Prime Minister, its movement is not steady, but it is buffeted around like a prostitute. The Prime Minister is more concerned about his power than about the welfare of the Parliament ... Prime Ministers are known to have made the Parliament do things merely for party advantage ... [15]

Lacking a *thekaana* that can constitute their separateness, the people and the ministers are here themselves mastered. 'These parliaments are a mark of the slavery of the people.'[16] Not sovereigns, thus, but slaves: such an assertion would well describe the stakes of the critique of representative democracy that takes place here in the name of *thekaana*.

From the perspective of *thekaana*, it can now be ventured, the sovereignty exercised through the restraint of a democratic state is violent in the sense of disordering by taking from any place, by disrupting boundaries. Instead, *thekaana* is proposed as a force that is not violent – because it keeps things and beings stay at their own place, in their separateness. *As such, the non-violence claimed by* thekaana *is not that of a more correct measure, but that of not requiring measure: it is in this sense that it can claim to be a force on the other side of violence.*

Keeping as control: the exclusions of thekaana

It is because of this conservative insistence on *thekaana* that the *veshya* and the sterile woman have to be rejected with such force. The sterile woman is not capable of playing a proper role as a fertile mother. And the *veshya*, even more constitutively than the sterile woman, is without *thekaana*.[17] Unlike the sterile woman, whose proper orientation it is to not to be able to bring things to their *thekaana*, the *veshya* is the figure who as her ownmost orientation refuses a *thekaana*, and practises a mobility that is outside the *thekaana*.

But what is the *thekaana* that the *veshya* is outside?

This *thekaana* is embodied by the *dhani* – a word, related to *dhan* (wealth), that is usually translated by Gandhi as master but carries connotations also of husband, lord, possessor. Both the ministers and the prime minister are identified as the *dhani* in relation to the *veshya*: 'And it is [like] a *veshya* because which(ever) ministry keeps [*raakhey*] it, it stays with [*paasey tey rahey*] that ministry. Today its *dhani* is Asquith, tomorrow Balfour, and the next day a third.' And also:

> It is appropriate that Parliament has been given the name of *veshya*. It does not have any *dhani*. It cannot have a one *dhani*. But the essence of what I am saying is not only this. When somebody does become its *dhani* – such as a Prime Minister – even then its gait is not steady [*eksarkhi*]. Like a ruined *veshya* – so does Parliament always remain.[18]

And as indicated by the metaphor of enslavement that we encountered in an earlier passage ('These parliaments are a mark of the slavery of the people'), the 'people' too retain the potential of being something other than slaves – they can become masters or *dhani*.

On too quick a reading of *Hind Swaraj* and other writings by Gandhi, it might seem that another *thekaana*, that of the mother, is as or more powerful as the *thekaana* of the *dhani*. Thus, even in the passage where the Parliament is identified as a *veshya*, the *veshya* seems to be contrasted to the mother – 'That which you speak of as the mother [*maata*] of parliaments, that parliament is a sterile woman and a prostitute'.[19] Gandhi did affirm the figure of the mother as a figure capable of love and suffering, and even himself adopting that persona – thus the title of Manu Gandhi's autobiography, *Baapu, my mother*. But motherhood as a political principle involved a male figure, the *brahmachari* or celibate. It is surely not accidental that Gandhi insisted that it was his *brahmacharya* or 'celibacy' that allowed women to trust him and regard him as a mother. *Brahmacharya* could be practised even within marriage: here, the *brahmachari* was the husband who was so strong that he could control his own sexuality and become the mother.[20]

Such, then, is the most evident ordering articulated in *Hind Swaraj*. In this economy, the *veshya* can only be a figure of ruin, necessarily kept outside every *thekaana*. (And the *veshya* is a pervasive figure – not only parliament but all those who do not stay at their *thekaana* are potentially *veshyas*, as is indicated by Gandhi's occasional use in his writings of 'prostitute' as a verb to describe the figures who are at other times weak *dhanis*.) Yet, though pushed to the margins, the *veshya* comes to ruin not just any particular *thekaana* but the thought of *thekaana* itself, most of all by raising questions about the violence that constitutes the separateness of the *thekaana*, or more precisely about the separation that the separateness that the *thekaana* must disallow. What emerges in attending to such questions is this – that even though the thought of *thekaana* initiates a critique of representative democracy, it nevertheless cannot carry this thought through.

To begin attending to these questions raised by the figure of the *veshya*, we need to reconsider the passage: 'And it is a *veshya* because which(ever) ministry keeps [*jey pan raakhey*] it, it stays with [*paasey tey rahey*] that ministry. Today its *dhani* is Asquith, tomorrow Balfour, and the next day a third.'[21]

One word and one phrase in this elliptical formulation deserve particular attention. The word is *raakhey*: the relationship of the *dhani* with both the *veshya* and the wife (*dhaniyani*, or more usually, *bayri*) can be described by the same word – *raakhey*, keep. (The phrase '*bayri raakhvu*', 'keep a wife', though no longer polite, was apparently common in at least central Gujarat till the mid-twentieth century.). The proper of the *dhani*, then, is thought primarily through keeping – the *dhani* keeps both the wife and the *veshya*.

Also, *raakhey* is related to *raakh*, *raakheli* or *raakhel* – a courtesan, concubine or mistress. The root of *raakh* as of *raakhvu*: *raksha* – protect, save or rescue (an English cognate?). Involved here, as this suggests, is a protecting that is a keeping outside, an exclusion. The *raakhel* is the figure who is protected only by the *dhani*, and who in this protection is excluded from legal institutions. Such exclusion is quite in contrast to the wife, who can in principle at least be the *dhaniyani* – the wife as a female *dhani*. While there is a subordination of the wife to the *dhani*, while she too is protected by the *dhani*, this protection and subordination takes place within the law, not outside the law as with the concubine. In this sense, the concubine stands as a figure of absolute subordination: kept only by the *dhani*, and incapable of being independent of the *dhani*. *Raakhvu*, then, is a distinctive kind of *raksha* or rescuing. As rescuing, it is a giving in the sense of patronage. But this giving of protection is not that of the gift: protecting through an exception, it becomes a keeping in domination. It is not surprising that, on two occasions, *raakhey* is translated as control, and that the English are described as keeping India.

The phrase is, *jey pan [raakhey] ... paasey tey rahey*. 'Whichever/whoever [keeps it/her] ... it/she stays with that.' The Parliament is not a *veshya* because it is kept, for one can be kept at one's *thekaana*, as the wife is supposed to be. Rather, it is a *veshya* because it resists being kept any *thekaana* – unlike, say, the concubine or mistress. Resisting such keeping, the *veshya* moves from one *thekaana* to another (Asquith, Balfour and then a third), ruining these *thekaaanas* themselves. This resistance is already signaled in the (para)phrase '*paasey ... rahey*' or stay with. That which has a *thekaana* does not stay with the *thekaana*; rather, it stays at the *thekaana*, is of it, or as the morpheme *sar* in '*thekaaneysar*' suggests, 'in accordance with' the *thekaana*. To stay with: this, paradoxical though it may sound, is to be without a *thekaana*.

The resistance is further emphasized by the *jey pan* (whichever or whoever – the word *jey* can be both which and who), which stresses that the staying with of the *veshya* is a mobility and promiscuity.[22] For Gandhi, promiscuity makes the Parliament as *veshya* incapable of separateness. Staying now with one and then with another, it nevertheless cannot give itself to that which it stays with because it does not have any *thekaana* (or consequently a *swa*) of its own, an itself to give. It can only give the measure of interest (which measures the immeasurable) or the heat of passion (which unites with that which it is passionate about); and both these forms of giving do not allow for separateness. Giving in this way, without having an itself to give, the Parliament as *veshya* pulls the *dhani* into a measure, equivalence and unicity that threatens the immeasurability of the *thekaana*; it makes the *dhani* a weak master.[23]

There are thus two ways of being outside the *thekaana* – those of the *veshya* and the weak master. Because her constitutive possibility raises the spectre of that which resists recuperation, because she threatens the *dhani*, the *veshya* is especially worrisome. Symptomatic of this is the alteration that the word *veshya* already undergoes in Gandhi's English translation. Here, the entire passage cited earlier ('It is appropriate. . . . always remain') is severely truncated: 'Parliament is without a real master. Under the Prime Minister, its movement is not steady but it is buffeted about like a prostitute.'[24]

In this formulation, the focus shifts away from the *veshya's* irrecuperability for any *thekaana* to the absence of a 'real master'. Like the *veshya*, the weak master also cannot stay at *thekaana*; unlike the *veshya*, however, he is not constitutively without a *thekaana*, and can be brought back to the *thekaana*. The *veshya* is thus always potentially only the pretext for a focus on the weak *dhani*.

This shift from the *veshya* to a stress on the lack of mastery and masculinity is not exclusive to the English translation – recall that in the Gujarati text the people, ministers and prime ministers are all cast as weak masters. And the emphasis on a weak masculinity resurfaces in Chapter 8, where Gandhi insists that the peace imposed by the English had made Indians *abada* ('without strength', also a word that was commonly used till the mid-twentieth century to describe women; we will later see the word used in this sense in *Hind Swaraj*), 'emasculated, effeminate, and cowardly'.[25]

This lack of masculinity is especially significant since *Hind Swaraj* sometimes seems to suggest that only a real master can practise *satyagraha*, and that a satyagrahi is marked by substantivity and worth – thus resorting to the very lexicon of equivalence and substance that *Hind Swaraj* at other places questions. Rejecting the reader's suggestion that satyagraha is an appropriate weapon for 'weak men [*nabada manas*]',[26] the editor insists: 'The strength and manliness that is required for *satyagraha* – that a cannon-force person can never have. Do you believe that a person without substance [*namaal*; *maal* – substance, *na*-not; 'coward'] can ever violate a law that he dislikes.'[27]

Even the English are admirable to the extent that, in their masculinity, they keep England. Thus the editor says that the English have 'one thing' (*ek vastu*; one quality very strongly developed): they will not let their country 'be lost' (*java na dey*). 'If any person were to cast an evil eye on it, they would make him stone-blind'.[28] Proposed here is a notion of letting, *dey*, which is simply the inverse correlate of *raakhey* or control – to let go would be lose control. Letting and losing in this sense is possible only with that which is possessed in the modality of *raakhey* as control.

In all of this, there emerges the precise sense in which the *thekaana* is conservative and substantive. Since a *thekaana* is constituted by *raakhey* as control, *to stay at a thekaana is necessarily to do a keeping*, most evidently of other *thekaanas* but also of one's own *thekaana*. The *dhani*, for example, stays at his *thekaana* by keeping his wife at her *thekaana*, and by excluding the *veshya*. Only through such a violent keeping in domination can the separateness of the *thekaana* be maintained. Thus, even though *Hind Swaraj* intimates that *thekaanas* give each other their own separateness, this giving turns out to be founded on relations of domination, and in that sense not a giving without measure. Despite its profound commitment to a constitutive multiplicity beyond the abstract equivalence of parliamentary democracy, the thought of *thekaana* necessarily practices its own measured violence rather than being a force on the other side of violence. (Of course, this violence is distinguished by its finitude from the violence involved in restraint.)

Perhaps it is an affirmation of this surreptitious violence that authorizes also the translation of *thekaana* as finality. As a keeping or *raakhey*, a *thekaana* is indeed final. It is incapable of that radical giving which – to anticipate the argument below – loses the *thekaana* itself, which keeps itself only in this radical giving. And perhaps even the desire to alter the word *veshya* belonged to this violence of *thekaana*: perhaps it was an effort (futile, of course) to banish the threat to the *thekaana* from that which constitutively resists recuperation; perhaps by altering the word *veshya*, Gandhi sought to affirm the programme of converting the weak master into the strong master of *thekaana* in the sense of control.

If this effort to institute *thekaana* as control had been successful and 'final', then the alteration of the word *veshya* would have little to give us. It could not be set aside; it would have to be simply dismissed. But the alteration of the word *veshya* ruins the concept of *thekaana*, and in this ruining opens up other possibilities.

Indeed, *raakhey* as control or keeping is already explicitly questioned in *Hind Swaraj*. For example, though the keeping of England by the English is affirmed (the one quality that the English have despite not being *thekaaneysar*), there is a rejection not only of the English keeping of India, but of control itself as the mode in which Indians should keep India. Thus, when the reader suggests that 'if they [the English] go [*teo gaya*], then I feel that we should keep [*raakhiye*] the constitution they created ... ', the editor rejects such control itself, famously describing such government as 'English rule without the Englishman'.

Hence the question that presses in on us: what is the relation between the *veshya* who rejects *raakhey* in the sense of 'control', and that editor who, rejecting the nationalist vision of the reader, also rejects *raakhey* as control, even when that control will keep Hindustan to its *thekaana*? And how would an alteration of the word *veshya* have altered this relation?

Keeping as letting stay: subaltern responsibility for subordination

To raise these questions is to open the possibility of thinking the *swa* otherwise than through the conservatism of *thekaana*; *it is to think a proper that is heterogeneous to any* thekaana. In order to pursue that possibility, consider the editor's response to the reader's question of how the English could take India. The editor insists: 'The English have not taken Hindustan, we have given it to them. They have not lasted in India on their own strength; we have kept [*raakhya*] them. ... In order to get rich fast, we welcomed them. We helped them. ... Hence it is more true to say that that we gave [*aapyo*] Hindustan to the English than that Hindustan was lost [*gayu*].' When the reader asks, repeating the sense of *raakhey* as control: 'Now tell me how the English could keep [*raakhi*] India', the editor responds by multiplying the emphasis on the other sense of *raakhey*:

> Just as we gave [it] to them, so do we let Hindustan stay with [*paasey raheva daiye*] them. Many amongst them say that they took [*lidhu*] Hindustan by the sword, and they even say they keep it by the sword. Both these statements [*vaat*] are wrong. To keep [*raakhvama*] Hindustan, the sword will be of little use; we alone let them stay [*raheva daiye chhe*]. [Gandhi's English translation: 'The sword is entirely useless for holding India. We alone keep them.']
>
> So if we keep [*raakhiye*] the English in India, this is only for our self-interest..
>
> To blame them is to perpetuate [*nibhav-va*] their power. ... we are the ones who help keep [*raakhvama*] them.[29]

What is involved in *raakhey* in this second sense? A first clue could be this: Gandhi uses the English word 'keep' to translate not only of *raakhiye* but also *raheva daiye*, 'let stay'. But *daiye* is also from *devu*, give. Here, to let stay also means to give staying. *Raakhey* in the second sense is to let stay or give staying – but what is this?

To begin, what it is not. Let us start with the statement, 'we have given it to them'. On too quick a reading of the editor's reply, it would be easy to (mis)understand the giving or letting in this and other remarks in terms of agency. It would then be easy assume that what is being said by the editor is that Indians were agential in their subordination, that it was not the greater power of the British which allowed them to take India. Rather, Indians let India be taken, even giving it to the British in exchange for material benefits. And Indians still 'keep' the British in the sense that they continue to exercise agency in an undesirable manner – they operate only with the measure of self-interest, and let the British stay.

If the letting is indeed that of agency, then the reader and the editor share the same vocabulary. The only difference would be the minor one that where the reader blames the British, the editor more judiciously blames Indians themselves; that where the reader says that India was *taken away* by the British, the editor disagrees and says that India was *taken* by the British because Indians gave it quite freely. If this is so, furthermore, the editor's argument could rightly be regarded as a precursor of that influential revisionist formulation in Indian historiography that has over the last few decades insisted that the colonized participated in their own colonization, that India was ruled by the English because of support from significant sections of Indians.[30]

But the distinction which sets the terms of debate in the problematic of agency – that between taking what is given freely and taking away – is not tenable here. To begin with, it is simply not faithful to the text: the editor does not say that the British did not take India *away*; he says that they did not *take* India.

If we nevertheless habitually practise this very crude infidelity to the text, and do not even notice it, this is because to not do so makes his argument seem preposterous, even ridiculous. After all, he does also say that Indians gave India to the British. How can India not be taken by the British even though it has been given by Indians? How can India be given such that it cannot be taken even in giving? And in what sense do the British rule India if they have not even taken India when it was given to them?

But if, rather than dismissing these questions, we take seriously what they give, this allows us to encounter the force of the phrase 'let stay'.

In the problematic of agency, the unstated assumption – regardless of whether the British took Hindustan by force, or Indians gave Hindustan to the English – is that Hindustan is an object. Only an object – that which we have a hold over – can be taken by force or taken and given in exchange. To give an object is simply to let go of it – which as remarked in the previous section is the correlate of *raakhey* as control.

But for the editor, Hindustan is not an object. This is the crux of his disagreement with the reader's nationalism. For the reader, 'because there are railways, today we see the spirit of one people [*ek praja*, 'new spirit of nationalism'] in Hindustan'. For the editor, however, 'if there had been no railways, the English could not have such a hold [*kaabu*] on Hindustan'.[31] Furthermore, he insists that 'the English have taught you that you were not one people [*praja*, "nation"] before ... [But] when the English were not in Hindustan, at that time [too] we were one people'. 'One people does not mean that we had no differences between us; but our leading men would travel throughout India either on foot or bullock-carts, they would learn each others' languages. ... '32

Contested here is the reader's constructivist idea of Hindustan, where the railways create the abstract time and space within which nationalism can emerge, or Hindustan can be made into an object of desire. The word *kaabu* is suggestive of this contestation, carrying as it does connotations of power over in a sense similar to *raakhey* as control – thus Gandhi's English translation 'hold'. The editor's hostility to the railways is because, enabling a hold in this sense, it facilitates and accelerates the making of Hindustan into an object.

What then is Hindustan for the editor? If we stress the suffix, Hindustan is a *sthaan* (etymologically associated also with *thekaana*) or place rather than an object. Furthermore, *praja*, the word that Gandhi here translates as 'nation', was earlier translated as 'people'. Hindustan, then, is the *thekaana* of the *praja* or people.

Here, the tension between *thekaana* as control and as the home of the proper flares up. The *swa* is the ownmost. As such a *thekaana*, Hindustan always remains one's own. As such a *thekaana*, can it be given or taken at all, and how?

When the editor says, 'The English have not taken Hindustan, we have given it to them', it is this question (rather than that of agency, where a finite amount of responsibility – the degrees of accountability of various actors in the conquest of India – is distributed) that he struggles with. 'We have given it to them' – this giving is neither of the gift, nor that of exchange of objects. What then is this giving?

'We have given it to them': here, the editor ventures a thought of *raakhey* ('we keep the English') as a *subaltern responsibility for subordination*. Unlike agency, which, as the property of the agent, can be taken away, such subaltern responsibility cannot be taken away or lost. True, responsibility here concerns a loss, as the chapter's title ('Why was India lost') intimates. But India has not been lost in the sense of being taken away. Because taking away involves measure, and because Hindustan is immeasurable, there is no circumstance in which the English can forcibly take Hindustan away from Indians – Hindustan can never be taken (though, as later discussion will suggest, it can be accepted as a gift). Through the term *raakhiye*, the editor tries to think a loss that is not a loss of agency (or of *thekaana*) but rather loss of responsibility; a subaltern responsibility for subordination.

Considered too quickly, this emphasis on a subaltern responsibility for subordination, and for the loss that such subordination necessarily entails, might seem an extremely dangerous move, a case of blaming the victim and exonerating the dominant. But this appears so only because in the commonsensical understanding (such as that of the reader in *Hind Swaraj*), responsibility is a finite totality, where if one party is responsible, then the other is less so.

Yet that is far from being the case here. In this insistence on subaltern responsibility for subordination, the violence practised by the dominant and the subaltern are *both* infinitely greater. Contrast the reader's and editor's understanding of the violence of colonial rule. While for the reader, it is possible to continue with British institutions in independent India, the editor rejects 're-form', or all colonial institutions. Then again, while the reader sees colonial violence as a zero sum situation where the British have gained, and Indians have lost, for the editor colonial violence is also directed at the English themselves. Re-form has caused the latter too to lose their *swa* or themselves (because they too have in trying to take Hindustan resorted to a logic of measure; and perhaps even because they keep or control not just Hindustan but England itself). In a similar vein, while for the reader the loss of India can be redressed by taking back Hindustan, for the editor a taking back of Hindustan through violence would get nothing back.

And, to point to an argument in *Hind Swaraj* that will not be developed here, *swaraj* or the rule of the proper is possible only through a subaltern responsibility for subordination – and *not* through the dominant taking responsibility for domination. It is surely not accidental that it is when Gandhi effectively denies such subaltern responsibility – as he does often enough for women and Dalits – that he also articulates some of his most conservative positions.[33] Without such subaltern responsibility, the *unilateral obligation* of *satyagraha* would become impossible.[34]

In the absence of any explicit discussion of subaltern responsibility for subordination in *Hind Swaraj*, it is necessary to be faithful to that essay's unthought (which is always the ownmost of a thought, and perhaps never more so than when fidelity to the unthought involves betraying the thought).

Let us start once again with the remark, 'we have given it to them'. If we understood this statement in the terms of *thekaana*, then we might say: Hindustan is a *thekaana*, and is characterized by having a *swa*. A *thekaana* cannot be given – the *swa* belongs to the *thekaana* in finality. 'We have given it to them' – this means, 'that which cannot and should not be given has been given'.

But what we are attempting to elicit here is not the problematic of *thekaana*, any more than it is that of agency. We are rather attempting to elicit that thinking which is *thekaana's* own unthought. In this unthought, I will be suggesting, the *swa* not only can be given, but can exist only in this giving. As such, the argument here must be understood differently. The argument is not 'that which cannot and should not be given and has been given', but rather: *the* swa *or proper has not been given in the way proper to it.*

To explicate this argument, let us consider two questions. To begin with: what is the manner of giving proper to the *swa*?

Very briefly, in anticipation of a more extended consideration on some other occasion, let me only insist for now on this axiom that organizes *Hind Swaraj's* unthought: *that a giving proper to the* swa *involves, before anything* else, the giving of separation itself. (It is this giving of separation that is arrested in the constative separateness of the thekaana.) This separation makes what is properly given into a gift.

We can think of this separation on two registers. First, there is what seems to be the separation of the giver from the recipient. But the other who is the recipient of the gift cannot be constituted empirically, *and is always instituted through the separation that passes through oneself.* Gifting is possible only as the other that one always is. (This is also why one can gift to oneself – because one is never only oneself. One cannot gift to oneself as oneself – that would be only a taking or a keeping as control.)

Second, there is the *separation of what is given from both the giver and the recipient.* Now, only what is of oneself can be given – the proper of the gift is always oneself, the giver. But to gift is also to separate oneself from what is given – which means to acknowledge that the giver cannot and will not control or revoke the gift. Since a gift is never an object (an object in itself – if such a contrary phrase may be momentarily entertained – cannot be gifted), to separate oneself from it is to let its proper or *swa* emerge (which is why the gift is the giver's proper and more, thus revealing the productivity proper to the *swa*). As such, to not control the gift does not mean to put the gift at the disposal of the recipient (as though the gift were empty); it is to give the proper of the gift to the recipient.

Having indicated the two registers of separation that constitute the manner of giving proper to the *swa*, we can now turn to the second question: how does the giving proper to the *swa* differ from the *raheva daiye* or giving of staying that has occurred with the British?

The latter giving has to be thought, it seems to me, as a transformation (or more precisely, extending the implications of *Hind Swaraj's* Gujarati term for 'modern civilization', a *re-form*) of the gift of separation that is proper to the *swa*. This re-form is what is questioned in the emphasis on the subaltern responsibility for subordination – on how 'we keep the British'. Struggling with the relation between the two forms of giving, *Hind Swaraj* effectively produces an argument about violence: *violence or re-form occurs when the proper, which can be given or taken only as a gift, without measure, has been given in measure.* What is thus given in measure, however, can also be taken by the recipient only in measure.

To think violence in this manner is to displace the commonsensical perspective that understands domination and subordination solely in terms of the work of reason and power. What power acts on has to be thought not only empirically, in its objectness, but rather in terms of how this power re-forms the proper or *swa*. Without the *swa*, in other words, there can be no sustained thinking of violence. This is why 'modern civilization' (or, rendered in another kind of fidelity to the Gujarati, 're-form') cannot have a concept of violence that is anything more than a statism.

How or in what manner does this re-form act upon the gift, or on the giving without measure proper to the *swa*?

> By not allowing the separations that constitute giving without measure, Indians seek to give Hindustan to the English in exchange. But Hindustan can be given in exchange only as an object – that which can be given and taken in measure, that with which Indians would have no constitutive relation. In the exchange of objects, nothing has a *swa* – not the giver, nor the recipient, and certainly not what is given – and no constitutive separation is therefore allowed.
>
> The paradoxical attempt to disallow what cannot be disallowed – this is what the editor struggles to think when he says, 'we keep [*raakhiye*] the English'.

> Now we can ask once again, more attentively, what does this phrase say?
>
> Thought in light of what has been argued above, does it not say this: Indians tried to give Hindustan as an object to the English. But Hindustan could not be separated out as an object from Indians, because it is their *swa*. Unable to separate themselves from the Hindustan that they give to the English, they give themselves to the English. Giving themselves to the English – this is how 'we keep the English'.
>
> A further question: who keeps – or, who is the 'we' that is the subject of 'keep'?

In a giving of oneself, no keeping as control is possible. In control, there is a oneself who stays apart from the giving, and does a keeping. In the giving of oneself all of oneself is given; here, the oneself who stays apart and keeps is annihilated. Therefore, if Indians give all of themselves, and still keep the British, then the oneself who is keeping can only be the *swa* – which cannot be given in exchange, and which stays distinct even in the giving of all.

But how or in what manner does the *swa* keep the English?

This keeping (which names nothing less than Gandhi's unthought concept of subordination) occurs, paradoxically, in the losing of the *swa*. 'We keep the English' – does not the phrase then say also this: *we lose ourselves*. Giving themselves to the English, giving in exchange what cannot be so given, the *swa* is lost. Indians lose their *swa* not in the sense that the English take it, but in the sense that they lose themselves by giving themselves without their *swa*.

To lose oneself: what this means is that the *swa* is separated from itself. We should not confuse this separation, which is the violence of re-form, either with the separateness of *thekaana* or with the two other separations that have figured in the argument so far – the separation that sustains the gift, and the separation from power. Indeed, it is absolutely crucial to understand both the difference *and* the relation between these three separations.

To lose oneself: *here the separation is from separation itself* – which is to say from the separation that sustains the proper gift. By giving in exchange that which cannot be so given, what is lost is precisely this separation that is constitutive of the gift. As such, this loss of oneself is abysally separated from the separation that founds the gift, where separation itself comes as a gift, where separation is not a loss.

To lose oneself: this separation is also separated, though in quite a different way, from the separation as loss invoked in the problematic of agency. In the latter, loss comes as a separation from power – as disempowerment and marginalization. Put in the terms of the argument 'we lose ourselves', we might say that the problematic of agency erroneously and in forgetting (and I will shortly return to this error-forgetting that Gandhi calls *bhool*) thinks of the separation as passing not through oneself but between oneself and what one gives of oneself as an object (and an object, recall, is defined by the logic of equivalence and can be possessed or controlled). Because of this error-forgetting, where Hindustan and 'we' are converted into objects and subjects, the problematic of agency thinks of separation not as from separation itself, but from power. The argument 'we lose ourselves' does not simply reject this agential problematic; rather, it sets this problematic aside as a forgetting, and thinks the loss more originarily as a separation from separation.

'We keep the English': to insist on a loss that is of ourselves, of our *swa* – this is to insist on the primacy of the separation that passes through ourselves. As such, it is also to insist that we are always capable of being responsible for our subordination, our loss of ourselves. Where there is no proper, there can also be no such responsibility – there can at most be agency, which can be taken away. To be possessed by a *swa* that cannot be erased even when it is gifted or lost – such is the mark of the figure who is responsible for the letting involved in both the gift and its re-form.

'We lose ourselves' – this is a vertiginous thought, and in some formulations of *Hind Swaraj*, there is a drawing back from it. *It is in this drawing back from* Hind Swaraj's *own thought that the* thekaana, *with its constitutive exclusion of the* veshya, *is instituted.*

Symptomatic of this is the surely unconscious but nevertheless striking relation between two very similar phrases – the 'stays with' (*paasey rahey*) of the *veshya*, and the 'let stay with' (*paasey raheva daiye*) by Indians which gives Hindustan to British.[35] 'We let Hindustan stay with them' – here the loss of Hindustan is not conceptualized as a loss of *swa*. Here, the letting occurs from a *thekaana* – that which is never given and can never be given to the British, which stays apart from any giving. Here, the figure who lets stay is conceptualized on the lines of the weak master, who does an inappropriate giving, but who despite himself cannot give the *thekaana*.

The *veshya* stays with who/whichever: the *veshya* cannot do a 'let stay with' because she is the converse mirror of the weak master, the figure who *does not have a* swa. In the violence of this insistence that the *veshya* does not have a proper, however, what comes undone is nothing less than *Hind Swaraj's* own thought of a subaltern responsibility for subordination. Central to that responsibility was the questioning of subordination through an insistence on the pervasiveness of a *swa* that even when lost remained one's own. But the case of the *veshya* suggests that the *swa* is not pervasive. Lacking a *swa*, incapable of the separation that passes through oneself, the *veshya* is incapable of responsibility for subordination, and thus incapable of subalternity itself.

This exclusion authorizes an immense violence against the *veshya*, a violence cannot even be recognized as violence. For since violence is possible only against those with a *swa*, against those capable of the separation of gifting, no force used against those who lack a *swa* would be a violence. *The veshya is excluded from the concept of violence itself – such is the violence practised on her.*

This violence is conceptually underwritten by the opposition of letting stay to staying with. But the *veshya's* practice of 'staying with' can be opposed to 'letting stay' only so long as the latter is thought through a substantive *thekaana*. When letting stay is thought as a loss of *swa*, as it is in the thought of a subaltern responsibility for subordination, then it is not only that opposition which crumbles. It is also the very concept of *thekaana* which crumbles, for the constitutive exception of the *veshya* which sustained that concept is no longer tenable.

With the thought of a subaltern responsibility for subordination, of subordination as a loss of the proper, we have seen, the *thekaana* itself crumbles. This thought is heterogeneous both to the *thekaana* and to the *veshya*, but is given by the *veshya's* ruin of the *thekaana*, by the emergence of the *swa* into the space left free by (and in) that ruin. This thought raises a new sheaf of questions. Most of all, there is this question: In the problematic of agency, subordination is resisted by seizing power back. In the problematic of *thekaana*, it is resisted by bringing things and beings back to their *thekaana*. *But how is subordination resisted in the thought of subaltern responsibility for subordination?* This question, which is a necessary consequence of an insistence on a subaltern responsibility for subordination, will have to be explored on another occasion. For now, I stop with only this: an alteration of the word *veshya* – would it have concealed the ruin of *thekaana*, the consequent thought of a subaltern responsibility for subordination, and of the resistance proper to such responsibility? Could it?

Notes

This essay is an attempt to respond to at least some of the pressing questions asked by students – especially Papori Bora, Emily Rook-Koepsel, Priti Misra and Julietta Singh – during my Spring 2005 course at the University of Minnesota on Gandhi. I would like to thank them for the gift of their scepticism. I also thank Leela Gandhi, Qadri Ismail, Sanjay Seth and Rajeshwari Sundar Rajan for discussions of the essay. I especially thank Vinay Gidwani for his meticulous and extensive comments on an earlier version; the very prose of many of his comments have become part of this version.

1. *CWMG*, Vol. 18, p. 69, 28 May 1919; *Akshardeha*, Vol. 15, p. 317. The Gujarati text uses both '*sudhaarva*' and '*badalva*' to translate 'alter'. Because there are so many English and Gujarati editions of HS, I have preferred to stick to the Akshardeha and CWMG versions. I have tried to make things easier for readers who don't have access to these versions by indicating the chapters in which the references occur.
2. *Akshardeha*, Vol. 10, p. 23, *Hind Swaraj*; *CWMG*, Vol. 10, p. 255. In cases where the writing was originally in English, as with *Hind Swaraj*, I have provided my own translation. In cases where there is a significant difference in translation, I have either provided Gandhi's translation of the relevant word or phrase in brackets in the text; occasionally, I have also footnoted his translation of the passage.
3. *Akshardeha*, Vol. 10, p. 23, *Hind Swaraj*; *CWMG*, Vol .10, p. 255.
4. Such a consideration could begin by exploring why 'there is still time' is translated into English as 'patience'. It would have to explore what would be involved in the urgent patience practised through satyagraha.
5. Gandhi's consistently translated *aadhunik sudhaara* or *aajkaalnu sudhaara* as 'modern civilization'. But a more common meaning of the word in the nineteenth century, as now, would be reform. Etymologically, sudhaar would concern the good (su) path (dhaara); as such it could be opposed to ku [bad] dhaara. Indeed, in a later chapter, Gandhi himself remarks that this *sudhaara* is *kudhaara*. But by the nineeenth century, as now, *sudhaara* had overwhelmingly come to mean reform in general, without necessarily carrying connotations of being good or bad. For instance, nineteenth-century reformists described themselves as engaged in *sudhaara*, and their opponents attacked *sudhaara* as undesirable. Gandhi identified a distinctive logic of re-forming involved in 'modern civilization'. I would therefore prefer to translate the word, in keeping with its other meaning, as 're-form', keeping the hyphen to distinguish it from the more conventional sense of reform.
6. *Samjhav-va*: the word is both persuade and explain.
7. Gandhi's English translation goes: 'That which you consider to be the Mother of Parliaments is like a sterile woman and a prostitute.' *Akshardeha*, Vol. 10, p. 23, *Hind Swaraj*; *CWMG*, Vol. 10, p. 256, *Hind Swaraj*.
8. I thank Vinay Gidwani for questions that foregrounded the issue of the relation between democracy and *swaraj*.
9. A caveat too may be in order. What will and should be abundantly evident in what follows is my profound obligation to many thinkers – both those who have written specifically on Gandhi, and those who have stayed with the questions that are the concern of this essay. If I have not explicitly acknowledged the innumerable places in this essay where there is such an obligation, this is because I have not wanted to be irresponsible. A responsible accounting of my obligation would require an engagement with these thinkers far more sustained than I can attempt within the limits of this essay. It would also involve a violence towards Gandhi's thought, which would then be even more likely to be understood by *analogy*.
10. *Akshardeha*, Vol. 10, p. 23, *Hind Swaraj*; *CWMG*, Vol. 10, p. 256. Gandhi's translation is: 'That Parliament has not yet, of its own accord, done a single good thing. Hence I have compared it to a sterile woman. The natural condition of that Parliament is such that, without outside pressure, it can do nothing.'
11. *Akshardeha*, Vol. 10, p. 24, *Hind Swaraj*; *CWMG*, Vol. 10, p. 256. Gandhi's translation is: 'The term "sterile woman" is not applicable. The Parliament, being elected by the people, must work under public pressure. This is its quality.'

12 *Akshardeha*, Vol. 10, p. 24, *Hind Swaraj*; *CWMG*, Vol. 10, p. 256. The CWMG version is: It is not possible to recall a single instance in which finality can be predicted for its work.
13 The relation of human rights, so central to this conception of liberal democracy, to a thinking of the proper is too complex an issue for me to address here. But it seems to me, very quickly, that the concept of human rights is an attempt to produce, through the state, a conception of the human that can take the place of the *swa*.
14 *Akshardeha*, Vol. 10, p. 24, *Hind Swaraj*; *CWMG*, Vol. 10, p. 257.
15 *Akshardeha*, Vol. 10, p. 25, *Hind Swaraj*; *CWMG*, Vol. 10, p. 257.
16 *Akshardeha*, Vol. 10, p. 28, *Hind Swaraj*; *CWMG*, Vol. 10, p. 261. The reference to the people is missing in the English version: 'Parliaments are really emblems of slavery.'
17 While the word *thekaana* is never used to describe the *veshya*, there are some indicators that such an extension of the word would not be violent. For example, 'steadfast' is Gandhi's translation of *thekaaneysar*; and in the citation above, the word 'steady' is from Gandhi's translation.
18 *Akshardeha*, Vol. 10, p. 24, 25 *Hind Swaraj*; *CWMG*, Vol. 10, pp. 256, 257. I will return below to the severely abridged version of this passage in the English version.
19 *Akshardeha*, Vol. 10, p. 23, *Hind Swaraj*; *CWMG*, Vol. 10, p. 256.
20 This is not to deny the significant differences between Gandhi's mother and the restrained mother invoked in the mainstream nationalism of *ankush*. The latter needed protection from the English, and was pre-social; she could become active and social only under the productive restraint of the people. Gandhi's mother, in contrast, has a *thekaana* and brings things to their proper places. This mother does not allow her sons to constitute her as pre-social, and plays a much more active role in Gandhian politics than in mainstream nationalism. Sociologically, there can be little doubt that the mother thought in this Gandhian produced a space for considerable participation by women – within, of course, sharply delimited roles – in the nationalist movement.
21 *Akshardeha*, Vol. 10, pp. 24, 25 *Hind Swaraj*; *CWMG*, Vol. 10, p. 255. Gandhi's translation of this is: 'It is like a prostitute because it is under the control of ministers who change from time to time. Today it is under Mr. Asquith, tommorow it may be under Mr. Balfour.'
22 The fear of *veshya's* mobility was surely related to Gandhi's fears of a promiscuous sexuality (which for the Gandhi of *thekaana* as control would have been any sexuality other than that of the celibate *brahmachari*, or at most the husband in a purely procreative relation with the wife). How this sexuality was outside the *dhani's* control and enslaved him, how it could mock and humiliate the *dhani* – these are recurrent themes in Gandhi's discussions of the 'occasions' when he 'went' or was 'taken to' a *veshya*. See, for example, his *Autobiography*, *CWMG*, V44, p. 108; also his account in Navjivan, 17.5.1925, *CWMG*, Vol. 31, p. 348.
23 Note how even here, the *veshya* is a symbol for the violence that the weak masters practise on themselves. It is they who cannot stay at their *thekaana*, and who keep the *veshya* by entering into this exchange. Wandering away from their *thekaana*, giving themselves in this equivalence, they practise a violence on themselves, and enslave themselves. This is why 'these parliaments are a mark of the slavery of the people'.
24 *CWMG*, Vol. 10, p. 257; cf. note 15.
25 *Akshardeha*, Vol. 10, p. 31, *Hind Swaraj*; *CWMG*, Vol. 10, p. 266. The Gujarati expression is: *namard, bayala* (from *bai* – woman) *aney bheeru*.

26 The Gujarati phrase is *nabada manasney theek kamno chhe* – is of good use to weak people. A cognate of *nabada*, recall, is *abada* – the word used also to refer to women.
27 *Akshardeha*, Vol. 10, p. 53, *Hind Swaraj*; *CWMG*, Vol. 10, p. 294. Gandhi's translation of this is quite different: Physical-force men are strangers to the courage that is requisite in a passive resister. Do you believe that a coward can ever disobey a law that he dislikes'?
28 *Akshardeha*, Vol. 10, p. 25, *Hind Swaraj*, Chapter 7; *CWMG*, Vol. 10, p. 258. Gandhi's translation of this is: 'pluck out his eyes'.
29 *Akshardeha*, Vol. 10, p. 29, *Hind Swaraj*, Chapter 7; *CWMG*, Vol. 10, p. 263.
30 Both this revisionist formulation and most criticism of it is conducted within the problematic of agency. By insisting that the colonized participated in their own colonization, by insisting on the miscibility of colonialism with both a pre-colonial past and with the colonized, the wound of colonialism is naturalized and denied, and colonialism is made an extension of what preceded it. (This mitigation of colonial domination, stressing as it does the agency of the colonized, has also found enthusiasts in a liberalizing middle-class India looking for a prehistory to Indian agency.) And many of those who attack such revisionist formulations understand the wound of colonialism as a loss of agency – which, as I shall be suggesting, is not Gandhi's argument.
31 *Akshardeha*, Vol 10, p. 32, *Hind Swaraj*, chapter 9; *CWMG*, Vol. 10, p. 267.
32 *Akshardeha*, Vol 10, p. 33, *Hind Swaraj*, chapter 9; *CWMG*, Vol. 10, p. 268. In this passage, the English text has 'us' where the Gujarati text has 'you'.
33 Gandhi was hostile to the idea of both women and Dalits undertaking satya-grahas against their subordination; he tried rather to bring about reforms amongst the dominant to redress their problems.
34 I discuss Gandhi's category of obligation in 'A politics without measure', forthcoming in Manu Bhagwan (ed.) *The Dynamics of Diversity: Nationalism and the Politics of Identity in South Asia*, edited volume under preparation.
35 The first occurs in the description of the *veshya*: 'And it is a *veshya* because which(ever) ministry keeps [*raakhey*] it, it stays with [*paasey tey rahey*] that ministry.' The second occurs in the description of how the British stay in India ('Just as we gave [it] to them, so do we let Hindustan stay with [*paasey raheva daiye*] them').

Bibliography

Gandhi, M.K., *Collected Works of Mahatma Gandhi*, Delhi: Publications Division, Ministry of Information and Broadcasting, 1958, 2nd edition.
—— *Akshardeha* [Collected Works in Gujarati], Ahmedabad: Navjivan Press,
Skaria, Ajay, 'A politics without measure', in Manu Bhagavan (ed.) *The Dynamics of Diversity: Nationalism and the Politics of Identity in South Asia*, edited volume under preparation.

Part III
Carrying Gandhi over
Global peace movements

Part III

8 Globalising Gandhi
Translation, reinvention, application, transformation

Sean Scalmer

For Gandhi, nonviolence was a universal aspiration.[1] Gandhi's Western interpreters also embraced this view,[2] and in the half-century since the Mahatma's passing, 'Gandhism' has enjoyed international influence. Indeed, Gandhi's methods have been applied by civil-rights campaigners in the US, pacifists in Britain, environmentalists in Australia, human shields in Iraq and peace brigades around the world.

In this chapter, I ask two questions. First, how, precisely, were Gandhi's methods exported? Who organised such diffusion? What did they do? What were the conditions that allowed them to do it? Second, what happened to the teachings of Gandhi in the process? Did they remain unchanged? Or were they transformed? Should the actions of Gandhi's disciples be understood as 'Gandhian'? As 'Gandhism'? Or did they stray too far from the master's path to merit such a designation?

These questions have long been ignored. 'Gandhian' scholars have often been more concerned to explore the particularity of the Mahatma's contribution than the breadth of his impact. Students of 'globalisation', for their part, have tended to adopt a Eurocentric viewpoint,[3] in which transnational flows from East to West have passed unexamined. As a result, the global impact of Gandhism has not received due consideration.

How should the globalisation of Gandhi's methods be understood? In the quest to find an answer, this chapter combines a case-study methodology, an historical approach and a theoretical perspective influenced by social-movement studies. First, I explore the global diffusion of Gandhi's methods through the detailed examination of a particular case: the nonviolent activism of British pacifists. The case-study method is well established in the social sciences, but why Britain? Beginning with Harold Steele's 1957 attempt to disrupt nuclear tests in the Pacific Ocean, British pacifists gained international celebrity with their adoption of 'direct action' techniques against nuclear weaponry. In 1958 the Easter march to the Aldermaston nuclear reactor helped give birth to a distinctive 'New Left'.[4] By 1960 the Committee of 100 was using civil disobedience in central London, and thereby helping to create a new era of 'independent social protest'.[5] Together, these activists developed a different kind of social movement for the West: theatrical, nonviolent, network-based, outside of the Party system.

This movement owed much to Gandhi. Although they eventually attracted a broad following, the first campaigns were led by a group of pacifists *directly inspired* by Gandhi's example. Key participants and subsequent histories have since emphasised the seminal importance of Gandhi's distinctive methods and career.[6] The export of nonviolence to Britain therefore offers a valuable opportunity to trace the diffusion and application of Gandhi's methods outside India. It should open a wider window on the general processes through which Gandhism has become a 'global' political presence.

On what evidence is this exploration based? My account draws on detailed primary research: India Office records; archival material from relevant organisations and individuals (including detailed institutional records and letters); contemporary newspapers, pamphlets and journals; campaign ephemera and published books.

What kinds of concepts does my explanation rest upon? Theoretically, this chapter applies and extends recent work in the study of social movements. In the last ten years, social-movement scholars have begun to investigate the diffusion of collective action across national boundaries. Briefly, they have emphasised two processes of particular relevance: translation and reinvention. First, a political technique must be *translated* before it can be transmitted.[7] An alien and foreign behaviour must become comprehensible. It must be restated in the local idiom. Translators attempt to rephrase the language of protest. They foster a sense of kinship and identification across national boundaries.[8] Their work makes the unknown familiar and thereby the unfamiliar possible.

Second, foreign political techniques are not simply copied. They are actually *reinvented*.[9] Local campaigners tinker and experiment with the tools that they have taken from overseas.[10] They improvise with the elements of a new performance, and remake its political rhythms. Invariably, discoveries occur. Therefore, diffusion is never imitation. It is a creative, difficult, and exploratory act. In the pages that follow, I explain the diffusion of Gandhism to Britain, focusing on the particular importance of translation and reinvention.

Translation

What was happening in India? What was Gandhi doing? The censorship of Indian newspapers made it difficult for Westerners to find out.[11] Gandhi's own writings offered one important source[12] and his public appearances in Britain another.[13] Both were insufficient. Western audiences were often unconvinced by Gandhi's oratorical style,[14] and his publications were sometimes hard to locate.[15] In 1946 one British pacifist surveyed the local situation: Gandhi's autobiography and central writings had been read by 'surprisingly few'; key commentaries were out of print or had 'curiously little impact'; Gandhi's newspaper, *Harijan*, could be considered only a 'negligible' influence. In sum:

> To say that Gandhi is available in English is an overstatement ... The British pacifist movement has no deep insight into the Gandhian approach; it has made no systematic study of his actual campaigns, and still less has it understood the thought and vision that inspired them.[16]

Not surprisingly, when Gandhi's example was contemplated during these years, it was invariably misquoted or misunderstood. As Richard Fox has recently argued, Gandhian protest was typically mistranslated through either the distorting lens of 'Orientialist hyper-difference' or the shallow framework of 'Western over-likeness'.[17] 'Hyper-difference' posited a great gulf between the Indian and the British. It suggested that the differences between the Mahatma and John Bull were so substantial that a British version of 'Satyagraha'[18] would be frankly impossible.

This version of 'Gandhism' was most associated with the translation of Gandhi's critics. It drew upon a wealth of 'orientalist' images. According to such an account, Gandhi was a representative of 'Oriental reaction'.[19] His personality was 'framed to baffle the Western mind'.[20] Gandhi's methods were based on the 'the mystic faith of the East', or the 'instinctive Buddhism of the East'.[21] They expressed the primacy of 'feeling and the emotions'.[22] The British were different, because their political system was apparently based on 'reason'.[23] As a result, they had nothing to learn from this 'strange little brown man'.[24]

Conversely, 'over-likeness' exaggerated the commonalities between the Indian and the British. This kind of translation was most associated with co-campaigners, anxious to build support for the struggle of Indians, but not deeply informed about its precise characteristics. This rendering emphasised Gandhi's status as a religious figure. Gandhi was a 'great saint',[25] perhaps the 'Greatest Christian today'.[26] His lessons embodied 'the spirit of Christ'.[27] The Gandhian approach represented 'the method of the Cross',[28] or 'the New Testament method against evil'.[29] Put simply, Satyagraha was a 'Christian thing'.[30] Understood in these terms, Gandhi's techniques lost their distinctiveness. They offered nothing more than the simple message of the carpenter from Galilee. As a result, there was no need to contemplate their direct application in Britain. Christian pacifists were already tilling this ground.

These misunderstandings continued to circulate in the public sphere for many decades. They were only corrected in the years after the Second World War. At this time, Britain's largest pacifist organisation, the Peace Pledge Union (PPU), became a hotbed of Gandhian discourse. Between 1946 and 1952 the PPU's newspaper, *Peace News*, published more than 160 articles that were dedicated to the discussion of Gandhi's relevance to the West.[31]

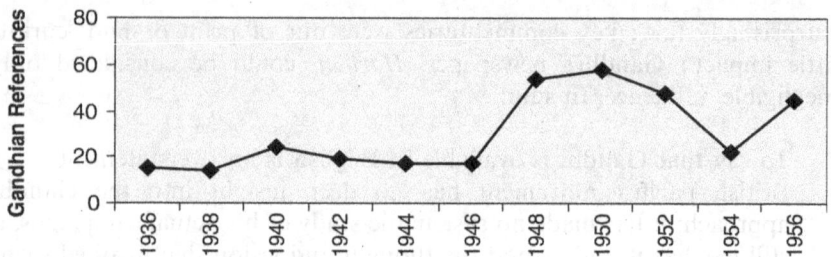

Figure 8.1 Number of Ghandian references.

Perhaps more importantly, the PPU also carved out a special space for the close study of nonviolence. It formed a 'Nonviolence Commission' in November 1949.[32] From January 1950, the Commission met regularly at Dick Sheppard House in London.[33] Here hopeful students struggled to come to grips with Gandhi's methods. As Kathleen Rawlins, a leading member, explained, they 'were not trying to teach the PPU nonviolence'. On the contrary, 'accepting one emphasis of the whole pacifist movement', they were 'trying to explore that particular aspect of pacifism'.[34] Gwyneth Anderson, another member, explained that the Commission focused on 'study' and 'self-training'. The object was ' ... "direct action" – that is action directed, however feebly, to the real demands of the situation'.[35]

To this end, bookish pacifists shared epigrams and swapped their cribbed notes. A 'travelling file' was compiled for those unable to attend meetings regularly,[36] made up of letters, suggestions, and newspaper cuttings.[37] Those who could make the trek to central London became entranced by the Mahatma. They studied and reported on Gandhi's nonviolent campaigns, and diligently sought to immerse themselves in the literature of the subject.[38] Over a number of years, the knowledge of Commission members began to grow. Slowly, they began to translate Gandhi's methods into the British environment.

Importantly, this translation always emphasised the practical application of Gandhi's ideas. Throughout the first two years of its existence, it was a common practice of the Nonviolence Commission to invite speakers 'who ha[d] taken part in nonviolence demonstrations' to share their experience and wisdom.[39] A core of around fifty members heard friends of Gandhi, such as Henry Polak and Mary Barr.[40] They listened eagerly to veterans of the passive resistance movement in South Africa, and African-American adherents of the nonviolent method.[41] Vera Brittain recalled her time with Gandhi's successors at the World Pacifist Meeting in India, and Welsh nationalists excitedly relayed their first embrace of nonviolent demonstrations.[42] The Commission became a site of 'brokerage', as proponents of Gandhism traded ideas and histories.[43]

Leaders of the Nonviolence Commission stressed that their task was to investigate the question of civil disobedience in particular.[44] As a result, the Commission soon developed into a forum for the discussion of schemes for direct action,[45] and fresh ideas for nonviolent protest, like organised income-tax refusal.[46] Indeed, this functional group rapidly became what sociologists call an 'abeyance structure', or a 'submerged network' – a place of shared critical discourse, in which the flame of future rebellion is sheltered and fuelled.[47]

'Submerged networks' are primarily places of discussion rather than action. In the case of the Nonviolence Commission, this was true for only a brief time, however. In the early 1950s the political opportunities open to pacifists began, ever slightly, to improve. The British Government's new testing of atomic weapons horrified many of those who had supported the Second World War.[48] 'Z Reservists' were called up for army service, and widespread opposition energised the peace movement.[49] At the same time, the left of the Labour Party tilted towards peace, with Aneurin Bevan's resignation over the Government's military expenditure.[50]

It was amid these events that some members of the Nonviolence Commission began to grow impatient with all the talk, and to wonder how it could ever be transformed into action. Ethel A. Lewis, the secretary of the Commission, captured the sentiment best in a letter to Kathleen Rawlins:

> I really feel that it is rather useless to merely meet pleasantly at intervals, to talk – waiting vaguely for the day when it might be useful to lay down in the road to demonstrate agst. [sic] 'something or other'.
>
> I may be wrong, but feel that if the members only joined – say – in a leaflet campaign, at least we should be doing something useful. I deplore this (to me) rather negative attitude, this detached position at which we appear to have arrived.
>
> I should be glad of your reactions to the matter, if you drop me a line, please.[51]

Ethel Lewis did not have long to wait. With the 'translation' of Gandhism well under way, a new phase of experiment and reinvention was about to unfold.

Reinvention

Once Gandhi's methods were more fully appreciated, how could they be applied? From the early 1930s, British pacifists had ventured a number of proposals. Among the most notable: pacifists should invade the 'drawing-rooms' of the authorities with the force of 'passive aggression', and demand signatures on a peace agenda;[52] a mass hunger-strike of PPU members should be used to compel disarmament;[53] nonviolent volunteers should travel to the continent as tourists and thence offer nonviolent resistance against dictatorship;[54] and a peace plough should make its way across the iron curtain and into Poland.[55] However, these plans remained hopelessly vague. It was only in December 1951 that a more detailed proposal for

Gandhian action was put forward. At a meeting of the Nonviolence Commission, a new political experiment, 'Operation Gandhi', was first ventured.

What was Operation Gandhi? As first imagined, it was a programme of direct action – a 'nonviolent struggle' for Britain. It had four aims:

1. The removal of American forces from Britain;
2. The abandonment of atomic weapons manufacture in Britain;
3. The withdrawal of Britain from the North Atlantic Treaty Organisation;
4. The disbandment of the British armed forces.

The architect of Operation Gandhi was the assistant-editor of *Peace News*, Hugh Brock. He argued that those taking part in Operation Gandhi had to be willing to face imprisonment, loss of income and other hardships.[56] Somewhat surprisingly, Brock's suggestions were embraced. Those who listened quickly agreed to undertake the project, to meet within the week, and to begin detailed planning.[57]

But what, precisely, would British Gandhians do? How would they protest? Brock himself had been very short on detail, arguing only that, ' A press sub-committee should be formed, and an operations sub-committee should arrange the mechanics and timetable for demonstration.'[58] Once 'the Operation' met, a wild divergence among would-be demonstrators quickly became apparent. Surviving archival material indicates a range of actions were entertained – protests at Grosvenor Square, Fleet Street, Whitehall, and at suburban Labour Exchanges, among others.[59] Three schemes were more seriously contemplated.

The first was an invasion of the House of Commons:

> Select evening session when appropriate matter is being discussed – trickle one by one to Central Lobby and ask to see our M.P.
>
> No given time (no signal), – as team squats in the passage from the Chamber to the Lobby, produce and display posters – and perhaps sing appropriate hymns.
>
> Remainder to act as observers only.
>
> When, if, first group ejected, and after short interlude for order to be restored, next group take up position and proceed as before. Meantime a further group – perhaps number of further groups, will arrive at House, by bus – having previously timed journey from a number of surrounding fire-off points – and will come into Lobby seeking M.P.s – and then follow as before ...
>
> Police to be told only that Operation Gandhi will visit on that particular evening.[60]

A second visualised a similar kind of shocking display, to be staged in a popular London church:

> Attend morning service and take part fully in it. At end of service squat in main exit, display appropriate posters, singing suitable hymns, handing out leaflets.
> Leaflet distributors in vicinity to go into action (well dispersed beforehand) when they see congregation begin to emerge.[61]

At the same time, Alex Comfort suggested a supplementary plan for agit-prop, entitled 'Umbrella Man', which involved theatrical displays of umbrellas, stickers and pickets all over London.[62]

As forms of political gimmick or media display, none of these schemes could be faulted.[63] However, their specifically Gandhian credentials were more seriously questionable. Although Hugh Brock praised the Umbrella Man scheme,[64] others were less easily impressed. A leading member of the Nonviolence Commission, Gwyneth Anderson, was highly suspicious of Alex Comfort, and counselled wariness.[65] Kathleen Rawlins also raised a number of concerns. First, she worried about the participation of communists – 'already working for the same objectives and by different means'.[66] Second, she emphasised that 'public opinion' was in favour of defence, security, and the fearful grinding of the war machine. As a result, any action needed to be accompanied by a 'simple leaflet', outlining the methods and aims of the protesters.[67] Others agreed, and the original plans presented by Brock were now considerably altered. The four initial objectives of 'Operation Gandhi' were quietly dropped.[68] Quickly, the drafting of the inaugural Operation Gandhi leaflet began.

The drafting of a common leaflet rapidly became a gigantic exercise in consensus-formation. In meeting after meeting, there was deep philosophical and practical discussion.[69] An unpublished, unattributed history of the early days of the group remembers the process well:

> Meetings ... were stepped up to about twice a week with daily consultation between the four or five members who were drawing up the leaflet which would be distributed during the demonstration.
> Whole evenings were given up to the discussion of the leaflet and planning of the timetable of the action. A draft idea ... by Kathleen Rawlins was remoulded by Alex Comfort. The renovated draft was cut to pieces by Kathleen and criticised by everybody else. One sentence would be upheld by some members of the group and objected to by others. The printer had to reset almost half the leaflet after we had given him what we thought was a final draft.[70]

What did these excited pacifists hope to communicate of 'Operation Gandhi'? Kathleen Rawlins' initial contribution established the first answer. As she saw it, the leaflet could only properly arouse one emotion. That emotion should be *shame*. 'Every Englishman' needed to be shamed out of quiescence and into the streets:

THIS IS THE MOMENT OF YOUR RESPONSIBILITY.
   If the decision is taken to use these weapons, your consent and mine will not be asked.
   IF WE ARE SILENT NOW WE HAVE GIVEN OUR CONSENT TO THEIR USE.[71]

Suffering and shame are frequent bedfellows. For Rawlins, the willingness of pacifists to suffer also needed emphasis:

   We try to ACT on the teaching of Jesus and Gandhi that men must be willing to suffer but not to hate or hurt each other.[72]

Such suffering served a practical purpose – it allowed for the conversion of others. Suffering produced shame in the observer, and therefore change:

   If we are arrested, we shall not pay fines! If we are imprisoned we shall be thankful, because our imprisonment may win YOUR understanding and support for the cause.[73]

The likeness to the concept of 'moral jujitsu' developed in Richard Gregg's *Power of Nonviolence* is easy to detect.[74] British Gandhians were on their own distinctive journey though. As Rawlins' initial draft was reread and remade, so a new consensus around a British version of Gandhism was hammered into shape. The drafting and redrafting of the leaflet produced a more sensitive and collective sense of Gandhism than had existed before.

By early January, agreement had been reached. Operation Gandhi came to agree on the essence of Gandhism-in-action. For this small, now-united group, it lay in the *making of an appeal to conscience*. The 'conscience of the British people' became the group's fundamental target.[75] This was an ethical appeal. As such, it required high ethical standards among the protesters. Members of the 'Operation Gandhi' experiment now came to agree that three elements of 'Gandhi's method' were therefore crucial:

1. Open strategies of organisation, with preliminary notification of any protest actions given to police and official authorities.
2. Complete personal nonviolence of behaviour.
3. Willingness to accept legal penalties for action 'knowing that the suffering of these penalties is our best means of persuasion'.[76]

As a result, the schemes for the House of Commons and church invasion were now rejected. So was a plan for pacifists to form a bus queue near the War Office in Central London, only sprinting into a sit-down position when Big Ben struck twelve.[77]

At the same time, the group's four original aims became one. A new coherence was evident:

> Operation Gandhi is a group of pacifists who want to secure the acceptance by the people of Britain of nonviolent resistance as the right and honourable course for the defence of their country.
> That is our specific objective.[78]

The first practical demonstration was organised soon afterwards, in January 1952. This protest adhered to all of the group's new wisdom. Eleven members of Operation Gandhi squatted on the steps of the War Office in London. Police were fully notified. Participants did not resist arrest, and they pled guilty to charges of obstruction and obstructing police. Complete nonviolence was evident in both word and deed.[79] Further actions followed rapidly. The newly drafted leaflet drew praise from non-participants,[80] and the confidence and energy of members lifted appreciably.[81] Similar protests were held at the Aldermaston nuclear reactor,[82] the U.S. base at Mildenhall Aerodrome,[83] the Porton microbiological research facility,[84] and Harwell atomic energy plant,[85] among many others. With its name changed to the 'Nonviolent Resistance Group',[86] the same basic cluster of activists expressed demonstrative support for the passive resistance movement in South Africa,[87] and took Gandhian performances to regional centres like Ilford and Colchester.[88] Suddenly, the wide-ranging use of 'Gandhism' seemed possible.

Application and transformation

'Operation Gandhi' brought disciplined nonviolent protest to Britain. Soon, however, unaffiliated citizens were also applying Gandhi's methods in new and idiosyncratic ways. Individuals started lone pickets of army bases,[89] 'war' movies such as *The Dam Busters*,[90] military tattoos,[91] and civil-defence displays.[92] One pacifist refused to pay her dog licence as a protest against the Government's war policy;[93] another walked through England and Wales in a Gandhian attempt to raise funds for Indian villages.[94] In 1956 Ipswich pacifists even began to adopt nonviolence in an attempt to break down local forms of racial segregation.[95]

By the later 1950s, the application of nonviolence was extending even further. As alarm about nuclear weapons spread widely, so Gandhi's political tools beckoned in the battle for peace. Harold Steele visited the 'Gandhi Shrine' on his way to stop nuclear testing at Christmas Island.[96] In late 1957, veterans of Operation Gandhi joined up with younger radicals to form the 'Direct Action Committee Against Nuclear War' (DAC).[97] The new organisation led nonviolent protests at rocket bases and military installations around the UK, including Swaffham, Harrington, Foulness, Finingley, and Holy Loch.[98]

Perhaps more importantly, it was also the DAC that proposed the first anti-nuclear march to the Aldermaston nuclear reactor, just outside London.[99] The Aldermaston march was rapidly backed by a larger and more moderate institution, the Campaign for Nuclear Disarmament (CND). In 1958 it was baptised with success.

From its first steps, the Aldermaston march attracted the previously apolitical.[100] A peak of six thousand participated in the original march.[101] Students mixed with bank clerks; West Indians with Welshmen.[102] This was widely seen as a 'new development' in contemporary politics.[103] Marchers were entertained by skiffle-groups and dancers; they dressed in bright scarves and beribboned hats.[104] Their 'calm and sober bearing' put onlookers to silence.[105] As Mervyn Jones noted, this was an event animated by a peaceful, loving, and dissenting spirit:

> [T]his is a campaign that urges people to reflect, not to destroy; to march a silent mile, not to shout; to dissent, not to obey; to be themselves, not to take sides; to love, not to hate; to live and let others live, not to kill or die.[106]

Jones was sure that the march was different to 'any other demonstration I have known'. In 1959 it attracted even greater numbers. This time the march set out from Aldermaston and terminated in London. At least 30,000 gathered in Trafalgar Square.[107] By the early 1960s, it was clear that Aldermaston was a major event. Some socialists admitted that it now outranked May Day.[108] A year later, it was openly described as an 'annual pilgrimage'.[109] By 1964 the name 'Aldermaston' suggested a political movement for peace, not a place devoted to the perfection of atomic weapons.[110] Indeed, it had become an important symbol of the presence of a 'New Left' in British cultural and political life.[111]

The growing popularity of Aldermaston expressed the more general acceptance of theatrical and challenging forms of political action. Beginning in 1961, a new organisation, the 'Committee of 100', organised mass civil disobedience in Central London. Whereas the Direct Action Committee had attracted scores, the Committee of 100 quickly attracted hundreds of participants.[112] Its 'sit-down demonstration' of September 1961 brought 12,000 to Trafalgar Square.[113] The political presence of so many dissenters was thought by authorities to signify 'mass resistance',[114] and the 'sit-down' soon became the object of widespread emulation. As the Committee put it in October 1961:

> In the 'sit-down' we have devised a useful tactic, which has already this summer been used by trade unions, Tenant's associations, etc., and in several other countries in issues other than nuclear disarmament.[115]

Nonviolence, it seemed, was 'all the rage'. Writing in the *British Weekly*, Derek Walker contemplated the possibility of 'Satyagraha in St. James Park':

> Satyagraha has not been confined to the East ... In Britain the Committee for Direct Action Against Nuclear War has staged its demonstrations at

rocket bases ... But the technique has also been used with little or no organisation for all kinds of reasons. Passengers in London tube trains staged sit downs in protest against bad service ... The list is probably far longer than even those who are interested in the subject imagine, for I do not think that anyone has yet attempted to draw it up. And to it there could be added several fascinating 'might' have beens.[116]

Walker's designation suggests that these actions were obvious members of the Gandhian family. 'Satyagraha' was, famously, Gandhi's favoured term for nonviolent political action.[117] Others, however, might be less certain. If members of Operation Gandhi had thought their way towards a 'British Gandhism', those who succeeded them typically lacked such experience. As 'nonviolence' spread, so its specifically Gandhian connections were also loosened.

Many new recruits to the campaign against nuclear weapons were unconvinced by the virtues of openness.[118] For them, secrecy was a tactical priority.[119] Some activists wondered whether nonviolent action was sufficiently revolutionary.[120] Others developed plans for 'mass civil disobedience' without a clear understanding of nonviolent traditions. April Carter, a veteran of the Direct Action Committee, noted these developments as early as September 1960:

> This problem is facing us here in England just now with [the] development of move toward mass civil disobedience by a number of individuals who don't believe in n.v. [nonviolence] in Satyagraha terms ... all sorts of ideas have been thrown up and abandoned and the whole thing is an unholy muddle.[121]

True, 'mass' civil disobedience promised to apply Gandhism more widely, and, in Carter's words, 'to break d.a. [direct action] right out of the pacifist "rut"'. But, at the same time, it also involved 'inevitable risks', as a 'small n.v. [nonviolent] movement' became a 'large one'.[122] While the protests of the early 1960s did draw greater numbers, they also diverged with increasing speed from the 'Gandhian' practice of the early 1950s.

The application of 'nonviolence' on a wide scale brought new problems. In a mass movement, tensions arose between the committed Gandhians (who believed in 'total' nonviolence), and the non-pacifists (who understood nonviolence as a 'tactical' expedient).[123] Younger radicals were angered by the violence of police, and began to react against them.[124] There were reports of 'swaying, jeering crowds' that 'shouted insults at police'.[125] New concepts like 'nonviolent pushing'[126] challenged the old philosophy of Satyagraha. Soon, explicitly violent strategies were up for debate. By the middle 1960s, many impatient radicals had set upon a new path:

> We have tried nonviolent civil disobedience and direct action to a point where the law of diminishing returns makes a demonstration almost

more damaging to us than to the state ... *Sabotage* could be the answer. It would indeed mean danger, conspiracy and anonymity, but it would be effective ... The resultant publicity would inevitably create and harden some hostility, but it would also make many more people begin to think about WHY we were doing it, in the same way sabotage by the Suffragettes, the Irish and Africans, led many people first to consider, then to espouse the causes of the saboteurs.[127]

Clearly, this was not nonviolence of any recognisable form. The children of 'Operation Gandhi' had strayed far from their parents. Here, the undulations of British politics connect up with a wider story. Indeed, the history of the Western Left in the 1960s is largely the story of the abandonment of nonviolence for more 'radical', 'revolutionary', and violent poses. The pantheon of the later 1960s was dominated by Che Guevara and Vladimir Illich Lenin; Paris '68 succeeded Aldermaston '58. Ho Chi Minh was preferred to Gandhi. Soon, Satyagraha seemed a creature of the past.

Radical historians have largely shared this view. As a result, the importance of nonviolent activism is only beginning to attain proper attention. Until now, the contribution of Gandhism to the British New Left has never been properly documented. Half a century after such fascinating events, what can we learn from this intriguing attempt to 'globalise' the teachings and methods of Mohandas K. Gandhi?

The globalisation of Gandhi offers many lessons to contemporary students of global and radical politics. First, 'global diffusion' is not at all novel; it greatly predates the 'anti-capital' or 'anti-globalisation' movement of the last few years. Second, the process of global diffusion is not at all automatic,[128] but is actually the outcome of a skilled labour of translation and reinvention. Third, it is a creative process. Gandhism was remade, not copied. Fourth, the 'Gandhism' produced by British pacifists was both portable and malleable. Nonviolence inspired by Gandhi passed across the polity and energised social movements of many kinds. However, this process produced new kinds of collective performance, with only a very limited connection to Satyagraha. If they rested upon a previous history of experiment with nonviolence, their specific form bore little resemblance to the acts of either Gandhi or of 'British Gandhians'. The rub of collective interaction coarsened nonviolent political routines; principles gave way to tactics. As new forms of violence promised excitement and dynamism, the old performances were quickly forgotten.

Does this mean that 'nonviolence' is best practised by small groups of dedicated activists? Or can it become a tool of mass politics? How can the committed possibly work together with the expedient? Can nonviolence be maintained over a cycle of protest, or is it inevitably displaced by the throb of collective passions? These were questions faced by Gandhi eight decades ago.[129] They remain to trouble, to confound, and to push us toward our own experiments today.

Notes

1 Gandhi's claim that Satyagraha was a universal force is reflected in Raghavan Iyer (ed.), *Moral and Political Writings of Mahatma Gandhi*, vol. 3, Oxford: Clarendon Press, 1987, p. 70. This claim was repeated to British audiences and reported in: n.a., 'Concerning the Fellowship', *Reconciliation*, vol. 9, no. 10, 1931, p. 445 and Hilda Clark, 'The Month in Retrospect', *New World*, vol. 2, no. 6, 1931, p. 3.
2 The most famous interpreters are: Richard Gregg, *The Power of Nonviolence*, second edn, London: J. Clarke, 1960, and Gene Sharp, *The Politics of Nonviolent Action*, Boston: Porter Sargent Publishers, 1973.
3 This is noted by: Sean Chabot and J.W. Duyvendak, 'Globalization and Transnational Diffusion between Social Movements', *Theory and Society*, 31, 2002, pp. 697–740.
4 On the history of the New Left, see Michael Kenny, *The First New Left: British Intellectuals After Stalin*, London: Lawrence and Wishart, 1995.
5 Michael Hanagan, 'Social Movements: Incorporation, Disengagement, and Opportunities – A Long View', in Marco G. Giugini, Doug McAdam and Charles Tilly (eds), *From Contention to Democracy*, Lanham and Oxford: Rowman and Littlefield, 1999, p. 25.
6 See, for example, Michael Randle, 'Nonviolent Direct Action in the 1950s and 1960s', in Richard Taylor and Nigel Young (eds), *Campaigns for Peace: British peace movements in the twentieth century*, Manchester: Manchester University Press, 1987; Richard Taylor and Kevin Ward, 'Community Politics and Direct Action: the non-aligned Left', in David Coates and Gordon Johnston (eds), *Socialist Strategies*, Oxford: Martin Robertson, 1983; Peter Brock and Nigel Young, *Pacifism in the Twentieth Century*, Syracuse, NY: Syracuse University Press, 1999.
7 Sean Scalmer, 'Translating Contention: Culture, History, and the Circulation of Collective Action', *Alternatives*, vol. 25, 2000, pp. 491–514.
8 David A. Snow and Robert D. Benford, 'Alternative Types of Cross-National Diffusion in the Social Movement Arena', in Donatella della Porta, Hanspeter Kriesi and Dieter Rucht (eds), *Social Movements in a Globalizing World*, London: Macmillan, 1999, pp. 23–39; Doug McAdam, '"Initiator" and "Spin-Off" Movements: Diffusion Processes in Protest Cycles', in Mark Traugott (ed.), *Repertoires and Cycles of Collective Action*, Durham, NC: Duke University Press, 1995, pp. 217–39.
9 Sean Chabot, 'Transnational Diffusion and the African-American Reinvention of the Gandhian Repertoire', *Mobilization: An International Journal*, vol. 5, 2000, pp. 201–16.
10 Sean Scalmer, 'The Labour of Diffusion: The Peace Pledge Union and the Adaptation of the Gandhian Repertoire', *Mobilization: An International Journal*, vol. 7, 2002, pp. 269–86.
11 Stephen Hobhouse, 'India's Message to the World', *Peace News*, 7/2/41, p. 2.
12 H.N. Brailsford, 'Saint Gandhi', *New Statesman and Nation*, 12 May 1951, pp. 540–41.
13 n.a., 'Concerning the Fellowship', *Reconciliation*, vol. 9, no. 12, December 1931, p. 485.
14 This is registered in n.a., 'Concerning the Fellowship', *Reconciliation*, vol. 9, no. 10, October 1931, p. 445.
15 The slowness of the shipment of Gandhi's publication *Harijan* is lamented in: n.a., 'The Current of Affairs', *The Christian Pacifist*, no. 3, March 1942, p. 43.
16 Roy Walker, 'Reflections on Nonviolence (1)', *The Christian Pacifist*, no. 49, January 1946, pp. 747–48.

17 Richard G. Fox, 'Passage from India', in Richard G. Fox and Orin Starn (eds), *Between Resistance and Revolution: Cultural Politics and Social Protest*, New Brunswick, New Jersey: Rutgers University Press, 1997, pp. 65–82. Fox focuses on the translation of Gandhi's concepts to the USA, but his concepts are still useful for students of British pacifism.
18 The term 'Satyagraha' was coined (in a competition organised by Gandhi) as an alternative to 'passive resistance'. It has been variously rendered in English as 'soul force', 'holding fast to truth', nonviolent resistance, and nonviolent direct action.
19 C.M. MacInnes, *The British Commonwealth and its Unsolved Problems*, London: Longmans, Green and Co., 1925, p. 124.
20 n.a., 'The Problem of Mr. Gandhi', *Nation and Athenaeum*, 18 February 1922, p. 746.
21 J.F.C. Fuller, *India in Revolt*, London: Eyre and Spottiswoode, 1931, p. 174; n.a. 'The Revolt of Passivity', *Nation and Athenaeum*, 6 August 1921, p. 670.
22 Glorney Bolton, *The Tragedy of Gandhi*, London: George Allen and Unwin, 1934, p. 15.
23 Ibid.
24 It should be noted that Fisher was critical of this view. See Frederick Bohn Fisher, *That Strange Little Brown Man Gandhi*, New York: R. Long and R,R. Smith, 1932.
25 A.K. Jameson, 'Gandhi's Early Years', *Peace News*, 15/12/50, p. 5.
26 n.a., 'Gandhi – "Greatest Christian"', *Peace News*, 1/5/37, p. 5.
27 E. Stanley Jones, *Mahatma Gandhi: An Interpretation*. London: Hodder and Staughton, 1948, p. 12.
28 John Hoyland, 'Gandhi's Message for the West', *Peace News*, 28/4/50, p. 3.
29 John Hoyland, *Gandhi: The Practical Peace Builder*. London: Peace Pledge Union, 1952, p. 7.
30 John Hoyland, *The Cross Moves East: A Study of the Significance of Gandhi's 'Satyagraha'*, London: George Allen and Unwin, 1931, p. 111.
31 This figure is based on systematic coding of *Peace News*. For details on the methods and data, see Sean Scalmer, 'The Labour of Diffusion: The Peace Pledge Union and the Adaptation of the Gandhian Repertoire', *Mobilization: An International Journal*, vol. 7, 2002, pp. 269–86.
32 n.a., 'Making the PPU a vital force for peace', *Peace News*, 11/11/49, p. 3. On the numbers attending, see n.a., 'Steps to Peace Conference', *PPU Journal*, no. 44, December 1949, p. 2.
33 n.a., 'Nonviolence group to meet in London', *Peace News*, 16/12/49, p. 8.
34 Kathleen Rawlins, cited in Stuart Morris, 'The Fourteenth AGM', *PPU Journal*, no. 62, June 1951, p. 14.
35 Gwyneth Anderson, 'Training in Nonviolence', *Peace News*, 18/8/50, p. 6.
36 Ethel A. Lewis, 'Report on Nonviolence Commission', *PPU Journal*, no. 60, April 1951, p. 19.
37 Ethel A. Lewis, 'Nonviolence Commission to have Travelling File', *Peace News*, 19/1/51, p. 8.
38 n.a., 'Peacemaking Through Education', *Peace News*, 2/11/51, p. 5.
39 Ibid.
40 On the numbers see Stuart Morris, 'The Fourteenth AGM', *PPU Journal*, no. 62, June 1951, pp. 7–8. On speakers, see Ethel A. Lewis, 'Report on Nonviolence Commission', *PPU Journal*, no. 60, p. 19.
41 Olwen Battersby, 'Work with Africans, not for them', *Peace News*, 17/10/52, p. 6. The impact of Bill Sutherland, an African-American, has been remembered as especially significant in an undated account, 'Operation Gandhi', in Hugh Brock's Papers, *Hugh Brock Papers*, Box 2, Folder 'Operation Gandhi Papers Selected by Hugh Brock', J.B. Priestley Library, University of Bradford.

42 n.a., 'Nonviolence Group', *PPU Journal*, no. 48, April 1950, p. 33; n.a., 'Peacemaking Through Education', *Peace News*, 2/11/51, p. 5.
43 For a theoretical analysis of social-movement diffusion that emphasizes the importance of brokerage, see Doug McAdam, Sidney Tarrow and Charles Tilly, *Dynamics of Contention*, Cambridge and New York: Cambridge University Press, 2001; Sean Chabot and Jan Willem Duyvendak, 'Globalization and transnational diffusion between social movements', *Theory and Society*, Vol. 31 Issue 6, December 2002, pp. 697–740.
44 Stuart Morris, 'The Fourteenth AGM', *PPU Journal*, no. 62, June 1951, pp. 14–15.
45 Gwyneth Anderson, 'Training in Nonviolence', *Peace News*, 18/8/50, p. 6.
46 n.a., 'Nonviolence', *PPU Journal*, no. 47, March 1950, p. 9.
47 For more on these concepts, see Verta Taylor, 'Social Movement Continuity: The Women's Movement in Abeyance', *American Sociological Review*, 1989, 54, pp. 761–75; Colin Barker, 'Empowerment and Resistance: "Collective Effervescence" and Other Accounts', in Paul Bagguley and Jeff Hearn (eds), *Transforming Politics: Power and Resistance*, Basingstoke and London: Macmillan Press, 1999, p. 21.
48 The PPU noted the positive response to its protests against the testing of a British A-Bomb: n.a., 'Britain's A-Bomb – Who Will Drop it?', *Peace News*, 10/10/52, p. 1.
49 n.a., '500 Z-Men Ask: How Do We Become COs?', *Peace News*, 16//51, p. 1; n.a., 'These Z-Men Know What They Want', *Peace News*, 23/2/51, p. 3.
50 The political possibilities for pacifists created by the resignation are noted in Editorial, 'Festival of Arms', *Peace News*, 4/5/51, p. 2.
51 Ethel A. Lewis, Letter to Kathleen Rawlins, n.d., stamped 29/1/51, *Hugh Brock Papers*, Folder: 'Pre-Operation Gandhi', J.B. Priestley Library, University of Bradford.
52 Fredoon Kabraji, 'Fighting by Turning the Other Cheek!', *Peace News*, 8/8/36, p. 4.
53 E. White, 'Strikes and Nonviolent Resistance', *Peace News*, 29/5/37, p. 10.
54 Kingsley Martin, 'The Peace Movement', *New Statesman and Nation*, 4/6/38, p. 946.
55 Hugh Brock, 'Nonviolent Project', *Peace News*, 1/7/49, p. 4.
56 Minutes, 'Nonviolence Commission of the PPU', 12/12/51, *Direct Action Committee and Committee of 100 Papers (April Carter)*, Folder 'PPU Nonviolence Commission', Commonweal Archives, J.B. Priestley Library, University of Bradford.
57 Minutes, 'Nonviolence Commission of the PPU', 12/12/51, *Direct Action Committee and Committee of 100 Papers (April Carter)*, Folder 'PPU Nonviolence Commission', Commonweal Archives, J.B. Priestley Library, University of Bradford.
58 Ibid.
59 A list of these and other sites as points of demonstration is found in Hugh Brock's papers, in three loose pages entitled 'Operation Gandhi', *Hugh Brock Papers*, Box 2, Folder 'Operation Gandhi Papers Selected by Hugh Brock', J.B. Priestley Library, University of Bradford.
60 Operation Gandhi Rejected Scheme – 'House of Commons', *Hugh Brock Papers*, J.B. Priestley Library, University of Bradford, Box 1, J.B. Priestley Library, University of Bradford.
61 'Operation Gandhi 2', *Hugh Brock Papers*, Box 2, Folder 'Operation Gandhi Papers Selected by Hugh Brock', J.B. Priestley Library, University of Bradford.
62 Alex Comfort, 'Umbrella Man', *Hugh Brock Papers*, Box 2, Folder: 'Operation Gandhi Papers Selected by Hugh Brock', J.B. Priestley Library, University of Bradford.

63 For more on the 'political gimmick' and media-attuned protest, see Sean Scalmer, *Dissent Events: protest, media and the political gimmick in Australia*, Sydney: UNSW Press, 2002.
64 Hugh Brock, Letter to Alex Comfort, 29/12/51, *Hugh Brock Papers*, Box 2, Folder: 'Operation Gandhi War Office Demo', J.B. Priestley Library, University of Bradford.
65 Gwyneth Anderson, Letter to Hugh Brock, 2/1/52, *Hugh Brock Papers*, Box 2, Folder, 'Operation Gandhi Papers Selected by Hugh Brock', J.B. Priestley Library, University of Bradford.
66 'Nonviolence Commission of the PPU Minutes', 9/1/52, *Direct Action Committee and Committee of 100 Papers (April Carter)*, Folder 'PPU Nonviolence Commission', J.B. Priestley Library, University of Bradford.
67 'Nonviolence Commission of the PPU Minutes', 12/12/51, *Direct Action Committee and Committee of 100 Papers (April Carter)*, Bay F, Folder 'PPU Nonviolence Commission', J.B. Priestley Library, University of Bradford.
68 The change to Brock's original plan is conceded in 'Nonviolence Commission of the PPU Minutes', 9/1/52, *Direct Action Committee and Committee of 100 Papers (April Carter)*, Folder 'PPU Nonviolence Commission', J.B. Priestley Library, University of Bradford.
69 Hugh Brock, Letter to Alex Comfort, 29/12/51, *Hugh Brock Papers*, Box 2, Folder 'Operation Gandhi War Office Demo', J.B. Priestley Library, University of Bradford.
70 n.a., 'Operation Gandhi', n.d., *Hugh Brock Papers*, Box 2, Folder 'Operation Gandhi Papers Selected by Hugh Brock', J.B. Priestley Library, University of Bradford.
71 Kathleen Rawlins, Letter to Hugh Brock, 19/12/51. The letter contains a draft of the leaflet.
72 Ibid.
73 Ibid.
74 Richard Gregg, *The Power of Nonviolence*, second edn, London: J. Clarke, 1960.
75 This is reflected in the text of the leaflet: '"Operation Gandhi – a call to you"', *PN*, 18/1/52, p. 3.
76 n.a., 'Pacifists Told Police and War Office: "We are Coming to Squat"', *PN*, 18/1/52, p. 1.
77 n.a., 'Operation Gandhi', n.d., *Hugh Brock Papers*, Box 2, Folder 'Operation Gandhi Papers Selected by Hugh Brock', J.B. Priestley Library, University of Bradford.
78 *Operation Gandhi Newsletter*, no. 1, p. 1.
79 n.a., 'Pacifists Told Police and War Office: "We are Coming to Squat"', *PN*, 18/1/52, p. 1.
80 Dorothy Glaister, Letter to Hugh Brock, 21/1/52, *Hugh Brock Papers*, Box 1, J.B. Priestley Library, University of Bradford.
81 Bill Lowe, 'Operation Gandhi', *PN*, 25/1/52, p. 4.
82 n.a., 'To Protest against A-Bomb', *PN*, 21/3/52, p. 8; n.a., 'Demonstration at Atom Plant', *PN*, 2/10/53, p. 1.
83 n.a., 'Armed Guards Turn Out for Pacifists', *PN*, 4/7/52, p. 5.
84 n.a., 'Coming Events', *PN*, 5/3/54, p. 6.
85 *Peace News* reporter, 'Protest at Atom Plant', *PN*, 24/4/53, p. 1 and p. 6.
86 The change did not reflect a growing distance from Gandhi, but the belief of Gandhi's family and closest friends that his name should not be associated directly with *any* political organisation.
87 *Peace News* reporter, 'Pacifists Demonstrate at S. Africa House', *PN*, 3/10/52, p. 4.
88 n.a., 'Colchester Hears the Pacifist Case', *PN*, 29/10/54, p. 6.
89 Sam Walsh, 'He marches to the barracks twice a week', *PN*, 30/10/53, p. 3.

90 Hugh Brock, 'From the Editor's Notebook', *PN*, 23/9/55, p. 3.
91 n.a., "Tattoo Protest Committee Formed in Leeds", *PN*, 4/6/54. p. 3.
92 n.a., 'Councillor Leads H-Bomb Demonstration in Salisbury', *PN*, 16/7/54, p. 5.
93 n.a., 'Rising Protests on H-Bomb Tests', *Peace News*, 26/10/56, p. 8.
94 n.a., 'Walking Through Britain to Help India', *Peace News*, 1/6/56, p. 1.
95 Martin Jackson, 'Ipswich Unites to End Discrimination', *Peace News*, 17/2/56, pp. 1–2; n.a., 'Rally at Ipswich', *Peace News*, 24/2/56, p. 6.
96 n.a., 'Harold Steele: Why I am going to the Pacific', *Peace News*, 17/5/57, p. 7.
97 Hugh Brock and Michael Randle, both veterans of Operation Gandhi, were the driving forces (together with April Carter and Pat Arrowsmith) behind the DAC.
98 'Demonstration at Swaffham Today', *Times*, 29/12/58, p. 4; '73 in custody after rocket base protest', *Times*, 4/1/60, p. 6; '21 Anti-nuclear Demonstrators Ask for Gaol Instead of Fines', *Times*, 26/4/60, p. 4; '18 People Refuse to be Bound Over', *Times*, 1/8/60, p. 10; 'Boarders Repulsed in Proteus "Battle"', *Times*, 22/5/61, p. 4.
99 From 1959, the march was reversed, so that it took off from Aldermaston and ended in London.
100 Llew Gardiner, 'The March of our Time', *Tribune*, 28 March, 1958, p. 8.
101 This is the conservative estimate of the London *Times*, '"A Wide Alliance" on the March to Aldermaston', *Times*, 5/4/58, p. 6.
102 Llew Gardiner, 'Man, this March – it's Beautiful', *Tribune*, 11 April 1958, p.6.
103 Donald Soper, 'My Faith in the Future', *Tribune*, 11 April 1958, pp. 6–7.
104 Mervyn Jones, 'Stop and Think',*Tribune*, 11 April 1958, p. 7.
105 Claud Coltman, 'The Field of Aldermaston', *Reconciliation*, vol. 35, no. 5, May 1958, p. 90.
106 M. Jones, 'The Time is Short', in Norman MacKenzie (ed.), *Conviction*, London: MacGibbon and Kee, 1958, p. 199.
107 Again, this is a conservative estimate. See '10,000 Marchers in Trafalgar Square', *Times*, 31/3/59, p. 4. There were an estimated 20,000 greeting the marchers.
108 n.a., 'Two Marches', *Solidarity: For Workers' Power* 2, no. 2, 1962, p. 1.
109 Douglas Brewood et al., 'Beyond Counting Arses', *Hannan Committee of 100 Papers*, Box 1, L/100/63/23, Commonweal Archives, J.B. Priestley Library, University of Bradford, p. 4.
110 n.a., 'Easter 1964', *Sanity*, January 1964, p. 6.
111 For example, Aldermaston was frequently discussed in attempts by New Left intellectuals to articulate the new mood, e.g. Editorial, 'Beyond the Bomb', *New Reasoner*, vol. 1, no. 4, Spring 1958, p. 1; Peter Smith, 'The Welfare State', *New Reasoner*, n.n., Summer 1958, p. 114; E.P. Thompson, 'Revolution', in E.P. Thompson (ed.), *Out of Apathy*, London: Stephens and Sons Ltd., 1960, p. 288.
112 The first demonstration attracted 800 – 'Lord Russell's message to demonstrators', *Times*, 1/5/61, p. 6.
113 '1314 arrrests in Trafalgar square disorders', *Times*, 18/9/61, p. 10.
114 This was the description offered by government prosecutors, cited in 'Prison for 32 ... ', *Times*, 13/9/61, p. 5.
115 'Notes on Future of Organisation, 4 October 1961, Folder 'Committee of 100, 1961' *Hannan Committee 100 Archives*, Box 1, Commonweal Archives, J.B. Priestley Library, University of Bradford.
116 Derek Walker, 'Satyagraha in St. James Park', *British Weekly*, 9/2/61, p. 3.
117 See Raghavan Iyer (ed.), *Moral and Political Writings of Mahatma Gandhi*, vol. 3, Oxford: Clarendon Press, 1987, Section 2 for a full discussion.
118 As noted in April Carter, letter to Francis Deutsch, 29/2/61, Folder 'Finningley', *Direct Action Committee*, Box DAC 3, Commonweal Archives, J.B. Priestley Library, University of Bradford.

119 'Minutes of Harrington Demonstrators Conference, February 27th 1960', in Folder, 'Harrington – London CND Groups', *Direct Action Committee*, Box DAC 6, Commonweal Archives, J.B. Priestley Library, University of Bradford.
120 Roger Murray, 'Direct Action: Confession of Impotence?', *Isis*, 2 March 1960, pp. 12–13.
121 April Carter, letter to Michael Randle 28/9/60, Folder 'Miscellaneous Papers', *Direct Action Committee*, Box DAC 7, Commonweal Archives, J.B. Priestley Library, University of Bradford.
122 April Carter, letter to Michael Randle 28/9/60, Folder 'Miscellaneous Papers', *Direct Action Committee*, Box DAC 7, Commonweal Archives, J.B. Priestley Library, University of Bradford.
123 This division is noted in 'Memorandum of the South West London Working Group', in bundle of documents 'Supporters Meeting', 14/11/62, Conway Hall, Folder, 'Committee of 100, 1962', *Hannan Committee of 100 Archives*, Box 1, Commonweal Archives, J.B. Priestley Library, University of Bradford.
124 This was especially noted in the demonstrations in support of Greek democracy, e.g. see 'Nonviolent Protest', *Sanity*, August 1963, p. 4.
125 This is reported in '1314 Arrests in Trafalgar Square Disorders', *Times*, 18/9/61, p. 10.
126 This concept was associated with Peter Cadogan. See a discussion in: 'Interview with Peter Moule', *Sanity*, August 1963, p. 11.
127 'Ulysses', 'Off with the Gloves!', *Resistance*, vol. 2, no. 9, 1/9/64, pp. 6–7.
128 This is the view of Sidney Tarrow, *Power in Movement: Social Movements and Contentious Politics*, Cambridge, 1998, p. 103.
129 For example, see his discussion on 'mass civil disobedience' from *Young India*, 4 August 1921, reproduced in Raghavan Iyer (ed.), *Moral and Political Writings of Mahatma Gandhi*, vol. 3, Oxford: Clarendon Press, 1987, pp. 93–95.

Bibliography

'Memorandum of the South West London Working Group', in bundle of documents 'Supporters Meeting', 14/11/62, Conway Hall, Folder, 'Committee of 100, 1962', *Hannan Committee of 100 Archives*, Box 1, Commonweal Archives, J.B. Priestley Library, University of Bradford

Minutes, 'Nonviolence Commission of the PPU', 12/12/51, *Direct Action Committee and Committee of 100 Papers (April Carter)*, Folder 'PPU Nonviolence Commission', Commonweal Archives, J.B. Priestley Library, University of Bradford.

'Minutes of Harrington Demonstrators Conference, February 27th 1960', in Folder 'Harrington – London CND Groups', *Direct Action Committee*, Box DAC 6, Commonweal Archives, J.B. Priestley Library, University of Bradford.

'Nonviolence Commission of the PPU Minutes', 12/12/51, *Direct Action Committee and Committee of 100 Papers (April Carter)*, Bay F, Folder 'PPU Nonviolence', J.B. Priestley Library, University of Bradford.

'Nonviolence Commission of the PPU Minutes', 9/1/52, *Direct Action Committee and Committee of 100 Papers (April Carter)*, Folder 'PPU Nonviolence Commission', J.B. Priestley Library, University of Bradford.

'Notes on Future of Organisation, 4 October 1961', Folder 'Committee of 100, 1961', *Hannan Committee 100 Archives*, Box 1, Commonweal Archives, J.B. Priestley Library, University of Bradford.

'Aldermaston', 'Beyond the Bomb', *New Reasoner*, vol. 1, no. 4, Spring 1958.

Anderson, Gwyneth, 'Training in Nonviolence', *Peace News*, 18 August 1950.

Anderson, Gwyneth, Letter to Hugh Brock, 2/1/52, *Hugh Brock Papers*, Box 2, Folder 'Operation Gandhi Papers Selected by Hugh Brock', J.B. Priestley Library, University of Bradford.
Barker, Colin, 'Empowerment and Resistance: "Collective Effervescence" and Other Accounts', in Paul Bagguley and Jeff Hearn (eds), *Transforming Politics: Power and Resistance*, Basingstoke and London: Macmillan Press, 1999.
Battersby, Olwen, 'Work with Africans, Not For Them', *Peace News*, 17/10/52. Hugh Brock, Hugh, 'Operation Gandhi', in Hugh Brock's Papers, *Hugh Brock Papers*, Box 2, Folder: 'Operation Gandhi Papers Selected by Hugh Brock', J.B. Priestley Library, University of Bradford.
Bolton, Glorney, *The Tragedy of Gandhi*, London: George Allen and Unwin, 1934.
Brailsford, H.N., 'Saint Gandhi', *New Statesman and Nation*, 12 May 1951.
Brewood, Douglas et al., 'Beyond Counting Arses', *Hannan Committee of 100 Papers*, Box 1, L/100/63/23, Commonweal Archives, J.B. Priestley Library, University of Bradford.
Brock, Hugh, 'Operation Gandhi 2', *Hugh Brock Papers*, Box 2, Folder 'Operation Gandhi Papers Selected by Hugh Brock', J.B. Priestley Library, University of Bradford.
Brock, Hugh, 'Operation Gandhi Rejected Scheme – 'House of Commons', *Hugh Brock Papers*, J.B. Priestley Library, University of Bradford, Box 1, J.B. Priestley Library, University of Bradford.
Brock, Hugh, Letter to Alex Comfort, 29/12/51, *Hugh Brock Papers*, Box 2, Folder 'Operation Gandhi War Office Demo', J.B. Priestley Library, University of Bradford.
Brock, Hugh, April, letter to Michael Randle 28/9/60, Folder 'Micellaneous Papers', *Direct Action Committee*, Box DAC 7, Commonweal Archives, J.B. Priestley Library, University of Bradford.
Brock, Hugh, 'Nonviolent Project', *Peace News*, 1/7/49.
Brock, Hugh, 'From the Editor's Notebook,' *Peace News*, 23/9/55.
Brock, Peter and Nigel Young, *Pacifism in the Twentieth Century*, Syracuse, NY: Syracuse University Press, 1999.
Cadogan, Peter. See a discussion in: 'Interview with Peter Moule', *Sanity*, August 1963.
Carter, April, letter to Francis Deutsch, 29/2/61, Folder, 'Finningley', *Direct Action Committee*, Box DAC 3, Commonweal Archives, J.B. Priestley Library, University of Bradford.
Chabot, Sean, 'Transnational Diffusion and the African-American Reinvention of the Gandhian Repertoire', *Mobilization: An International Journal*, vol. 5, 2000, pp. 201–16.
Chabot, Sean and J.W. Duyvendak, 'Globalization and Transnational Diffusion between Social Movements', *Theory and Society* 31, 2002, pp. 697–740.
Coltman, Claud, 'The Field of Aldermaston', *Reconciliation*, vol. 35, no. 5, May 1958.
Comfort, Alex, 'Umbrella Man', *Hugh Brock Papers*, Box 2, Folder: 'Operation Gandhi Papers Selected by Hugh Brock', J.B. Priestley Library, University of Bradford.
Fisher, Frederick Bohn, *That Strange Little Brown Man Gandhi*, New York: R. Long and R.R. Smith, 1932.
Fox, Richard G., 'Passage from India', in Richard G. Fox and Orin Starn (eds), *Between Resistance and Revolution: Cultural Politics and Social Protest*, New Brunswick, New Jersey: Rutgers University Press, 1997.

Fuller, J.F.C., *India in Revolt*, London: Eyre and Spottiswoode, 1931.
Gardiner, Llew, 'The March of our Time', *Tribune*, 28 March 1958.
Gardiner, Llew, 'Man, This March – It's Beautiful', *Tribune*, 11 April 1958.
Glaister, Dorothy, Letter to Hugh Brock, 21/1/52, *Hugh Brock Papers*, Box 1, J.B. Priestley Library, University of Bradford.
Gregg, Richard, *The Power of Nonviolence*, second edn, London: J. Clarke, 1960.
Giugini, Marco L., Doug McAdam and Charles Tilly (eds), *From Contention to Democracy*, Lanham and Oxford: Rowman and Littlefield, 1999.
Hanagan, Michael, 'Social Movements: Incorporation, Disengagement, and Opportunities – A Long View', in Marco G. Giugini, Doug McAdam and Charles Tilly (eds), *From Contention to Democracy*, Lanham and Oxford: Rowman and Littlefield.
Hobhouse, Stephen, 'India's Message to the World', *Peace News*, 7 February 1941.
Hoyland, John, *The Cross Moves East: A Study of the Significance of Gandhi's 'Satyagraha'*. London: George Allen and Unwin, 1931.
Hoyland, John, 'Gandhi's Message for the West', *Peace News*, 28/4/50.
Hoyland, John, *Gandhi: The Practical Peace Builder*, London: Peace Pledge Union, 1952.
Iyer, Raghavan (ed.), *Moral and Political Writings of Mahatma Gandhi*, vol. 3, Oxford: Clarendon Press, 1987.
Jackson, Martin, 'Ipswich Unites to End Discrimination', *Peace News*, 17/2/56.
Jameson, A.K., 'Gandhi's Early Years', *Peace News*, 15/12/50.
Jones, E. Stanley, *Mahatma Gandhi: An Interpretation*, London: Hodder and Staughton, 1948.
Jones, Mervyn, 'Stop and Think', *Tribune*, 11 April 1958.
Jones, Mervyn, 'The Time is Short', in Norman MacKenzie (ed.), *Conviction*, London: MacGibbon and Kee, 1958.
Kabraji, Fredoon, 'Fighting by Turning the Other Cheek!', *Peace News*, 8/8/36.
Kenny, Michael, *The First New Left: British Intellectuals After Stalin*, London: Lawrence and Wishart, 1995.
Kingsley, Martin, 'The Peace Movement', *New Statesman and Nation*, 4/6/38.
Lewis, Ethel A., 'Nonviolence Commission to have Travelling File', *Peace News*, 19/1/51.
Lewis, Ethel A., Letter to Kathleen Rawlins, n.d., stamped 29/1/51, *Hugh Brock Papers*, Folder: 'Pre-Operation Gandhi', J.B. Priestley Library, University of Bradford.
Lewis, Ethel A., 'Report on Nonviolence Commission', *PPU Journal*, no. 60, April 1951.
Lowe, Bill, 'Operation Gandhi', *PEACE NEWS*, 25/1/52.
MacInnes, C.M., *The British Commonwealth and its Unsolved Problems*, London: Longmans, Green and Co., 1925.
McAdam, Doug, ' "Initiator" and "Spin-Off" Movements: Diffusion Processes in Protest Cycles', in Mark Traugott (ed.), *Repertoires and Cycles of Collective Action*, Durham, NC: Duke University Press, 1995.
McAdam, Doug, Sidney Tarrow and Charles Tilly, *Dynamics of Contention*, Cambridge and New York: Cambridge University Press, 2001.
Morris, Stuart, 'The Fourteenth AGM', *PPU Journal*, no. 62, June 1951.
Murray, Roger, 'Direct Action: Confession of Impotence?', *Isis*, 2 March 1960.
n.a., '500 Z-men ask: How do we become COs?', *Peace News*, 16//51.
n.a., 'Colchester Hears the Pacifist Case,' *Peace News*, 29/10/54.

n.a., 'Coming Events', *Peace News*, 5/3/54.
n.a., 'Councillor leads H-bomb Demonstration in Salisbury,' *Peace News*, 16/7/54.
n.a., 'Easter 1964', *Sanity*, January 1964.
n.a., 'Gandhi – 'Greatest Christian'', *Peace News*, 1/5/37.
n.a., 'Harold Steele: Why I am Going to the Pacific', *Peace News*, 17/5/57.
n.a., 'Making the PPU a vital force for peace', *Peace News*, 11/11/49.
n.a., 'Nonviolence Group to Meet in London', *Peace News*, 16/12/49.
n.a., 'Nonviolence Group', *PPU Journal*, no. 48, April 1950.
n.a., 'Nonviolence', *PPU Journal*, no. 47, March 1950.
n.a., 'Pacifists Told Police and War Office: "We are Coming to Squat"', *Peace News*, 18/1/52.
n.a., 'Peacemaking Through Education', *Peace News*, 2/11/51.
n.a., 'Rally at Ipswich', *Peace News*, 24/2/56.
n.a., 'Rising Protests on H-Bomb Tests', *Peace News*, 26/10/56.
n.a., 'Two Marches', *Solidarity: For Workers' Power*, no. 2, 1962.
n.a., 'To Protest Against A-Bomb', *Peace News*, 21/3/52, p. 8.
n.a., 'The Revolt of Passivity', *Nation and Athenaeum*, 6 August 1921.
n.a., 'Armed Guards Turn Out for Pacifists', *Peace News*, 4/7/52.
n.a., 'Britain's A-Bomb – Who Will Drop it?', *Peace News*, 10/10/52.
n.a., 'Concerning the Fellowship', *Reconciliation*, vol. 9, no. 12, December 1931, This is registered in: n.a.., 'Concerning the Fellowship', *Reconciliation*, vol. 9, no. 10, October 1931.
n.a., 'Steps to Peace Conference', *PPU Journal*, no. 44, December 1949.
n.a., 'Tattoo Protest Committee Formed in Leeds', *Peace News*, 4/6/54.
n.a., 'The Current of Affairs', *The Christian Pacifist*, no. 3, March 1942.
n.a., 'The Problem of Mr. Gandhi', *Nation and Athenaeum*, 18 February 1922.
n.a., 'Walking Through Britain to Help India', *Peace News*, 1/6/56.
Peace News editorial, 'Festival of Arms, *Peace News*, 4/5/51.
Peace News reporter, 'Pacifists Demonstrate at S. Africa House', *Peace News*, 3/10/52.
Peace News reporter, 'Protest at Atom Plant', *Peace News*, 24/4/53.
Peace News reporter, 'Demonstration at Atom Plant', *Peace News*, 2/10/53.
Randle, Michael, 'Nonviolent Direct Action in the 1950s and 1960s', in Richard Taylor and Nigel Young (eds),*Campaigns for Peace: British peace movements in the twentieth century*, Manchester: Manchester University Press, 1987.
Rawlins, Kathleen, cited in Stuart Morris, 'The Fourteenth AGM', *PPU Journal*, no. 62, June 1951.
Scalmer, Sean, 'Translating Contention: Culture, History, and the Circulation of Collective Action', *Alternatives*, Vol. 25, 2000, pp. 491–514.
Scalmer, Sean, *Dissent Events: protest, media and the political gimmick in Australia*, Sydney: UNSW Press, 2002.
Scalmer, Sean, 'The Labour of Diffusion: The Peace Pledge Union and the Adaptation of the Gandhian Repertoire', *Mobilization: An International Journal*, vol. 7, 2002, pp. 269–86.
Sharp, Gene, *The Politics of Nonviolent Action*, Boston: Porter Sargent Publishers, 1973.
Smith, Peter, 'The Welfare State', *New Reasoner*, n.n., Summer 1958.
Snow, David A. and Robert D. Benford, 'Alternative Types of Cross-National Diffusion in the Social Movement Arena', in Donatella della Porta, Hanspeter Kriesi and Dieter Rucht (eds), *Social Movements in a Globalizing World*, London: Macmillan, 1999.

Soper, Donald, 'My Faith in the Future', *Tribune*, 11 April 1958.
Tarrow, Sidney, *Power in Movement: Social Movements and Contentious Politics*, Cambridge, 1998.
Taylor, Richard and Kevin Ward, 'Community Politics and Direct Action: the non-aligned Left', in David Coates and Gordon Johnston (eds), *Socialist Strategies*, Oxford: Martin Robertson, 1983.
Taylor, Verta, 'Social Movement Continuity: The Women's Movement in Abeyance', *American Sociological Review*, 1989, 54, pp. 761–75.
Thompson, E.P., 'Revolution', in E.P. Thompson (ed.), *Out of Apathy*, London: Stephens and Sons Ltd., 1960.
'Ulysses', 'Off with the Gloves!', *Resistance*, vol. 2, no. 9, 1/9/64.
Walker, Roy, 'Reflections on Nonviolence (1)', *The Christian Pacifist*, no. 49, January 1946.
Walker, Derek, 'Satyagraha in St. James Park', *British Weekly*, 9/2/61.
Walsh, Sam, 'He Marches to the Barracks Twice a Week,' *PEACE NEWS*, 30/10/53.
White E, 'Strikes and Nonviolent Resistance', *Peace News*, 29/5/37.

9 Gandhiji in Burma, and Burma in Gandhiji

Penny Edwards

> This is a religious battle ... to revolutionize the political outlook ... to spiritualize our politics.
> (M. K. Gandhi, speech at Mirzapur Park, Calcutta, 23 January 1921)

On 24 September 1932, Rabindranath Tagore visited Mohandas Gandhi in Yeravada prison. Entering Poona, he found 'armoured cars and machine guns being paraded on the military grounds' and soldiers stationed along the city roads. Four days earlier, contemplating Gandhi's stand, Tagore had written: 'Today there are thousands in India, confined in prisons indefinitely and without trial, inhumanly treated ... there can be no doubt that not only are they a heavy burden upon the Government but they permanently lower its dignity.'[1] Were we to substitute Yangon for Poona, Myanmar for India, and Aung San Suu Kyi for Gandhi, these musings on colonial injustice and the deeply spiritual fight for right (and rights) could easily be mistaken for an account of life under military rule in contemporary Burma.

In her own writings, Aung San Suu Kyi has contrasted the military bearing of her father, Aung San, architect of Burma's Independence and 'the founder of a national army' with the pacifism of Gandhi, 'that great apostle of nonviolence', while likening their mettle and their courageous stance against British authoritarianism. A later recipient of the Jawaharlal Nehru prize, Suu Kyi saw in both the qualities identified by Nehru as '*abhaya*, fearlessness, not merely bodily courage but absence of fear from the mind'.[2] But this was no blind hero worship. Suu Kyi tempered her admiration for Gandhi with recognition that, by the twentieth century, the universal approach and renaissance ideals she admired in the literature of Tagore had begun to narrow in such 'men of action'. It is disturbing, she wrote, 'when a man of Gandhi's vision casually writes of English women as wandering in the streets and slaving away in factories'.[3] Impressed by the energy of Burmese women on his first visit in 1902, Gandhi had developed a particular vision for Burmese women as the producers and consumers of Burmese-made cloth and parasols by the time of his third, longest and last visit to Burma in 1929. One can only speculate as to how he would have viewed himself, some seventy years later at an exhibition in Delhi, framed alongside Suu Kyi in the composition 'Suu Kyi and Gandhiji', created by the artist-in-exile Sitt Nyein Aye in homage to Gandhi's influence on Suu Kyi's 'nonviolent Satyagraha against one of the world's most tyrannical military dictatorships', a viewpoint reflected in his work on Suu Kyi and Gandhiji.[4]

Since Aung San Suu Kyi faced off a military state in 1988, comparisons between her and Gandhi have ranged from media caricatures of Suu Kyi as 'Burma's Gandhi' to sophisticated tributes by the Nobel Committee in 1991, to recognition of Gandhi's intellectual influence by Suu Kyi herself, to academic debate between non-Burmans as to the extent of that legacy. Neglected in most such discussions are Gandhi's own three sojourns in Burma and their impact on both his own thinking and on the philosophy and practice of Burmese nationalists.

The first two visits, in 1902 and 1915, impressed Gandhi with particular views of Buddhism, Burmese women, and the complicity of the Indian diaspora in the British occupation. The third, shortly before the Salt March and Gandhi's imprisonment in Poona, was more significant, and took Gandhi to Rangoon, Prome, Moulmein, Pynimana and Mandalay, bringing him into contact with monastic and lay Burmese nationalist leaders, Burmese students and members of the Indian community. As Gandhi's motorcade traversed Rangoon on this, his last and longest trip to Burma, the Burmese writer Paragu recalled, 'a young boy watching up in a palm tree clapped his hands with glee, and fell down'.[5] Some sixty years later, at Aung San Suu Kyi's first public rally in front of Shwedagon, onlookers shinned up palm trees to get a better view across the dense crowds. One such tree-climber, moved to loud applause by Suu Kyi's words, lost his grip, and tumbled down.[6] This little bit of history repeating is the subject of this chapter.

If being Indian today, as Amitav Ghosh recently reflected, is 'a truly global experience' which involves carrying the experiences of Indians 'everywhere', then in Gandhi's lifetime that experience was not so much global as imperial.[7] However transcendental, universal and timeless Gandhi's philosophy now appears, his preaching and practice were forged along colonial parameters, loosely contained within the boundaries of British empire and the trajectories of Indian diaspora. In the 1920s and 1930s, the itineraries of nationalist monks in India and of Gandhi and other Indian nationalists in Burma created conduits and circuits of political and cross-cultural knowledge and exchange. Today, Gandhian interventions, echoes or legacies are manifest in three specific sites of resistance utilised by Aung San Suu Kyi's opposition party: the boycott, the body and clothing. In what follows, I trace the cross-cultural lineage of these modalities of resistance and their refashioning in a postcolonial world. Gandhian ideology and praxis percolated into Burmese political history and thinking long before the birth or rise to prominence of Aung San Suu Kyi. But perversely, Gandhi owes as much a debt to Aung San Suu Kyi as she to him. This is not to deny the universality of his message today, but to historicise it along specific geographic axes.

Gandhi, Burma and Indian diaspora

Historian Nalini Ranjan Chakravarti has described the history of Indians in Burma as 'the sad story of a minority race' whose industry and contribution to Burma over several generations and a century of British rule was rewarded with their eviction. Here, the diversity of past lives morphs into the tragic tale of a 'poor man, contemptuously called *kala*, who hopefully migrated to a country whose "golden pagodas" transmitted the concept of Ahimsa – love and compassion for all living beings', a doctrine shared by the "majority of Indians and Burmans"'.[8] Anxious to highlight the 'loyalty' and law-abiding characteristics of the Indian community, Chakravarti contrasts the broad social spectrum of Indians in Burma, from temporary, impoverished migrant labourers to long term, wealthy residents, with the antics of 'terrorist ... young educated Indians' and such 'extremists' as Gandhi and Tilak.[9] Under a 'prisoner-exchange' programme, Lokmanya Bal Gandadhar Tilak (1856–1920) was jailed in Burma in 1908, in Meiktila jail and then in Mandalay. Here, from 1911 to 1914, he produced his *Gita Rahasya*, his Hindu exposition of the Bhagvad Gita from Sanskrit. In the history and mythology of Indians in Burma, Tilak's antithesis is his jailor: the 'loyal' Indian caricatured by Orwell in *Burmese Days*, through the figure of the ardently pro-British Dr Veraswami, whose duties included offering medical advice at executions. A more recent critical representation of the 'loyal' Indian can be found in Amitav Ghosh's *The Glass Palace* where he writes about the 'innocent evil' of the sepoys and soldiers who marched into Burma with British troops.[10]

Conspicuous in mid-nineteenth century sketches of the storming of Rangoon, the Indian sepoys were by no means the first Indians in Burma. But after Rangoon was secured in the Second Anglo-Burmese War of 1852, new trading and commercial opportunities in this rapidly expanding colonial seaport encouraged the consolidation of a new Indian immigrant community. By the early 1880s, the Hindu population of Rangoon numbered 44,908, and its Muslim population 21,000, making a minority not only of the British but also of the Burmese in the new colonial capital.[11] Indian peasant migration to cultivate lower Burma was also encouraged. The preponderance of Indians, particularly from Madras and Bengal, in domestic service and the commercial sector meant that, by the 1890s, 'Hindustani' had become the 'tongue of most utility for ordinary needs', and was spoken equally in colonial homes, barracks, offices, along the railways and in market places. Domestic service with the British was largely shunned by the Burmese. Indians, particularly Madrassis and Bengalis, served as butlers, cooks and 'boys'. As subaltern clerks and domestic staff, Indians provided more than a military buffer between British and Burmese. Many possessed a smattering of English, meaning that most British had no need to learn Burmese, much less to interact with them.[12]

In Burma more than in South Africa, Gandhi was confronted with direct complicity by Indians in the coercion and imprisonment of both Burmese and Indian activists, and in the exploitation of economic opportunity. The moral ambivalence of these bodyguards of empire no doubt honed both his vision for a moral reformation of the Indian nation and his formulation of Swaraj as a means of bringing dignity to those Indians fighting with and for the British. Under Swaraj, he pledged in 1921, Indian soldiers would not be 'hirelings' used to 'cut down offensive Turks or Arabs or to quell inoffensive Chinese or Burmese in the East'.[13] He was equally apprised of their role as underwiters of empire. 'Just as Bombay was not India', Gandhi realised on his 1902 visit, 'Rangoon was not Burma, and ... just as we in India have become commission agents of English merchants, even so in Burma we have combined with the English merchants, in making the Burmese people our commission agents.'[14] This scenario was complicated by the fact that Indian merchants in Burma effectively emerged as Gandhi's commission agents for his Satyagraha movement in Burma and beyond. While quick to condemn the deeply ambivalent position of Burma's Indians as profiteers, Gandhi was logistically and financially dependent, in his Burma tours, on such benefactors. His prime patron was Dr P. J. Mehta, the cosmopolitan scion of a Rangoon-based diamond-trading clan.

It was Pranjivandas Mehta who had welcomed Gandhi off his first passage from India to England, proffering medical advice and suggestions as to how to gain 'experience of English life and customs'.[15] Mehta subsequently visited him in Durban, where he treated his rheumatism and, in the years before the First World War, sponsored Sorabji Adajania, 'Gandhi's comrade in jail and a Satyagrahi', to study law in London, to qualify as a barrister and take Gandhi's place on return to Africa.[16] By the late 1920s, Mehta had emerged as a primary sponsor of Gandhi's movement.[17]

Gandhi, Buddhism, hunger strikes and boycotts in Burmese nationalism

The brutality of Britain's conquest of Burma, through three wars in 1824, 1852, and 1885, fuelled heavy resistance. From the 1820s to the 1930s, as Michael Adas has shown, 'the defense of Buddhism was used by princely pretenders, prophets and nationalist leaders alike to rally peasant supporters to their cause'.[18] On his initial visit to Burma in 1902, Gandhi appeared largely ignorant of the political potential of Buddhism, and his superficial encounters with Burmese monks, as an Indian tourist in Rangoon, were marked more by repulsion than reverence. Visiting Shwedagon, arguably the most sacred site in Burmese Buddhism, in 1902, Gandhi's visceral reactions echoed common colonial condemnations of the *sangha*. He is 'pained' by the 'lethargy' of the monks; the 'innumerable little candles' burning at Shwedagon kindled only discomfort, and his aversion to the rats at this sacred site echo colonial conflations of indigeneity and pestilence. Four years after Gandhi's visit, the Young Men's Buddhist Association was established in Rangoon by young western-educated middle-class Burmese.

Often seen as the harbinger of modern Burmese nationalism the YMBA was largely socio-religious in orientation, preferring discussions and debates to the walk-outs and demonstrations used by the Indian National Congress.[19] It was not until 1908 that Burma's first overtly political organisation emerged: the Burma Provincial Congress Committee (BPCC). Its founder was Gandhi's mentor P. J. Mehta, who had by this juncture established himself as 'a prominent social worker ... highly respected by all the communities in Burma'.[20] His helpers included Pundit Madanjit, a full-time Congress worker, and several other Burmese Indians and local Burmese.[21]

In 1915, Gandhi again visited Rangoon and stayed with Mehta, whose home he described as 'good as my own'.[22] Gandhi's autobiography reveals little of this visit, but he may well have heard from Mehta, over his vegetarian table, of plans for a monastic boycott of a new colonial heritage law which sought to establish European heritage protocols over sacred monuments and active places of worship. It was against this highly charged atmosphere, which became further politicised by protests against Europeans wearing shoes to temples, that a young Burmese monk named U Ottama left Burma to study in India. He returned to Burma in 1918 deeply influenced by India's *satyagraha* movement. U Ottama's encounters with Gandhi's ideology and praxis coincided with the search by an energetic, frustrated and intellectually gifted group of youth, for new forms of resistance. Attracted by 'the Indian rethinking of the aim and methodology of the politics of gaining *swaraj*', U Ottama and others were enticed into the world of 'practical politics'. Gandhi's philosophy and social activism offered a refreshing alternative to the predominantly British schooled, and clothed, secular leaders of Burma's nationalist movement. While Burmese monks were visiting India, some members of the Indian diaspora were applying Gandhian strategies in Burma. One boycott of the Duke of Windsor's visit to Burma, which features in Burma's nationalist narrative,[23] was arranged by Mr Tyabji, an elected member of the legislature from Gujarat, who had proposed a 'counter demonstration to draw attention to India's political needs', for which he was imprisoned for a fortnight.[24] This incident became an iconic moment in Burma's nationalist narrative.[25] Soon after, Gandhi recommended a boycott of the visit of the Prince of Wales to Bombay.[26] The following year, a student strike at Rangoon University won massive popular support and derailed new elitist provisions for restricted university access. In 1921, the General Council of Buddhist Associations (GCBA), an amalgam of YMBA and other associations, staged a boycott of a parliamentary committee led by Sir Frederick Whyte of the Indian Legislative Assembly.[27]

Inspired by Gandhi's ideology, and fired by popular support for such boycotts, a young Burmese named U Chit Hlaing harnessed growing disillusionment with the western bias of the predominantly British schooled and clothed secular leaders of Burma's nationalist movement into a new and vibrant campaign: the Thakin or 'masters' movement. Roughly equivalent to 'Sahib', the term 'Thakin' was an honorific for Europeans: in marking themselves as Thakins, U Chit Hlaing and others were stating their birthright to Burma and their preparedness for *swaraj*. Suu Kyi has dubbed the 1920s the 'wunthanu' era, wunthanu denoting the conservation of one's lineage and patriotism in the shape of the rejection of 'foreign' things and the retention of traditional values.[28] The influence of India's swadeshi movement, she writes, was also clearly discernible. A member of the Indian National Congress, U Chit Hlaing favoured the use of boycott and, like Gandhi, saw strength in unity, believing that continued attachment to India would help achieve home rule more rapidly. U Chit Hlaing joined forces with two monks, Venerable U Ottama and Venerable U Vossara who looked to India for political ideas and tactics. Their monastic training, energy and fearlessness earned them popular respect and the epithet, '*dhammatatikas*' or dhamma-activists.[29] Mingled with this rejection of the foreign and the embrace of swaraj was increasing unease at the economic and demographic preponderance of Indians. The implicit tensions between these two orientations, first couched in nationalist songs, would surface in violence after Gandhi's last and longest visit to Burma.[30]

By the early 1920s, Burma's nationalist leaders were polarised tactically, between those committed to constitutional struggle, and those rejecting it for Gandhian *satyagraha*, and strategically, between those who saw separation from India as the fastest way to fully representative government, and those who shared Gandhi's belief that strength would come from unity, and that Burma should subordinate its fight to India's struggle for home rule. Elections at the General Council of Buddhist Associations in July 1922 formalised this split into the U Chit Hlaing faction and the 21 Party, which campaigned for separation as the only fast-track to a fully representative government. The British government had little patience for either faction, but was especially anxious to insulate Burma from Indian nationalism and its discontents. Lieutenant-Governor Richard Craddock urged 'young Burmans' not to 'be misled by extremists into selling their birthright for a mess of Indian pottage'. If 'young Burma' joined hands with the Indian National Congress and 'their shibboleths sinking all originality of their own', Craddock warned in the 1920s, Britain would not look kindly on their aspirations to Independence.[31]

Despite such warnings, contacts continued between the Indian National Congress and Burmese nationalist leaders, and the British government's arrests of U Ottama and U Vissara for making seditious speeches galvanised further support for their movement among both monks and laity. The sangha openly demonstrated its support for U Ottama on his first incarceration in 1921. To protest the government's prohibition on wearing monk's robes in prison, U Vissara adopted another Gandhian tactic, engaging in a hunger strike which lasted 166 days, until his death.[32]

In 1929, U Chlit Haing joined the throngs of Burmese and Indians greeting Gandhi at Rangoon port. The colonial government arrested them for making seditious speeches against the British, but the arrests only increased support.[33] It was not until 1929 that Gandhi made a conscious effort to appeal to audiences in Burma. In 1929, the year in which Gandhi was arrested for burning foreign cloth in India, he visited Burma for two weeks, initially staying with his old friend P. J. Mehta in his impressive residence near the Shwedagon pagoda. It was Gandhi's first and last overtly political visit to Burma. Touring Rangoon, Mandalay, Moulmein and Toungoo, Gandhi gave numerous public addresses to audiences in the thousands, comprising Burmese monks and laity as well as Indian diaspora. Although he once again reprimanded Burma's Indian community for their role in assisting colonialism, they proved his major hosts and sponsors. Described by the historian Chakravarti as an attempt to 'collect money for his Khaddar scheme', Gandhi's Burma tour appeared to be much more.[34] In the opinion of the Burmese writer Paragu, who composed the following account from conversations with U Ottama, Venerable U Nageinda and others, Gandhi's visit touched a political and spiritual chord with Burmese monks and nationalists:

> At Brooklyn Road (now Bogalay Bazaar Road) Port Gate, before six a.m, a huge mass gathered and waited eagerly for someone. For whom were they waiting? This was an informal gathering, a crowd of not only Indians but also Burmese men and women. Among them was the Rangoon Municipality Chairman Mr. Rafi, Gandhiji's friend and medical advisor Dr. Mehta, Dr. Dugai, the Burmese nationalists U Chit Hlaing and U Pan Tun Ilater Saw Paw Tun) and city elders. When the Oceanliner anchored at the jetty, the crowd cried out 'Long Live Mahatma Gandhi!'
>
> When Gandhiji's motorcade drove along the Signal Pagoda road, one of the young Indianmen who was at the top of a coconut tree, clapped his hands with joy. He lost his grip and fell down. In the afternoon, Gandhi gave a long speech at Fytche Square, now Mahabandoola Garden. A Burmese Buddhist monk named Venerable Ashim Nageinda gave a blessing speech first, and hundreds of people attended the welcome ceremony later.[35]

In a commemorative verse dedicated to his wife, B. C. Guha, one Indian resident of Burma who appears to have shared the secular clothing and legal training of Burma's early nationalists, and was Honorary Secretary of Hindu Maha Shabha cum Congress, remembered Gandhi's 1929 visit to Pynimana and the interchange between U Hla Bu, a lawyer who was Chairman of the Gandhi Reception Committee, and who acted as Gandhi's Burmese translator:

> U Hla Bu, a sparkling wit, with knowledge of several languages, translated Mahatma's speech in Hindi, to a crowd of about ten thousand people.

Mahatma Gandhi tapped U Hla Bu on the shoulders and said 'Friend, you are a wonderful man. Your translation seems to be more appealing than my speech. Hear the frequent hand clappings.'[36]

At Pyinmana, Gandhi stayed in the house of the millionaire Dr B. K. Haldar, and received a substantial donation of 6,500 rupees to start the Mahatma Satyagraha Movement. In Toungoo, he welcomed many 'yellow robed monks and Burman sisters and brothers' in the crowd, and spoke to them of Ahimsa in explicitly Buddhist terms. Describing Ahimsa as 'one of the most active forces in the world' he noted how

Gautama himself, whenever he saw oppression, injustice and death around him, and when he saw darkness in front of him, at the back of him and on each side of him, went out in the wilderness and remained there fasting and praying in search of light.

Urging self-purification and penance on laity and monks alike, he exhorted the latter to 'revolutionise life' by rejecting rigid traditions and the stranglehold of scriptures, 'interpreting the message of Buddha' through their hearts and so revealing the 'hidden meaning lying behind the written word'. In Mandalay, 18 March 1929, Gandhi urged the Buddhists in his audience to 'explore the limitless possibilities of nonviolence', and to study the doctrine of Ahimsa – 'one of the greatest truths the world can ever have' – and to practise it 'in every act of your lives'.[37]

On his departure from Burma in late March 1929, Gandhi addressed large crowds in Mandalay, and reminded them of Lokmanya Tilak's incarceration. 'It was [Tilak] who gave India the mantra of swaraj', Gandhi claimed. 'In India, it is a common saying that the way to *swaraj* is through Mandalay.'[38] It was the women alone who made a favourable impression on Gandhi during his first Burma visit in 1902. 'The freedom and energy of the Burmese women charmed just as the indolence of the men pained me', he wrote in his *Autobiography*.[39] Impressed by the artistic superiority of the Burmese spinning wheel, Gandhi preached *swadeshi*. Urging a boycott of cloths of foreign manufacture, he addressed women in particular, urging them to discard foreign silks and English umbrellas for homespun *longyees* and paper parasols. On 13 March 1929, he advised students in Rangoon that to become real patriots and 'guardians of the purity of every girl and woman in Burma' they must first purify their hearts.[40] Here, Gandhi was indirectly addressing a nationalist prohibition, enshrined in the charter of the GCBA and in song, of marriages between Burmese women and Indian men.[41] To Gandhi, it seemed women offered both the means and the platform for the success of swadeshi; they could weave their national essence and then wear it. His attitudes to the widespread practice of smoking by Burmese women also smacked of the Temperance Movement and his own preoccupations with bodily purity. Addressing Burmese ladies in Moulmein,

Gandhi chastised them for smoking and for wearing foreign silks: praising their industry, dexterity and organisational capacity, he asked them to strive for simplicity. In Paunde and Prome, he lauded Burmese spinning wheels as superior, cheaper and lighter than Indian versions, and urged the crafting of more spinning wheels from bamboo. Weavers should display patriotism, he lectured, revive the art of hand-spinning, and so reconnect with the villagers who produced the yarn.[42]

These were not new messages. U Ottama had urged a boycott on foreign cloth and promoted homespun clothing, in counterpoint to the British-educated, suited barristers who dominated Burmese nationalism in the 1910s, and this tactic was adopted by the Thakin movement.[43] Historian Michael Gravers speculates on the contrast between the Thakin outfit and the lawyers whose European attire clothed a nationalism which was an 'attempt to construct a form of self-determination upon British premises'.[44] But there was one area where Gandhi appears to have lent new meaning to a longstanding accoutrement: a Burmese traditional, broad-brimmed, bamboo, farmers hat known as the *kamauk*. Pictorial records suggest that Gandhi adopted the *kamauk* on his Burmese tour to symbolise the practical utility of *swadeshi*. While members of the Thakin movement favoured Burmese headwear, they embraced a white cloth turban, associated with the Burmese mandarinate and literati, rather than the *kamauk* with its agrarian semiology. All headwear is prohibited for members of Burma's sangha, and we can thus speculate that Gandhi acted as a conduit for the *kamauk* to become part of the symbolism of resistance, resilience and freedom later adopted by Suu Kyi.

On 29 March 1929, days after Gandhi's departure from Burma, the General Council of Buddhist Associations disintegrated at its sixteenth conference, at once revealing the strength of factionalism in Burmese nationalism and creating a vacuum on which ethnic chauvinism would feed in coming months.[45] The unifying anticolonial rubric of 'Thakin' was increasingly overshadowed by that movement's identification as the 'We Burma Association' (*Do-bama Asaiyone*). U Nageinda, who had given the blessings on Gandhi's welcome to Rangoon, was subsequently jailed and sent to India. Presumably sensing the urgent need for new monastic leadership and direction, the monk Dhammananda Kosambi Bhikku travelled to India and persuaded U Ottama to return to Burma. Arriving in Rangoon, U Ottama gave a courageous public speech urging people to struggle for Independence and praising Gandhi. 'Gandhi is so kind, not suitable for the colonists; Imperialism and colonialism are no match for Gandhi', he declared.[46]

On 19 September of 1929, U Vissara died in Rangoon Jail following a 166-day hunger strike, protesting the colonial prohibition on wearing monk's robes in prison. In his moving account of U Vissara's ordeal, Burmese novelist Sankaing Han Tin described how, when prison doctors tried to force food on him in the first week of his hunger strike, U Vissara replied: 'Gandhi can stay with bones and flesh only.' Pointing to his ample cover, he declared 'with this body I can stay at least one year'.[47] The hunger strike provided a spiritual, moral, political and physical tactic of resistance which drew heavily on the cosmology and iconography of Buddhist fasting and asceticism, and as such its roots long predated Gandhi. In such acts, monks such as U Vissara would have also drawn their energy from Burma's strong tradition of Buddhist meditation. The power of the hunger strike as a political weapon lay both in its martyrdom of opponents and in its tangible repudiation of the legitimating framework of benevolence and paternalism claimed by all colonial states. Through starving and fasting, the symbolic emasculation and eventual termination of the colonial subject represented the utmost denial of the claimed beneficence, benevolence and paternal feelings of the state. U Vissara's death stoked anti-British feeling and nurtured further disillusionment among activist monks as to the utility of civic protest, laying the groundwork for a millenarian movement of the type identified by Adas as a conduit of nationalism. Despite Gandhi's exhortations to *ahimsa*, in a climate whose volatility was exacerbated by the increasingly strident ethnic chauvinism of the Dobama movement, conditions were now ripe for violent change.

Indo-Burmese tensions and the rejection of *ahimsa*: from the riots of 1930 to independence in 1947

U Vissara's death presaged several years of intense violence during which time Gandhian tactics were fused with extreme ethnic nationalism. On receiving news of Gandhi's arrest during the Salt March on 5 May 1930, Indians in Rangoon shut up their shops. Later that night, an earthquake struck. The jewelled pinnacle of the Shwedagon Pagoda shifted sideways, and, in the ensuing panic, ran one account, a crowd of Indians ran through the streets crying 'Victory to the Holy Gandhi'. Although Burmese did not apparently connect the earthquake with the arrest of Gandhi, it was seen as a portent of significant events to come.[48] Three weeks later, riots broke out between Burmese and Indian dockers in Rangoon and quickly spread throughout the capital in a wave of gang violence against Indians, whose primary victims were poor coolies, waste-pullers and manual labourers from Madras. Although none of the Burmese political associations explicitly endorsed the violence, the *Dobama Asaiyone* was quick to manipulate heightened tensions. A rousing new manifesto reframed *swadeshi* as an explicitly pro-Burman and implicitly anti-Indian tactic, calling upon Burmese to be united, set up their own shops and buy only Burmese products. A remake of its theme tune, the popular Dobama (we-Burmans) song, celebrated Burma's historic conquest of Indians.[49] The gunning down of Burmese prisoners in a Rangoon jail by Indian prison-guards, sporadic incidents of Indo-Burmese violence beyond Rangoon, and the beheading of Burmese collaborators with Britain by participants in a rebellion led by the millenarian monk Saya San and Britain's predictably violent response all point to the non-cohesion of Gandhi's doctrine of *ahimsa* in Burma. After 1932, following the crushing of the Saya San rebellion, 'most of the powerful Buddhist monks had either died or were disappointed in the turn of events and declined to take active part in the nationalist movement'.[50]

Despite their songs and manifestos, the Thakin movement had not openly associated itself with the violent Indo-Burmese riots. In the early 1930s, the *Dobama Asaiyone* sent delegations to the Indian National Congress, and so forged close links with Gandhi, Nehru, the socialist Jay Prakash Narain, and Indian communist leaders. These contacts further encouraged the Thakins to adopt Gandhi's nonviolent techniques and the political programme of the Indian Socialist Party.[51] In 1936, Thakin Thein Pe, a friend of Aung San's then studying in India, travelled to Lucknow to report on the 1936 Indian National Congress for the Myanma Alin newspaper, and met with leaders of the Indian Communist Party. Thakin Thein Pe subsequently invited Puranda, a Bengali member of the Indian Communist Party, to Rangoon to unite the Indian and Burmese Marxist study groups in Rangoon into a party cell. In 1937, U Ottama participated in the Calcutta Conference. That year, Burma was officially recognized as an 'independent' colony, no longer subordinate to the administration of India.

From March to April 1940, Aung San led a *Dobama Asaiyone* delegation to the Indian National Congress at Bihar, where he met with Gandhi, Nehru, Subhash Chandra Bose and other leaders. The delegation toured many Indian provinces and major cities, educating Indians about the DAA, announcing its decision to cooperate with Indian people in fighting the British Imperialists. On 2 April 1940, Aung San told the people of Lahore that to gain independence it would probably be necessary to sacrifice flesh and blood.[52] Two years later, Japan's aerial bombardment of Burma led hundreds of thousands of Indians to evacuate Burma on a harrowing march that claimed countless lives. Allied forces restored British rule in 1945 with their own controversial bombing campaign whose targets included the Mandalay palace where Tilak had served penance. In 1947, the young general Aung San successfully negotiated Burma's independence. Weeks later, he was gunned down by unidentified assailants, leaving behind his wife and their two year old daughter, Suu Kyi. His death was closely followed by that of Gandhi.

Remembering Gandhi: official discourses of Gandhi in postcolonial Burma, 1947–69

On 30 January 1948 – forty years before the military junta turned fire on Aung San Suu Kyi's democracy movement, and a year after her father was murdered by his political opponents in Rangoon – Gandhi was assassinated. The Burmese Indologist and prolific writer Baragu, then a monk studying in Benares, still remembers the melancholy melody of the song *Rajaputira Raja Ramsa* fusing with the cries of students and faculty, through his hostel in the ensuing days of mourning. Only the previous year,

Gandhi had commemorated Aung San at prayer meetings organized across India.[53] In early February, an obituary in the Burmese journal *Dido* (The Owl) labelled Gandhi's killer an 'enemy of *Ahimsa*'. Next to a cartoon of a hooded, dagger-bearing assassin, an editorial explicated Gandhi's concept of *Satyagraha*, praised the Salt March, and lamented that on this propitious anniversary of Burmese Independence 'the friend of Burma's struggle for Independence is ascending heaven'.

After Burmese Independence, good relations and mutual admiration between Nehru and U Nu fostered a memorial narrative which celebrated Gandhi as an icon of independence and freedom from colonial rule. The Mahatma Gandhi Memorial Association was founded in the late 1950s or early 1960s by U Nu, Nehru, and the Indian Ambassador to Burma, and the Gandhi Memorial Hall built at a prestigious site in the centre of Rangoon. After the 1962 coup, General Ne Win nationalised businesses, prompting the departure of some 200,000 South Asians. Like successive military regimes Ne Win sought legitimacy in Buddhism by sponsoring the construction of pagodas as displays of Buddhist piety and a conduit to national and personal 'merit'. But despite this emphasis on Burmese Buddhist Socialism, and his obvious lack of empathy for the plight of dispossessed Indian diaspora, Ne Win's government saw no reason to censor Gandhi or dilute his message. In 1968 and 1969, to celebrate Gandhi's Jayanti, a book entitled 'Gandhi in Burma' – translated from Hindu to Burmese by the prolific writer and Indologist Baragu – was distributed in the Gandhi Memorial Hall, where photos and news-cuttings from Gandhi's Burma visits, and his *kamauk*, were placed on display.[54] Although Gandhi might have disproved of this glorification of his life, as a proponent of the educational and economic value of exhibitions promoting *swadeshi* and *khadi* goods he would probably have approved of the forum.[55] Meanwhile, in New York, in 1969, the Burmese Secretary General of the United Nations U Thant (1909–74) commemorated Gandhi's centennial with a speech declaring that the UN charter was based on the principle of *satyagraha*. Defining *satyagraha* as the principles of nonviolence and democracy, U Thant declared these the dual characteristics for humankind, and claimed that one day *satyagraha* would make a good witness for world peace and stability.[56] Ten years later, the Indian Embassy in Rangoon again celebrated past ideological connections with its bilingual publication *Gandhi in Burma*. The cover shows Gandhi in a *kamauk*, kneeling before a Burmese spinning wheel, against a silhouette of the Shwedagon. A similar constellation appears in one of the book's photographic illustrations, which depicts a *kamauk*, the Gita, a spinning wheel and a vase containing Gandhi's ashes.[57]

Burma's Gandhi? Aung San Suu Kyi and Gandhi's legacy for Burmese resistance

From 1962 to 1964 Aung San's widow was posted to Delhi as Burmese Ambassador to India. Her daughter Suu Kyi's first exposure to Gandhi's ideology has been traced to her studies in political science at Delhi University during this time. But from a much earlier age, her father and his legacy had impressed upon her a deep reverence for Gandhi, and awareness of such leaders as Tilak and Bose, while her own literary leanings led her to read widely in the works of Gandhi and Tagore. In her own writings, Suu Kyi has cited the importance of the Buddhist concept of *saddha* – confidence in moral, spiritual and intellectual values – to laity, and lectured against the dangers of political exigencies obscuring or nullifying 'essential spiritual aims'.[58]

In his stimulating discussion of the role of Buddhism in Suu Kyi's philosophy, anthropologist Gustaaav Houtman argues against the notion that Suu Kyi's spiritualisation of politics derives from such Indian sources as the *Bhagavad Gita* or Gandhi's concept of *Satyagraha* and *Ahimsa*. Though she admired Gandhi and Tagore, and was well aware of Burma's history of Indianisation and shared colonial history with India, this does not, Houtman declares, remotely touch the core of Burmese sensibilities about her spirituality. Arguing that Suu Kyi has engaged Burmese people in terms of the traditions and resources of her own society he emphasises her 'spiritual revolution' in terms of Burmese Buddhism and points to Suu Kyi's dedication of the Shwedagon as the 'soul of the nation' at her first public rally, in front of the Shwedagon, on 12 August 1988, when she asked her audience of half a million to observe silence for students fallen in the struggle so as to 'share the merit' of their deeds.[59]

But Shwedagon is as much an icon of Burma's political history and its mixed ethnicity as it is a palladium of a specifically Burmese Buddhist nation. Indeed, Shwedagon is layered with multiple beliefs, sponsors, histories of protest, violence, resistance, foreign occupation and colonialism's demerits, and its structures and atmospherics encompass Burma's pantheon of 37 animist Nats, the remains of Christian soldiers, shrines sponsored by Chinese, and its own monuments to earlier protests, including the student boycott of 1920.[60] Shwedagon can at once signify Buddhism and the multiplicity of histories of those who passed and crossed it, including Gandhi. In their desire to obliterate and eclipse those earlier histories and so to dilute this historic effervescence, the military government has made a concerted, lavish and widely broadcast campaign of temple renovation at the Shwedagon and elsewhere seeking legitimacy as sponsors of Buddhism in a far more extravagant style than Ne Win. 'Myanmar resembled a house that tumbled down. The Tatmadaw [army] had to pick up the pieces and build a new one', explained one of many metaphors current in military propaganda following the 1988 'unrest'. Devoid of moral legitimacy or spiritual appeal, since 1989 the government has invested in a spate of museum building and the museumification of pagodas. Houtman compares this literal emphasis on state and nation-building with Burma's particularly strong emphasis, among both monastic and lay practitioners, on Buddhist meditation. This practice represents a lived allegiance to the teachings of Buddha:

> I have passed in ignorance through a cycle of many rebirths, seeking the builder of the house. Continuous rebirth is a painful thing. But now, housebuilder, I have found you out. You will not build me a house again. ... All your rafters are broken, your ridge-pole shattered. My mind is free from active thought, and has made an end of craving.

While the military government has become an ardent sponsor of temples, meditation centres and an International Buddhist University, they have produced no spiritual or philosophical doctrine to rival that offered Suu Kyi whose spiritual revolution takes the mind as its centre-point, pitting a *universalist mental culture* with the *bounded material cultural stance of the military*.[61] We can trace this lineage to Buddha and his teachings, but there is also a case for arguing that these notions were mediated by Gandhi and Tagore. Speaking in Harare in 1921, Gandhi declared: 'I do not want my house to be walled in on all sides and my windows to be stuffed. I want the cultures of all lands to be blown about my house as freely as possible.' Ten years later, days before he set off to visit Gandhi in Poona, Tagore equated the 'contemptuous vindictiveness ruthlessly pursued against political prisoners', reflected on the cruel confines of the 'moral prison' which governments create by setting 'narrow limits to a man's self-respect' and noted that 'a dungeon does not solely consist of brick and mortar confinement'.[62] But brick and mortar also have their practical application, and it was at the Gandhi Memorial Hall that the National League of Democracy met over several days in late July 1990, before unanimously adopting and issuing their Gandhi Hall Declaration, which echoed Gandhian strategies and colonial histories of resistance and negotiation, declaring the 'practice of peaceful means' an essential policy, and stressed the importance of 'spiritual' as well as the physical happiness of the people.[63] In the months following the massacre of students and supporters of the democracy movement of which Aung San Suu Kyi emerged the head, monks across Burma showed a savvy sensibility for history. Reinventing earlier tactics of resistance, monks in Mandalay and elsewhere adopted the strategies of U Ottama, U Vissara and Gandhi, shifting the currency and targets of their boycott from foreign merchants and rupees to Burmese rulers and Buddhist merit, by refusing to receive alms from members of the military government.

In the 1980s, the *kamauk* emerged as the symbol of the National League for Democracy, together with clothing associated with 1920s and 1930s members of the U Chit Hlaing faction and the later *Thakibn* movement. Suu Kyi and her supporters teamed a close-fitting jacket or *pinni* with a *longyi*. They added ethnic diversity to their message with Suu Kyi adopting minority dress in some regions and many men in the NLD wearing dark-coloured kachin *longyis* which had been favoured by student demonstrators in 1988. Types of *longyi* and initials or patterns on shoulder bags offer discreet means of sartorial resistance which defy no written law. In contrast, the military government, like the British rulers defied by Gandhi, sport trousers and military caps, a simulacrum of uniforms once worn by British officers, Indian sepoys and Japanese occupying troops. The regime's security forces, many of them drafted from rural areas, have abandoned the *kamauk* for rounded metal helmets.

Ironically, although members of government do not wear their xenophobic policies on their sleeves and dress in 'western'-inspired military uniforms, the population, and particularly women, are encouraged by official policies enforcing 'Myanmar' cultural tradition to wear the *longyis, pinnis* and other attire that is associated with the Democracy Movement in the international eye. Here the junta has unsuccessfully adapted Gandhian strategies of *swadeshi* to the ideological and cultural plane, launching its own stifling boycott of 'foreign' ideas and associated attempts to slur Suu Kyi for her western associations. Where once Winston Churchill belittled Gandhi as a 'half-naked fakir', today the military government derides Suu Kyi as an under-dressed imposter. In 1996, the government newspaper *New Light of Myanmar* reported that members of the opposition had supposedly lost their strength, postulating that Suu Kyi's 'western' skirts had the power to destroy their *hpon* (a specifically cultural concept of intrinsic, male-based power and glory) on contact.[64]

In October 1995, Suu Kyi expressed her 'personal joy' on accepting the Gandhi Award from the Canadian Friends of Burma, and acknowledged Gandhi among her 'most revered teachers' whose life and works had inspired her since her childhood. Quoting Gandhi's emphasis on discipline and his warnings against compulsion from a 1930 Issue of *Young India*, she continued:

> Gandhiji taught that united action by a people armed merely with the principles of justice and nonviolence can achieve far greater results than the vast institutions of a state that is not upheld by the consent of the populace. He holds out across the barriers of time and space a blazing torch of hope and courage to those who struggle against overwhelming odds that their people may live in dignity and security.[65]

In her struggle of spiritual attrition against the military state, Aung San Suu Kyi has been imprisoned for close to twenty years. She shares Gandhi's proclivity for the *kamauk* and Burmese cloth, and has embraced Gandhian tactics, including the boycott. In the postcolonial world, she has called on international figures and Burmese diaspora to boycott the current government, recognising the limitations for action by its subject-citizens. Where Gandhi once frowned upon the political apathy of Indians in Burma, he would have welcomed the widespread support for Suu Kyi in India, which was the only regional country to openly call for her release and for the recognition of her party's mass majority in the 1990 election results.

But her thinking and tactics are not only indebted to Gandhi. As we have seen, they draw on Buddhist philosophy and on a long history of monastic involvement in resistance. The junta's own recognition of the moral high ground occupied by Aung San Suu Kyi and its continuum with anti-colonial paths of resistance once taken by U Ottama, U Vissara and Gandhi is reflected in its rigid suppression of such past histories of resistance. Fearful of the weight of spiritual example, government censorship extends, in practice if not in any written law, to research on U Ottama, mention of Aung San outside the lukewarm tributes trotted out on national days, and to a continuing and suspicious silence around the legacy of Gandhi. Despite offers of renovation by the Indian Embassy, the Gandhi Memorial Hall today evinces an air of shabby decay.[66]

Not all Burmese have taken the path of Suu Kyi. Her extreme tenacity, spiritual resilience and uncompromising commitment to ethics, like those of Gandhi, are hard to translate into the everyday. Instead, their distaste for the current government translates into a spectrum of muted forms of quotidian resistance. Across Burma a myriad invisible acts of *ahimsa*, of covert non-compliance with a violent regime, allow the interpretation of apathy, detachment from one's official post, deliberate underachievement, as a form of pyschological *satygraha*, a non-buying of regime policies. As interpreted by one resident of Rangoon, the concept of *satyagraha* here offers a means of making sense of an existence which is seen by members of the opposition outside Burma as collaboration and surrender. Their apparent complicity may have infuriated Gandhi, yet Gandhi offers a vital handle to steer those who care to think differently through such corridors of complicity.

As Monique Skidmore shows in her new study of the cultural logic of life in contemporary Burma, the military regime by muzzling the public sphere and saturating it with propaganda, 'creates grey spaces of confusion in which complicity may begin'.[67] Gandhian ideology, its identification with Aung San Suu Kyi, and the linguistic and cultural underpinnings of such concepts as *Ahimsa* in Theravadan Buddhist cultures, offer room for a number of pyschological strategies through which Burmese people can survive life under an authoritarian regime. These strategies involving resistance, collaboration and complicity muddy traditional motivational analyses. As Skidmore shows, invisible, anonymous acts of *Ahimsa* can coexist with those 'layers or veneers of conformity that Burmese people present to each other and, most especially, to the military regime'.[68]

Looking back and forward

In their creative interpretation of merit, Buddhism and boycotts, and their elastic interpretation of *satyagraha* to span a spectrum of inaction, those now living in Burma and choosing to differ from the military regime, owe much to Gandhi's memory and legacy. Burma had other Gandhis, in the figures of U Ottama and U Vissara, who combined his ascetic realism with a commitment to social justice and spiritual purity. In their lifetime they were superseded by advocates of violent resistance, such as Saya San and

Aung San Suu Kyi's father, Aung San. That violent legacy, itself a product of the violence imposed on Burma in three successive wars by imperial Britain, is alive in Burma today.

While we cannot draw a line down or across the ideological trajectories and spiritual travelogue which intertwined Gandhi and Burma from his first visit in 1902, a mid way point is as good as any to look to and through this cross-cultural history. In 1949, a Burmese student was travelling by train in England when he met an Englishman who muddled Burma, Bangkok and Gandhi. Playing upon his confusion, the youngster claimed to hail from 'Bangkok, the golden city of Burma; Burma the land of pagodas and smiling people and saintly men like Gandhi'. Nodding in hearty assent, his fellow traveller retorted: 'Gandhi ... A very nice man. A very good man indeed. He is a man to watch.' The gentleman was not 'far wrong in fact', decided the student who went on to become a leading historian. 'Though Gandhi was then ten months dead, his spirit is deathless and to it men of all nations will for ever continue to say, "Lead, kindly Light."'? In his geographic confusion, the Englishman was also not far wrong.[69] Although Gandhi is commonly identified as an Indian nationalist icon, his intellectual wanderlust fuelled a peripatetic lifestyle, and in his life as in his afterlife transcended national boundaries. But those wonderings, and wanderings, were largely trammelled by a British imperial grid yoking England, India, South Africa and Burma. In some strange historic symmetry infused with spiritual synchronicity, Aung San Suu Kyi's embrace of Gandhian thinking and tactics has broadened their resonance in Theravada Southeast Asia. Alongside Martin Luther King and Nelson Mandela, she has reinvigorated the power and postcolonial applicability of *ahimsa*, giving Gandhi's legacy a truly global dimension.

Notes

1 Rabindranath Tagore, *Mahatmaji and the Depressed Humanity; East and West*, New Delhi: Rupa, 2002, p. 25.
2 Aung San Suu Kyi, *Freedom from Fear*, London: Penguin Books, 1991, p. 184.
3 Ibid.
4 Sitt Nyein Aye, www.mizzima.com.
5 Private communication with Baragu, 2004.
6 Author interview, Rangoon, 2004.
7 Sibree Bron, 'Probing the Deep Silence of the Indian Diaspora', *Panorama*, 18 August 2001, p. 4.
8 Nalini Ranjan Chakravarti, *The Indian Minority in Burma: The Rise and Decline of an Immigrant Community*, London, New York and Bombay: Oxford University Press, 1971, pp. xv, xvii, p. 49.
9 Ibid., p. 100.
10 George Orwell, *Burmese Days*, Penguin: London, 1989, pp. 38–39; Amitav Ghosh, *The Glass Palace*, London: Flamingo, 2002, pp. 26, 30.
11 R. Pearn, *A History of Rangoon*, Rangoon: American Baptist Press, 1939, p. 243.
12 E.D.Cuming, *In the Shadow of the Pagoda: Sketches of Burmese Life and Character*, London: W.H. Allen 1893, pp. 14–15,

13 Dhananjay Keer, *Mahatma Gandhi: Political Saint and Unarmed Prophet*, Bombay: Popular Prakashan, 1973, p, 409.
14 Ibid.
15 M.K. Gandhi, *An Autobiography or The Story of My Experiments with Truth*, Ahmedabad: Navijavan Trust, 2001 reprint of 1927 first edition, p. 39.
16 Ibid., pp. 8, 39.
17 More information on the Mehta family's Gandhi connections can be found at www.kamdartree.com.
18 Michael Adas, 'Bandits, Monks and Pretender Kings: Patterns of Peasant Resistance and Protest in Colonial Burma, 1826–1941', in Robert P. Weller and Scott E. Guggenheim (eds), *Power and Protest in the Countryside: Studies of Rural Unrest in Asia, Europe, and Latin America*, Durham, North Carolina: Duke University Press, 1989, p. 78.
19 Chakravarti, *The Indian Minority in Burma*, pp. 99–101.
20 Ibid., p. 99.
21 Ibid., p. 9.
22 Gandhi, *An Autobiography*, pp. 322–23.
23 Maung, *Sangha to Laity: Nationalist Movements of Burma, 1920–40*, Australian National University Monographs on South Asia No. 4, 1980, p. 42.
24 Keer, *Mahatma Gandhi*, p. 409.
25 Maung, *Sangha to Laity*, p. 42.
26 Maurice Collis, *Trials in Burma*, London: Faber and Faber, pp. 107–8.
27 Than Htut, 'Two Songs', *Myanmar Historical Research* Journal (8), December 2001, p. 41.
28 Suu Kyi, *Freedom from Fear*, pp. 142–43.
29 Maung, *Sangha to Laity*, pp. 61–62.
30 Htut, 'Two Songs', p. 43.
31 Chakravarti, *The Indian Minority in Burma*, pp. 102–3.
32 Christina Fink, *Living Silence: Burma Under Military Rule*, London: Zed Books, 2001, pp. 18–20.; M. Gravers, *Nationalism as Political Paranoia in Burma: An Essay on the Historical Practice of Power*, Copenhagen: Nordic Institute of Asian Studies Reports 11, 1992, p. 35.
33 Fink, *Living Silence*, pp. 18–20; Gravers, *Nationalism as Political Paranoia in Burma*, p. 35.
34 Chakravarti, *The Indian Minority in Burma*, p. 130.
35 Baragu, *Mahatma Gandhi and Burma*, Rangoon.
36 B.C. Guha, *Shwedagon: Coronation of Burma's Shingottara Kon,* Ragoon: Burma Art Press ltd, 1960, pp vi–vii.
37 A.N. Bose, Preface to *Gandhi in Burma*, Rangoon: Information Service of India, 1979, pp. 7–8.
38 Bose, p. 2.
39 Gandhi, *An Autobiography*, p. 99.
40 Information Service of India, pp.14
41 Htut, 'Two Songs', pp.: 43–44.
42 Bose, op cit, pp 15–16
43 Fink, *Living Silence*, pp. 18–20.
44 Gravers, M., *Nationalism as Political Paranoia in Burma*, p. 35.
45 Maung, *Sangha to Laity*, pp. 61–63.
46 Author interview, Rangoon, 2004.
47 Sankaing Han Tin, 'With tears and anguish written our history', 1934 clipping from his serialised short story of that name in an unidentified journal, held at Yangon Universities Central Library.
48 Collis, *Trials in Burma*, pp. 138–40.
49 Htut, 'Two Songs', pp. 42–43, 45.

50 Maung, *Sangha to Laity*, p. 63.
51 Angelene Naw, *Aung San and the Struggle for Burmese Independence*, Bangkok: Silkworm, 2001, pp. 52–54.
52 Ibid., pp. 47–54.
53 Private communication with Baragu, 2004.
54 Author interview, Rangoon, 2004
55 Lisa Travedi, 'Visually Mapping the Nation: Swadeshi Politics in Nationalist India, 1920–30', *Journal of Asian Studies* 62 (1), February 2003, p. 11.
56 Kamboza Sangw in 1998, *India: Thoughts of Gandhi*, Para. 14, U Thant.
57 Author interview, Rangoon, 2004
58 Suu Kyi, *Freedom from Fear*, p. 184.
59 Gustaaf Houtman, *Mental Culture in Burmese Crisis Politics: Aung San Suu Kyi and the National League for Democracy*, Tokyo: Study of Languages and Cultures of Asia and Africa Monograoh Series No. 33, Tokyo University, 1999.
60 Craig Reynolds, 'Icons of Identity as Sites of Protest', talk given at the CCR Seminar Series on 'Iconographies from Asia', Australian National University, May 2002.
61 Houtman, *Mental Culture in Burmese Crisis Politics*.
62 Tagore, *Mahatmaji and the Depressed Humanity*, p. 9.
63 National League for Democracy Gandhi Hall Declaration, 29 July 1990: http://www.ibiblio.org/obl/docs/Gandhi_Hall_Declaration.htm
64 Houtman, *Mental Culture in Burmese Crisis Politics*, p. 138.
65 'May we be able to go forward together in disciplined strength', Aung San Suu Kyi, Acceptance Speech www.dassk.org/contents.php?id-609.
66 Author visit, Rangoon, April 2004
67 Monique Skidmore, *Karaoke Fascism: Burma and the Politcs of Fear*, Philadelphia: University of Pennsylvania Press, 2004, p. 71.
68 Ibid.
69 Maung, *Sangha to Laity*, p. 14.

Bibliography

Adas, Michael, 'Bandits, Monks and Pretender Kings: Patterns of Peasant Resistance and Protest in Colonial Burma, 1826–1941', in Robert P. Weller and Scott E. Guggenheim (eds) *Power and Protest in the Countryside: Studies of Rural Unrest in Asia, Europe, and Latin America*,Durham, North Carolina: Duke University Press, 1989.
Baragu, *Mahatma Gandhi and Burma*, Rangoon.
Bose, A.N., Preface to *Gandhi in Burma*, Rangoon: Information Service of India,1979.
Bron, Sibree, 'Probing the Deep Silence of the Indian Diaspora', *Panorama*, 18 August 2001.
Chakravarti, Nalini Ranjan, *The Indian Minority in Burma: The Rise and Decline of an Immigrant Community*, London, New York and Bombay: Oxford University Press, 1971.
Collis, Maurice, *Trials in Burma*, London: Faber and Faber, 1938.
Cuming, E.D., *In the Shadow of the Pagoda: Sketches of Burmese Life and Character*, London: W. H. Allen, 1893.
Fink, Christina, *Living Silence: Burma Under Military Rule*, London: Zed Books, 2001
Gandhi, M.K, *An Autobiography or the Story of My Experiments with Truth*, Ahmedabad: Navijavan Trust, 2001 reprint of 1927 first edition.

Ghosh, Amitav, *The Glass Palace*, London: Flamingo, 2002.
Gravers, M., *Nationalism as Political Paranoia in Burma: An Essay on the Historical Practice of Power*, Copenhagen: Nordic Institute of Asian Studies Reports 11, 1992.
Guha, B.C, *Shwedagon: Coronation of Burma's Shingottara Kon*, Ragoon: Burma Art Press, 1960.
Houtman, Gustaaf, *Mental Culture in Burmese Crisis Politics: Aung San Suu Kyi and the National League for Democracy*, Tokyo: Study of Languages and Cultures of Asia and Africa Monograoh Series No. 33, Tokyo University, 1999.
Keer, Dhananjay, *Mahatma Gandhi: Political Saint and Unarmed Prophet*, Bombay: Popular Prakashan, 1973.
'National League for Democracy Gandhi Hall Declaration, 29 July 1990': http://www.ibiblio.org/obl/docs/Gandhi_Hall_Declaration.htm.
Naw, Angelene, *Aung San and the Struggle for Burmese Independence*, Bangkok: Silkworm, 2001.
Orwell, George, *Burmese Days*, Penguin: London, 1989.
Pearn, R., *A History of Rangoon*, Rangoon: American Baptist Press, 1939.
Reynolds, Craig, 'Icons of Identity as Sites of Protest', talk given at the CCR Seminar Series on 'Iconographies from Asia', Australian National University, May 2002.
Sankaing Han Tin, 'With Tears and Anguish Written our History', 1934, clipping from his serialised short story of that name in an unidentified journal, held at Yangon Universities Central Library.
Skidmore, Monique, *Karaoke Fascism: Burma and the Politics of Fear*, Philadelphia: University of Pennsylvania Press, 2004.
Suu Kyi, Aung San, *Freedom From Fear*, London: Penguin Books, 1991.
—— 'May we be able to go forward together in disciplined strength', Acceptance Speech: www.dassk.org/contents.php?id-609
Tagore, Rabindranath, *Mahatmaji and the Depressed Humanity: East and West*, New Delhi: Rupa, 2002.
Than Htut, 'Two Songs', *Myanmar Historical Research* Journal (8), December 2001.
Travedi, Lisa, 'Visually Mapping the Nation: Swadeshi Politics in Nationalist India, 1920–30', *Journal of Asian Studies*, Vol. 62, No.1, February 2003.
U Maung Maung, *Sangha to Laity: Nationalist Movements of Burma, 1920–40*, Australian National University Monographs on South Asia No.4, 1980.

10 Nonviolence and long hot summers
Black women's welfare-rights struggles in 1960s' Baltimore

Rhonda Y. Williams

In Baltimore, Maryland, USA, a cadre of low-income black and white women who depended on government financial support for their families formed a welfare rights coalition. The coalition included the city's first welfare rights group, Mother Rescuers from Poverty, which informed 'welfare recipients of their rights to welfare and to work for a minimum standard of living with dignity'.[1] Mother Rescuers and other local welfare rights groups laboured to fulfil the National Welfare Rights Organization's imperative to fight for jobs, better welfare services, and dignity. Founded in 1966 in the United States, this national organization, clearly echoing black rights and freedom struggles of the day, implored low-income women to: 'Know your rights, demand your rights, protect your rights, link up with Welfare Rights.'[2]

In 1969, the Baltimore coalition attended a meeting at the city's welfare headquarters. Protesting mothers, who had children in tow, wanted the welfare agency to act on a series of demands aimed at improving their quality of life. They not only sought to meet immediate needs such as an adequate income, food, clothing, and shelter, but also to participate in and thereby change what they perceived as a 'paternalistic' and 'dictatorial' bureaucracy that structured their daily lives and attacked their human dignity.[3]

But the meeting at the welfare agency did not proceed as smoothly as might have been desired by either activists or local agency officials. It turned into an overnight protest – a sleep-in at welfare headquarters. That day in May 1969, Rudell Martin, a Cherry Hill Homes' tenant and welfare rights' activist, told a newspaper reporter that the welfare director '[Esther] Lazarus told us last week to come back Monday for an answer. ... Well when we got here today she told us she couldn't answer us till Thursday.'[4] Lazarus, who worked to dispel 'popular but baseless misconceptions' of welfare clients, in fact, had approved most of their demands including allowing coalition members to represent recipients upon request and to set up a 'welfare rights advisory service' inside the agency. But a few of the demands had required state approval and thus the wait.[5]

The mothers who had sacrificed money and time to attend the meeting at the welfare department held vigil throughout the night, vowing to stay 'until we get action'.[6] Rudell Martin recalled that people gathered outside once they knew that the mothers would camp out in the building. Supporters from a local church and other civil rights groups brought the protestors food, drinks, and blankets and kept in touch with them through walkie-talkies. Police confronted the demonstrators but made no arrests, apparently upon the request of Lazarus – a wise action given that police mistreatment of welfare recipients, civil rights activists, and black citizens in general had escalated out of control in other cities over the previous five years.[7] In Boston, for instance, police beat welfare recipients who staged a sit-in at the welfare department; the women's screams 'from the windows to the streets below' provoked 'three days of rioting'.[8] An advisor to the contingent from Baltimore's Cherry Hill Homes, Charles Henry, maintained that the sleep-in, which resulted in positive action on the remaining demands, exemplified 'people power ... This is something Malcolm X and the late Martin Luther King were working towards.'[9]

This essay explores the influence of Mohandas K. Gandhi's nonviolent philosophy on a specific articulation of black American politics – welfare rights activism – and examines the complex interaction and often simultaneous operation of nonviolence, self-defence, and counter-violence on the ground.[10] Against the backdrop of decades of black civil disobedience in the post-1930s era, nonviolent direct action at the grassroots had become a folkloric, or customary, strategy of activist import among everyday people.[11] Welfare rights activism, which exposed urban-based social justice imperatives and low-income women's concerns, provides a context for exploring the disparate and multiple strategies adopted by working-class people at the grassroots. Welfare rights activists engaged in political lobbying, litigation, educational programming, leadership development, coalition and institution building, and direct action campaigns.

From the mid-1960s when the first local groups and national organization emerged through the 1970s, these direct-action campaigns had different forms and tenors. The fluid and embedded nature of welfare rights protest direct-action tactics (from sleep-ins, marches and door-to-door organizing) and utterances (from cooperation to threatening hot summers) exemplifies how Gandhian nonviolence operated as a situational liberation technique – one of many purposefully and ably deployed by a group of black women who had not been regarded as ideologically astute political actors.[12] In fact, the popular image portrayed them as leeches comfortable with their life on the government 'dole'.

Welfare rights activists, however, were not content, and their engagement in campaigns to publicly expose and confront unjust and undemocratic state programmes served as unarguable evidence of their disgruntlement. In the 1969 sleep-in, nonviolence as a strategy and language found expression among low-income black women – as it had for numerous civil rights activists for decades. But nonviolence did not monopolize welfare rights activism or black freedom politics. Aggressive self-determination and vocalized threats of violence also existed at the grassroots – often times used by the same activists who sought to challenge power through peaceful protest. In their daily battles, low-income black women enacted divergent strategies and verbal postures to secure better services, adequate income, dignified treatment, democratic participation, and 'a constitutionally and humanely just system'.[13]

These philosophical complexities, tactical flexibility, and the eventual public concern about self-defence and counter-force details the nuances of black struggle and conjure up a decades-old debate about whether 'Gandhi's unequivocal commitment to nonviolence' translated well to black people's then contemporary conditions in the United States – thereby exposing the way liberation philosophies travelled internationally and operated domestically.[14]

Black Americans, East Indians, and liberation

In the first decade of the twentieth century, news of Gandhi's heroism and Indian people's struggles against British colonials travelled the globe, landing in Europe, South Africa, Asia, and Australia. Returning to India from South Africa in 1915, Gandhi challenged repressive British policies and led campaigns for self-rule. At age 46, Gandhi, who became the leader of the Indian National Congress, protested the British partition of Bengal in East India, organized non-cooperation campaigns including the anti-tax Salt March of 1930, and contested the marginalization and stigma of 'Untouchables' or Harijan peoples.[15] Reports of the audacity of this determined 'little man with spectacles' – a former British-trained lawyer – who dared to contest British power and domination similarly reached the United States where African Americans engaged in their own battles against racism and exclusion.

As early as the 1900s, black Americans learned of Gandhi and the anti-colonial struggle in India. Author, activist, co-founder of the National Association for the Advancement of Colored People (NAACP), and 'father' of pan-Africanism, W.E.B. Du Bois expressed global 'racial solidarity' with Indian freedom fighters and other subjugated people of colour. In 1919, Du Bois wrote: 'We are all one – we the Despised and Oppressed, the "niggers" of England and America.'[16] Mary Church Terrell, an esteemed black middle-class clubwoman, and Marcus Garvey, the black nationalist Jamaican founder of the Universal Negro Improvement Association (UNIA) and political progenitor of the Nation of Islam and Malcolm X, also publicly supported India's freedom struggle in the 1920s.[17] Black journals, including the NAACP's *Crisis* and UNIA's *Negro World*, and newspapers such as the Baltimore *Afro-American*, Pittsburgh *Courier*, and Chicago *Defender*, all carried news about Gandhi and his country's struggle against British colonials. The *Defender* went so far as to describe 'India's concepts of equality and freedom' as 'the world's ideals'.[18] Already possessing a tradition of religiously driven activism and 'civil disobedience to unjust systems', black people showed an interest in and receptivity to Gandhian strategies and the travails of Indian peoples.[19]

In the 1930s and 1940s, on the tail of the Depression, the rise of fascism, the government's espousal of democratic liberalism, and continued racist and colonial oppression, several black men, who would emerge as nationally recognized civil rights leaders in the United States, had visited India and even met Gandhi and began discussing nonviolent direct action as a tool to bring about mass struggle and social change. Mordecai Johnson, the president of Howard University, and Channing Tobias, a clergyman and future member of the NAACP Board of Trustees in the 1940s, both travelled to India and met with Gandhi.[20] So did Howard Thurman, a Howard University dean, and well-respected black intellectual and theologian who remained a strong voice for social justice based on Christian liberation theology. In an effort to end the exclusion of black people from wartime industry jobs underwritten by the federal government, A. Phillip Randolph consciously drew on Gandhi's nonviolent protest strategy by threatening a mass march on Washington, DC.[21] Pacifist and anti-Jim Crow activist, Bayard Rustin, learned about Gandhian nonviolence through the Christian, interracial, and pacifist Fellowship of Reconciliation (FOR). The Gandhian philosophy of social change – *satyagraha* – based on truth (*satya*), resolute persuasion (*graha*), and non-injury (*ahimsa*), included deploying strategies such as direct action, mass peaceful protest, and non-cooperation campaigns.[22] Rustin expressed a commitment to 'the struggle for racial equality, a peaceful international order, and a democratic economic system'. John D'Emilio's recent biography of Rustin credits him with insinuating 'nonviolence into the heart of the black freedom struggle'.[23] And like Gandhi, Rustin enacted nonviolence as a principled way of living, not primarily as a strategy for black freedom on the US battleground.

Inspired both by Thurman's teaching and FOR's philosophy, James Farmer called for 'a creative use of Gandhi's philosophy tailored to American conditions' and initiated the creation of the Congress of Racial Equality (CORE) in 1940s' Chicago. CORE spearheaded nonviolent, direct action campaigns in the United States, organizing sit-ins and boycotts in the 1940s and freedom rides in 1947 and 1961. By the 1960s, CORE had participated in campaigns with SNCC and the popular and most recognized 'prophet' of nonviolence, Dr Martin Luther King Jr. and his Southern Christian Leadership Conference (SCLC). Both Martin Luther King and Coretta Scott King had visited India in 1959, four years after the Montgomery Bus Boycott and eleven years after Gandhi's murder.[24]

In 1953 a CORE chapter was established in Baltimore. An eastern city with an inner harbour, Baltimore had a vibrant industrial and commercial economy during World War II. As the northernmost southern city, its political economy reflected de facto and de jure racial segregation, state control, and financial conservatism – all of which worked to limit black advancement and opportunity. The local chapter's initial group of 25 to 30 members included middle-class whites and blacks such as a minister and his wife and a 'significant contingent of upwardly mobile black trade unionists who were active in the International Ladies' Garment Workers' Union'.[25] While some members believed in direct action in the early years, others were reticent about doing anything to cause 'potential embarrassment' and feared the 'limelight'. In general, however, men and women civil rights' protestors experimented with sit-ins and marches to open up jobs, restaurants, and theatres as early as the 1930s. In particular, the Interstate Route 40 campaign, organized by the national CORE with indispensable aid from the Baltimore chapter, highlighted the idiocy of a logic that excluded US black people from public accommodations, but not African diplomats – the latter often confused with the former to the US government's great embarrassment. In 1961, the Route 40 Freedom Riders came through Baltimore, revitalizing what had become a relatively unstable and lethargic chapter.[26]

This broad-based, interlocking constituency and agenda provide early evidence of the direct activist linkages at the grassroots level among race, religion, rights, and labour that undergirded the developing association of nonviolent resistance against colonialism, black subjugation, economic discrimination, and eventually women's marginalization both locally and nationally. In fact, one of CORE's former national officers, George Wiley, helped to found the NWRO in 1966. This relationship between civil rights' workers and low-income grassroots women's activists, in particular, not only helped to transmit nonviolence as a protest strategy, but also foster its folkloric status in welfare rights organizing.

While black Americans journeyed to India, the exchange of ideas and people did not just occur in one direction. Between the early 1900s and the mid-1940s, numerous Indian scholars visited US black educational institutions, and Indian officials had toured Jim Crow cities, including Baltimore. In 1914 Lala Lajpat Rai as a political exile and member of the Hindu self-government movement, Arya Samaj, came to the United States. During his five-year stay, Rai developed a relationship with Du Bois and other black political activists and publicly gave intellectual witness to the 'analogy between the Negro problem in the United States of America and the problem of depressed classes [Untouchables and members of tribal groups] in India'.[27] While Rai was not singularly devoted to nonviolence, exposing the contested nature of the philosophy even in India, another Indian traveller, Haridas T. Muzumdar, who reached the states in the 1920s, worked to spread the power of Gandhi and *satyagraha*.[28] In 1937, J.J. Singh, who participated in Gandhi's Salt March to the Sea, came to the United States and headed the India League of America.[29] And in 1945 during the United Nations' first meeting, Madame Vijaya Lakshmi Pandit, the leader of the Indian Congress Party, Jawaharlal Nehru's sister, and an outspoken anti-racist and women's rights activist, toured the United States. A future ambassador to the United States and the first woman president of the UN

General Assembly, Pandit had refused to speak at the Lyric Theater, Baltimore's premier music hall, because of its segregationist policy when she visited the city.[30]

In this post-1930s age of continued white supremacy, imperialism, colourism, and caste, black activists identified with Gandhi's battle. And Gandhi not only knew this, but also recognized the struggles of black Americans and the potential power nonviolence could have through their freedom movements. In fact, after a 1936 meeting in India between Gandhi and Thurman, who argued black people possessed a religious tradition 'conducive to Gandhi's philosophy and that they were ready to practice it', Gandhi stated: 'Well, if it comes true, it may be through the Negroes that the unadulterated message of nonviolence will be delivered to the world.'[31]

Inspired by the success of Gandhi's non-cooperation campaigns, CORE, SCLC, and SNCC leaders and organizers helped spread nonviolent protest strategies among thousands of black activists, who participated in mass public accommodations' demonstrations and voter education campaigns. By the 1960s, nonviolence as a strategy, as a political technique, was affirmed, although not uncontested. The philosophy had penetrated the civil rights movement and, with the growing reach of television, provided the stark footage that depicted nonviolent protestors in battle with violent state authorities and galvanized national and international sympathy for black people in America.

While many of the most publicized nonviolent civil rights campaigns did not address deep-rooted racism and the dire economic needs of impoverished black residents, particularly in the North, the strategy of nonviolence had influenced activism in cities nationwide. And some of these grassroots activists applied similar tactics against government authorities. Welfare rights' activists, most of them black women, assumed a nonviolent politics of confrontation to achieve their goals – not because they necessarily knew of or revered Gandhi, but because nonviolence had become a widespread quotidian tactic in the search for equality and social change. By then, narratives of the movement often celebrated sit-ins and marches as tools of mass resistance. The dissemination of strategic nonviolence, then, did not travel a direct or inviolable linear path from Gandhi to grassroots black women activists. Many grassroots organizers, including welfare rights activists, reshaped and creatively domesticated the strategy to the US political economy and citizenry needs by waging, for instance, sleep-ins, lie-ins, and even shop-ins.[32] Moreover, when several of these women activists reminisced about their politicization and discussed their confrontational ethos and activism, they recalled not Gandhi as had Rustin, King, and Farmer, but the influences of family members, then contemporary grassroots urban activists, or simply the urgency of daily life. For instance, Goldie Baker recollected being dragged from demonstrations to meetings to picket lines by her grandmother and mother in 1940s' Baltimore. Low-income black women's historical memory, family legacy, and components of Gandhian philosophy incorporated into black protest traditions infused their activism, and the attendant strategies were mediated through black prophetic leaders and grassroots organizers.[33]

But the questioning of suitable and honourable strategies for black liberation caused a significant public furore in the 1960s, particularly with the popularization of Malcolm X and media coverage of the incendiary rhetoric of student activists like Stokely Carmichael and H. Rap Brown of the Student Nonviolent Coordinating Committee (SNCC). While the rhetoric and ideologies of these men actors precipitated public discomfort and new rifts in movement politics, the overarching debate regarding effective and appropriate strategies had a history that involved both men and women. The long view of African-American resistance has demonstrated the consistent existence of the all-important question: What methods should black people employ to attack and dismantle racial exclusion and violence? After the 1930s the harnessing of nonviolence in the United States reflected the spread of a black liberation politics that combined homegrown protest traditions including self-defence, religious sentiments with a growing familiarity with Gandhi and nonviolence in the Indian liberation movement.[34] The name of the premier black students' rights group in the 1960s – the Student *Nonviolent* Coordinating Committee (SNCC) – signified this. But the black political terrain was a complicated and shifting one. For just as SNCC organizers would increasingly harness self-defence and counter-violence, especially in the face of state-fomented police brutality, murders, and social oppression, so did working-class women activists who contested their own forms of state violence.

Nonviolence, self-defence, and counter-violence

While nonviolent strategies infused black women's activism, these women also drew on other black traditions such as self-defence and threats of violence – as signified by Charles Henry's pairing of King (known for his nonviolent stance) with Malcolm X (known for his support of self-defence) during the low-income women's welfare rights protest in 1969.[35] While in popular perception self-defence was often conflated with or confusedly understood as inextricably intertwined with violence, historian Emilye Crosby has argued: 'Self-defense is not the opposite of nonviolence nor the equivalent of violence.'[36] Neither were self-defence claims, threats of violence, and nonviolence necessarily mutually exclusive or antithetical; for some, they represented available options on a tactical continuum. Historian Simon Wendt's work on black protective clubs in Tuscaloosa, Alabama, for instance, revealed the simultaneous operation of and lack of conflict among 'God, Gandhi, and Guns' in local movement politics.[37] In fact, while self-defence experienced popular resurgence in the late 1960s, it also had a long history, stretching at least as far back to anti-lynching crusader Ida B. Wells. In her well-known treatise *Southern Horrors: Lynch Law and All Its Phases*, published in 1892, Wells maintained:

The only times an Afro-American who was assaulted got away has been when he had a gun and used it in self-defense. The lesson this teaches and which every Afro American should ponder well, is that a Winchester rifle should have a place of honor in every black home and it should be used for that protection which the law refuses to give.[38]

Low-income black women's use of various traditions reaffirms the ways in which nonviolence had become a political technique and an embedded practice, but just one of many.[39] In Cambridge, Maryland, grassroots activist Gloria Richardson challenged the unequivocal acceptance of nonviolence in a multilayered movement confronting a wily violent state. In June 1963, violence erupted between armed activists and gun-wielding Cambridge authorities.[40] A good friend of Rustin's, Ella Baker, who helped run King's SCLC and founded SNCC, similarly viewed nonviolence as a strategy. A radical humanist who believed in fundamental social change through the democratic participation of everyday people, Ella Baker in speaking of Rustin, and by extension nonviolence, said: 'He had a history of dedication to the concept of nonviolence. I have no such history; I have no such commitment.' In other words, Ella Baker 'accepted nonviolence as a tactic'. But she departed from the moral *de rigueur* of Gandhian philosophy and 'never internalized the concept as a way of life or made it a defining feature of her worldview'.[41] Their words exemplify the stance of many black Americans who did not witness the emergence of a beloved community in the aftermath of nonviolent protests in the 1950s and 1960s.

Between 1964 and 1968, in particular, when welfare rights organizations proliferated and flourished in cities, urban residents experienced police power, witnessed urban rebellions, and confronted systemic inequality that posed as 'normal' social relations. The Civil Rights Act of 1964 and Voting Rights Act of 1965, after years of protest and lost lives, had provided legal equality, but had not alleviated entrenched economic inequality. During these years, militant civil rights, Black Power, and New Left activists made cities their new activist targets. For instance, CORE, the Black Panther Party of Self-Defense, and SDS-ERAP operated in cities, including Baltimore, where embattled low-income women confronted the harshness of state power and heard about state assaults on black protestors. These women did not allow the notions of orderliness, bourgeois deportment, and demeaning stereotypes delimit their activist postures. Low-income women in Baltimore and elsewhere sometimes used nonviolent language and other times discarded it – depending on the perceived needs and effectiveness for their particular urban-based, racialized, gendered, and working-class issues. Welfare rights groups not only engaged in resistance based on truth, but also vigorously spoke truth to power thereby exposing the limits of the liberal state's individualized, gradualist reforms and wilful inaction, and its simultaneous repressive reaction to marginalized people's demands.

Mother Rescuers from Poverty, which had participated in the 1969 sleep-in protest, followed the strategy of a 'civil rights organization', the Union for Jobs or Income Now (U-JOIN). Founded years earlier by an integrated cadre of SDS-ERAP student organizers concerned about poverty, U-JOIN had a 'reputation of getting in the Establishment's hair and pulling hard'. Founded by U-JOIN and inspired by its unrelenting defiance of state authority, Mother Rescuers confronted bureaucrats and commanded the public eye by frequently marching and passing out leaflets. In order to lure other low-income women to their cause, the group regularly protested outside the welfare department office when welfare cheques were issued – once even using a sound truck to encourage people to join their picket line. Recipients' outspokenness and their demonstrations garnered attention from the press, and in the first six months of their existence, their protests resulted in meetings with municipal and state welfare officials and legislators.

On occasion, they also deployed an aggressive stance to secure their rights, to convey a strong sentiment of self-determination, and to confront a legacy of government inequality. In this they exposed the existence of state violence and the particular forms it took in the lives of low-income black women and their families. Gandhi may not have encouraged violence or threats of violence as liberation strategies, but he was quite familiar with state sponsorship of it.[42] Popularly imagined as a martyr of moral righteousness, Gandhi was more than a symbol of redemption; he was also a vocal critic of imperial power. Until his death in 1948, Gandhi challenged British imperialism and its violent antecedents. The demands for political autonomy, nationhood, and self-determination, which suffused both the Gandhian-led anti-colonial movement and black freedom struggles, in fact, represented a path away from violence. Gandhi critiqued American democracy and its underlying hypocritical treatment of black people.[43] Motivated by the similar forces of state power, race, and caste, Gandhi's movement, like the contentious battles against Jim Crow, even exalted the language of 'open rebellion' and called for 'a mass movement on the widest possible scale'.[44]

As the 1960s proceeded, working-class black women activists, and their middle-class sympathizers, increasingly defined state violence broadly. Violence no longer meant only those acts that resulted in immediate bodily harm such as slavery, lynchings, Ku Klux Klan vigilantism, massive resistance in the wake of *Brown vs. Board of Education*, and police brutality. It extended to dehumanization and oppression in its many forms. Echoing the sentiments welfare rights organizers had expressed for years, Coretta Scott King conveyed this expansive view at a Mother's Day March of welfare recipients in May 1968 during the second phase of the Poor People's Campaign, which followed on the heels of her husband's assassination. At the end of a 12-block march culminating in a rally, Scott King reaffirmed a commitment to interracial, nonviolent activism and encouraged 'black women, white women, brown women, and red women – all the women of this nation – [to join] in campaign of conscience'. But while Scott King stressed nonviolence, she also knew it did not represent 'an easy way, particularly in this day when violence is almost fashionable, and in this society, where violence against poor people and minority groups is routine'. She continued:

> I must remind you that starving a child is violence. Suppressing a culture is violence. Neglecting school children is violence. Punishing a mother and her family is violence. ... Ignoring medical needs is violence. Contempt for poverty is violence. Even the lack of will power to help humanity is a sick and sinister form of violence.[45]

This timely remark redefined violence and exposed the interaction of non-violent and violent rhetoric.

But even before Scott King's incisive public comment before 5,000 people in the nation's capital, such violence had infiltrated low-income black women's lives, their families' lives, their historical memories, and their relationships with government authorities and programmes – as well as the lives of some fellow black men activists. Walter Lively, the leader of Baltimore's U-JOIN, had grown up in poverty in public housing in Philadelphia. Stories of abusive treatment by social-service workers and the systems they represented existed much earlier than the 1960s heyday of welfare rights activism. Even Malcolm X, the charismatic and intellectual icon of black-power activists, argued that the belittling of his mother by a white welfare worker in the 1930s led to his mother's nervous breakdown and the break-up of their family. Goldie Baker remembers her grandmother and mother contesting unfair welfare agency policies in the 1940s and 1950s. Given the activist and daily realities of the 1960s, the violent dehumanization of welfare recipients through debasing stereotypes disseminated as truth, and the sometimes overzealous response of frightened public welfare and government officials to assertive protestors, it was not surprising that the threat of violence emerged as a strategic call.[46]

The relationship between expressions of violence and nonviolence in welfare rights' activism, however, differed from that in other black-freedom organizations. In several southern cities in Alabama, North Carolina, and Louisiana, black civil rights activists developed self-defence units and rifle clubs that actively protected demonstrators and freedom workers with rifles and arms.[47] The Black Panther Party for Self-Defense and US, both founded in the mid-1960s in California, also established paramilitary units of their organizations.[48] Welfare rights activists, in contrast, did not express their belief in self-defence through the development of such organizational sub-units. Instead these women engaged in rhetorical posturing. In Baltimore and elsewhere, low-income black women activists exhibited a willingness to deploy aggressive language and utilize the spectre of urban uprisings and black radical confrontation as they negotiated their demands.

In 1967, one year prior to Coretta King's Mother's Day statement and two years before the Baltimore sleep-in, the welfare rights struggle began to intensify, particularly with increased national coordination of poor mothers' actions and more widespread critiques of poverty including by Martin Luther King.[49] In Baltimore in February, Mother Rescuers geared up for a battle to reinstate money for rent, food, and clothing that Maryland's governor, Spiro T. Agnew, had cut from his budget. Handfuls of women marched to Annapolis, the state capital, to demand the restoration of cut items and challenge a '"slap in the face" wholesale cutting of the State welfare budget'.[50] Viewing the governor's policy as physical assault, welfare rights activists responded with the rhetoric of physical aggression. A month later during another march in Annapolis on 22 March, dubbed Poor People's Independence Day, Margaret McCarty, the Mother Rescuers' chair, threatened legislators with a 'long, hot, angry summer'.[51] Unlike other major cities, Baltimore had escaped the rebellions that had exploded over the last two years, and municipal and state officials wanted to keep it that way. Organizers knew this and not only exploited officials' fears, but, in a sense, issued a warning: continuous government inaction would chip away at civility.

That same year in August at the NWRO's first national convention, a 1,000-member singing and shouting delegation including Baltimore women protested the federal government's proposed bill that would force mothers who received welfare to work or remove them from the rolls. NWRO organizers invited Senators to meet with them, but none did. Protestors vented their disappointment and outrage in a protest at the Health, Education, and Welfare building in DC and a rally on the Mall. Both protests drew heavy police details, so much so that even a *Washington Post* reporter wrote: 'The Capitol and metropolitan police were present in unusual force.'[52]

Organizers did not mince words. Lambasting the insanity of spending billions on the Vietnam War while spending a pittance on social programmes, welfare rights activists characterized the restrictive welfare bill as 'a betrayal of the poor, a declaration of war upon our families, and a fraud on the future of our nation'.[53] At the rally on the Mall, McCarty aroused the national delegation, drawing resounding applause when she bellowed that 'lousy, dirty, conniving, brutes' devised the welfare bill to 'take us back to slavery'. In her emphatic statement, McCarty connected the historical memory and brutality of slavery and racial discrimination to contemporary violent state oppression. She continued in her statement: 'It's another form of slavery, baby. But I'm black and I'm beautiful. They're not going to take me back.'[54] McCarty then stated that if the protestors' collective voices did not motivate officials to change the laws and welfare system, maybe 'force' would. At the time, to protestors, the threat of violence and the doom of urban rebellions seemed to be the only language to which the government paid attention. For several summers in a row, pent-up frustrations had exploded into full-scale uprisings. During 1967, urban rebellions in Newark, New York, Cleveland, Chicago, Atlanta, and Detroit were still fresh, and summer had not ended yet.

Mothers felt the proposed bill penalized them for their poverty and would force them to abide by a less than fair policy. In fact, they claimed that government officials treated them as less than second-class citizens. The potentiality of citizenry retaliation and real government repression mediated political relations. Responding to the physical and political presence of government force, Beulah Sanders, vice-chair of NWRO and a New York City resident, similarly deployed the rhetoric of counter-force at the Mall rally, saying protestors' money 'paid for the Capitol' and they should 'tear it down if they don't listen to you'. Other NWRO figures echoed McCarty's and Sanders' sentiments. George Wiley, the former CORE organizer and NWRO founder, conjured up more starkly the urban rebellions: 'If this country does not listen to poor people after what happened in Detroit and Newark and New Haven you haven't seen nothing yet.'[55] And Johnnie Tillmon 'said it was time officials understood the meaning of the long hot summer'. The *Evening Star* newspaper, which covered the rally, blared in its headline: 'Welfare Rally Threatens Riots'.[56] In an era ripe with urban uprisings, law and order claims, and police attacks on black activists, state force met the people's threat of counter-force.

Conclusion

Throughout the 1960s and 1970s, the struggles of welfare rights activists drew on various traditions of grassroots empowerment – and black struggles inflected by Gandhian nonviolence represented one of them. In fact, these women's activism exemplifies Emilye Crosby's point that 'nonviolent direct action and self-defense were not mutually exclusive, but were often used by the same people in different situations'.[57] Low-income women's combined strategic use of nonviolent resistance, aggressive confrontation, and threats of force reaffirm the complexity of the unfolding of history. The strategies and rhetoric exemplify not only the existence of folkloric, Gandhian-inflected civil disobedience and direct action strategies, but also the malleability of nonviolence and the creativity of black activists who purposefully shaped it to provoke responsiveness from a government that excluded them. An examination of their protests helps to bring women center stage. Moreover, low-income women's stories expand our understanding of black freedom struggles and working-class protest in post-Depression and post-industrial cities beyond the charismatic leader, and the formal and popularly recognized black political organizations. By forcing us to deal with how women enacted their issues and pushed the boundaries of accepted political practice, low-income women's struggles unveil a much fuller picture of whom the activists were and of the activist traditions they fostered.

Welfare rights activism that bridged nonviolence, self-determination, and threats of forceful action had an impact on low-income women's lives 'in the moment'. Contending with marginalization by the government, poverty, and gender and racial discrimination, these low-income black women activists refused to be marginalized as political actors and US citizens. While not middle-class intellectuals manipulating sophisticated theoretical propositions, as organizers engaged in the activist process these low-income black women wielded skilfully the language of citizenship and rights, self-defence and force, and nonviolence in their grassroots battles. And they won some of them. They garnered increased benefits from the state and carved out an official public space of representation on local and state government boards and in welfare agencies. For welfare rights activists not only fought for subsistence rights and a better quality of life, but they also sought to participate in government decision-making and to contest the state's discriminatory and violent stance against its low-income citizens – a stance that that remains all too present decades later in this the twenty-first century.

Notes

I would like to thank Pam Brooks, Peniel E. Joseph, and Karen Sotiropoulos for reading this essay in its entirety and offering useful suggestions for revisions; conference organizers John Docker and Debjani Ganguly for inviting me to participate in the 'Gandhi, Nonviolence and Modernity' Conference at the Humanities Research Centre of the Australian National University in Canberra, Australia, in 2004; and fellow conference participants for a wonderfully rich intellectual exchange.

1 State Board of Public Welfare, Minutes of Meeting Minutes, 18 April 1969. For greater detail on many of the incidents of activism and low-income women's stories referenced in this essay, see Rhonda Y. Williams, *The Politics of Public Housing: Black Women's Struggles Against Urban Inequality.* Transgressing Boundaries Series (New York: Oxford University Press, 2004).

2 NWRO, 'Bill of Welfare Rights', 1966, Folder 5: Membership Miscellany, 1967–72, Box 8, George Wiley Papers, Wisconsin Historical Society, Madison, Wisconsin. For a rich discussion of the national movement, see Premilla Nadasen, *Welfare Warriors: The Welfare Rights Movement in the United States* (New York: Routledge, 2005).

3 'Goals for a National Welfare Rights Movement', The Report of Worskshop 2, National Welfare Rights Meeting, Chicago, Illinois, 6–7 August 1966, Folder 7: Founding Meetings, Box 7, George Wiley Papers.

4 'Welfare Sit-in Protests Delays', Baltimore *Morning Sun*, 13 May 1969. Also see, regarding the involvement of O'Donnell Heights' IMPACT, Memos to Van Story Branch from Jacob Fisher, 3 April 1969, 13 June 1969, Folder: O'Donnell Heights – Monthly Reports, 1965–70, Box 39, Series 14, RG 48.

5 Mueller resigned in 1971. See State Department of Public Welfare, Minutes of Meeting, 19 March 1971.

6 Lee Lassiter, 'Welfare: Reform or Revolt', Baltimore *News American*, April 1969, Folder 16: Welfare – DSS, Box 22, Series 24, BCP; 'Welfare mothers sleep-in at DPW', Baltimore *Afro-American*, 13 May 1969. In Detroit, demonstrating welfare mothers closed offices for four days. See Frances Fox Piven and

Richard A. Cloward, *Poor People's Movements: Why They Succeed, How They Fail* (New York: Vintage, 1977), 265.

7 'Welfare mothers sleep-in at DPW', Baltimore *Afro-American*, 13 May 1969; 'Welfare Sit-in Protests Delays', Baltimore *Morning Sun*, 13 May 1969; Rudell Martin, Betty Keaton and Geraldine Randall, interviews by author.

8 Piven and Cloward, *Poor People's Movements*, 274.

9 John C. White, 'Welfare Mothers Sleep-In at DPW', Baltimore *Afro-American*, 13 May 1969.

10 See, for instance, Clayborne Carson, *Malcolm X: The FBI File* (New York: Carroll & Graf Publishers, Inc., 1991), 48–49; Emilye Crosby, ' "This Nonviolent Stuff Ain't No Good. It'll Get You Killed": Teaching About Self-Defense in the African-American Freedom Struggle', *Teaching the American Civil Rights Movement: Freedom's Bittersweet Song*, edited by Julie Buckner Armstrong, Susan Hult Edwards, Houston Bryan Roberson, and Rhonda Y. Williams (New York: Routledge, 2002), 159–69; Simon Wendt, 'God, Gandhi, and Guns: The African American Freedom Struggle in Tuscaoloosa, Alabama, 1964–65', *Journal of African American History* 89, Winter 2004: 36–56.

11 I'd like to thank Dr. Mary Bivins for suggesting the term 'folkloric' as a way to think about the indirect conveyance and expression of nonviolent action among grassroots black women activists.

12 With regard to the use of Mohandas Gandhi and the deploying of his nonviolent philosophy, Leela Gandhi, a scholar and familial descendant, described Mohandas Gandhi as an 'experimental subject' that had 'utter usability', 'domesticating possibilities', and 'malleability in a variety of global places'. Leela Gandhi's comments during the closing session of the 'Gandhi, Nonviolence and Modernity' Conference, Humanities Research Centre (HRC), Australian National University (ANU), 3 September 2004, Canberra, Australia. During this same session, scholar Debjani Ganguly similarly raised the question of Gandhi's seemingly 'infinite malleability'.

13 'Goals for a National Welfare Rights Movement,' The Report of Worskshop 2, National Welfare Rights Meeting, Chicago, Illinois, 6–7 August 1966, Folder 7: Founding Meetings, Box 7, George Wiley Papers.

14 Quote appears in Brenda Gayle Plummer, *Rising Wind: Black Americans and U.S. Foreign Affairs, 1935–1960* (Chapel Hill: University of North Carolina Press, 1996), 29. This quote refers to clergyman, Channing Tobias, but Benjamin E. Mays and Ralph Bunche among others also expressed concern about Gandhian nonviolence in the US context – some thirty years before similar debates arose in the 1960s, emblematic in SCLC–SNCC exchanges over strategies and tactics. Also see Marc Gallicchio, *The African American Encounter with Japan and China: Black Internationalism in Asia, 1885–1945* (Chapel Hill: University of North Carolina Press, 2000), 44; Sudarshan Kapur, *Raising Up a Prophet: The African-American Encounter with Gandhi* (Boston: Beacon Press, 1992), 89, 95, and particularly Chapter 5.

Even in India, lower castes, Marxists, and those who preferred or saw the utility of violence contested Gandhi and his nonviolent philosophy. Dipesh Chakrabarty's comments during the closing session of the 'Gandhi, Nonviolence and Modernity' Conference, HRC, ANU, 3 September 2004.

15 Kapur, *Raising Up a Prophet*, 13–16. Harijan means 'children of God'.

16 Ibid., 11.

17 In his work on Aboriginal politics, Garveyism, and resistance strategies, scholar John Maynard explores the connections of Gandhian and Garveyite rhetoric and activist formations. ' "Be the Change That You Want to See": The Awakening of Cultural Nationalism – Gandhi, Garvey and the AAPA',

paper presentation at the 'Gandhi, Nonviolence and Modernity' Conference, HRC, ANU, 2 September 2004.
18 Kapur, *Raising Up a Prophet*, 16–23, 38–39; Penny M. Von Eschen, *Race Against Empire: Black Americans and Anticolonialism, 1937–1957* (Ithaca: Cornell University Press, 1997), 31.
19 Kapur, *Raising Up a Prophet*, 3.
20 Ibid., 7.
21 August Meier, 'On the Role of Martin Luther King', *The American Civil Rights Movement: Readings and Interpretations*, edited by Raymond D'Angelo (McGraw Hill, 2001), 195.
22 Leela Gandhi argues that even though ahimsa has a 'love your opponent' component, it also has a language of violence – 'vivisection'. Leela Gandhi paper presentation, 'Ahimsa: The Genealogy of An Immature Politics,' HRC, ANU, 2 September 2004.
23 John D'Emilio, *Lost Prophet: The Life and Times of Bayard Rustin* (Chicago: University of Chicago Press, 2004), 1. Also see Kapur, *Raising Up a Prophet*, 117, 139.
24 Martin Luther King drew heavily on Gandhian nonviolence principles and practices. See his speeches and writings between 1957 and 1968 in *Testament of Hope: The Essential Writings and Speeches of Martin Luther King, Jr.*, edited by James M. Washington (San Francisco: HarperCollins, 1986), 5–72.
25 August Meier and Elliott Rudwick, *Core: a Study in the Civil Rights Movement, 1942–1968* (New York: Oxford University Press, 1973), 57.
26 Meier and Rudwick, *Core*, 162–63.
27 Kapur, *Raising Up a Prophet*, 14.
28 Kapur, *Raising Up a Prophet*, 16. Kapur provides rich detail and analysis of the exchange of black and Indian intellectuals and activists between India and the United States.
29 Plummer, *Rising Wind: Black Americans and U.S. Foreign Affairs, 1935–1960*, 33, 93. Also see Kapur, *Raising Up a Prophet*, 7–8.
30 Gallicchio, Marc, *The African American Encounter with Japan and China*, 208. On Pandit and United Nations anti-oppressive stances, see Kapur, *Raising Up a Prophet*, 127–32.
31 Kapur, *Raising Up a Prophet*, 89–90. Also see William Stuart Nelson, 'Gandhian Values and the American Civil Rights Movement', *The Meanings of Gandi*, edited by Paul F. Power, Honolulu: University Press of Hawaii, 1971, 155.
32 See, for instance, Marilyn Salzman Webb, 'Week of Welfare Protests', *Guardian*, Folder 9: 'Live on Welfare Budget' Weeks and Dinners, 1969–71, Box 24, Wiley Papers. Also see Nadasen, 118; Felicia Kornbluh, 'To Fulfill Their "Rightly Needs": Consumerism and the National Welfare Rights Movement', *Radical History Review* 69 (Fall 1997), 76–113.
33 Gandhi's philosophy is based on satyagraha or 'nonviolent resistance based on truth and non-sentimental love of the opponent'. Kapur, *Raising Up a Prophet*, 4.
34 Kapur, *Raising Up a Prophet*.
35 Interestingly, Clayborne Carson argued that, 'Debates over the use of violence are unproductive without recognition that all effective political movements combine elements of persuasion and coercion', *Malcolm X: The FBI File*, New York: Carroll & Graf Publishers, Inc., 1991.p. 49.
36 Crosby, ' "This Nonviolent Stuff Ain't No Good. It'll Get You Killed"', 160.
37 Simon Wendt, 'God, Gandhi, and Guns: The African American Freedom Struggle in Tuscaoloosa, Alabama, 1964–65', *Journal of African American History* 89, Winter, 2004.

38 In Jacqueline Jones Royster (ed.), *Southern Horrors and Other Writings: The Anti-Lynching Campaign of Ida B. Wells, 1892–1900* (Boston: Bedford Books, 1997), 70.
39 In 1971, a black member of the American Friends Service Committee and a dean at Howard University, who met with Gandhi in India in the pre-World War II era, William Stuart Nelson maintained that the 'Negro rights movement has become a mass movement with an arsenal of techniques'. Nelson taught a course at Howard University entitled: 'The Philosophy and Methods of Nonviolence'. He died in 1977. Nelson, 'Gandhian Values and the American Civil Rights Movement', *The Meanings of Gandi*, edited by Paul F. Power (University Press of Hawaii, 1971), 153–63.
40 Paula Giddings, *When and Where I Enter: The Impact of Black Women on Race and Sex in America* (New York: Quill, 1984), 290–92; Sharon Harley, '"Chronicle of a Death Foretold": Gloria Richardson, the Cambridge Movement, and the Radical Black Activist Tradition', *Sisters in the Struggle: African-American Women in the Civil Rights–Black Power Movement*, edited by Bettye Collier Thomas and V.P. Franklin (New York: New York University Press, 2001), 174–96. Also see Peter Levy, *Civil War on Race Street: The Civil Rights Movement in Cambridge, Maryland* (Gainesville: University Press of Florida, 2003).
41 Barbara Ransby, *Ella Baker & the Black Freedom Movement: a Radical Democratic Vision* (Chapel Hill: University of North Carolina Press, 2003), 193.
42 Gandhi also did not unilaterally dismiss violence or retaliation as an option. According to writings examining his philosophy, Gandhi consistently maintained that if there was a choice between violence and cowardice, violence should win out. See for instance, Karl H. Potter, 'Explorations in Gandhi's Theories of Nonviolence,' *The Meanings of Gandhi*, 91–117.
43 Penny M. Von Eschen, *Race Against Empire: Black Americans and Anticolonialism, 1937–1957* (Ithaca: Cornell University Press, 1997), 31.
44 Gandhi's statement in *Pittsburgh Courier* as reprinted in Von Eschen, *Race Against Empire*, 31.
45 'Activists Gather in Washington', *Welfare and the Poor*, edited by Lester A. Sobel (New York: Facts on File, Inc., 1977), 28–29. Maurice Friedman in his 1970 essay, 'The Power of Violence, the Power of Nonviolence', argued that 'racism, poverty, and war are already violent by their nature and by their origin', His essay appears in *Gandhi, India, and the World: An International Symposium*, edited by Sibnarayan Ray, (Philadelphia: Temple University Press, 1970), 319. Friedman, a conscientious objector and religious studies professor, also argued and lamented the fact that 'the movements both of civil rights and peace have turned away from nonviolence toward violence' (326). A popular perception of the movement withstanding, his assessment does not convey the complexity of struggle and the simultaneous use of black strategies for liberation in the 1960s.
46 For instance, see Piven and Cloward, *Poor People's Movements*, 274–75.
47 Crosby, ' "This Nonviolent Stuff Ain't No Good. It'll Get You Killed" '; Lance Hill, *The Deacons of Defense: Armed Resistance and the Civil Rights Movement* (Chapel Hill: University of North Carolina Press, 2004); George Lipsitz, *A Life in the Struggle: Ivory Perry and the Culture of Opposition* (Philadelphia: Temple University Press, 1988); Timothy B. Tyson, *Radio-Free Dixie: Robert F. Williams and the Roots of Black Power* (Chapel Hill: University of North Carolina Press, 1999); Wendt, God, Gandhi, and Guns'.
48 Scot Brown, *Fighting for US: Maulana Karenga, the US Organization, and Black Cultural Nationalism* (New York: New York University Press, 2003); Robert O. Self, *American Babylon: Race and the Struggle for Postwar Oakland* (Princeton: Princeton University Press, 2003), especially Chapter 6.
49 See Martin Luther King, Jr., *Where Do We Go From Here: Chaos or Community?* (New York: Harper & Row, 1967); Nick Kotz and Mary Lynn Kotz,

A Passion for Equality: George A. Wiley and the Movement (New York: W.W. Norton, 1977); Premilla Nadasen, Welfare Warriors: The Welfare Rights Movement in the United States (New York: Routledge, 2005); Williams, The Politics of Public Housing: Black Women's Struggles Against Urban Inequality.
50 Agnew set aside $300 million in supplemental budget, but McCarty called this a 'drop in the bucket'. See 'Rescuers from Poverty take fight to Agnew', Baltimore Afro-American, 21 February 1967; 'Protests Set on Welfare Cuts', Baltimore Afro-American, 21 March 1967.
51 'Protest Set on Welfare Cuts', Baltimore Afro-American, 21 March 1967; Kotz and Kotz, A Passion for Equality, 218.
52 Joseph A. Loftus, '1,000 on Welfare Lobby at Capitol', Washington Post, 27 August 1967, Folder 7: Founding Meetings, Box 7, George Wiley Papers. Also see 'Welfare Recipients Demonstrate', Welfare & the Poor, 25–26.
53 Ibid.
54 Betty James, 'Welfare Rally Threatens Riots', The Evening Star, 29 August 1967, Folder 7: Founding Meetings, Box 7, George Wiley Papers.
55 Carol Honsa, 'Welfare Bill Called "Betrayal of Poor"', Washington Post, 29 August 1967, Folder 7: Founding Meetings, Box 7, George Wiley Papers.
56 Ibid.; James, 'Welfare Rally Threatens Riots'.
57 Crosby, ' "This Nonviolent Stuff Ain't No Good. It'll Get You Killed" ', 160.

Bibliography

Anon, 'Protest Set on Welfare Cuts', Baltimore Afro-American, 21 March 1967.
Brown, Scot, Fighting for US: Maulana Karenga, the US Organization, and Black Cultural Nationalism, New York: New York University Press, 2003.
Carson, Clayborne, Malcolm X: The FBI File, New York: Carroll & Graf Publishers, Inc., 1991.
Crosby, Emilye, '"This Nonviolent Stuff Ain't No Good. It'll Get You Killed": Teaching About Self-Defense in the African-American Freedom Struggle', Teaching the American Civil Rights Movement: Freedom's Bittersweet Song, edited by Julie Buckner Armstrong, Susan Hult Edwards, Houston Bryan Roberson, and Rhonda Y. Williams, New York: Routledge, 2002.
D'Emilio, John, Lost Prophet: The Life and Times of Bayard Rustin, Chicago: University of Chicago Press, 2004.
Friedman, Maurice, 'The Power of Violence, the Power of Nonviolence', in Gandhi, India, and the World: An International Symposium, edited by Sibnarayan Ray, Philadelphia: Temple University Press, 1970.
Gallicchio, Marc, The African American Encounter with Japan and China: Black Internationalism in Asia, 1885–1945, Chapel Hill: University of North Carolina Press, 2000.
Giddings, Paula, When and Where I Enter: The Impact of Black Women on Race and Sex in America, New York: Quill, 1984.
'Goals for a National Welfare Rights Movement Goals for a National Welfare Rights Movement', The Report of Workshop 2, National Welfare Rights Meeting, Chicago, Illinois, 6–7 August 1966, Folder 7: Founding Meetings, Box 7, George Wiley Papers.
Harley, Sharon, ' "Chronicle of a Death Foretold": Gloria Richardson, the Cambridge Movement, and the Radical Black Activist Tradition', Sisters in the Struggle: African-American Women in the Civil Rights – Black Power Movement, edited by

Bettye Collier Thomas and V.P. Franklin, New York: New York University Press, 2001.
Hill, Lance, *The Deacons of Defense: Armed Resistance and the Civil Rights Movement*, Chapel Hill: University of North Carolina Press, 2004.
Honsa, Carol, 'Welfare bill Called "Betrayal of Poor"' *Washington Post*, August 29, 1967, Folder 7: Founding Meetings, Box 7, George Wiley Papers.
James, Betty, 'Welfare Rally Threatens Riots,' *The Evening Star*, August 29, 1967, Folder 7: Founding Meetings, Box 7, George Wiley Papers.
Kapur, Sudarshan, *Raising Up a Prophet: The African-American Encounter with Gandhi*, Boston: Beacon Press, 1992.
King, Martin Luther, Jr., *Where Do We Go From Here: Chaos or Community?*, New York: Harper & Row, 1967.
King, Martin Luther, Jr.,*Testament of Hope: The Essential Writings and Speeches of Martin Luther King, Jr.*, edited by James M. Washington, San Francisco: Harper Collins, 1986.
Kornbluh, Felicia, 'To Fulfill Their "Rightly Needs": Consumerism and the National Welfare Rights Movement', *Radical History Review* 69 (Fall) 1997.
Kotz, Nick and Kotz, Mary Lynn, *A Passion for Equality: George A. Wiley and the Movement*, New York: W.W. Norton, 1977.
Lassiter, Lee, 'Welfare: Reform or Revolt,' Baltimore *News American*, April 1969, Folder 16: Welfare – DSS, Box 22, Series 24, BCP.
Levy, Peter, *Civil War on Race Street: The Civil Rights Movement in Cambridge, Maryland*, Gainesville: University Press of Florida, 2003
Lipsitz, George, *A Life in the Struggle: Ivory Perry and the Culture of Opposition*, Philadelphia: Temple University Press, 1988.
Loftus, Joseph A., '1,000 on Welfare Lobby at Capitol', *Washington Post*, 27 August 1967, Folder 7: Founding Meetings, Box 7, George Wiley Papers. Also see 'Welfare Recipients Demonstrate'.
Maynard, John, '"Be the Change That You Want to See"': The Awakening of Cultural Nationalism – Gandhi, Garvey and the AAPA,' Paper presentation at the 'Gandhi, Nonviolence and Modernity', Conference, HRC, Australian National University, 2 September 2004.
Meier, August, 'On the Role of Martin Luther King', *The American Civil Rights Movement: Readings and Interpretations*, edited by Raymond D'Angelo, McGraw Hill, 2001.
Meier, August and Rudwick, Elliott, *Core: a Study in the Civil Rights Movement, 1942–1968*, New York: Oxford University Press, 1973.
Nadasen, Premilla, *Welfare Warriors: The Welfare Rights Movement in the United States*, New York: Routledge, 2005.
Nelson, William Stuart, 'Gandhian Values and the American Civil Rights Movement', *The Meanings of Gandi*, edited by Paul F. Power, Honolulu: University Press of Hawaii, 1971.
NWRO, 'Bill of Welfare Rights', 1966, Folder 5: Membership Miscellany, 1967–72, Box 8, George Wiley Papers, Wisconsin Historical Society, Madison, Wisconsin.
Piven, Frances Fox and Richard A. Cloward, *Poor People's Movements: Why They Succeed, How They Fail*, New York: Vintage, 1977.
Plummer, Brenda Gayle, *Rising Wind: Black Americans and U.S. Foreign Affairs, 1935–1960*, Chapel Hill: University of North Carolina Press, 1996.
'Protest Set on Welfare Cuts', Baltimore *Afro-American*, 21 March 1967.

Ransby, Barbara, *Ella Baker & the Black Freedom Movement: a Radical Democratic Vision*, Chapel Hill: University of North Carolina Press, 2003.
Royster, Jacqueline Jones (ed.) *Southern Horrors and Other Writings: The Anti-Lynching Campaign of Ida B. Wells, 1892–1900*, Boston: Bedford Books, 1997.
Self, Robert O., *American Babylon: Race and the Struggle for Postwar Oakland*, Princeton: Princeton University Press, 2003.
Tyson, Timothy B., *Radio-Free Dixie: Robert F. Williams and the Roots of Black Power*, Chapel Hill: University of North Carolina Press, 1999.
Von Eschen, Penny M., *Race Against Empire: Black Americans and Anticolonialism, 1937–1957*, Ithaca: Cornell University Press, 1997.
Webb, Marilyn Salzman, 'Week of Welfare Protests', *Guardian*, Folder 9: 'Live on Welfare Budget' Weeks and Dinners, 1969–71, Box 24, Wiley Papers.
'Welfare Sit-in Protests Delays', Baltimore *Morning Sun*, 13 May 1969, 19 March 1971.
Wendt, Simon, 'God, Gandhi, and Guns: The African American Freedom Struggle in Tuscaoloosa, Alabama, 1964–65', *Journal of African American History* 89, Winter, 2004.
White, John C., 'Welfare Mothers Sleep-In at DPW', Baltimore *Afro-American*, 13 May 1969.
Williams, Rhonda Y., *The Politics of Public Housing: Black Women's Struggles Against Urban Inequality*. Transgressing Boundaries Series, New York: Oxford University Press, 2004.

Part IV
Interlocuting with modernity
Gandhi at home and in the world

Part IV

11 Josephus
Traitor or Gandhian *avant la lettre*?

John Docker

And I prayed unto the LORD my God, and made my confession, and said, O Lord, the great and dreadful God, keeping the covenant and mercy to them that love him, and to them that keep his commandments;

We have sinned, and have committed iniquity, and have done wickedly, and have rebelled, even by departing from thy precepts and from thy judgments:

Neither have we hearkened unto thy servants the prophets, which spake in thy name to our kings, our princes, and our fathers, and to all the people of the land.

O Lord, righteousness belongeth unto thee, but unto us confusion of faces, as at this day; to the men of Judah, and to the inhabitants of Jerusalem, and unto all Israel, that are near, and that are far off, through all the countries whither thou has driven them, because of their trespass that they have trespassed against thee.

(Daniel 9:4–7)

... the language in which I record the events will reflect my own feelings and emotions; for I must permit myself to bewail my country's tragedy. She was destroyed by internal dissensions, and the Romans who so unwillingly set fire to the Temple were brought in by the Jews' self-appointed rulers, as Titus Caesar, the Temple's destroyer, has testified. For throughout the war he pitied the common people, who were helpless against the partisans; and over and over again he delayed the capture of the city and prolonged the siege in the hope that the ringleaders would submit. If anyone criticizes me for the accusations I bring against the party chiefs and their gangs of bandits, or my laments over the misfortunes of my country, he must pardon my weakness, regardless of the rules of historical writing. For it so happened that of all the cities under Roman rule our own reached the highest summit of prosperity, and in turn fell into the lowest depths of misery; the misfortunes of all other races since the beginning of history, compared with those of the Jews, seem small; and for our misfortunes we have only ourselves to blame.

(Josephus, Preface, *The Jewish War*)[1]

Josephus is famous, or infamous, as the author of *The Jewish War*, one of the most remarkable and controversial works of antiquity. He wrote the book first in Aramaic for his fellow Jews of the eastern Diaspora, and then translated it into Greek, the common language of Asia Minor, Syria, and the eastern part of north Africa in the ancient world for over three centuries. It was thus made accessible to the peoples of the Roman Empire, and indeed it became a classic from antiquity to the present day. The book was written in the mode of Western history as bequeathed by Thucydides, focusing on history as crisis, on political and military events, with many set speeches that the historian believes *could* have been made at the time by the various protagonists, but which are also infused with rhetoric and literary art. Like Thucydides in relation to the Peloponnesian war in fifth-century Greece BCE, Josephus promised to narrate as completely as he could the details of a war in which he himself was a participant and observer.[2] *The Jewish War* evokes the Jewish rebellion against the Roman Empire that began in 66 CE; Jerusalem, the centre of the revolt, was defeated and overrun by Roman forces led by Titus in 70 CE. The Temple was destroyed. Three years later the rebellion's final act occurred at Masada, a fortress not far from Jerusalem, when the Jewish warriors known as the Sicarii committed mass suicide rather than submit to Roman rule.[3] In the twentieth century and into the twenty-first, in official and popular Israeli culture and the Zionist movement generally, the mass suicide at Masada has been celebrated as one of the great defining episodes of Jewish history, iconic of the undying desire Jews have for their own nation and independence; in Zionist rhetoric, the heroic spirit of Masada is reborn in the modern Israeli state.[4]

Because he went over to the Roman side during the war, Josephus has always been regarded as a historical traitor to the Jewish people.[5] Writing this essay gives me the opportunity to do something I've long wanted to do: defend Josephus.[6] I argue, on the basis of a Gandhian reading of *The Jewish War*, that Josephus was *not* a traitor; on the contrary. I suggest that *The Jewish War* raises questions about the wisdom of armed revolt, and about nationalist violence and political leadership. I also draw attention to Josephus's musings on nonviolence as part of Jewish tradition. I make this intervention in the spirit of Walter Benjamin suggesting, in fragment XVII of his 'Theses on the Philosophy of History', that the historian should 'blast a specific era out of the homogeneous course of history – blasting a specific life out of the era or a specific work out of the lifework'.[7] Accordingly, I will arrange conversations between past and present, with Gandhi most crucially, but also with the radical theologian and cultural theorist Daniel Boyarin and contemporary Jewish Cultural Studies, including Boyarin's concern with gender.

In terms of method, I will follow Tessa Rajak in focusing on Josephus' own self-presentations, approaching *The Jewish War* in terms of creation of character, genre, drama, and narrative.[8] I will also follow Benjamin's urgings in the prologue to *The Origin of German Tragic Drama* that the critic fragment the text into distinct and separate particles, seeking out extremes, an awareness of discontinuity, of the need for digression. In particular, I will explore how *The Jewish War* disperses 'Josephus' its narrator into a number of disparate figures, of historian, philosopher, high-born priest, warrior, military leader and strategist, trickster, apocalyptic prophet, redeemer and saviour, angry denouncer, anguished mourner of a lost world.[9]

Gandhi on Zionism

A conversation between Gandhi in modernity and Josephus in antiquity suggests itself. Gandhi, we know, had a cosmopolitan, pluralist, and critical interest in many religions, in Hinduism, Christianity, Islam, Buddhism, Judaism. In South Africa, three of his closest Western co-workers were of Jewish ancestry: Henry S.L. Polak, Herman Kallenbach, and his secretary, Sonya Schlesin; and later, in 1939, Kallenbach visited Gandhi and stayed with him at the Sevagram ashram.[10] In a 1938 essay 'Zionism and Anti-Semitism', Gandhi writes that he has learnt much from his Jewish friends about their 'age-long persecution', in particular persecution by Christians, which he compares to the treatment of untouchables by Hindus. In this essay Gandhi denounces Hitler and anti-Semitism in Germany, indeed he comes close to supporting war against Hitler's 'religion of exclusive and militant nationalism': 'if there ever could be a justifiable war', Gandhi declares, 'in the name of and for humanity, a war against Germany, to prevent the wanton persecution of a whole race, would be completely justified.' But, Gandhi continues, 'I do not believe in any war'.[11]

Despite his sympathy and understanding of Jewish experience of persecution, in this and other essays Gandhi is also highly critical of the Zionist movement and what it was doing in British-Mandated Palestine. He is not impressed by the Zionist call for a Jewish return to Palestine which is supposedly sanctioned by the Bible, a call that affords, Gandhi notes, 'a colourable justification for the German expulsion of the Jews'.

> Palestine belongs to the Arabs in the same sense that England belongs to the English or France to the French. It is wrong and inhuman to impose the Jews on the Arabs. What is going on in Palestine today cannot be justified by any moral code of conduct. . . . Surely it would be a crime against humanity to reduce the proud Arabs so that Palestine can be restored to the Jews partly or wholly as their national home.[12]

Gandhi suggests that the 'Palestine of the Biblical conception is not a geographical tract', rather it lies in Jewish hearts. He observes that the Zionists are trying to make Palestine their national home 'under the shadow of the British gun': the Zionists are 'co-sharers with the British in despoiling a people who have done no wrong to them'; the Jews can 'settle in Palestine only by the goodwill of the Arabs', and they 'should seek to convert the Arab heart'. Gandhi adds, in reference to a book by Cecil Roth called *The Jewish Contribution to Civilization*, that while Jews have enriched the world's literature, art, music, drama, science, medicine, and agriculture, he wishes they could add 'nonviolent action' to their historical achievements.[13] Gandhi is critical, in another 1938 essay, 'Questions on the Jews', of the Old Testament for its discourse of violence, an eye for an eye and a tooth for a tooth.[14]

Interestingly, Gandhi in the essay 'Zionism and Anti-Semitism' wishes the Palestinian Arabs had 'chosen the way of nonviolence in resisting what they rightly regard as an unwarrantable encroachment upon their country'.[15]

In a 1946 essay 'Jews and Palestine', Gandhi again criticises the Christian world for singling out Jews for prejudice, 'owing to a wrong reading of the New Testament'.[16] Again he also attacks the Zionists for recent violence: 'they have erred grievously in seeking to impose themselves on Palestine with the aid of America and Britain and now with the aid of naked terrorism'. Gandhi exhorts the Jews to instead adopt the 'matchless weapon of non-violence whose use their best prophets have taught and which Jesus the Jew who gladly wore the crown of thorns bequeathed to a groaning world'.[17]

In acknowledging that there may be support for nonviolence in Jewish tradition, Gandhi is here reprising a major theme of Josephus' speeches to his fellow Jews two millennia earlier.

The case against Josephus

It is nonetheless no easy task to defend Josephus. As a historian he is accused – unlike the austere and detached Thucydides – of being inaccurate, an exaggerator particularly of numbers, and self-interested. His moral character as he reveals it in his own words has been judged harshly by posterity. Let's quickly review his life as he presents it. He was born in 37 CE to an aristocratic priestly family.[18] Destined for the priesthood, he was educated in a rabbinic school in Jerusalem, under Roman rule since 6 CE. At about the age of sixteen he spent some months studying successively with the Pharisees, the Essenes, and the Sadducees, and in *The Jewish War* there is a fascinating summary of their varying beliefs and positions, suggesting that Jewish thought in antiquity, as in the Hellenistic world of thought more generally, was differentiated into competing schools. In this portrait, Jewish thought can be viewed as sharing with Greek, Egyptian and Indian philosophy an interest in the notion of the immortality of the soul, and indeed there was a belief in the ancient world, including by a pupil of Aristotle, that the Jews were descended from Indian philosophers.[19]

Revealing as a teenager an interest in bodily renunciation that Gandhi surely would have admired, Josephus went to live with a hermit in the desert for three years' meditation, returning to Jerusalem at the age of nineteen, now a declared Pharisee.[20] Josephus says the Pharisees were counted as the leading sect of the time and were held to be the most authoritative exponents of the Law. In common with the Greek philosophers Pythagoras and Plato, they believed in reincarnation and the transmigration of souls; as Josephus phrases it, every 'soul is imperishable, but only the souls of good men pass into other bodies, the souls of bad men being subjected to eternal punishment'.[21]

Just as Gandhi would cross the dark waters to the centre of empire and to explore many strands of thought, Eastern and Western, so Josephus at the age of twenty-six sailed to Rome on a minor diplomatic mission, to gain release for some Jewish priests held by Nero. He succeeded in getting his friends acquitted, through the good offices of Nero's wife Poppaea, to whom he was introduced by an actor of Jewish descent he had met on landing in Italy, Rome having a sizeable Jewish population, and seems to have stayed in Rome for the next couple of years.[22] When he returned to Jerusalem in 66 CE, he was travelled and worldly, possessing a cosmopolitan ease with different cultures, including Greek literature and mythology.[23] But the city was on the point of revolt against the Roman Empire; since the annexation of Judaea sixty years before, Jewish nationalists had chafed under Roman rule, which they considered oppressive. As a Pharisee Josephus aligned himself with the moderate party in Jerusalem, which tried to prevent the revolt, warning that the outcome of war with Rome would inevitably be calamity and disaster. The moderate forces, however, lost out to the extreme nationalists, including the Zealots, who now took control of the city; the moderates like Josephus had to go along with the revolt, and Josephus was appointed commander of the most northerly of the regions, Galilee. In 66–67 CE Josephus did everything he could *not* to engage with Roman forces, to the anger of the extremist Jewish leaders in the area, but in spring 67 CE when a large Roman force invaded Galilee and his army ran away, Josephus retreated into the town of Jotapata along with the extremists.[24]

The Roman siege of Jotapata lasted for nearly two months, Josephus proving an able military commander, impressing the attacking Romans led by Vespasian. He was finally captured in circumstances which have always been regarded as highly discreditable. As Josephus himself explains, when the town fell, the Romans, remembering what the siege had cost them, showed neither mercy nor pity, slaughtering everyone they came across, except women and babies, with many even of Josephus' picked soldiers driven to suicide so that they would not die at Roman hands. Josephus meanwhile had jumped into a cave which could not be seen by the Roman soldiers above. With him were 'forty persons of importance'. When the Roman leader Vespasian discovered where he was, he offered Josephus safe conduct and kindness. His companions, however, realizing that Josephus was about to accept Vespasian's invitation to surrender, said they would kill him if he did not commit suicide with them to avoid being enslaved. In this scene as he evokes it Josephus attempts to dissuade them. He argues that 'suicide is hateful in God's sight', an act of 'sheer impiety'. As a Pharisee, Josephus here expresses his belief in reincarnation and transmigration of souls. He tells his companions that, if they suicide, their souls, instead of proceeding upon death to unsullied bodies and further lives on earth, will be cast into Hades.[25]

Josephus fails in his attempt to persuade his companions against mass suicide. Thinking quickly, Josephus then suggests that if they have chosen to die, they should all draw lots and kill each other, one man to the next; as it turns out, Josephus and another man are the last two left alive, and Josephus makes a pact with him so they can both stay alive.[26] Josephus forever after has been accused of despicable duplicity and unworthy trickery for this act. Perhaps it was – Josephus says that either divine providence or luck looked after him[27] – though I can't see why he should be blamed for not committing suicide, given that as a Pharisee he opposed suicide on religious and philosophical grounds and he made his opposition clear to his companions.[28] Arguably as well, the scene of his escape as Josephus describes it belongs to the trickster genre, a narrative mode and figure of great antiquity: the trickster, who had somehow made sure there were only two people left, defeats death; to defeat death is the trickster's ultimate test, and out-tricking death gives hope not only for his own survival against the ravages of fate but also for humanity, hope that fate is not necessarily ordained towards misery and failure.[29] In the drama of *The Jewish War* Josephus here as trickster had to escape, because he also has a prophetic and indeed apocalyptic mission: to survive in order to attempt to save his country and his city from imminent destruction.

Josephus had just before his escape from death been thinking about the 'terrifying images of his recent dreams', dreams by which 'God had forewarned him both of the calamities coming to the Jews and of the fortunes of the Roman emperors'. Moreover, he adds, he was 'in the matter of interpreting dreams' capable of 'divining the meaning of equivocal utterances of the Deity'. Suddenly understanding the awful meaning of these dreams, he had sent a secret prayer to God:

> Inasmuch as it pleaseth Thee to visit Thy wrath on the Jewish people whom Thou didst create, and all prosperity hath passed to the Romans, and because Thou didst choose my spirit to make known the things to come, I yield myself willingly to the Romans that I may live, but I solemnly declare that I go, not as a traitor, but as Thy servant.[30]

Josephus as prophet is like the biblical Daniel, interpreting dreams in order to foretell of the future, a future that might be desolation or hold out hope of salvation.[31] But, in the drama of *The Jewish War*, will Josephus, the trickster who has survived to be prophet, be listened to, will he be heeded by his own people?

Taken to Vespasian, Josephus tells the Roman leader that he has prophetic powers, and he predicts both he and Titus will become emperors of Rome: prophecies that turn out to be true.[32]

Defending Josephus

Josephus spends the rest of the war with the Roman forces, with Vespasian indeed becoming emperor of Rome in 69 CE, his son Titus then taking over as commander in Palestine. It is in this context, as a kind of intermediary for the Roman army, that Josephus makes a remarkable as it were Gandhian speech to the nationalists who were resisting the Roman siege and scorning as well Titus' offers of leniency if they would surrender. The alternative, Titus had suggested to the nationalists, with the city already in a state of famine and starvation, was eventual complete destruction of the city, death of their men, and the enslaving of the women and children.[33]

Outside the walls of Jerusalem, before the hostile nationalists throwing missiles and screaming execrations at him, Josephus speaks eloquently against violence. It betrays, he says, Jewish tradition at its ethically finest and most sacred. He tells the nationalists that, in continuing the rebellion till final destruction was guaranteed, they would inevitably endanger Jerusalem's holy places. Further, in choosing violence they were fighting not only the Romans but God as well, who should be trusted to come to the assistance of the Jews when he chooses to. Josephus then points to key moments in the Jewish past as evoked in various biblical stories. He observes that when the Egyptian pharaoh Necho descended on the Jews with a vast army and seized Sarah their Princess, mother of their nation, Abraham did not respond by force of arms, but waited for God to intervene. And indeed, the very next evening the Egyptians sent back Sarah while the Egyptians themselves, shaken by terrible dreams, fled. Josephus then refers to the Jews' sojourn in Egypt, which lasted four hundred years. Though the Jews could have resisted with weapons, they instead committed their cause to God, who finally came to their assistance with plagues directed against the Egyptians. The Jews could then leave, Josephus says, 'with no bloodshed and no danger, led forth by God to establish His temple-worship'. Josephus reminds his howling interlocutors that when the Jews were taken in bondage to Babylon and lived there in exile for seventy years, they never tried to shake off the yoke till Cyrus granted them liberty as an offering to God.[34]

In short, Josephus declares, 'on no occasion did our fathers succeed by force of arms, or fail without them after committing their cause to God. If they took no action, they were victorious as it seemed good to their Judge: if they gave battle they were beaten every time.' It was never intended, Josephus says, 'that our nation should bear arms, and war has inevitably ended in defeat'. He urges the nationalists to surrender before it was too late, for all the Romans were demanding was the customary tribute which their fathers had always paid. When the tribute was paid, Josephus reassures them, they will neither sack the City nor lay a finger on the holy places: 'they will give you everything else, the freedom of your children, the security of your property, and the preservation of your holy Law'.[35] Josephus here reminds the nationalists – anticipating Freud in *Civilization and Its Discontents* – that the Hellenistic Roman Empire was pluralist in relation to its many communities, religions, and diverse cults.[36] In this internationalist pluralistic world, Jews were not outsiders and pariahs, the despised and persecuted, as they would later frequently become in European Christian history.

Josephus ends with a plea to the nationalists to save Jerusalem, a plea reminiscent of the great lamentation speeches near the end of *The Iliad* prophesying the devastation of Troy: 'at least', says Josephus, 'pity your families, and let each man set before his eyes his wife and children and parents, so soon to perish by famine or the sword'. In a later speech inside Jerusalem, as the nationalists faced final defeat and the city faced destruction, Josephus spoke again to the citizens remaining, reminding them of the 'splendid example' of Jehoiachin, king of the Jews, who, when the king of Babylon made war on him, left the city of his own accord before its capture, and with his family submitted to voluntary imprisonment rather than surrender the holy places to the enemy and see the House of God go up in flames.[37]

As it turned out, Josephus was ignored, the revolt continued, and the siege of Jerusalem ended in mass death, atrocity, horror, deportation, and enslavement, a catastrophe, as Josephus warned, including destruction of the Temple, for one of the world's great and most renowned cities.

After the war, Josephus left for Rome, where he was given the house in which the emperor Vespasian had lived as a private citizen, a pension for life, Roman citizenship, and enjoyed friendships with non-Jews. Here he wrote his first work, *The Jewish War* (75–79).[38] In Rome, in exile from Palestine the land of his birth, Josephus became a diasporic writer and intellectual and produced more books, including a Jewish history and an autobiography. In the last two decades he has become an increasingly important figure in many fields of Jewish, Greco-Roman, and Christian history.[39]

Josephus, Daniel Boyarin, and gender

Josephus opposed armed revolt against a ruling power, suggesting in *The Jewish War* that armed rebellion always leads to domination *within* a community by the most violent of the political leaders. He tells us that the nationalists, including the fearsome Zealots, had spent much of their time during the revolt murdering or imprisoning the moderates within Jerusalem who appealed for peace, including Josephus' own family.[40]

Among the extreme nationalists in and outside Jerusalem were the Sicarii, or dagger men, the nationalists who committed mass suicide at Masada in 73 CE. In *The Jewish War* Josephus refers to the Sicarii as assassins and marauders, people who, contrary to later Zionist mythologising, were the reverse of heroic, murdering in broad daylight in the middle of Jerusalem;

taking up residence in Masada in 66 CE, they engaged in raids and looted and set on fire nearby Jewish settlements that were prepared to submit to Rome.[41] Against the nationalists, Josephus urged the citizens of Jerusalem to find salvation in nonviolence and arts of accommodation to ruling secular power, here that of the Roman Empire.

In his dislike of nationalist violence, Josephus is being valued more highly in some recent anti-Zionist critique. In contemporary theory, in the New Jewish Cultural Studies, Daniel Boyarin opposes Zionism confusing mind and spirit with territory, and for its stress on masculinity. In an essay entitled 'Tricksters, Martyrs, and Collaborators: Diaspora and the Gendered Politics of Resistance' (2002), Boyarin feels that Josephus should be reassessed in modernity, noting particularly Josephus' undermining of the Masada myth by drawing attention to the murderousness of the Sicarii.[42]

Boyarin positions gender at the centre of his opposition to Zionism. In these terms, he contrasts Zionism with the rabbinic Judaism of late antiquity, a diasporic Judaism existing precariously within the Roman Empire after the destruction of Jerusalem. He argues that the thinking of late nineteenth-century Jewish intellectuals like Herzl and Nordau who initiated the Zionist movement was very much shaped by their historical context, in particular by general European prizing of the nation-state, and influential conceptions of masculinity that contrasted effeminate Jews with what should be considered proper ideals of manliness in a nationalist and imperial age. Boyarin argues that 'essentialization of the male role' became 'typical of Zionist ideology', indeed is the 'very goal of Herzlian-Nordovian Zionism', and such 'exacerbation' of 'male domination' is clearly related to Zionism as a form of aggressive nationalism.[43]

Boyarin suggests that Zionist ideals of masculinity actually draw on a long tradition in non-Jewish thought of admiration for the phallus, in and from Greco-Roman times to the present. Here he brings into focus twentieth-century Zionism's attraction to the story of Masada and mass suicide as told in the final pages of Josephus' *The Jewish War*.[44] So familiar and prominent has Masada become as Zionist myth and collective memory, that it is surprising to recall, Boyarin reminds us, that its provenance is quite recent, from early in the twentieth century.[45] Boyarin notes that it was Christians who preserved Josephus' text through the centuries until its highly selective and belated discovery by Zionism. The Zionist misuse of Josephus's evocation of Masada is, Boyarin reflects, highly ironic. While the 'Masada myth' became paradigmatic for Zionist notions of 'manliness', honourable death by suicide rather than surrender and submission to slavery was, Boyarin observes, a long-established *Roman* ideal; the Masada leader El'azar's pro-mass suicide speech supposedly reported by Josephus is an historiographical fiction, modelled on Roman exemplars, and perhaps created in this way by Josephus so that the Roman audience for his work could sympathise and empathise with it as a concluding note to his history.[46]

Boyarin compares Josephus' *The Jewish War* with a particular tale told in the Babylonian Talmud which refers to the siege of Masada (perhaps, he speculates, the only allusion to Masada there is in rabbinic literature). Where Josephus' closing evocation of Masada creates the Sicarii as heroes, the Talmudic text expresses anger at them as 'hooligans' and links them to the extreme nationalists in Jerusalem: such nationalism is perceived, says Boyarin, 'as more of an enemy than Rome itself and its Emperor Vaspasian'. In this Talmudic story the Sicarii in Masada and the 'zealots' in Jerusalem prefer death to making 'peace with Rome', yet such peace would have ensured continuing life for the Jews of Jerusalem, and where there is continuing life there can be continuing Jewishness. The Talmudic story, Boyarin adds, perhaps even parodies the Masada mass suicide, for in it one of the rabbis pretends to be dead and hopes to be taken out alive in a coffin in order to give himself up to the Romans.[47] Such trickster actions of cheating death directly recall – though Boyarin himself doesn't point this out – Josephus's own trick whereby he escapes the mass suicide that his companions had tried to force on him at Jotapata.

Boyarin regards as highly significant the Talmudic narrative opposing the Masada mass suicide and the nationalist revolt of Jerusalem. He feels it embodies the 'Babylonian founding myth of the rabbinic movement', the creation-story of all of rabbinic literature, established in the story's encoding of an 'exact reversal of values'. It exactly reverses Roman and later Zionist codes of manliness, for in the story the 'Rabbis prefer slavery to death', for even in slavery Jews could work out a 'resistant strategy for remaining alive and continuing as Jews'. And a key part of such strategy is a discourse of 'femminization', a neologism which, Boyarin tells us in an enigmatic endnote, is 'based on "femme" as in butch/femme'; it indicates the 'constructed and nonessentialist character of the "feminization" imputed to these sociocultural practices'. Faced with the 'tyranny of the Roman Empire', the Diaspora Jews of late antiquity positioned themselves as akin to a certain conception of femaleness. Like the powerful and honoured Jewish women of ancient Israel such as Esther, Ya'el, and Judith, Jewish men in Diaspora chose to practise 'dissimulation, intrigues, tricks, and lying' when they served the purpose of survival. Such is rabbinic Judaism's 'femminized self-understanding', which is not to be confused, Boyarin clarifies, with actual gender relations between Jewish men and women in late antiquity: 'This did not cash out as a better life for human wives.'[48]

In the Talmudic texts, creating stories and characters, often humorous, what Boyarin refers to as 'Roman phallic masculinity' is always being defeated: here is Jewish culture at its wisest, for whereas Zionism attempts to enforce gender as normatively patriarchal, for Boyarin it is 'precisely that discourse of natural gender roles that ... Jewish culture helps dislocate'. Such diasporic Jewish culture demystifies the phallus for what it is, a 'violent and destructive ideological construct'. Where in late nineteenth-century Europe and in Zionism the absence of the phallus is considered pathological, a signifier of disease, in Jewish diasporic history, with its 'marked images of femminized men', the absence of the phallus can be viewed as a 'positive product'. Indeed, Boyarin speculates, such images represented a challenge to the Roman Empire, a site of cultural crisis that, 'it could be argued, led eventually to its breakdown'.[49] The implication is that such a challenge to Zionism's gendered politics may also help lead to its breakdown.

Such practices in relation to oppressive power are in direct opposition to strategies of martyrdom and masculinist defiance. In one rabbinic story the theme is, says Boyarin, that 'Torah is incompatible with the sword', that there is an 'opposition between the Torah and modes of violence per se'.[50] In these formulations, Boyarin comes very close to Josephus' vision of the importance of nonviolence in Jewish tradition.[51]

Uncertain conclusions: Josephus and Gandhi

Josephus in antiquity and Gandhi in modernity shared many positions concerning nonviolence and the course of history. Both believed that history was overseen by God. In his appeal to the nationalists from outside the walls of Jerusalem, Josephus reports that he told them that at this period 'the might of Rome was invincible', with 'submission to her an everyday experience'. Their ancestors, he tells them, far superior to the partisans in wisdom, had rightly chosen to submit to Rome, 'which they could not have borne to do if they had not known that God was on the Roman side'. God, he points out, 'who handed dominion over from nation to nation round the world, abode now in Italy', in a situation where the Romans were the 'lords of the whole world'.[52] Josephus was suggesting that at some future stage God would favour another nation, that Rome was not destined for ever to enjoy God's favour.[53] Gandhi, too, suggested that Britain would one day be abandoned by God. In his 1922 essay 'Shaking the Manes', Gandhi writes:

> No empire intoxicated with red wine of power and plunder of weaker races has yet lived long in this world, and this British Empire, which is based upon organized exploitation of physically weaker races of the earth and upon a continuous exhibition of brute force, cannot live if there is a just God ruling the universe.[54]

There are differences between Josephus and Gandhi we can ponder. Unlike Josephus, Gandhi represented a popular mass movement and enjoyed the support of other leaders, whereas Josephus by his own account was reviled by the nationalists when he attempted to intervene and stop the revolt. Nonetheless, we can also qualify this difference. Gandhi struggled to avert the horrifying violence that accompanied Partition, and he was assassinated by Indian nationalists – a fate perhaps that Josephus might have met with if the nationalists could have captured him and if he did not have Roman protection.[55]

Another apparent difference is that Gandhi felt affection for the Indian masses, whereas it is generally held that Josephus, proud of his claimed aristocratic ancestry and imbued with the belief that society – Jewish but also to be emulated by others – attained an ideal harmony when guided by a priesthood who could bring knowledge of God's intentions to the world, had nothing but relentless contempt for the masses. Tessa Rajak writes, for example, that a 'blanket contempt for the masses (*plethos* or *demos*) runs through Josephus's thinking', including in *The Jewish War*, where he identifies the masses with the rebels, both of whom inspire in him only disgust, and she compares Josephus' attitudes in this respect to Hellenistic thought, as in Plato's disdain for the ignorance of the multitude, or Thucydides' observations of the ways the multitude are given to civil discord.[56] Perhaps, however, *The Jewish War* is more ambivalent than Rajak suggests. Certainly there is a Thucydidean thread running throughout *The Jewish War* commenting on the gullibility of the masses, especially when 'the mob' is willing to be deceived by false prophets. In this thread, history is perceived as frequently farcical, the 'mob' so easily misled by the not infrequent appearance of impersonators, parvenus, and imposters.[57]

Yet Josephus, during the final stages of the siege, notices the contempt the 'war-party' in Jerusalem, in conditions of famine and starvation, had for the common people, who were dying from hunger:

> ... the partisans welcomed the destruction of the people: it left more for them. The only people who deserved to survive were those who had no use for peace and only lived to defeat the Romans: the masses who opposed them were a mere drag, and they were glad to see them go.

Josephus refers here to the 'innocent' ordained to perish by the actions of the partisans.[58] Josephus also writes warmly, as we can see from our epigraph, of Titus who 'throughout the war ... pitied the common people' and repeatedly called on the ringleaders of the revolt to submit to prevent the carnage that would destroy the masses along with the extremists.[59]

Some differences between Josephus and Gandhi relate directly, I think, to differences across the millennia between the two empires they inhabited as their known worlds, the Roman and British. Josephus' *The Jewish War* reminds us of a pre-modern imperial world without nation-states, where city states had a choice between paying tribute or violent revolt, in which case they faced the prospect of catastrophe. If they did pay tribute, the Jews in Jerusalem and surrounding areas could be counted as one community amongst others in an overarching mosaic, where local communities could retain considerable legal, cultural and religious self-governance – as indeed would occur later with the Arab and Ottoman empires, successors of the pluralisic Roman empire. The British empire worked by settler colonialism as in its colonization of North America, New Zealand, Australia, and South Africa, and colonialism of extraction as in India. Britain always regarded its own society as ideal, the civilizational model to be followed by all and imposed on all in the territories within its power. Further, Britain itself, the metropolitan centre of the empire, was a nation-state which, like every modern nation-state in European history after 1492, was conceived as an ideal unity, of culture, language, ethnicity, and religion.[60]

In his situation, Josephus urged his fellow Jews to pay tribute and continue their customary community; if they were faced with situations of dire oppression, they should choose inaction until God intervened. This may remind us of a comment of Gandhi's, which he made in 1937 to two African-American visitors: 'there may be action in inaction. And action may be worse than inaction.' In this same interview Gandhi also urges patience, saying that he knows that victory through nonviolence and civil disobedience may not come in his lifetime.[61] It was Gandhi's genius, his legacy of wisdom, his contribution to history, to think through the question of resistance without violence, opposing 'passive resistance', and favouring creative and imaginative forms of direct action.

Yet the danger of Gandhi's desire for India to achieve national independence was the spectre of the modern nation-state itself. Clearly Gandhi did not seek a purity and unity of culture, language, ethnicity, and religion in a new India and he always celebrated India's historical diversity as one of its great civilizational achievements. Nor was Gandhi opposed totally to the British Empire, or at least to a supra-national entity like an empire. He admired, for example, as he wrote in his 'Farewell Speech' to South Africa in 1914, the liberal 'ideals' of the 'glorious British Constitution'[62] – an admiration that anticipates Mandela's respect for such ideals in his *Autobiography*. In his 1922 essay 'Shaking the Manes' Gandhi writes approvingly of the British Empire being quietly transformed into a 'true Commonwealth of free nations, each with equal rights and each having the power to secede at will from an honourable and friendly partnership'.[63] Here Gandhi supports a kind of pluralistic commonwealth of nations. Yet, it would very much appear, despite Gandhi's opposition to Partition, that the historical logic of the nation-state, with its inherited suspicion of those designated internal enemies and desire to exclude those regarded as others, overtook the new Indian state on independence, in the disaster of Partition itself and the consequent establishing of two nation-states India and Pakistan, and then later in the rise and political power – until recently anyway – of Hindu fundamentalism. To continue eternally to be in the power of the British Empire was intolerable for Gandhi, but the alternative, the establishing of a nation-state or indeed now three nation-states, has involved various kinds of violence – state and communal.

In a world still marked by national and religious violence, nonviolence as argued for by Josephus in antiquity and Gandhi in the first part of the twentieth century – and by Daniel Boyarin in his musings on rabbinic Judaism, Josephus, and the Zionist myth of Masada – remains the only hope for humanity in a disastrous world.

Notes

1. Josephus, *The Jewish War*, trans. G.A. Williamson, revised edition with a new introduction by E. Mary Smallwood (Penguin, London, 1981), p. 28.
2. Josephus, *The Jewish War*, Smallwood's introduction pp. 20, 23–24; Josephus, *The Jewish War*, preface, p. 29. Concerning Thucydides and Josephus, see Tessa Rajak, *Josephus: The Historian and His Society*, second edition (Duckworth, London, 2002 (1983)), pp.5, 9, 80, 155; apropos Thucydides and historiography, see Ann Curthoys and John Docker, *Is History Fiction?* (UNSW Press, Sydney, 2005), ch. 2.
3. Josephus, *The Jewish War*, pp. 266, 398–405.
4. See Nachman Ben-Yehuda, *The Masada Myth: Collective Memory and Mythmaking in Israel* (University of Wisconsin Press, Madison, 1995), and Yael Zerubavel, *Recovered Roots: Collective Memory and the Making of Israeli National Tradition* (University of Chicago Press, Chicago, 1995).
5. Ben-Yehuda, *The Masada Myth*, pp. 28, 89, 267, 294.
6. This essay was originally given as a paper for HRC Conference, *Gandhi, Non-violence, and Modernity*, ANU, 1–3 September 2004; convenors John Docker and Debjani Ganguly.
7. Walter Benjamin, *Illuminations*, trans. Harry Zohn, introd. Hannah Arendt (Schocken, New York, 1969), p. 263.
8. Tessa Rajak, *Josephus: The Historian and His Society*, pp.ix, xi, xiv–xv, 6, and 'The *Against Apion* and the Continuities in Josephus's Political Thought', in Steve Mason (ed.), *Understanding Josephus: Seven Perspectives* (Sheffield Academic Press, Sheffield, 1998), pp. 222–46.
9. Walter Benjamin, *The Origin of German Tragic Drama*, trans. John Osborne (London, Verso, 1996), pp. 28–29, and John Docker, *1492: The Poetics of Diaspora* (Continuum, London, 2001), p. 247. Rajak in her essay in *Understanding Josephus* refers to the way Josephus constructs 'various personae' (p. 222).
10. Homer A. Jack (ed.), *The Gandhi Reader* (Grove Press, New York, 1956), p. 317.
11. Ibid., 'Zionism and Anti-Semitism', pp. 317–18.
12. Ibid., 'Zionism and Anti-Semitism', p. 318.
13. Ibid., 'Zionism and Anti-Semitism', pp. 321–22.
14. Ibid., 'Questions on the Jews', p. 322.
15. Ibid., 'Zionism and Anti-Semitism', p. 321.
16. Gandhi, perhaps because of his admiration for the Jesus of the Sermon on the Mount, is too charitable to the Gospels, especially the Gospel of John, which in its notorious chapter eight denounces 'the Jews' as no longer God's chosen people and as children of the devil, a passage which proved fatefully influential in European anti-semitic violence in both the Crusades and Nazi Germany; see Robert Carroll, *Wolf in the Sheep Fold: The Bible as a Problem for Christianity* (SPCK, London, 1991), pp. 90–98, 102, 110, 114.
17. Jack, 'Jews and Palestine', pp. 324–26.
18. Cf. Rajak, *Josephus*, ch. 1, 'Family, Education and Formation', pp. 14–21.
19. *The Jewish War*, ch. 7, pp. 133–38; concerning India and Indian philosophy, see pp. 400–401 and p. 459 note 39. See also Rajak, *Josephus*, pp. 34–37, 109–12, and Joseph Sievers, 'Josephus and the Afterlife', in Steve Mason (ed.), *Understanding Josephus: Seven Perspectives*, pp. 20–31; on p. 31 footnote 14 Sievers refers to Josephus and Indian philosophers.
20. *The Jewish War*, Smallwood introduction, pp. 9–10. Rajak, *Josephus*, pp. x–xi, notes the qualifying argument of Steve Mason, *Flavius Josephus on the Pharisees: A Composition-Critical Study* (Brill, Leiden, 2001), that Josephus was merely referring to a temporary political connection with the Pharisees. Mason

concludes his study by suggesting that while Josephus portrays the philosophy of the Pharisees along with that of the Essenes and Sadducees as part of the richness and diversity of Jewish thought, he disliked the Pharisees on political and ethical grounds, preferring instead the Essenes as the most pious and virtuous of the schools. In Mason's view, Josephus agrees with the Pharisaic (and Essene) beliefs in fate and immortality, but nevertheless regards the Pharisees as a constantly destructive force in Jewish history; because, however, Josephus recognised the Pharisees as the dominant religious group who enjoyed mass support, he felt compelled to side with them when he returned to Jerusalem from his retreat, however later he lamented their power, actions, and popularity. See 'Conclusion to the Study', pp. 372–75.

21 *The Jewish War*, pp. 137 and 427 note 15.
22 Cf. Rajak, *Josephus*, p. 43, concerning the actor Aliturus and Poppaea.
23 *The Jewish War*, p. 199; Rajak, *Josephus*, pp .3–4, suggests that Josephus and his family belonged to a cosmopolitan, outward-looking stream in Jewish life, in general accepting of Roman power, competent in Greek, and ready to mix with Greeks.
24 *The Jewish War*, Smallwood introduction, pp. 10–11, 16. Martin Goodman, *The Ruling Class in Judaea: The Origins of the Jewish Revolt against Rome A.D. 66–70* (Cambridge University Press, Cambridge, 1995 (1987)), pp. 18–20 and chs 7 and 9, argues that some factions of the ruling class supported the revolt, more than Josephus allows, and that a precipitating factor in war breaking out in the first place was a power struggle within the Jewish ruling class, with some faction leaders hoping to win power for themselves within the new independent Jewish state they envisaged (p. 175). Cf. Rajak, *Josephus*, p. xi.
25 *The Jewish War*, Smallwood introduction p. 11; *The Jewish War*, pp. 137, 215–19, 427 note 15, 440 notes 14 and 15.
26 *The Jewish War*, p. 220.
27 *The Jewish War*, p. 220.
28 Concerning suicide and Jewish tradition, see discussion in Zerubavel, *Recovered Roots*, pp. 200–201 and 292 note 31.
29 Cf. John Docker, *Postmodernism and Popular Culture: A Cultural History* (Cambridge University Press, Melbourne, 1994), p. 217.
30 *The Jewish War*, p. 217.
31 See Per Bilde, 'Josephus and Jewish Apocalypticism', in Steve Mason (ed.), *Understanding Josephus: Seven Perspectives*, pp. 41–56. See also Robert Hall, *Revealed Histories: Techniques for Ancient Jewish and Christian Historiography* (Sheffield Academic Press, Sheffield, 1991), and Rebecca Gray, *Prophetic Figures in Late Second Temple Jewish Palestine: The Evidence from Josephus* (Oxford University Press, New York, 1993), also Rajak, *Josephus*, p. xii. Rajak, 'The *Against Apion* ... ', pp. 235–36 refers to Josephus' admiration for Moses' prophetic identity as a man through whom God spoke; Rajak argues that in Josephus' view God as the supreme ruler of the universe delegated power to the priesthood.
32 *The Jewish War*, p. 221.
33 *The Jewish War*, pp. 314–17.
34 *The Jewish War*, pp. 318–19.
35 *The Jewish War*, p. 321.
36 Sigmund Freud, *Civilization and Its Discontents*, trans. James Strachey, introd. Peter Gay (W.W. Norton, London and New York, 1989), p. 73: 'To the Romans ... religious intolerance was something foreign'. Cf. Jan Assmann, *Moses the Egyptian: The Memory of Egypt in Western Monotheism* (Harvard University Press, Cambridge, Mass., 1997), p. 136, who refers to the 'kind of cosmopolitanism and its belief in the translatability of religious ideas and

denominations which flourished in the Roman Empire'. See also John Docker, 'The Challenge of Polytheism: Moses, Spinoza, and Freud', in Jane Bennett and Michael J. Shapiro (eds), *The Politics of Moralizing* (Routledge, New York, 2002), pp. 215–17, and my essay 'In Praise of Polytheism', *Semeia* 88, 2001, pp. 168–69.
37 *The Jewish War*, pp. 322, 345.
38 See Rajak, *Josephus*, Table of Events at beginning of book; also p. 12.
39 *The Jewish War*, Smallwood introducion, pp. 16–17; Rajak, *Josephus*, 'Introduction to the Second Edition', pp.ix–xv, also 6–7; Steve Mason, ' "Should any wish to enquire further" (*Ant.* 1.25): The Aim and Audience of Josephus's *Judean Antiquities/Life*', in Mason (ed.), *Understanding Josephus*, pp. 64–103; Rajak, 'The *Against Apion* ... ', p. 224.
40 *The Jewish War*, pp. 147, 188, 266, 393, 405, 407, 462.
41 *The Jewish War*, pp. 147, 166, 266, 393, 462. Yael Zerubavel, *Recovered Roots*, pp. 25, 129, 198–99, relates that the Zionist movement worked hard to rehabilitate the Zealots and Sicarii as positive figures in Jewish history; Israeli archaeology also became a vehicle for the nationalist legitimizing of Masada and groups like the Zealots (pp. 66–67).
42 Jonathan Boyarin and Daniel Boyarin, *Powers of Diaspora: Two Essays on the Relevance of Jewish Culture* (University of Minnesota Press, Minneapolis, 2002), chapter by Daniel Boyarin, 'Tricksters, Martyrs, and Collaborators', pp. 48–49, 135 note 11, 137 note 19.
43 Daniel Boyarin, 'Tricksters, Martyrs, and Collaborators', pp. 44–45, 53, 69, 91–92, 135 note 10, 136 note 18, 137 note 19, 138 note 26, 142 note 51.
44 *The Jewish War*, pp. 393–405.
45 Ben-Yehuda, *The Masada Myth*, includes near its beginning a 'Prologue: Masada – A Chronology', which suggests that the first discernible Zionist interest in recent times was in 1912. See also Zerubavel, *Recovered Roots*, 'The Rediscovery of Masada', pp. 62–68.
46 Daniel Boyarin, 'Tricksters, Martyrs, and Collaborators', pp. 46–48, 135 note 12.
47 'Tricksters, Martyrs, and Collaborators', pp. 50–52, 101–2.
48 'Tricksters, Martyrs, and Collaborators', pp. 37–38, 40, 46, 52–53, 134 note 5.
49 'Tricksters, Martyrs, and Collaborators', pp. 38–40, 45–46, 52–54, 64, 78, 100–101.
50 'Tricksters, Martyrs, and Collaborators', pp. 55–56, 59, 61–66, 80, 83, 101.
51 See John Docker, 'Re-"Femminising" Diaspora: Contemporary Jewish Cultural Studies and Post-Zionism', *Holy Land Studies*, vol. 4, no. 2, November 2005, pp. 71–90 for a more extended critique of *Powers of Diaspora*.
52 *The Jewish War*, p. 317; also p. 217.
53 Rajak, 'The *Against Apion* ... ', pp. 233, 238.
54 *The Gandhi Reader*, p. 196.
55 Concerning Partition, see Maulana Abul Kalam Azad, *India Wins Freedom: An Autobiographical Narrative* (Orient Longman, Bombay and London, 1959), pp. 190–227; cf. esp. p. 215: 'Gandhiji's distress was increasing every day. Formerly, the whole nation had responded to his slightest wish. Now it seemed that his most fervent appeals were falling on deaf ears. ... ' (My thanks to Subhash Jaireth for the reference to Azad's autobiography.)
56 Rajak, 'The *Against Apion* ... ', pp. 239–40. Cf. also Thucydides' view of the fickleness of the multitude in relation to Pericles, *History of the Peloponnesian War*, 2.65.
57 *The Jewish War*, pp. 120–21, 128, 130–31, 147, 162–63, 184.
58 *The Jewish War*, pp. 315–16.
59 *The Jewish War*, p. 28.

60 See John Docker, *1492: The Poetics of Diaspora* (Continuum, London and New York, 2001), ch. 10, 'The Disaster of 1492 in World History'.
61 Mahadev Desai, 'Nonviolence and the American Negro', *The Gandhi Reader*, pp. 311–12; Desai reports the conversation between Gandhi and Dr Channing Tobias and Dr Benjamin Mays.
62 Jack, 'Farewell Speech', *The Gandhi Reader*, pp. 99–100.
63 Jack, 'Shaking the Manes', *The Gandhi Reader*, p. 196.

Bibliography

Assmann, Jan, *Moses the Egyptian: The Memory of Egypt in Western Monotheism*, Cambridge, Mass.: Harvard University Press, 1997.
Azad, Maulana Abul Kalam, *India Wins Freedom: An Autobiographical Narrative*, Bombay and London: Orient Longman, 1959.
Benjamin, Walter, *Illuminations*, trans. Harry Zohn, introd. Hannah Arendt, New York: Schocken, 1969.
—— *The Origin of German Tragic Drama*, trans. John Osborne, London: Verso, 1996.
Ben-Yehuda, Nachman, *The Masada Myth: Collective Memory and Mythmaking in Israel*, Madison: University of Wisconsin Press, 1995.
Boyarin, Jonathan and Daniel Boyarin, *Powers of Diaspora: Two Essays on the Relevance of Jewish Culture*, Minneapolis: University of Minnesota Press, 2002.
Carroll, Robert, *Wolf in the Sheep Fold: The Bible as a Problem for Christianity*, London: SPCK, 1991.
Curthoys, Ann and John Docker, *Is History Fiction?* Sydney: UNSW Press, 2005.
Desai, Mahadev, 'Nonviolence and the American Negro', *The Gandhi Reader*, ed. Jack Homer, New York: Grove Press, 1956.
Docker, John, *Postmodernism and Popular Culture: A Cultural History*, Melbourne: Cambridge University Press, 1994.
—— *1492: The Poetics of Diaspora*, London: Continuum, 2001.
—— 'In Praise of Polytheism', *Semeia* 88, 2001.
—— 'The Challenge of Polytheism: Moses, Spinoza, and Freud', in Jane Bennett and Michael J. Shapiro (eds), *The Politics of Moralizing*, New York: Routledge, 2002.
Freud, Sigmund, *Civilization and Its Discontents*, trans. James Strachey, introd. Peter Gay, London and New York: W.W. Norton, 1989.
Goodman, Martin, *The Ruling Class in Judaea: The Origins of the Jewish Revolt against Rome A.D. 66–70*, Cambridge: Cambridge University Press, 1995 (1987).
Gray, Rebecca, *Prophetic Figures in Late Second Temple Jewish Palestine: The Evidence from Josephus*, New York: Oxford University Press, 1993.
Hall, Robert, *Revealed Histories: Techniques for Ancient Jewish and Christian Historiography*, Sheffield: Sheffield Academic Press, 1991.
Homer, A. Jack (ed.), *The Gandhi Reader*, New York: Grove Press, 1956.
Josephus, *The Jewish War*, trans. G.A. Williamson, revised edition with a new introduction by E. Mary Smallwood, London: Penguin, 1981.
Mason, Steve, *Flavius Josephus on the Pharisees: A Composition-Critical Study*, Leiden: Brill, 2001.
Rajak, Tessa, Josephus, 'The *Against Apion* and the Continuities in Josephus's Political Thought', in Steve Mason (ed.), *Understanding Josephus: Seven Perspectives*, Sheffield: Sheffield Academic Press, 1998.

—— *Josephus: The Historian and His Society*, second edition, London: Duckworth, 2002 (1983).

Sievers, Joseph, 'Josephus and the Afterlife', in Steve Mason (ed.), *Understanding Josephus: Seven Perspectives*, Sheffield: Sheffield Academic Press, 1998.

Zerubavel, Yael, *Recovered Roots: Collective Memory and the Making of Israeli National Tradition*, Chicago: University of Chicago Press, 1995.

12 Homespun wisdom
Gandhi, technology and nationalism

Anjali Roy

In an institution set up in the high noon of his institution building spree, it is but natural that Pandit Jawaharlal Nehru, the first Prime Minister of India, should be the most visible presence in the Indian Institute of Technology (IIT) Kharagpur. Nehru's shadow looms large in IIT Kharagpur, the first of the 'higher technical institutions' established in post independence India to translate the Nehruvian vision of a modern industrialized nation. From his signature engraved on the foundation stone of the Main Building and recordings of his speech at the first Convocation to the establishment of the Nehru Museum of Science and Technology recently, Nehru continues to be the patron saint of the four hundred and fifty odd scientists and technologists enjoined to 'modernize' India.[1]

The 'Father of the Nation', Mahatma Gandhi, either remains silent, or his voice is heard only in routine invocations to technology's social responsibility and goals. But the ecological rediscoveries of Gandhi and his appropriation in new social movements in the last two decades has made the repressed Gandhi return in the fashionable talk of appropriate technology in the IITs. In this essay, I propose to read Gandhi's *Hind Swaraj* together with the Report of the Sarker Committee that laid the blueprint for the Indian Institutes of Technology, to mark Gandhi's pronounced absence in the construction of one of Nehru's 'temples of modern India'. I shall show that the repressed Gandhian text in the policy document of the institution, embodying Nehru's nation-building dream, returns like a disturbing trace in the sporadic soul-searching that accompanies the celebration of the strengths and achievements of the IITs. Does the Gandhian trace in the appropriate technology talk at the premier Indian institution disrupt the metanarrative of technology and technical education? Considering that the IITian's new role model is neither Nehru nor Gandhi but Bill Gates, who recently hailed the IITs as Microsoft's partners, can Gandhi speak in the digital decade without being brand-marketed as a new age messiah? I must mention at the very outset that both Gandhi and Nehru have been portrayed as totemic figures embodying two disparate models of development in the critiques of modernity appearing in India in the last two decades.[2] This essay draws on this literature in projecting the two leaders' complex visions of Indian modernity and the ideological imperatives shaping them as a simplified opposition. Following Ashis Nandy's explanation that 'Gandhi was not *one* single critic of the modern West; he represents a whole class of critics of the modern civilization', I read Gandhi as an embodiment of the developmental alternatives rejected in India after independence in favour of what has come to be known as the 'Nehruvian' model.[3]

Howard Perlmutter and Eric Trist, in 'Paradigms for Social Transition', define social architecture as 'the process of consciously building legitimate and viable institutions infused with new and relevant meaning' and regard institution building as related to the concept of paradigm or 'the overall framework embracing several determinants of behaviors'. Comparing three world views or paradigms, Industrial (I), De-Industrial (D) and Symbiotic (S), they see the socioeconomic and sociocultural configuration of advanced growth societies premised on industrial growth as approximating to paradigm I and attribute the emergence of D to environmental degradation and resource scarcity in the present. They identify two versions of D — one Arcadian and the other spiritual of which they consider Gandhi as the best example. Permutter and Trist maintain that while India might have abandoned Gandhi after Independence, the present crisis in the West may lead many versions of Paradigm D to emerge in the lifestyles chosen by people. There is no doubt that I was preferred over the Gandhian version of D in the building of 'higher technical institutions' in post-Independent India and continues to dictate both the teaching and research priorities of the IITs.[4]

The Honourable Members of the Sarker Committee, among whom were luminaries such as Sir J. C. Bose and S. S. Bhatnagar, could not possibly have come together to implement the policy on higher education without adequate deliberation. Ashis Nandy and Sudhir Chandra testify to the existence of vernacular responses in the nineteenth century that did not demand exclusivist rejection or acceptance of the West but incorporated the West in indigenous designs.[5] Similarly, Gyan Prakash has uncovered a discourse on science and technology that had emerged in India in the nineteenth century, which included heated discussions on the appropriateness of Western science to India.[6] These critiques of Western science and modernity account for the availability of several alternatives to the Nehruvian vision of Indian modernity beside the Gandhian. But the team of scientists advising Nehru on the setting up of the institutions betrays no self-doubts or reservations that could suggest their acquaintance with this debate. While the Report uses dispassionate, denotative prose, its proposal to set up a Higher Technical Institution is clearly underwritten by the nationalist dream of an industrialized India based on the Western developmental paradigm that Permutter and Trist define as I. Patrick Colm Hogan and Lalita Pandit in 'Rabindranath Tagore: Universality and Tradition' point out that the establishment of an institution that would rival western science and engineering and the modernization of industry and the pursuit of a rational, scientific goal through technical education was far removed from the Gandhian vision of a grassroots movement towards cottage industry.[7]

Since policy statements are expected no more than to implement decisions already taken, it might be inappropriate to compare a document of this nature with one that was intended to be and is still read as a definitive Gandhian text on development. But the specific agenda of the Sarker Committee Report, which it proceeds to address quite efficiently, appears to be unambiguously underwritten by the Nehruvian ideology while it maintains a high-bred silence on Gandhi. The Report's terms of reference are stated clearly, namely, to ensure 'an adequate supply of technical personnel which will be required for post-war industrial development in this country'.[8] However, the urgency of the requirement for technical personnel emerges from a world crisis, the unavailability of specialists after the Second World War. Notwithstanding the acknowledged haste that marks the skipping of certain standard procedures in the submission of the Interim report, such as undertaking a survey of existing facilities, the need for qualified technical personnel is predicated on the heavy industries model credited to India's first Prime Minister. Breaking down the specific requirements of particular industrial houses and government projects follows the statement of objectives. Discussion and deliberation is invited only on logistics such as the number and location, the staff and faculty, the costs and so on. But the Report's terms of reference expertly sidestep the issues Gandhi had raised about four decades before in The *Hind Swaraj*, and had stubbornly held on to even in the reprint issued in 1938.

The meaning of the Report can be constructed only in relation to what it does not refer to and in the specific difference of its agenda from the Gandhian schema. The presence of the Gandhian alternative is inscribed in the Report's terms of reference that seem to be formulated in relation to the Nehruvian vision of Indian modernity. It must be understood that the conflict between tradition and modernity is often polarized through the figures of the two founding fathers of the Indian nation and that the translation of the Science and Technology dream requires a simplification of the first Prime Minister's own complex narrative of modernization and technology. The official technology document, thus, becomes a site of a polarized conflict between the two leaders on the meaning of development. The terms reiterated throughout the text – *industrial*, *development*, *machinery*, *education*, *technical* and *technology* – acquire added resonance when read through the traces of the absent querulous Gandhi.

The key words in the Report, beginning with the notion of *Higher Technical Education*, uncannily evoke Gandhian discussions on education. 'What is the meaning of education?' Gandhi asks in Chapter XVIII of the *Hind Swaraj* and examines it in its common understanding as literacy or grounding in the three Rs at the primary level. 'It simply means a knowledge of letters.'[9] Gandhi's ideal subject is the Indian peasant and he rejects literacy as inadequate and inappropriate for providing him life-skills or values. However, his use of the word *niti* to point out the limitations of literacy resonates with echoes of the original *nitishastra*, *The Panchtantra*. Here, Vishnu Sarma, the learned Brahmin, had taken up the challenge of educating the daft sons of King Amarsakti in six months. But the term the eighty-year-old Brahmin had used to describe education shows that his promise was one of 'awakening the intelligence' of the princes and not of making them memorize the rules of grammar. In *Hind Swaraj*, Gandhi, too, mourns the fact that, in modern India, literacy skills have taken precedence over *niti* or intellectual awakening. He blames western education models for it: 'Carried away by the flood of western thought we came to the conclusion, without weighing pros and cons, that we should give this kind of education to the people.'[10] Yet when it comes to higher education, Gandhi juxtaposes against the Western educational model not an oriental alternative but Huxley's views on liberal education. He argues that he has never been able to use science for 'controlling my senses', echoing the Huxleyian test of true education.[11] The concerns in the discipline of science had infinitely expanded in 1947 from the ones enumerated by Gandhi in 1908. But neither the list of basic undergraduate courses nor the specialized postgraduate courses cited in the Report have anything to do with 'the control of senses'. In the conversation that follows in *Hind Swaraj*, Gandhi touches upon several themes, such as linguistic and discursive indenturement and concern for ethical values, that have become staples of postcolonial resistance.

The Gandhian distinction between literacy and education was beyond the instrumental brief given to the Sarker Committee 'for ensuring the supply of technical personnel'. Other than in the letter of transmittal, the synonyms for 'education' reiterated through the rest of the Report are 'training' and 'instruction'. The repeated use of these terms connotes a view of higher education totally at odds with those of Huxley and Russell's liberal model that Gandhi invokes in defining education. Considering the specific mandate the Sarker Committee was given, the syllabi and the course content had to be designed 'to teach him[the student]the fundamental principles and theories of engineering'.[12] The Report returns time and again to the need for hands-on experience through knowledge of practical work 'as would assist the student in realistic appreciation of engineering principles as applied in practice'.[13] Thus, education is interpreted in the Report as a sound grounding in the fundamentals of engineering, which must be combined with rigorous practical training.

It is in 'The General Principles in the Design of Under-Graduate Course of Study' in Part IV, expressing a commitment to providing 'a combination of a fundamental scientific training with a broad human outlook', that Russellian echoes of liberal education may be heard.[14] The General Principles invoke Russellian principles in shaping the IITian, 'whose intellect is a clear, cold, logic engine with all its parts of equal strength and in smooth working order' and 'whose mind is stored with a knowledge of the fundamental truths of nature'.[15] The first principle is character building or *niti*, that Gandhi saw as fulfilling the objective of true education. But it is disengaged from Gandhi's 'ancient school system' and annexed to the national project of citizen-making. Item four, point (b), introduces the importance of project work in the form of a thesis to provide 'opportunities for exercising initiative and thought'.[16] Gandhi's emphasis on the use to which education should be put is thus reiterated but only in terms of closing the gap between theory and praxis through applied knowledge. The mention of religious instruction in an institution priding itself on its commitment to the secular democratic ideal would have been utterly sacrilegious. And it was clearly beyond the Sarker Committee's brief – the production of the ideal techno-subject – to ask, along with Gandhi, if the training and instruction so provided will 'make men[or women] of us' or 'enable us to do our duty'.[17]

When Gandhi wrote the *Hind Swaraj*, the 'tech' prefix had not yet entered the Indian consciousness. The meaning of technical and technology, the two words reiterated in the report, must be read in consonance and dissonance with that of the machine, the word Gandhi prefers. But the Report also carries specific references to machines and includes courses on machines in the courses outlined in the Appendices. These would have an instant recall value for the reader familiar with Gandhi's chapter on Machines in the *Hind Swaraj*. The absent Gandhi returns in the enthusiastic inclusion of the knowledge of machines of every conceivable kind in the syllabi. The celebration of the machine as the symbol of industrial progress and modernization shaping the Report's plan of action evokes its opposite, the Gandhian horror of the machine for the kind of development it would usher. 'Machinery is like a snake-hole which may contain from one to a hundred snakes. Where there is machinery, there are large cities; and where there are large cities, there are tram-cars and railways; and there only does one see electric light.'[18] As J D Sethi argues, Gandhi's pronouncements on science and technology, far from systematic, are 'both narrower and broader than any modern framework on the subject'.[19] Gandhi speaks only of machines not of technology. But Gandhi sees urbanization, industrialization, and capitalism all of a piece linking them with the worship of the machine, which he defines negatively in relation to the happiness quotient thus anticipating the post-industrial critiques of technology.

Yet the Sarker Committee Report (that views Machines as the route to industrial development) and *Hind Swaraj* (that views the Machine as evil) complement one another in the rhetoric of nation-building, in interesting ways. Reading the Report together with Gandhi's thoughts on the machine contextualizes the contesting visions of modernization as envisaged by the two giants of Indian nationalism – Nehru and Gandhi. Gandhi's exposition is not based simply on a critique of the competitive edge gained by advanced machines and tools over manual labour. Like the other symbols Gandhi deployed in his critique of colonialism and modernity, his denunciation of machinery is a symbolic resistance against modes of living he considered destructive. As interpretations of the *Hind Swaraj* demonstrate, Gandhi's rejection of machinery is really directed at the concentration of wealth in Industrial Capitalism and the materialism of Rationalism. 'Beware and avoid me', Gandhi's warning voice may be heard beneath the elaborate planning of machine-centred learning in the Sarker Report.[20]

The disparity between the Report's thrust areas and the kind of industry Gandhi found comparatively tolerable, highlights the clash between the big and small development ideologies represented by the two leaders. The clearly stated agenda of the Report, 'industrial development', and the specific industries selected to fulfil this mission, are both reflected in the course-work. Apart from the general reference to industrial needs, the Report singles out certain specific industries and government departments that underline the heavy industry slant in the developmental paradigm adopted by the new nation. The main branches of Technology are named as Aeronautical, Chemical, Civil and Sanitary Engineering, Electrical Engineering, Mechanical Engineering, Architecture, Metallurgy, Botany, Meteorology, and Geology and Geophysics. Certain courses such as Hydraulics are tailor-made for the specific requirements of departments such as the Central Public Works Department and the Ordnance Unit. But it is the doubts expressed in Brigadier Woolf's letter (about the industries prioritized) to Dr John Sargent, Educational Adviser to the Government of India, dated 12 April 1945 and appended to the Report, that reflect the strategic planning that preceded the tabling of the Report. Brigadier Woolf's consternation that the Sarker Committee Report should choose to develop new industries instead of consolidating the already existing industrial infrastructure shows that technological self-reliance in core heavy industry was independent India's carefully considered move towards import substitution. Woolf's list of Indian industries, developed, partially developed, or capable of development, which are not catered for in the Report includes textiles, fibres, vegetable drugs, dyes and chemicals, lumber, detergents and edible oils, pharmacy, fuel, tanning, ceramics, and glass. What might also be of interest in this context is that many of the institutions named in the Report, the Railways, the Central Public Works Department, the Electricity Board, the Ordnance Unit, figure in Gandhi's list of non-essentials.

The blueprint for India's capital-intensive industrialization and urbanization through the establishment of centralized teaching and research institutions such as the IITs in the vicinity of urban, industrial centres evokes its opposite, the rural, decentralized, low-cost cottage industry that Gandhi had envisaged. Against the large-scale plan of automation and mechanization is the appeal of the 'homegrown' and 'handmade' that Gandhi sees as the bedrock of Swadeshi. The sole reference to Gandhi's village economy and artisanship is in the Report's acknowledgement of the 'essentially rural and agricultural background' of the students in the emphasis given to workshop and practical training as compared to Western universities. But, despite the inclusion of traditional skills like carpentry, smithy, welding, masonry, and foundry, the Report makes it clear that 'an engineer is not a craftsman nor is expected to possess the same degree of manual skill as an artisan'.[21] It certainly misses out the link between artisanship, the development of the body and the ethic of bread labour that is essential to the Gandhian system. Neither the control of the senses nor the training of the body through skill development, the twin goals of Gandhian/liberal education, are included in the training of technical personnel.

The concept of global benchmarking in the Report that has helped the IITs to evolve into world-class institutions over the years is in opposition to the decolonizing purpose Gandhi had in mind by eschewing the Western model. Though the West shifts from Europe to America as a 'Central institution' is proposed in the Report, modelled on the Massachusetts Institute of Technology, the ghost of the West looms large in formulating the eligibility criteria, the syllabi, the fee structure, and so on. The Institution is enjoined to benchmark against 'the first class institutions abroad'. Among the two institutions that the new Higher Technical Institutions are modelled on, Manchester's inclusion rings with an un-Gandhian echo. Gandhi's attribution of the role played by textile industries in Manchester in destroying indigenous crafts is well known. Gandhi had clearly staged the clash between Manchester and Swadeshi as a symbolic battle between indigenous and non-indigenous, big and small, industrial and traditional. But his caveat against 'reproducing Manchester in India' was really directed at the price that industrial capitalism would extract from us. 'Our very moral being will be sapped', he had warned.[22] If Manchester could be read as the signifier of a certain kind of industry, the Manchesterian allusions in the Report may be read as embodying the heavy industrialization model that engendered the Higher Technical Institutions.

The theories of technology underpinning the Report define technology solely in terms of growth. They also reverberate with a form of technological determinism. The entry of technical progress in economic theory after World War Two is reflected in the preoccupation of the policy makers with economic considerations, such as the rate of return, cost, and benefit and change in the production functions. Technological progress is related in the Report mainly to the production function, which is again defined in technical terms. While technology was later found to be only one of the factors in the production function, development is construed here as a structural shift that places a great emphasis on technology in the switchover from traditional to modern technologies in manufacturing and from agriculture to industry in general. The transforming effect of technologies is restricted to the availability of technical personnel within the scope of the Report and it steers clear of Research and Development. Even a pure cost–benefit economic analysis of the investment assumes the beneficiary to be the modern sector that concerns itself only with capital, technology, and education. But the Report's axiomatic narrative of technology as neutral and as linked to development acquires meaning only in relation to the Gandhian, in which technology, man, and nature are interlinked.

While the Report, like all good reports, is generically equipped to avoid doubt and ambiguity in the articulation of its objective, its enthusiastic reiteration of terms and ideas abhorrent to Gandhi in *Hind Swaraj* sounds almost like a reaction to his caveats against technology. Though the Report lists 'other relevant questions' in the list of items to be discussed, the question of the social or spiritual benefits of technology that Gandhi had raised time and again is not deemed relevant. In fact, repeated allusions to the west and western institutions, including universities and industry, suggest a fetishization of the West and Western models of development that Gandhi had warned against. When read together with *Hind Swaraj*, innocuous references to places and institutions, such as Manchester or the Railways, in the Report begin to reverberate with particularly un-Gandhian undertones. Its omission of a section on problems and gap areas in the translation of its objectives in the light of this intertextual dialogue foregrounds the limitations of the policymakers in understanding the complete impact of the task they set themselves. As these questions haunt the Institutes in the years to come, the lacunae and silences in the Report become doubly obvious. The most important of these, in the light of Gandhi's appropriation in contemporary critiques of modernity, is that relating to the metanarrative of progress based on doctrines of materialism and instrumental rationality, the belief in scientific and technological progress, large-scale methods of production and so on that Gandhi had seen as opposed to his own idea of civilization predicated on alternative morality.

Since 1951, the IITs have produced nearly a hundred thousand graduates who have 'supplied' the 'technical manpower' not only for India's development but also for the developed West. Every year, many of these graduates migrate to the US and Europe. Fifty years later, the agenda of the Sarker Committee Report appears to have been more than fulfilled not only with respect to achieving the industrialization mission through training technical persons, but also through having approximated to the global benchmark in terms of undergraduate excellence. The Golden Jubilee celebrations of the IITs in the Silicon Valley, where it was hailed by the Microsoft founder Bill Gates as 'an incredible institution', substantiates the claim about the IITs having become a global brand. The *IIT Story: Issues and Concerns* published in *Frontline* raises a number of issues such as the claims of primary versus higher education, opportunity for the socially disadvantaged, and brain drain; but the success and failures of the 'institute of national importance' are still largely evaluated in terms of the Nehruvian dream of nation-building. It must not be forgotten that despite the overplayed difference between Nehru and Gandhi on the sector that ought to be developed, the two were in complete agreement on the social benefits of technology. However, the large IIT exodus to the United States of America and the globalized economy complicates the Nehruvian programme of nation-building and value-addition. It would appear that the diverse meanings of contribution to the national wealth as defined by IITians in the new millennium might force a revision of the Nehruvian ideal as well. IITians contributing to the global economy or to increasing global wealth and welfare in preference over that of the nation is well beyond what Nehru might have envisaged. But the Gandhian alternative of development achieved through a different pedagogical tradition had never been incorporated into the educational technology favoured by the IIT system.

Neither the Report nor periodic appraisals of the IIT system transcend the limited concern with the scope and uses of technology that they locate in the context of national development to interrogate the ideological imperatives that informed the establishment of these edifices of technology. Gandhi's broader concern with technology that cannot be separated from its social, economic, political, and even philosophical impact cannot be voiced in the idiom of modernization and development based on technological advancement, industrialization, and urbanization that still dictate the agendas of policymakers as well as the alumni. When the list of sponsored research projects being conducted by the various IITs is circulated, the criterion for achievement is the financial bottom line rather than social utility. Similarly, nonchalant IITian redefinitions of value and returns geared to present requirements betray little awareness of alternative developmental options. Technology is commonly read in these celebratory stories solely in relation to growth. It is assumed that the IITian *dharma* is to increase wealth through the use of advanced technologies and allow its benefits to percolate to the economically disadvantaged.[23] Gandhi's selective adoption or rejection of technology becomes particularly pertinent in this context because, more than choosing the right technology, his questioning of the goals of technology leads to the interrogation of the goals of development.

The IIT dream, both in the N R Sarker Report tabled in the heyday of Indian Independence and in Vision 2020 presented fifty years later, is essentially a 'progressive', forward looking narrative. But the ghostly presence of the 'regressive' Gandhi may be felt in the unsaid, the silences, and the occlusions. For this reason, Gandhi can make a 'lateral entry' in the IIT system subsequently in the critiques of the IIT system that emerge time and again.[24] Gandhi's voice may be heard in these critiques, which supplement the exogenous narrative of technology underwriting the Sarker Committee Report by doing a technology audit in relation to society and nature. At the Golden Jubilee of the system, the Directors of the six IITs indulged in a critical self-appraisal and came to the conclusion that the self-congratulatory tone of producing a world-class institution must be tempered with a recognition of its failure in fulfilling the nation-building goal. While the IITian goal, 'the pursuit of excellence', has inspired the vision and mission of the IITs throughout their history, the questions relating to the applications and the benefits of excellence and the socio-economic model so produced still remain unanswered. While evaluating the IIT programme, it is extremely important to note the discrepancy in the IIT system between the objectives of teaching – of producing a world-class techno-elite – and those of research – development of indigenous, local, low-cost technologies. While the IIT programme is designed to and has produced techno-engineers and techno-manager who may be employed in sophisticated industries and research laboratories in the world, the social objectives of the premier institute of science and technology are defined in relation to rural masses. The irreconcilable goals of teaching and research account for the dissonance between the focus on the development of appropriate technologies that is in conflict with the pedagogic aspirations of the undergraduate programme. This contradiction is also reflected in the bifurcation of the syllabi and methodologies of undergraduate and graduate programmes. While undergraduates are prepared to grapple with the most advanced technologies employed in the developed world, the masters and research students are enjoined to contribute to the research goals of the developing nation.

The IITs have certainly produced better engineers than any other institution in India but the silence on whether they have 'made better men [or women]' of students and 'enabled us [students] to do our duty' returns as a disturbing note at every routine stock-taking.[25] With a pronounced metropolitan, even global outlook, the bias towards meritocracy and scholastic perfection has sidelined issues of social responsibility, particularly to the rural sections or the disadvantaged, which have not been sufficiently addressed at the systemic level. Though examples of individuals dedicated to rural improvement or empowerment of the disadvantaged may be cited, how many IIT graduates have opted to bring the benefit of their education to the masses? How many of the technologies developed or research projects embarked on are directed towards the alleviation of poverty or improvement of the life of the common people? Is the image of the elitist institution that IITs have come to acquire inscribed by its anti elitist opposite? The issue of discursive indenturement that Gandhi foresaw in imitating Western models continues to haunt the national elite. The construction of the techno elite by the IIT system needs to be evaluated against Gandhi's critique of the English educated elite in *Hind Swaraj*. The IITs elitist thrust might not seem 'compatible with local cultural and social environments'[26] as 'maximizing social welfare'.[27] In fulfilling their specific brief 'to supply technical personnel', the IITs depart from Thormann's definition of appropriate technology as being economical 'in the use of scarce factors, capital and highly trained personnel'.[28] But their agenda still conforms to that of Bourrieres who held that 'while technology must correspond as closely to actual manpower supply, teaching and training methods should endeavor to improve that supply so as to meet the requirements of the most productive technologies'.[29]

The Gandhian caveat buried in the structure of the Institution returns surreptitiously in the ritual references to appropriate technologies in the IITs, which seem innocent of their Gandhian etymology.[30] Those influenced by the slogan of 'small is beautiful' might not be aware of Schumacher's indebtedness to Gandhi who Rybczynski names the 'first, authentic, appropriate technologist' and considers even more radical than the renowned economist.[31]

It must be recalled that the appropriate technology discourse to which the Gandhian vision of technology has been annexed is ridden with divergences on the meaning of 'appropriateness'. Does appropriate technology mean 'small', 'for the poor', 'relevant', 'ecologically conscious', 'sustainable' or something else? What criterion should be used to define appropriate technologies? Critics of appropriate technology consider it as a top-down movement, located in a Western philosophical problem, flowing from the universities and academies in the developed world to Third World countries. This critique is relevant to the appropriate technology talk at the IITs that flows from Western metropolitan labs and institutions through projects, funding, collaborations, conferences, and faculty exchanges. IITians have come home to the ecological, social or psychological costs of technologies after their sojourns at universities in Europe and America. Appropriate technologies are interpreted in a near literal fashion in IITspeak to mean any technology that is suited to specific conditions. But the multiple meanings of appropriate technologies that derive from the Gandhian understanding of technology and the body of knowledge, techniques, and the underlying philosophy that shaped it remain largely unexplored. Even so, the debate on appropriate technology, into which IITs have been drawn, puts the narrative of technology in the Sarker Report under erasure.

Gandhi's approach looks forward to both strains in the appropriate technology argument, the importance of 'intermediate technologies' and the radical critique of technology as development.[32] Gandhi's own selective appropriation of technology slips through all these meanings as well as through the indigenous/western dichotomy. It is more important to understand the philosophy behind rejections and acceptances of technologies rather than to reconcile his anathema for one technology or the other. 'The spinning wheel is also machinery. It is a beautiful work of art. It typifies the use of machinery on a universal scale. It is machinery reduced to the terms of the masses', Gandhi had said.[33] The spinning wheel, or the *charkha*, the most celebrated emblem of Gandhian development, offers us the most apt example to enter the appropriate technology argument and explore its multiple meanings as 'intermediate', 'progressive', 'alternative', 'light-capital', 'labour-intensive', 'indigenous', 'appropriate', 'low-cost', 'community centred', 'soft', 'radical', 'liberatory', and 'convivial'.[34] The Gandhian strategy rests on a manipulation of the symbolic significance of the most ordinary act, be it breaking the Salt Law or advocating the use of the spinning wheel and boycotting mill-made fabrics to gain political advantage. In the symbolic signification that the *charkha* has acquired as the rural, non-technologized, low-cost form of production, it is often forgotten that the spinning wheel is also a technology. But evidence of the existence of the spinning wheel in the Harappan age establishes its autochothonous origins and makes it the perfect tool for postcolonial resistance. Unlike new technologies, it is both cost-saving and labour-intensive and thereby appropriate to the low-capital labour-intensive development required by the rural sector in India. Its benefits are physical as well as psychological, the pleasure of labour and the advantage of health. Being small scale, it is environmentally friendly and produces the intimate *gemeinshaft* community compared to alienating and polluting technologies. Finally, the *charkha* is not only aesthetically fulfilling in its concrete output as khadi but emancipates the weaver and wearer from the enslaving networks of global capital. Without suggesting that the technology missions be redesigned for the propagation of the *charkha* or khadi, one could use the *charkha* concept to examine the appropriateness of technologies used or developed in or by the IITs.

Rather than borrowing *charkha* ideology to the letter, the spirit in which Gandhi had proposed it as an alternative to the Western model could be used as a guideline to determine the appropriateness or inappropriateness of technologies. Gandhi's definition of *charkha* allows room for an expansion of its metaphorical value in relation to altered circumstances. *Charkha* need not be deployed in its literal sense as rural, low-cost, indigenous technology but the symbolic value possessed in a colonized state to strike at imperialist hegemony may be appropriated to reply to neo-imperialist structures of domination. Rather than viewing appropriate and modern technologies as oppositional or even complementary, 'their relative suitability for specific purposes or situations' might be used to define different technologies.[35] Following Jequier's solution, that appropriate and modern technologies be seen as complementary rather than oppositional, could be one way that IITs can reconcile their global ambitions with Gandhian local concerns. The two contradictory objectives in the vision and mission of the IITs, to produce world-class scientists and engineers and provide state-of-the-art facilities while developing technologies that are attuned to the needs of the masses, can be achieved if *charkha* is reinscribed as 'best-fit' rather than rural or indigenous technology.

In the list of Technologies Developed and Ready for Commercialization at the Indian Institute of Technology Kharagpur, small technologies, particularly those designed for the rural or domestic consumption, match the big.[36] At least fourteen technologies innovated by IIT Kharagpur have been transferred to industries and have gone into commercial production. The humble 'Explosion Puffing Machine for Food Grains' shares space with those such as 'Cost Effective Servo Controlled Charging Circuit for Large SC Coils Used in Superconducting Magnetic Energy Storage System used as UPS'. Whether these could be regarded as intermediate technologies until Indian research institutions can develop the capability for creating bigger technologies or as small village technologies, the ratio of small technologies developed at Kharagpur to those with application in core or heavy industry seems larger. As research interests and capabilities are a reflection of funding priorities, it is equally possible that the selection criteria of funding bodies like the Department of Science and Technology (DST) and the Council for Scientific and Industrial Research (CSIR) dictate the technologies that are being developed at the IITs. But the list appended at the end of the paper is an indication of the small-scale scope of many of the technologies developed locally. Several of these technologies would directly fit Gandhi's charkha concept of homegrown appropriate technology. The technology of 'Moulding Machine to Make Leaf Plates and Leaf Bowls', whose salient features are 'simplicity, affordability, portable nature of the device, less drudgery to operators, and locally available raw materials', definitely falls into this category.[37] However, the criticism of appropriate technologies such as whether these technologies are profitable, efficient, sophisticated, congenial to growth and workplace productivity, and conducive to improving standards of living, is equally applicable here.

Second, while these rural, low-cost technologies might be promoted officially, there is a suggestion that they are 'inferior' technologies that might consolidate the Western nations in their socioeconomic and technological dominance over the Third World. Despite politically right invocations to appropriate technologies and tokenist inclusions of Rural Development Centres at the IITs, the IITs display greater pride in developing 'high technologies' that are believed to make Indian globally competitive. To cite one example, the authorities at IIT Kharagpur regard the National Semiconductor Corporation sponsored VLSI (very large-scale integration) lab, which has produced 12 cutting-edge chips in the past two years (2003), as its 'most astounding success'. But the target user of this technology, 'the global infotech market', brings to mind mass and community orientedness as one of the criteria for defining appropriate technology. Probably none of the characteristics included by Jequier and Blanc (1983), for example, can be applied to such technologies:

> Appropriate technology (AT) is now recognized as the generic term for a wide range of technologies characterized by any one or several of the following characteristics: low investment cost per workplace, low capital investment per unit of output, organizational simplicity, high adaptability to a peculiar social and cultural environment, sparing use of natural resources, low cost of final product or high potential for employment.[38]

It must be remembered that not all the technologies developed at the IITs can be accommodated in the *charkha* ideal of low-cost, labour-intensive, indigenous oriented to the rural masses. As Anderson pointed out, 'scale, complexity and expense are not always positively correlated. It is possible for a large machine to be both simple and cheap and for a small one to be highly complex and expensive.'[39] An 'appropriate technology' project currently being conducted at the Computer Science and Engineering Department at IIT Kharagpur problematizes the polarization between big and small, capital intensive and labour intensive, low cost and high cost, indigenous and Western in the debates on appropriate technologies. Called *Sparsha*,[40] this project began with the development of a Low Cost Tactile

Braille Reader in 1999. The involvement of the Ministry of Information Technology to develop a complete Braille Information System for Indian language documents and the tie-up with an industrial partner, Webel Mediatronics Limited, made the Bharati Braille Transliteration System available to thirty schools for the Visually Challenged. The availability of the software in Indian languages now ensures that the benefits of the project are not confined to the English-speaking elite. The Principal Investigator of the project, Anupam Basu, claims '*Sparsha* is a very successful project if the metric be the feedback from the users'.[41] However, when the issue of costs comes up, the product that Basu sees as being directed at the economically disadvantaged begins to ring with the scepticism about the top-down-flow critique of appropriate technologies. At the moment, *Sparsha's* assembly and distribution is free of cost but requires 'low-end PCs and Braille embossers to be purchased, and often that is beyond the reach of its intended users'.[42] Basu plans to involve non-governmental organizations for making this possible but feels that the government should step in to support this effort to reach the disadvantaged. But Basu's 'assistive' technologies for the physically challenged are being financed with support from MediaLab Asia and other funding agencies. The objective of the Media laboratory, 'to develop affordable technology for bridging the digital divide', it appears, can be fulfilled only if it fits in with global priorities. Gandhi would approve of the 'coming together of technology, people and values, an effort to direct scientific research towards the needs of the underprivileged' in this project if Basu could only cut down costs. After all, one of the criteria for appropriate technologies in the Third World context is low cost. Yet the project illustrates that there cannot be a simple correlation between the small and low cost as appropriate and the capitalist intensive as inappropriate because the big might be as intended for social benefit as the small. Appropriate technology is not always small, simple, cheap, and labour-intensive to all advocates of appropriate technology. For example, to P V Indiresan, a former Director of IIT Chennai and Coordinator of the Pura project, 'Appropriate technology is always profitable. If it's not profitable and does not give the employee reasonable remuneration, it's not appropriate. It is reasonable high technology which ensures growth.'[43]

The notion of relativity, often invoked in the discourse of appropriate technology, is important in resolving the confusing inconsistencies in Gandhi's own allusions to machines. Gandhi's preferences for big or small machines, as J. D. Sethi points out, were 'contextual, historical, temporal, conscious and purposive, and thus *essentially relative*'.[44] Gandhi's advocacy of small technologies, like Schumacher's, ought to be seen as provisional because he was not entirely opposed to high technologies as he is believed to be but even recommended their deployment in the public sector. Besides, his suggestion that large-scale, capital-intensive industrial enterprise should supplement and reinforce the development of small-scale industries and agriculture in the hinterland confirms his support for technological diversity as a solution to solving the problems of developing nations.

> If I can convert the country to my point of view, the social order of the future will be based predominantly on the Charkha and all it implies. It will include everything that promotes the well-being of the villagers. I do visualize electricity, ship-building, ironworks, machine-making and the like existing side by side with village handicrafts. But the order of dependence will be reversed. Hitherto, the industrialization has been so planned as to destroy the villages and the village crafts. In the State of the future it will subserve the villages and their crafts ... [45]

The prioritizing of the traditional sector, emphasized by Gandhi, cannot be dictated by any special virtues of the traditional sector. But the asymmetry between the traditional and the modern through the emphasis on urban, advanced, capital-intensive technological developments in post independence India should be removed. Similarly, the correlation between small technologies for the rural and urban marginalized and advanced for the elite cannot be established simplistically. Advanced technologies might be equally employed for rural development as evident in the drive to use Information and Communication Technologies for developing regional communities. Critiques of appropriate technology as inefficient and expensive will have to be juxtaposed against its uses and benefits. The equation between job creation and the optimum use of existing skills and resources and appropriate technologies is complicated by the job opportunities provided by the large sector and the need for the constant redefinition of existing skills and resources.

The appropriate technology argument, therefore, cannot be predicated on any single definition, or the big/small, low cost/ high cost, capital intensive/ labour intensive or any other dichotomies. Akubue is of the opinion that 'appropriate technology cannot be seen simply as some identifiable technical device; rather, it is an approach to community development consisting of a body of knowledge, techniques, and an underlying philosophy'.[46] What is important is that one understands appropriate technology not as a 'homogeneous phenomenon' but as a heterogeneous collection of social and technical options. The objectives and the uses determine the meaning of appropriateness. Just as the term 'appropriate' is open to interpretation, other givens such as development, growth, community, and the notion of the good also need to be deconstructed in order to determine the best fit and the best alternative for the specific needs of specific regions.

As Gandhi continually modified his views on technology that were contradictory to begin with, he would have found no dichotomy between the small and the big, the advanced or the primitive, labour intensive or capital intensive, provided that they contributed to the welfare of all sections of society and the surrounding environment. IITs seem to have redefined the notion of the appropriateness of technologies and technologists by addressing the nation's needs. The prevailing logic in the IITs today is that the prestige and wealth created through the IIT alumni would improve the economic condition of the nation that would, in turn, transform the traditional sector and the less advantaged. But Gandhian reservations that engage with the larger issues of environmental depredation, alienation, consumerism, minimization of needs, continue to form a disturbing undercurrent at each self-congratulatory exercise. The ghost of the Father of the Nation returns as the father of appropriate technology to ask the same uncomfortable questions that the IITs would prefer not to answer with their gaze being fixed elsewhere.

Appendix: technologies developed and ready for commercialization

Process technology for tomato powder
Production of gallic acid utilizing mixed agricultural residues by co-culture method
Novel catalytic process for preparation of diallyl trisulfide and important transformation product of garlic
Bioprocess for herbal skin–nourishing gel
Bio-process for sandalwood somatic seedling production
Design and development of a doppler ultrasonography system
Process for preparation of al–ti–b master alloys for grain refinement of aluminium and its alloys
Device for transmitting pressure and differential pressure signals
Explosion puffing machine for food grains
Process technology for making ready-to-eat dehydrated puffed potato cubes
Process technology for enriched quick-cooking rice
Process technology for making dehydrated instant potato
See-saw bioreactor
Process technology for production of mango milk-based fruit bar
Process technology for production of fruit-juice powder
Libb (layered insulating building block)
Tractor-mounted air-carrier sprayer using axial flow blower
Polyamide films and a process for producing such films
Quick-setting polyurethane compositions for composite application
Automated irrigation controller
Continuous soil-moisture recorder
Granular matrix soil-moisture sensor (g m s)
Low-cost computer-controlled automated irrigation system
Soil-moisture sensor for automated micro irrigation system
Portable infusion pump
Preparation of polysaccharide blended slow-release urea
Recovery of lead metal through green technology

Preparation of nano-sized titanium oxide from mineral or crude source
Preparation of sulfides of rare-earth metals
Metabrowser (multimedia e-book on brasses)
Metabrowser – ii (multimedia e-book on tool steels)
Virtual alloys (software)
Clock-controlled sun-tracking system for solar photovoltaic and solar thermal collectors
symbols2000
Flotilla connector
Overloading indicator for mechanized country boats
Speed-control system for mechanised country boats
High-performance flocculating agents and viscosifiers based on hydrolysed Polyacrylamide grafted amylopectin and polyacrylamide grafted carboxymethyl cellulose
Application of grafted amylopectin in reduction of energy requirement of sprinkler irrigation system
High-performance flocculating agents based on hydrolyzed and unhydrolyzed Hydroxypropyl guar gum and polyacrylamide
Application of grafted amylopectin for wastewater treatment
High-performance flocculating agents based on carboxymethyl cellulose and polyacrylamide
Fibrillisation of liquid crystalline polymer (lcp) vectra-950a in poly(ether ether)ketone (peek) matrix.
High-performance flocculating based on hydrolysed and unhydrolysed guar gum-g-polyacrylamide
Novel technique for manufacture of instant tea
Tea-production technology for non–traditional areas
Zerotree encoding of wavelet data
Method of compressing a colour image
Enzymatic polishing of rice
Reagent for application in combinatorial chemistry for complex mixture of ti^{4+}, nb^{5+}, ta^{5+} and other ions for synthesis of ferroelectric materials.
Development of nano-intermetallic dispersed al–matrix composites from the al–cu– x ternary metastable precursors
Indigenously developed real-time digital simulator (powerdraw)
Near toll quality speech coder at 2.4 kbps
Processing of a set of plasma sprayed caramic coatings on metal substrates
Synthesis route for processing of fe-tic composite materials by thermit reduction
High-performance cbn abrasive wheel
Application of grafted amylopectin n deduction of energy requirement of sprinkler irrigation system
Novel and inexpensive isolated gate drive circuit for igbts and mosfets for certain industrial electronics application

Novel electronic circuit for fast detection and protection of sc magnet coil during quench

Cost-effective servo controlled charging circuit for large sc coils used in superconducting magnetic energy storage system used as ups

Design and construction of superconducting solenoidal magnet for smes-ups application; hull form

Use of chlorinated waste tire rubber as filler in polyvinylchloride

Discrete wavelet transform based computationally efficient video compression scheme Preparation of mechanically ground waste rubber and useful compositions

Abrus seed lectin based aqueous immuno adjuvant for the production of high titre antibody in experimental anima

Modified bubble column for the simultaneous scrubbing of particulate and gaseous matters

New method with al–surface hydrolysis for forming a metalloceramic gel and corrosion resistant encapsulated metal nanoparticles

Discovery of a natural chemical route for recovering a pure metal powder from metal salts

Processing a single phase c-zro2 nanopowder form a transparent amorphous ceramic gel

Processing finely divided loose zno nanopowder from usual salts through a chemical route with nabh4

Low-fat absorbing self–supporting films made from food grade starch and other edible materials

Notes

1 The Director of IIT Powai S.P. Sukhatme's speech 'The Growth of an Institute for Higher Technological Education' on the Golden Jubilee celebrations on 27 July 2005 begins with an invocation to the Nehruvian vision just as the report of the former Director of IIT Chennai and Director of IIT Delhi P.V. Indiresan and N.C. Nigam 'Indian Institutes of Technology: An Experience in Excellence' (to be published by OUP for the World Bank) concludes with a quote from Nehru:.talkevax.ucsd.edu/vijay/iit.html. (accessed on 26 January 2007).

2 See Sudhir Chandra, *The Oppressive Present: Literature and Social Consciousness in Colonial India*. Delhi: OUP, 1992, Ashis Nandy, *The Intimate Enemy: Loss and Recovery of Self under Colonialism*. Delhi: OUP, 1983, Ashis Nandy, *Alternative Sciences: Creativity and Authencity in Two Indian Sciences*. ND: Allied. 1979.

3 Ashis Nandy, *Traditions, Tyranny, and Utopia : Essays in the Politics of Awareness*. Delhi: OUP, 1987, p. 129.

4 Howard Perlmutter and Eric Trist, 'Paradigms for Social Transition', *Human Relations*, Vol. 39, No. 21, 1986. 1–27, p. 2.

5 Chandra, *The Oppressive Present* and Nandy, *The Intimate Enemy*.

6 Gyan Prakash, 'Science between the Lines', in *Subaltern Studies IX*, ed. Shahid Amin and Dipesh Chakrabarty. Delhi: Oxford University Press, 1996.

7 Patrick Colm Hogan, Lalita Pandit, *Rabindranath Tagore: Universality and Tradition*. Madison: Fairleigh Dickinson University Press,. 2003, p. 89.

8 See 'Development of Higher Technical Institutions in India' (Report of Sarker Committee), Central Bureau of Education India, March 1948, Reprint 1951 (Shimla, Manager of Government of India Press), p. 1. Henceforth, RSC.
9 *Hind Swaraj*, Ahmedabad: Navjivan Publishing House, translated by Amritlal Thakoredas Nanavati, 1948, p. 71. Henceforth, HS.
10 HS, p. 72.
11 HS, p. 73.
12 RSC, 1951, p. 18.
13 RSC, p. 19.
14 RSC, p. 18. But to understand the guiding principles for achieving this combination one has to turn to Item 3.
15 HS, p. 72.
16 RSC, p. 19.
17 HS, p. 73.
18 HS, p. 80.
19 J.D. Sethi, *Gandhi Today*, New Delhi: Vikas Publishing House Pvt Ltd, 1979, p. 51.
20 HS, p 81.
21 RSC, p. 19
22 HS, p 78.
23 Consider the views of Rekhi and Mashruwala, for instance. 'To me, creating wealth is a noble activity. I don't consider this to be a trivial or cheap thing to do', says Kanwal Rekhi, an IIT Bombay graduate who sold his company ExceLan to software giant Novell for $200 million and now often backs companies started by younger IIT graduates. 'They are building major trade relationships which will help India more than if they had stayed in India', says Mashruwala. 'Twenty years from now, the IITs will be recognized as the one single entity that generated the single most amount of wealth in India. They will be recognized as the wisest decision' (Alexander Salkever, 'Technical Sutra', salon.com. 6 December 1999). www.salon.com/books/it/1999/12/06/indian/index1.html. (accessed on 26 January 2007).
24 Lateral entry is the system in the IITs through which students, unable to qualify for the five year MSc programme in science disciplines through the Joint Entrance Examination, may be admitted to the same course in the fourth year.
25 The phrases in inverted commas are from HS, p. 73. R Natarajan, Director IIT Chenna underlined the need for changing the IITs terms of reference but defined the future goals of IITs in terms not very different from those underlying the Sarker Report.

> To review the vision, mission and goals of the IITs and strategies for achieving them taking into consideration the current and future national priorities and emerging global scenario, we must combine national relevance the India's intrigue research along with the global scenario because internationalization EETO, GATT, all of them are steering us in the phase. Second one would be to review the performance of IITs relating to the vision, to review the extent and intensity our linkages and introduction with industry, to review the management structures and governance mechanism we have in order to get the maximum productivity. Then to review the faculty recruitment to tension and development process is to review the procedures of students' admission to the different programmes maintaining the constitutional provisions and designing facilitating systems for assisting disadvantage sections of society without compromising the high standard of academic and research performance because we are functioning in a milieu, which has special social characteristics, political

characteristics, industry and commercial characteristics, all of them have to be addressed.

R Natarjan. *Panel Discussion, Golden Jubilee Foundation Day*, IIT Kharagpur, 18 August 2001.

26 P. Thormann, 'Proposal for a Program in Appropriate Technology', in A. Robinson (ed.), *Appropriate Technologies for Third World Development*, New York: St. Martin's Press, 1979, pp. 283–84.
27 D. Morawetz, 'Employment Implications of Industrialization in Developing Countries: A Survey', *The Economic Journal*, 84 (333), 1974, p. 517.
28 Thormann, 'Proposal for a Program in Appropriate Technology'.
29 Bourrieres, 'Adaptation of Technologies to Available Resources', in A. Robinson (ed.), *Appropriate Technologies for Third World Development*, New York: St. Martin's Press, 1979, p. 5.
30 Gandhi has been named the 'father' of appropriate technology and the 'first appropriate technologist' even though the term gained usage much after Gandhi's time. M. J. Betz, P. McGowan, and R.T. Wigand (eds), *Appropriate Technology: Choices and Developments*, Durham, NC: Duke University Press, 1984; Witold Rybczynski, *Paper Heroes: A Review of Appropriate Technology*, Garden City, NY: Anchor Press/Doubleday, 1980.
31 Anthony Akubue, 'Appropriate Technology for Socioeconomic Development in Third World Countries', *Journal of Technology Studies*, Winter–Spring 2000, p. 35.
32 Schumacher coined the term intermediate technology in relation to the needs of developing countries, particularly India. 'Such an intermediate technology would be immensely more productive than the indigenous technology ... but it would be immensely cheaper than the sophisticated, highly capital-intensive technology of modern industry' (E.F. Schumacher, *Small is Beautiful: Economics as if People Mattered*, New York: Harper & Row, 1973, p. 180).
33 Akubue has interpreted Gandhi's distinction between 'mass produced' and 'produced by masses' to mean that the former is goods-centred and that the latter is people-centred. In Gandhi's scheme, the masses are also consumers of the goods they produce. But in the present context, the masses who produce and those who consume might be quite different. Similarly, as the question of the community has now been extended as much by migration as by globalization of the economy, the question of contributing to community becomes extremely complicated just as the big/small dichotomy cannot be the sole criterion for determining appropriateness (Akubue, 'Appropriate Technology for Socioeconomic Development in Third World Countries').
34 All these aspects of appropriate technologies are examined by Akubue, 'Appropriate Technology for Socioeconomic Development in Third World Countries'.
35 K.W. Willoughby, *Technology Choice: A Critique of the Appropriate Tchnology Movement*. Boulder, CO: Westview Press. 1990. p. 6.
36 Details are appended at the end of the essay.
37 'Rural Technologies', *Technology Linked Business Opportunity Publications* http://www.tifac.org.in/offer/tsw/rural63.htm. (accessed on 26 January 2007).
38 N. Jequier and G. Blanc, *The World of Appropriate Technology*, Paris: Organization for Economic Cooperation and Development, 1983, p. 10.
39 Anderson, M.B., 'Technology Transfer: Implications for Women'. In C. Overholt, M.B. Anderson, K. Cloud, and J.E. Austin (eds), *Gender Roles in Development Projects*, West Hartford, CT: Kumarian Press, 1985, pp. 57–77, 68.
40 Project Name: Empowering the Visually Handicapped through Speech Synthesis for Multilingual Indian Environment(EVHS), Client: MediaLab.Asia, Mumbai, Consultant: Prof. Anupam Basu. Co-consultant(s): Prof. A.K. Majumdar, Dr Sudeshna Sarkar.

41 Rasika, Dhavse, 'Reaching Out with Valuable Technology', indiatogether.org, http://www.indiatogether.org/2004/feb/hlt-sparsha.htm, February 2004, 6 April 2005.
42 Quoted in Dhavse, 'Reaching Out with Valuable Technology'.
43 A government National Project on Biogas Development in 1981 brought needed relief to many in rural India. For instance, biogas in Pura, a village in south India, has been meeting the water-pumping, electric-lighting, cooking, and fertilizer needs of this village's 485 inhabitants. According to P. Sampat, about 2 million biogas digesters have been installed in India since 1981, 'and although the program has had its share of problems, it has made substantial progress, ('India's Low-tech Energy Success'. *World Watch*, 8 (6), 1995, p. 21, quoted in A. Akubue, 'PV Indiresan interviewed by Ashutosh Bhardwaj', on 10 January 2007, New Delhi. IndianNGOS.com. www.indianngos.com/interviews/indiresan.htm
44 Sethi, *Gandhi Today*, p. 76.
45 Bhatt, V.V., 'The Development Problem, Strategy, and Technology Choice: Sarvodaya and socialist approaches in India'. In F. A. Long and A. Oleson (eds), *Appropriate Ttechnology and Social Value – A Critical Appraisal*, Cambridge, MA: Ballinger, 1980, p. 172.
46 Akubue, 'Appropriate Technology for Socioeconomic Development in Third World Countries'.

Bibliography

Akubue, Anthony, 'Appropriate Technology for Socioeconomic Development in Third World Countries', *Journal of Technology Studies*. Winter–Spring 2000.
Betz, M. J., McGowan, P., and Wigand, R.T. (eds), *Appropriate Technology: Choices and Developments*, Durham, NC: Duke University Press, 1984.
Bourrieres, P., 'Adaptation of Technologies to Available Resources', in A. Robinson (ed.), *Appropriate Technologies for Third World Development*, New York: St. Martin's Press, 1979.
'Development of Higher Technical Institutions in India' (Report of Sarker Committee), *Central Bureau of Education India*, March 1948 Reprint, Simla: Manager Government of India Press, 1951.
Dhavse,Rasika, 'Reaching Out with Valuable Technology', indiatogether.org, http://www.indiatogether.org/2004/feb/hlt-sparsha.htm, February 2004, 6 April 2005.
Gandhiji, Mahatma, *Hind Swarajya*, translated by Amritlal Thakoredas Nanavati, Ahmedabad: Navjeevan Parakashan Mandir, 1948.
Harrison, P., *The Third World Tomorrow*, Harmondsworth: Penguin Books, 1980.
Jequier, N. and Blanc, G., *The World of Appropriate Technology*, Paris: Organization for Economic Cooperation and Development, 1983.
Gandhi, Mahatama, *Hind Swaraj and Indian Home Rule*, Ahmedabad: Navjivan Publishing House, Electronic Version compiled by Hinal Kariya.
Morawetz, D., 'Employment Implications of Industrialization in Developing Countries: A Survey', *The Economic Journal*, 84(333) 1974, 491–542.
Pellegrini, U., 'The Problem of Appropriate Technology'. In A. De Giorgio and C. Roveda (eds), *Criteria for Selecting Appropriate Technologies under Different Cultural, Technical and Social Conditions*, New York: Pergamon Press, 1979, pp. 1–5.
Ramashray, Roy, *Gandhi: Soundings in Political Philosophy*, Delhi: Chanakya Publication, 1984.
Schumacher, E.F., *Small is Beautiful: Economics as if People Mattered*, New York: Harper & Row, 1973.

Sethi J. D., *Gandhi Today*, New Delhi: Vikas Publishing House Pvt Ltd, 1979.
Terchek, Ronald J., *Gandhi: Struggling for Autonomy*, New Delhi: Vistaar Publications, 1995.
Thormann, P., 'Proposal for a Program in Appropriate Technology', in A. Robinson (ed.), *Appropriate Technologies for Third World Development*, New York: St. Martin's Press, 1979.
'Top 10 Colleges – Engineering', *India Today Magazine*, 2 June. http://www.indiatoday.com/itoday/20030602/index.html (accessed 6 April 2005).

13 Vernacular cosmopolitanism
World historical readings of Gandhi and Ambedkar

Debjani Ganguly

> But Gandhi does not belong only to India.... He is ... a world figure, a man who belongs to us all.
>
> Horace Alexander

> The mighty shadow of the Mahatma lay across the world. The mighty man in Ambedkar was exposing man's inhumanity to man and the ruthless strokes of his hammer resounded throughout the world.
>
> Dhananjay Keer

Mohandas Karamchand Gandhi (1869–1948) led India's struggle for independence from colonial rule and committed his life to the social reconstruction and regeneration of India. Bhimrao Ramji Ambedkar (1891–1956) fought to eradicate India's internal apartheid manifested in the pernicious caste practice of untouchability and was committed to a vision of modernized India free of caste and colonial oppression. Both were champions of untouchables or dalits, both considered untouchability the most shameful smear on the Indian social fabric and both thought that social reform in India ought to precede political freedom. Both were also highly charismatic national leaders who carried the masses with them. Historian Judith Brown's comment that masses reacted to Gandhi 'with a mixture of religious adulation and millenniary anticipation'[1] could apply as well to Ambedkar. They have both been compared reverentially to the Buddha and were hailed as prophets of their times. Further, their respective paternal honorifics – *Bapu* for Gandhi and *Babasaheb* for Ambedkar – testify to the affection of their followers.

Yet during their lifetimes, as has been well documented, they differed fundamentally on many social and political issues and occasionally even fought bitterly about their respective roles as champions of dalit masses. These quarrels are now part of national lore. D.C. Ahir, in his book *Gandhi and Ambedkar*, succinctly sums up the most common nationalist perception of their differences:

> Gandhi christened victims of untouchability as Harijans, Children of God. Ambedkar, however, wanted to see his people as full-fledged

'Children of the Soil' with equal rights and privileges and not merely as 'touchables' under the guise of another name.[2]

Ambedkar's biographer Dhananjay Keer characterized the differences between them as a clash of titans. As he dramatically put it: 'Gandhi and Ambedkar were temperamentally what Vashistha and Vishwamitra or Voltaire and Rousseau were to each other!'[3] From the late 1920s to the 1940s, the differences between them were serious enough to be manifested not only at national, but also international forums such as the two Round Table conferences in London in the 1930s and the famous meeting with the King Emperor, where the apocryphal dalit narrative has the King infinitely more impressed with Ambedkar than with Gandhi:

> Gandhi, with his ascetic mind and khadi apparel, stood exposed before the August Assembly by a man comparatively younger in age, but full of irreverent audacity, and who spoke with a cultivated ferocity and the fervour of an iconoclast.[4]

Other depictions of the same event portray Gandhi in an admirable light and simply make no reference to Ambedkar. For instance, Viscount Templewood's *Nine Troubled Years*[5] gives us this account of Gandhi's meeting with the King Emperor:

> When the conversation was drawing to an end, the King, the most conscientious of monarchs, evidently thought it was his duty to warn Gandhi of the consequences of rebellion. Just, therefore, as Gandhi was taking leave, His Majesty could not refrain from uttering a grave warning. 'Remember Mr. Gandhi, I won't have any attacks on my Empire'. I held my breath in fear of an argument between the two. Gandhi's *savoir faire* saved the situation with a grave and deferential reply. 'I must not be drawn into a political argument in Your Majesty's palace after receiving Your Majesty's hospitality'[6]

Templewood's is an eyewitness account for he escorted Gandhi to meet the King Emperor.

My aim in this essay is not to create yet another inventory of dissonance – mythic or real – between the two figures or even to compare their respective achievements from a nationalist matrix. It is rather to widen the lens beyond the nationalist framework and cast the two personages, not as two political leaders and social reformers who differed on Indian societal arrangements, but rather as interlocutors of modernity on the world stage. I suggest that histories of the Indian nation-state focus on their differences, while a world-historical approach shows deep points of convergence between them. World history, in other words, provides a different optic on the same set of historical events. As Geoffrey Barraclough put it in his

History in a Changing World, 'World history cuts into reality at a different angle from other types of history; and because its angle is different, it cuts across the lines they have traced.'[7] My attempt to place Gandhi and Ambedkar on the stage of world history is based not so much on arguments to do with their respective global legacies after their deaths, as on a mining of their political vocabularies to unearth a critical mass of articulations demonstrating a cosmopolitical sensibility, one that invested deeply in the affective politics of living in and connecting with a larger world.

I intend to argue two propositions in the essay. One, the tense relationship between Gandhi and Ambedkar can be recast as a dialogic exchange between two idioms of non-European cosmopolitanism – *nonviolence* as hybridized Hindu life-practice, and *democratic development* as a non-hierarchical Buddhist orientation to life. Two, the sharp differences between them notwithstanding, both Gandhi and Ambedkar, along with other nationalist leaders from Asia and Africa, were engaged in projects of world democratization in the era of the decline of modern European colonialism.

In his bird's eye view of what he called 'the short twentieth century', *Age of Extremes 1914–1991*, historian Eric Hobsbawm talks of the importance of the 1930s as a crucial decade in the democratization of not just the Third World, but the globe as a whole. The imperial powers – France, Britain – were besieged by both economic and political woes in the form of the Great Depression and the emergence of fascism in Europe. With the globalization of industrial capitalism in the age of Empire, these developments adversely impacted on the already disgruntled colonies:

> The Great Slump of 1929–33 shook the entire dependent world. For practically all of it the era of imperialism had been one of continuous growth, unbroken even by the world war from which many of them remained remote. ... The Great Slump changed all this. For the first time the interests of dependent and metropolitan economies clashed visibly, if only because the prices of primary products, on which the Third World depended, collapsed so much more dramatically than those of the manufactured goods which they brought from the West. For the first time colonialism and dependency became unacceptable even to those who had hitherto benefited from it ... for the first time ... the lives of ordinary people [in the colonies] were shaken by earthquakes plainly not of natural origin, and which called for protest rather than prayer. A mass basis for political mobilization came into existence.[8]

The mobilization of colonized masses in Asia and Africa under an anti-imperialist umbrella throughout the thirties was paralleled by the mobilization of both liberal and socialist regimes in Europe under an anti-fascist umbrella. These developments had the radical impact of catapulting democratic impulses of various hues onto the world stage and for enabling, perhaps, for the first time in world history, a democratic political vision that was truly global. To paraphrase Hobsbawm, in the 1930s one could see the emerging outlines of a mass politics of the future that would envelop the globe. As modernity's interlocutors among their mass followers, both Gandhi and Ambedkar were key participants in this emergent global democracy.

Gandhi and Ambedkar in world history

Attempts to write about India, especially modern India, from the perspective of a world historical model is bound to attract much scepticism, not least because till recently such a model was scaffolded to a narrative of European imperial formations. India in such a formulation entered 'world' history as a British colony and as a 'footnote' to the history of Britain. World history was interpreted as the globalization of European domination from the late eighteenth to mid-twentieth century. One early expression of this is found in David Thompson's 'What is World History?' (1963):

> One feature of recent history is the spread of European power and influence throughout the world, and the manifold consequences of this both for Europe and for the other five continents. The result today is a world in which any momentous event anywhere really matters, within a relative short time, to all other parts of the world ... a war, breaking out initially between groups of nations in Europe, tends to spread until it entangles nearly every other people on the globe. It seems possible, therefore, for the historian of world history not to write the history of the continents separately[9]

In spite of his claims that world historians could now write about all continents together, the structure of Thompson's book relegates decolonization in Asia and Africa to a chapter in the final stages of his book. Since Thompson there have been many attempts to redress this Eurocentric bias in theorizations of world history.[10] Nevertheless, in the context of India, there is still much scepticism about these efforts. For instance, historian Vinay Lal notes that, while in recent times, there has been a widening of India's 'world horizon', not only through the history of the Indian diaspora since World War Two, but also through globalization discourses that see India and China as major global economic and political players in the twenty-first century, world history even today is not much more than 'the history of the West energizing the rest of the world'.[11]

While one does not doubt his proposition that the West is far from being provincialized even in current attempts to write world history, many recent projects re-imagine colonial histories in a global context by breaking out of the 'nations and empire' mould or the 'colonizer's model of the world' and refocussing attention on cultural traffic among imperial centres and colonies. This has had the effect of bringing together the mundane and monumental aspects of imperial systems in intricate networks of not only trade, military power and politics, but also cultural practices, social formations and knowledge-making. Tony Ballantyne and Antoinette Burton use the metaphor 'webs of empire' to describe these networks. As they put it, 'the web ... conveys something of the double nature of the imperial system. Empires, like webs, were fragile and prone to crises where important threads were broken or structural nodes destroyed, yet also dynamic, being constantly remade and reconfigured through concerted thought and effort.'[12]

While Ballantyne and Burton's focus on the networked nature of empires does to some extent counter Vinay Lal's pessimism that world history invariably re-centres the West, there is one aspect of Lal's analysis that has a bearing on my attempt in this essay to read Gandhi and Ambedkar from a world historical perspective. Lal draws our attention to India's extensive connections with the world in pre-colonial times and highlights the makings of another kind of world history for India, one that connected her to vast regions in Asia, Africa and the Mediterranean through both trade and cultural-religious enterprises. He cites Janet Abu-Lughod's monumental work on the pre-European expansion of world systems in the second millennium in which India was part of a vast trading network. The Coromandel Coast in the south-east, the Malabar Coast in the south west and the ports of Gujarat in western India had active trade connections expanding from south-east Asia to eastern Africa, the Persian Gulf and the Mediterranean. The Gujarati trading class, to which Gandhi belonged, had a long pre-colonial history of extensive contacts with the world:

> Classical sources suggest that Gujarati merchants may have been present in Eygpt in remote antiquity, and their presence in the ports of the Persian Gulf and the Red Sea, along the Arab littoral, and on the east coast of Africa, where there seems to be some evidence of Indian settlements from around the tenth century, is well documented. By the late Middle Ages, they appear to have gained dominance in the trade with East Africa, and obtained control over the ports ... along the Coromandel coast.[13]

Apart from trade, other world historical connections of pre-colonial India included those related to the spread of Buddhism in China, Sri Lanka and south-east Asia much before Christianity and Islam, and what the renowned Indologist Sheldon Pollock has called 'the Sanskrit Cosmopolis'. The millennium-long temporal stretch of this latter from AD 300 to 1300 had an awesome political and cultural reach from Afghanistan in the West to Vietnam and Central Java in the east. According to Pollock, the cosmopolis was a 'new kind of vast zone of cultural interaction, what some might name an ecumene'.[14] But since the dominance of empire-led world history, the Sanskrit cosmopolis has remained a little known world cultural formation. Further, India's pre-colonial links with vast swathes of Asia and Africa are now mediated through an epistemology that foregrounds the history of European colonialism and the rise of the West as normative. In short, the insertion of India into a world history dominated by the making of European empires has had the effect of shrinking the horizon of India's total historical contact with the world to the history of its relationship with the West.

Can then one effectively bypass this conundrum in reading two modern Indian figures against a world historical background? Not wholly perhaps, but the conundrum can be addressed if one argues for the world historical provenance of both Gandhi and Ambedkar not just in terms of British imperialism, but also in terms of traces of India's pre-colonial links to the world that their respective cosmopolitical projects carry. The rest of my essay will place Gandhi and Ambedkar in world history precisely in these terms. The argument here is that Gandhi's peripatetic life and work in the context of his genealogy in the old global Gujarati thalassocracy, and Ambedkar's attempts to revive Buddhism in India and reconnect with the rest of the Buddhist world, when inserted into a narrative of their interventions in global democracy in the age of Empire, unsettle assumptions of modern India being engulfed by an Euro-American dominated world history.

In the sections that follow, I trace the 'world' orientation of Gandhi and Ambedkar in two ways. First, I delineate their deep engagement with world events during the period of empire and focus on their commitment to global democracy. Second, I briefly trace the vernacular and cosmopolitan idioms of their respective political projects – *nonviolence* as a vernacular Hinduised life-practice in Gandhi and *democratic development* for Ambedkar as a non-hierarchical Buddhist orientation to life. I suggest that these can be read productively in complementary rather than in oppositional terms for both Gandhi and Ambedkar offered resistance to the oppositional way in which the discourse of 'normative modernity'[15] read the *vernacular* in relation to the *cosmopolitan*, with the later invariably valorized over the former. In doing so, I argue for the provenance of these two thought figures in the domain of a 'critical modernity' that bears witness to not just the achievements but the horrors of colonial modernity's civilizing mission, and that continues to carry traces of pre-colonial modes of connecting with the world. The reading is, in the final analysis, postcolonial in the complex historicist sense of the term, intertwining discrepant temporalities and articulating the pull of the vernacular and the push of the cosmopolitan in one single gesture.

Conversing democratically in the age of empire:

In an interview with the *New York Times* on 27 April 1940 Gandhi was asked to comment on the future of India in the context of the Allied struggle in World War Two. In a global democratic gesture linking nationalist struggles in the colonies with the western world's fight against European fascism, his response categorically connected the democratic future of India to a world free of both fascism and colonialism:

Of what value is freedom to India if Britain and France fail? If these powers fail, the history of Europe and the history of the world will be written in a manner no one can foresee. ... [At the same time] by doing justice to India, Britain might ensure victory of the Allies because their cause will then be acclaimed as righteous by the enlightened opinion of the world.[16]

Throughout his political career, Gandhi never thought of India's freedom from colonial rule in isolation from world events. Empire, he believed, needed to be challenged globally, not merely nationally or territorially. As so many Gandhi scholars have noted, his early experience of the colonial race divide in South Africa was the crucible that honed his cosmopolitical vision of a world free of all forms of inequities and bondage. Sifting through his voluminous corpus of books, letters and essays, one finds evidence of a mind constantly at pains to address colonial, communist and fascist excesses in all corners of the globe – Turkey, South Africa, Palestine, Israel, Germany and Russia.

One of the earliest manifestations of Gandhi's commitment to take the fight against imperialism onto the world stage can be seen in his mobilization of Indian masses on behalf of the Caliphate of the defeated Ottoman Empire in World War One. According to the Treaty of Versailles, the British as victors of the war had promised not to abolish the Caliphate claimed at the time by the Ottoman Emperor in Turkey. The Caliphate symbolized for the Muslim world, even if in a tokenistic way, a spiritual and temporal authority uniting the Muslim *ummah*. So as to ensure that the British kept their promise, an already besieged global Muslim leadership appealed to Indian Muslim leaders to join forces with them and keep up the pressure on colonial authorities. Hence was launched the Khilafat Movement in India to which Gandhi mobilized the masses and provided his wholehearted support, convinced as he was of the necessity to resist the juggernaut of British colonial authority decimating all non-Western political and socio-cultural formations. The Khilafat Movement's three primary objectives were: to preserve the Turkish Caliphate, to maintain the unity of the Ottoman Empire within its 1914 frontiers and to maintain Islamic protection over the Holy Places of Islam including Palestine.[17] The movement, which did not gain the desired momentum from the very beginning, suffered its fatal blow when, in 1924, Turkey's new secular republican leader, Kemal Ataturk, overthrew the Ottoman Sultan himself and relinquished the Turkish state's claim to a universal caliphate. In most accounts of this movement Gandhi's role is seen in strategic terms as a bargain with the Indian Muslims, pledging his support for this pan-Islamic movement in return for their support towards Hindu–Muslim unity in his call for *swaraj* or total freedom on home ground. This is broadly the thrust of Gail Minault's argument in her fine and detailed account of the movement, *The Khilafat Movement: Religious Symbolism and Political Mobilization in India* (1982).

However, if one turns from this nationalist focus and places Gandhi's articulations on Khilafat within the wider ambit of an imperial globalism taking shape in the early years of the twentieth century, one begins to trace a dialogue between Gandhi and the world that has hitherto not been too audible in this specific context.[18] Why does Gandhi, for instance, say in his *Young India* essay of 10 March 1920 that 'the Khilafat Question has now become a question of questions? and 'an imperial question of the first magnitude'?[19] Why does he refuse to equate the Jallianwallah Bagh massacre in 1919 with the international importance of the Khilafat Movement, as when he says, 'However grievous the wrong done in the Punjab, it is after all a domestic affair ... the Punjab grievance does not arise out of the peace [the Versailles Treaty] terms as does the Khilafat question. We must isolate the Khilafat question if we wish to give it its proper value'?[20] Surely statements such as these cannot be read purely in instrumentalist terms as trying to 'win over' Indian Muslims to his nationalist cause. In fact, his relegation of the Amritsar massacre to a 'domestic' concern could hardly have endeared him to the masses, either Hindu or Muslim. A clue to Gandhi's global orientation in the matter of the Caliphate lies in his invocation of a rich Islamic pre-Europe-dominated geopolitical and geocultural space and time that was now under threat of extinction from the modernizing machinations of a colonialist-capitalist enterprise: 'The Great Prelates of England and Mahomedan leaders combined have brought the question to the fore. The Prelates threw down the challenge. The Muslim leaders have taken it up.'[21]

In a fascinating recent reading of Gandhi in the context of the Khilafat Movement, Faisal Fatehali Devji[22] notes Gandhi's resistance to the rhetoric of liberal interest and state arbitration in arguing the case of the Ottoman Empire. He cites these words of Gandhi to make his case:

> Oppose Turkish misrule by all means, but it is wicked to seek to efface the Turk and with him Islam from Europe under the false plea of Turkish misrule. ... Was the late war a crusade against Islam, in which the Mussalmans of India were invited to join?[23]

Devji offers a reading of the Gandhian stance in terms of 'prejudice' and a 'politics of friendship' towards Islam and Muslims that are not reducible to either the rhetoric of nationalist brotherhood or the rational rhetoric of liberal interest. To that extent he upholds Gandhi as an exemplary articulator of the limits of liberalism in the context of empire, a relationship brilliantly explored by Uday Mehta a few years ago in his book *Liberalism and Empire.*[24] While such a reading provides another fillip to my attempt to situate Gandhi in a dialogic relationship with the imperial world, it is another comment that Devji makes merely as an aside to his main argument that has a more significant bearing on the way I wish to place Gandhi in a world historical context. It also relates to a point made in an early part of this essay about pre-colonial world historical formations that a Eurocentric world history has all but erased from collective global memory.

Devji refers to Gandhi's 'antiquated geographical imaginary', derived from pre-colonial Indian Ocean trade routes dominated by Arabs and Gujaratis, that ever so often impinged on his readings of British imperial territoriality.[25] So much so that Gandhi's rhetoric in his early writing subconsciously linked his passages to London and subsequently South Africa in a continuum with journeys of the old Gujarati thalassocracy rather than in terms of the routes of colonial capital. These old Islamic routes were part of his collective history that he could not orient himself out of simply because the European imperial order charted and controlled them in different ways. It is not an exercise in anachronism or even nostalgia, I submit, to read Gandhi's conception of his and India's involvement in the Khilafat movement in terms of his vision of a clash between old Islamic world formations and a new imperial globalism dominated by Europe. The clash may have been decisively settled in favour of the latter, but no historicist account of Europe's triumph over pre-modern life worlds, can take away from the reality of their survival in collective imaginaries across vast swathes of the non-European world.

The complexity in worlding Gandhi, however, is not so easily resolved by marking his orientation towards Islamic world formations at a time of their imminent ruin. For Gandhi was as eloquent and forceful in identifying himself as a serious player in the British Empire and in world events as a whole. As he put it famously in 1920, 'I serve the Empire by refusing to partake in its wrong'.[26] His critiques of communism with its highhanded statism, of Zionism with its dispossession of Palestinians or of anti-colonial nationalism with its elitist stance towards the masses can certainly be read in this light.

The carnage of World War Two evoked in turn exasperation and anguish from him. 'Europe seems to be heading for another war. It's not sufficiently exhausted', he told Louis Fischer after the atomic Holocaust in Hiroshima and Nagasaki.[27] In his personal correspondence with Mira Behn he expressed sorrow at the bombing of London. On 22 May 1941 he wrote to her: 'War news continues to be sensational. The news about the destruction in England is heart-rending. The Houses of Parliament, the Abbey, the Cathedral seemed to be immortal. And yet there is no end. ...'[28] He coped with his anguish by occasionally comparing the war with the epic battle in the *Mahabharata* and drawing on the message of the *Bhagvad Gita* to be philosophical about victory and defeat. His letter to Rajkumari Amrit Kaur on 25 May 1940 is reminiscent of Krishna's exhortation to Arjuna not to grieve over the death of his loved ones in the war:

> Why should you feel depressed? The Allies seem to be losing everywhere. These are the fortunes of war. You must not grieve over these things. The slaughter is awful but it is part of the game. All parties know what is what.[29]

The war was a prime test of his ethical stance on the non-negotiable nature of nonviolence. The atrocities of Nazi Germany on the one hand and the threat to India's borders through Japanese invasion on the other demanded more than just a pacifist response. His writings are scattered with his thoughts on the Nazi persecution of Jews. Obviously not able to imagine that the sheer monstrosity of anti-Semitism and the venality of the Nazi bureaucratic machine far exceeded the excesses of British rule in India, Gandhi urged the Jews to resist Nazis nonviolently, through *Satyagraha*, just as the Indians did in South Africa. In 1938 he wrote in the *Harijan*:

> If there ever could be a justifiable war in the name of and for humanity, war against Germany to prevent the wanton persecution of a whole race would be completely justified. But I do not believe in any war. ... If I were a Jew and were born in Germany and earned my livelihood there, I would claim Germany as my home even as the tallest gentile German might. ... The Jews of Germany can offer *satyagraha* under infinitely better auspices than the Indians of South Africa. The Jews are a compact homogeneous community in Germany. They are far more gifted than the Indians of South Africa. And they have organized world opinion behind them. I am convinced that if someone with courage and vision can rise among them to lead them to nonviolent action ... what has today become a degrading manhunt can be turned into a calm and determined stand offered by unarmed men and women possessing the strength of suffering given to them by Jehovah.[30]

In response to the panic among members of the Indian National Congress about an imminent Japanese invasion of the east coast of India, Gandhi pleaded with the INC to exercise restraint and not think in terms of an armed conflict. A troubled Nehru wrote:

> The approach of the war to India disturbed Gandhi greatly. It was not easy to fit in his policy and program of nonviolence with this new development. Obviously civil disobedience was out of the question in the face of an invading army or between two opposing armies. Passivity or acceptance of invasion was equally out of the question. What then?[31]

In 1942, Gandhi had already dispatched his trusted lieutenant Mira Behn to Orissa to 'prepare' as Mira Behn put it, 'the masses for nonviolent, non-cooperative resistance to the probable Japanese invasion of the east coast'.[32] From Orissa Mira Behn sent a detailed report to Gandhi on *The Question of Invasion and Occupation by the Japanese.*[33] The report outlined nonviolent strategies that the people of Orissa would be persuaded to adopt in the event of an invasion. The course of history did not allow Gandhi to have his way, not only because the Japanese did not get beyond India's North East, but also because negotiations with Nehru and Congress compelled

Gandhi to 'swallow the bitter pill' and accept that the 'primary function of the provisional government of free India would be to throw all her great resources in the struggle for freedom against aggression and to cooperate fully with the United Nations in the defence of India with all the armed and other forces at her command'.[34]

While Gandhi went along temporarily with Nehru's pragmatic position that India's cooperation in regard to the Japanese invasion would expedite her freedom from British rule, he remained convinced of the long-term efficacy of his nonviolent stance in resisting world-wide colonialism and bondage. Tied to this commitment was his very radical vision of democracy that plumbed the very depths of what it was to be human in those fraught times. Calling himself a 'born democrat', he added, 'I make that claim, if complete identification with the poorest of mankind, longing to live no better than they, and a corresponding conscious effort to approach that level to the best of one's ability can entitle one to make it'.[35] It is worth reading this radical Gandhian democratic gloss on the ethicality of being poor retroactively into a recent exposition of the 'poor' as 'the common denominator of life, the foundation of the multitude' found in Michael Hardt and Antonio Negri's *Empire*.[36] What kind of democracy was Gandhi espousing and why was identifying with the poorest of mankind such a radical gesture that unsettled discourses of liberal democracy then circulating in the colonies? Hardt and Negri's exposition on the poor helps us answer these to some extent:

> In each and every historical period a social subject that is ever-present and everywhere the same is identified, often negatively but nonetheless urgently, around a common living form. ... The only non-localizable 'common name' of pure difference in all eras is that of the poor. The poor is destitute, excluded, repressed, exploited – and yet living!. ... This common name, the poor, is also the foundation of every possibility of humanity.[37]

For Gandhi, to live democratically was not merely a matter of reaping the benefits of electoral politics and representative government. It meant putting oneself in touch with the very root or foundation of what made humanity possible – the condition of being poor, bereft, destitute, a condition of pure difference in all eras and yet a common living form.

To turn now to Ambedkar's links with the world in the age of empire, by even the most sympathetic of accounts he did not command the presence that Gandhi did in the global order of things. Nevertheless, over his lifetime he displayed a unique cosmopolitical sensibility, one forged during his graduate study days in New York and London during World War One when he began to imagine perhaps for the first time in the history of India's untouchable castes, the dalits, the possibility of a genuine global democratic revolution that would link dalit freedom from the shackles of untouchability to the overthrow of racism against coloured and black people across the world. Ambedkar's intervention on behalf of Indian dalits, in fact, can be inserted in any twentieth-century political and legal narrative of the global passage of the notion of rights from 'civil rights' to 'human rights'. Even though he would later make fine distinctions between caste and race, this aspect of his legacy has remained with the dalit movement and was given global articulation at the UN Conference on Racism in Durban in 2001. Ambedkar's biographer, Dhananjay Keer, notes the impact on him of the Fourteenth Amendment declaring freedom of African Americans when he was a student of John Dewey and Edwin Seligman from 1913–16. Keer also notes how affected Ambedkar was by the death in 1915 of the African-American reformer and educator Booker T. Washington. What did not happen, however, was the quick transformation of the student into a revolutionary, and this in spite of the presence of the Indian Gadar Party revolutionary leaders such as Lala Har Dayal and Lala Lajpat Rai in New York at the time. Ambedkar preferred to concentrate on his studies at the time. After three years at Columbia University, he proceeded to the University of London to do his doctorate.

But he could not maintain his detachment from colonial politics for long. His doctoral thesis called *The Problem of the Rupee*, which he submitted to the University of London in 1922, caused a furore for it offended his imperial examiners and they demanded that he rewrite it. In the thesis Ambedkar argued that in the final settlement of the currency problem the exchange rate between the rupee and the pound was manipulated to the greater advantage of the pound and that this would lead to further impoverishment of Indians. While his pragmatism made him revise the thesis to some extent, he refused to modify his conclusions and stood his ground. A few weeks earlier he had spoken passionately to the students' union at his University about the responsibilities of the colonial government in India. His paper was later circulated among University staff and students and it evoked an alarmed response from Professor Harold Laski who commented on the "revolutionary nature" of Ambedkar's exposition.[38]

Unlike anarchist tendencies in Gandhi's response to nation-making, Ambedkar's academic training in law, economics and political science oriented him towards arguing for the importance of the constructionist role of the state. He researched liberal-democratic frameworks and aspired to a form of representational governance that spoke the language of identity-based politics. This implied, for him, not just recognition of minoritarianism on the basis of religion, but also of caste. The untouchables, he argued, could never hope to participate in nation-making unless they had special political representation. This was the basis of his disagreement with Gandhi who aspired to a non-fragmented Hindu constituency and who believed that the untouchable cause could be redressed through revolutionary transformations in the domain of civil society. Gandhi could not conceive of a political scenario where the untouchables stood *outside* Hindu representation, even though the social reality through millennia was precisely that the untouchables were located *outside* the bounds of Hindi sociality. Gandhi was steadfast in his conviction that his commitment to and identification with the destitute, which constituted the cornerstone of his democratic vision, would be sufficient to transform Hindu society and eradicate untouchability. Ambedkar's social-scientific and legally trained mind was deeply suspicious of Gandhi's emotive and sentimental take on the problem of untouchability, especially when Gandhi announced in the same breath that he was and would always remain a *Sanatani Hindu*. Theirs was a critical dialogue on competing visions of representational democracy and resolution of minoritarian questions – liberalism, socialism Marxism, anarchism – in the era of fledging nation-building in the colonized world. The rest of twentieth-century politics would continue to resonate with these meta-themes and agonistically witness radical manifestations of democratic life forms across the postcolonial world.

For more than half his life, Ambedkar negotiated the dialectic between nation and the world through conversations on democracy with Indian nationalist leaders, with the colonial government and with the vast tomes of political, social and legal philosophy in which he immersed himself from his early youth. But he eventually found his home in the world by recuperating for India a link with a pre-colonial world historical formation in the form of Buddhism. In the concluding section of this chapter, I propose to read his conversion to Buddhism in terms of a vernacular cosmopolitical act that drew on the cosmopolitical genealogies of the non-Christian world[39] while at the same time resisting both antiquarianism and indigenism. Here I very briefly want to foreground Ambedkar's renewal of India's connections with the world through Asia, which, as we saw in early parts of this chapter, were severed with the advent of colonial rule. Ambedkar's determination to lead untouchables out of the Hindu fold and into a more egalitarian religion, Buddhism, was tied to a desire to bring Buddhism back to the land of its birth and make India once again an important node, if not the central one, in Asian Buddhist transnationalism. For this purpose, all through the late 1940s right up to his death in 1956, he travelled to many parts of Buddhist Asia – Sri Lanka, Burma, Tibet and Japan – in order to forge spiritual alliances and bring to life once again an Asian world formation that could converse with modernity in tongues both sacred and secular. His dialogic uptake on Marxism through the teachings of the Buddha was the substance of his intervention at the World Buddhist Conference in Kathmandu in 1949 and again in 1956. He spent many days in Sri Lanka in 1954 to specifically study Sinhalese Buddhist practices. He subsequently attended the Rangoon World Buddhist Conference. In these years, he also frequently conversed with an English monk, Denis Lingwood (Sangharakshita), who was then based in a monastery in north-eastern India. His letters to Sangharakshita exhorted the young English monk to take the message of Buddha to the western world. Sangharakshita subsequently founded the

Friends of the Western Buddhist Order (FWBO) in the UK in 1969 which now has branches all over the world. In one of those recursive ironies that so characterize world history, after Ambedkar's death in 1956, the role of FWBO has been critical in keeping Buddhist religious practices alive among neo-Buddhist dalits in India, especially in Maharashtra, Ambedkar's home state.[40]

The precariousness of vernacular cosmopolitics

In the concluding section of this chapter I wish to bring together the various lines that have so far traced the world historical roles of Gandhi and Ambedkar on to a conceptual matrix that I call, after Bhabha, 'vernacular cosmopolitanism'.[41] While I do draw on Bhabha's assertion that the phrase best applies to the orientation of embattled leaders and thought figures of the non-White, non-Western world – Du Bois, Gandhi, Ambedkar, Fanon, Morrison – who attempt to 'translate between cultures and across them in order to survive, not in order to assert the sovereignty of a civilized class or the spiritual autonomy of a revered ideal',[42] in my reading of Gandhi and Ambedkar, I wish to explore the phrase a little further both conceptually and historically. The term at first glance is an oxymoron. For 'vernacular' connotes an affiliation to a domain that is local, finite, while 'cosmopolitan' invokes an orientation to a world larger than one's own immediate *habitus*. How then does one yoke them together? What does this oxymoronic adjacency generate? Before I attempt to answer these questions, I would also like to note that the origins of the word 'vernacular' lie in the term 'verna' which etymologically denotes the language of slaves in Roman Republics. The circulation of the term 'varna' in the Indian context further complicates its meaning, for in Sanskrit *varna* literally means 'colour'. A philological reading of 'vernacular', one that traces its embeddedness in historical practice, cannot help carrying signs of subjugation – slavery of course, but also racial subjugation if *colour* is refracted on to *race* in the age of Empire. The passage of meaning from subjugation to a finite, local boundedness is not hard to imagine. So, I ask again, what does its yoking together with 'cosmopolitanism' – a term that connotes a 'world' orientation facilitating a free crossing of boundaries – achieve in the context under discussion?

One yokes them together, I submit, in order to mark critical moments of historical conjunction when historically disenfranchised 'small' narratives engage in dialogue with firmly entrenched 'world-enveloping' ones to generate radical transformations in both. So that, for instance, liberalism when translated or carried over to the domain of the colonized through the lexicon of Gandhian *ahimsa* or Ambedkarite-Buddhist *dhamma*, becomes a term loaded with plural histories of the individuating self and its relationship with community and the State. In the domain of Empire, liberalism, as Uday Mehta has shown, repeatedly confronts its limits in other non-European political narratives and is willy-nilly forced to hybridize itself. Again, notwithstanding the 'ancient' cultural repertoire from which Gandhi and Ambedkar draw their political lexicon, their own deployment of predominantly 'vernacular' Hindu and Buddhist terms is shot through with modern hybrid genealogies that bespeak the historical and cultural permeability of modernity's multiple practices. Such a reading breaks through the dichotomy of a modernizing cosmopolitanism and a vernacular traditionalism. Let me briefly illustrate this argument with examples from the writings of Gandhi and Ambedkar.

In enunciating his principle of nonviolence through terms such as *ahimsa, satyagraha and sarvodaya*[43] Gandhi is constantly at pains to foreground the 'vernacular' connotative force of these concepts, to highlight that they are not exactly recuperable in English through terms such as 'passive resistance'. On 11 June 1917, he writes to an English friend, Esther: 'You may not know that the *Gujarati* for passive resistance is truth-force. I have variously defined it as truth-force, love-force or soul-force.'[44] In 1914, he writes about truth-force and soul-force in the *Indian Opinion*:

> It is totally untrue to say that it is a force to be used only by the weak so long as they are not capable of meeting violence by violence. This superstition arises from the incompleteness of the *English* expression. It is impossible for those who consider themselves weak to apply this force. Only those who realize that there is something in man which is superior to the brute nature in him, and that the latter always yields to it, can effectively be Passive Resisters. This force is to violence and, therefore, to all tyranny, all injustice, what light is to darkness.[45]

Gandhi's emphasis on the power of the *Gujarati* term *satyagraha* which the English translation cannot convey, however, does not prevent him for invoking Socrates, Christ, Tolstoy, Thoreau, Ruskin, Emerson, and many ancient Indian philosophers, to account for its complex etymology. In doing so, I argue, he seeks to distil into his Gujarati use of the term the combined connotative force of global registers of nonviolence available to him as his peripatetic inheritance and training. In another essay in this volume, Leela Gandhi's chapter discusses yet another aspect of the complex etymology of Gandhian nonviolence and locates some early influences on Gandhi in a radical fringe late Victorian animal-welfare and vegetarian movement. During his student days, Gandhi imbibed from this movement a critique of imperial masculinity, a resistance to modern forms of governmentality and a regard for multiple forms of relationality that included strangers in radical ways. Leela's argument is not only that these can be read as constituting part of the vocabulary of Gandhian nonviolence, but that their very 'integrity' and 'organicity' can themselves be read under the comprehensive sign of *ahimsa*. Each gets translated into the other. This resonates strongly with the line of argument I have pursued, that the vernacular cosmopolitics of a Gandhi or an Ambedkar is about generating transformation in the assured global registers of the political through their translations into and from myriad *petit* registers.

Ambedkar's mining of Buddhist discourse to seek in it points of convergence and dialogue with modern political philosophy, especially Marxism, socialism and liberalism, can be seen precisely in terms of such a vernacular cosmopolitical practice. As an aside I also wish to note that, like Gandhi, he wrote in a register that was truly vernacular, truly accessible to ordinary men and women who invested so much faith in him. He did not allow his specialist training in legal and political philosophy and his vast erudition to come in the way of writing in an accessible manner. One very good example is his attempt to read the principles of the French Revolution into Buddha's social message in terms of four rhetorical questions:

> Did the Buddha teach justice?
> Did the Buddha teach liberty?
> Did the Buddha teach equality?
> Did the Buddha teach fraternity?[46]

He then goes on to impatiently mark a lacuna in esoteric traditionalist interpretations of Buddha's message by adding, 'These questions are hardly ever raised in discussing the Buddha's Dhamma'.[47] His famous ahistoricist comparison of Marx and Buddha, written in a register suspect to academic specialists, was actually delivered at a World Buddhist Conference in 1956 with the express intention of translating a possible dialogue between the two thought figures to the world at large in terms of a truly inclusive ethics of universal humanity. What is significant about this piece of writing is not so much Ambedkar's successful demonstration through a series of syllogisms that Buddhism has ethically more to offer than Marxism in terms of a democratic world order, but its subtext that the world is that much poorer for not taking into account (or merely dismissing as traditional) other legitimate and ethical ways of dwelling democratically on earth in the present.

In an earlier part of this chapter, we read Ambedkar's place in world history not only in terms of his attempt to forge along with Gandhi a democratic vision for India and the world in the age of Empire, but also in terms of his efforts to re-establish India's links with the Asian world through Buddhism. His translational cosmopolitical efforts were thus, directed, not just westwards towards Euro-American life-worlds, but also towards an aspired Buddhist cosmopolis that would be truly global in its reach and vision. Likewise, Gandhi's nonviolent resistance to the imperial regime was an effort to globalize the forces of soul, truth and love through acts of active translation in disparate tongues and registers, especially those disenfranchised by the British imperial machine. In spite of drawing deeply from the wellsprings of India's spiritual heritage, neither was antiquarian, nor indigenist in his response to the horrors of colonialism. In treading the faultlines of seismic political and cultural upheavals in the twentieth century, especially from the side of the vanquished, both were acutely aware of the precariousness of their cosmopolitical vision. But they were equally convinced of the sheer urgency of their moral and political enterprise in an age that stood at the threshold of a global democratic revolution of the kind never witnessed before.

Notes

1 Judith Brown, *Gandhi's Rise to Power: Indian Politics 1915–1922*, Cambridge University Press, 1972, p. 345.
2 D.C. Ahir, *Gandhi and Ambedkar: A Comparative Study*, New Delhi: Blumoon Books, 1995, p. 96.
3 Brown, *Gandhi's Rise to Power*, p. 182.
4 Dhananjay Keer, 'War with Gandhi' in *Dr Ambedkar: Life and Mission*, Bombay: Popular Prakashan, 1962, p. 182.
5 Cited in Horace Alexander's *Gandhi Through Western Eyes*, New Delhi: Asia Publishing House, 1969.
6 Ibid., p. 82
7 Cited in Benedikt Stuchtey and Eckhardt Fuchs (eds), *Writing World History 1800–2000*, Oxford University Press, 2003, p. 44.
8 Eric Hobsbawn, *Age of Extremes: The Short Twentieth Century 1914–91*, London: Abacus Books, 1995, pp. 212–14.
9 David Thompson, *World History from 1914 to 1961*, London: Oxford University Press, 1963, p. 2.
10 Books such as Stuchtey and Fuchs (eds), *Writing World History 1800–2000* and Philip Pomper et al.(eds), *World History: Ideologies, Structures, Identities*, Blackwell, 1998 contain details of this shift.
11 Vinay Lal, 'Provincialising the West: World History from the Perspective of Indian History', in Stuchtey and Fuchs (eds), *Writing World History 1800–2000*, p. 287.
12 Tony Ballantyne and Antoinette Burton, 'Bodies, Empires and World Histories', in Ballantyne and Burton (eds), *Bodies in Contact: Rethinking Colonial Encounters in World History*, Durham: Duke University Press, 2005, p. 3.
13 Lal, 'Provincialising the West: World History from the Perspective of Indian History', p. 277.
14 Sheldon Pollock, 'The Sanskrit Cosmopolis, 300–1300: Transculturation, Vernacularisation, and the Question of Ideology', in Jan E.M. Houben (ed.), *Ideology and Status of Sanskrit: Contributions to the History of the Sanskrit Language*, Leiden, 1996, p. 199.
15 See my deployment of the term in my book *Caste, Colonialism and Countermodernity*, London and New York: Routledge, 2005.
16 *The Moral and Political Writings of Mahatma Gandhi*, Volume III, ed. Raghavan Iyer, Oxford: Clarendon Press, 1987, p. 309.
17 See Gail Minault's *The Khilafat Movement: Religious Symbolism and Political Mobilization in India*, New York: Columbia University Press, 1982 for details of the movement in the Indian nationalist context. See also reference to the three objectives in Eric Hobsbawm's *Age of Extremes*, p. 201.
18 One exception is Faisal Fatehali Devji's brilliant reading of Gandhi's role in the Khilafat Movement. See his 'A Practice of Prejudice: Gandhi's Politics of Friendship', *Subaltern Studies XII*, ed. Shail Mayaram, MSS Pandian and Ajay Skaria, New Delhi: Permanent Black and Ravi Dayal, 2005, pp. 78–98.
19 Gandhi, 'The Question of Questions', *Young India*, 10 March 1920, p. 145.

20 Gandhi, 'All-India Khilafat Conference', *Young India*, 13 December 1919, pp. 140–41.
21 Gandhi, 'The Question of Questions', p 145.
22 See Devji, 'A Practice of Prejudice: Gandhi's Politics of Friendship', pp. 86–87.
23 Gandhi, 'The Meaning of the Khilafat', *Young India*, 8 September 1921, p. 190.
24 Uday Mehta, *Liberalism and Empire*, Chicago: University of Chicago Press, 1999.
25 Devji, 'A Practice of Prejudice: Gandhi's Politics of Friendship', p. 86.
26 Gandhi, "How to Work Non-Co-operation", *Young India*, 5 May 1920, p 192
27 Ibid., p. 581.
28 *Bapu's Letters to Mira [1924–1948]*, Ahmedabad: Navajivan Publishing House, 1949, p. 329.
29 *Letters to Rajkumari Amrit Kaur*, Ahmedabad: Navajivan Publishing House, 1961, p. 181.
30 Cited in Ved Mehta's *Mahatma Gandhi and His Apostles*, Harmondsworth: Penguin, 1976, p.166.
31 Jawaharlal Nehru, *Nehru on Gandhi: A Selection, Arranged in the Order of Events, from the Writings and Speeches of Jawaharlal Nehru*, New York: John Day, 1948, p. 127.
32 See Gandhi, *Bapu's Letters to Mira*, p. 335.
33 Ibid., pp. 336–40
34 Nehru, *Nehru on Gandhi*, pp. 115.
35 Cited in ibid., p. 189.
36 Michael Hardt and Antonio Negri, *Empire*, Cambridge, Mass.: Harvard University Press, 2000, p. 156.
37 Ibid.
38 Cited in Keer, 'War with Gandhi', p. 49.
39 See Sheldon Pollock, Homi Bhabha et al., 'Cosmopolitanisms', *Public Culture*, 12(3), 2000, p. 582.
40 See my paper, 'Yet Another English Gift: The Role of English Bhikkhus in Indian Dalit Buddhist Conversions (1970–90)', *JNU Journal of the School of Language, Literature and Culture Studies*, No. 4, Autumn, 2005, pp. 97–110.
41 See his conversation with John Comaroff, 'Speaking of Postcoloniality in the Continuous Present', in David Theo Goldberg and Ato Quayson (eds) *Relocating Postcolonialism*, Oxford: Blackwell, 2002, pp. 23–24.
42 Ibid., p. 24.
43 Rough translations of which are, 'non-violence', 'truth-force' and 'welfare of all' respectively
44 *The Moral and Political Writings of Mahatma Gandhi*, Vol. 3, pp. 23–24, emphasis added.
45 Ibid., p. 21, emphasis added
46 See Ambedkar's 'Does Buddha have a Social Message?', in *The Essential Writings of Ambedkar*, ed. Valerian Rodrigues, New Delhi: Oxford University Press, 2002.
47 Ibid.

Bibliography

Ahir, D.C, *Gandhi and Ambedkar: A Comparative Study*, New Delhi: Blumoon Books, 1995.
Alexander, Horace *Gandhi Through Western Eyes*, New Delhi: Asia Publishing House, 1969.

Ambedkar, B.R, 'Does Buddha have a Social Message?', in *The Essential Writings of Ambedkar*, ed. Valerian Rodrigues, New Delhi: Oxford University Press, 2002.
Ballantyne, Tony and Antoinette Burton, 'Bodies, Empires and World Histories', in Ballantyne and Burton (eds), *Bodies in Contact: Rethinking Colonial Encounters in World History*, Durham: Duke University Press, 2005.
Bhabha, Homi and John Comaroff, 'Speaking of Postcoloniality in the Continuous Present', in David Theo Goldberg and Ato Quayson (eds), *Relocating Postcolonialism*, Oxford: Blackwell, 2002.
Brown, Judith, *Gandhi's Rise to Power: Indian Politics 1915–1922*, Cambridge University Press, 1972.
Devji, Faisal Fatehali, 'A Practice of Prejudice: Gandhi's Politics of Friendship', *Subaltern Studies XII*, ed. Shail Mayaram, MSS Pandian and Ajay Skaria, New Delhi: Permanent Black and Ravi Dayal, 2005.
Gandhi, M.K, *Letters to Rajkumari Amrit Kaur*, Ahmedabad: Navajivan Publishing House, 1961.
—— 'All-India Khilafat Conference', *Young India*, 13 December 1919.
—— 'The Question of Questions', *Young India*, 10 March 1920.
—— 'How to Work Non-Co-operation', *Young India*, 5 May 1920, p. 192.
—— 'The Meaning of the Khilafat', *Young India*, 8 September 1921, p. 190.
—— *Bapu's Letters to Mira [1924–1948]*, Ahmedabad: Navajivan Publishing House, 1949.
—— *The Moral and Political Writings of Mahatma Gandhi*, Volume III, ed. Raghavan Iyer, Oxford: Clarendon Press, 1987.
Ganguly, Debjani, 'Yet Another English Gift: The Role of English Bhikkhus in Indian Dalit Buddhist Conversions (1970–90)', *JNU Journal of the School of Language, Literature and Culture Studies*, No. 4, Autumn, 2005.
—— *Caste, Colonialism and Countermodernity: Notes on a Postcolonial Hermeneutics of Caste*, London and New York: Routledge, 2005.
Hardt, Michael and Antonio Negri, *Empire*, Massachussetts: Harvard University Press, 2000.
Hobsbawn, Eric, *Age of Extremes: The Short Twentieth Century 1914–91*, London: Abacus Books, 1995.
Keer, Dhananjay, 'War with Gandhi' in *Dr Ambedkar: Life and Mission*, Bombay: Popular Prakashan, 1962.
Lal, Vinay, 'Provincialising the West: World History from the Perspective of Indian History', *Writing World History 1800–2000*, in Benedikt Stuchtey and Eckhardt Fuchs (eds), *Writing World History 1800–2000*, Oxford University Press, 2003.
Mehta, Uday, *Liberalism and Empire*, Chicago: University of Chicago Press, 1999.
Mehta, Ved, *Mahatma Gandhi and His Apostles*, Harmondsworth: Penguin, 1976.
Minault, Gail *The Khilafat Movement: Religious Symbolism and Political Mobilization in India*, New York: Columbia University Press, 1982.
Nehru, Jawaharlal, *Nehru on Gandhi: A Selection, Arranged in the Order of Events, from the Writings and Speeches of Jawaharlal Nehru*, New York: John Day, 1948.
Pollock, Sheldon, 'The Sanskrit Cosmopolis, 300–1300: Transculturation, Vernacularisation, and the Question of Ideology', in Jan E.M. Houben (ed.), *Ideology and Status of Sanskrit: Contributions to the History of the Sanskrit Language*, Leiden, 1996.
Pollock, Sheldon, Homi Bhabha, Carol Breckenridge and Dipesh Chakrabarty, 'Cosmopolitanisms', *Public Culture*, Vol. 12, No. 3, 2000.

Pomper, Philip, Richard Elphick and Richard Vann (eds) *World History: Ideologies, Structures, Identities*, Oxford: Blackwell, 1998.
Stuchtey, Benedikt, and Eckhardt Fuchs (eds), *Writing World History 1800–2000*, Oxford University Press, 2003.
Thompson, David, *World History from 1914 to 1961*, London: Oxford University Press, 1963.

Index

aadhunik sudhaara 166
Abdulla, Dada 101
abjection 54
abstinence 6, 46
Abu-Lughod, Janet 249
Adajania, Sorabji 166
Adam, Moosa Hajee 104
Adas, Michael 166, 172
affective affiliation 26
affective anti-colonialism 18
affective consubstantiality 27
affinity 26–27, 52, 59
afflicted *strangers* 42, 55
African Americans 144, 185, 189, 217, 256
African-American resistance 189
ahimsa 1, 165, 178; meaning of 19–20, 24, 33; and Gandhi 10, 32, 85, 170, 172, 259; and practice of caregiving 48, 52; rejection of 170, 173–74; Gandhian ahimsa 4–5, 18, 175, 179, 186, 258
Ahir, D.C. 245
Ahmedabad 91, 94, 96; Ahmedabad textile mills 6, 66, 68, 71, 73–74, 76
Akubue, A. 237
Aldermaston march 141, 149–50, 152
Alexander, Horace 245
alimentary 40, 44–45 47; see anti-alimentary
All India Village Industries Association (AIVIA) 95
allopathic 49
Alter, Joseph 42, 51, 53, 57
amateur curing 38, 61
Ambedkar, Bhimrao Ramji 6, 12–13, 245–50, 255–60
Ambedkarism 12
American democracy 191

anarchy 20, 26
Anderson, Gwyneth 144, 147
animal rights 20, 22, 26
anthropocentric dominion 21
anti-alimentary 43–44, 52
anti-colonialism 4, 18–20, 24, 27, 29, 33
anti-fascist 247
anti-imperial 4, 18, 247
anti-Indian legislation 8, 101–2, 104
anti-medical 38–39, 45–46
anti-medical economy 38
anti-oral 40
anti-pharmacological 40, 52
anti-Semitism 207–8, 254
apad-dharma 40, 47, 49
aparigraha 43
appropriate technologies 13, 223, 232–33, 235–38
Aristotle 208
ascesis 6, 38, 57, 61
ashrams 7, 52, 84, 86, 91–93, 96
Asian Buddhist transnationalism 257
Ataturk, Kemal 251
Attenborough, Richard 83
ayurveda 5, 40
ayush 47

Bajaj, Jamnalal 8, 85–86, 94–97
Baker, Ella 190
Baker, Goldie 188, 192
Ballantyne, Tony 249
Baltimore 11, 183, 185–88, 190, 192–93
Banker, Shankarlal 66, 68, 70
Baragu 173–74
Bardoli 95
Barr, Mary 144
Barraclough, Geoffrey 246
Basu, Anupam 236
Beagle 29–30

266 *Index*

Besant, Annie 19, 115
Behn, Mira 253–54
Benjamin, Walter 206
Bentham, Jeremy 5, 21–22, 25–26, 28, 32
Bevan, Aneurin 145
Bhagavad Gita 175
Bhave, Vinoba 85, 94
Bhikku, Dhammananda Kosambi 171
the Bible 207
bioethical 38, 51, 56, 61
bioethics 5, 42, 52, 60
bioethics of proximity 42, 52
biography 84, 87, 186
biomoral politics 61
biotherapies 48
Bissicks, Ada 87
black civil disobedience 184, 186, 194
The Black Panther Party 190, 192
black women's activism: see Black Women's movement
Black Women's movement 11–12, 184–85, 188, 192, 195
Blanc, G. 235
Boer War 41, 56
Bose, Subhash Chandra 173, 175
Boyarin, Daniel 206, 212–15, 217
brahmacharya 56, 123
Briggs, Asa 23
British 29, 207; Government 145–46, 152, 163, 168, 176–77, 251; un-British 108, 172
British colonialism 3, 100, 115–16, 169, 185; *see* British occupation and rule
British Constitution 41, 108, 217
British Empire 29, 41, 164, 166, 215–17, 253
British Gandhism 9–10, 142–44, 146, 148, 150–52
British imperialism 173, 179, 191, 248–50, 253, 260
British occupation and rule 11, 32, 128–33, 164–66, 254–55
British pacifists 9–10, 141–43, 145, 152
British Weekly 150
British-Mandated Palestine 207
Brittain, Vera 144
Brock, Hugh 146–47
Brown, Judith 245
Bu, U Hla 169, 170
Buddhism 11–13, 143, 164, 247, 249–50, 257–60; in Burma 166, 168–70, 172–78
Buddhist cosmopolis 260

Burma 9–11, 163–64, 178–79, 257; and Indian diaspora 165–66; hunger strikes and boycotts 166–72; Indo-Burmese tensions 172–73; discourses in postcolonial Burma 173–74; Aung San Suu Kyi and Gandhi's legacy 174–78
Burmese Days 165
Burmese monks 10–11, 166–67, 169
Burmese nationalists 10, 164, 169
Burmese spinning wheels 171
Burton, Antoinette 249
Butler, Judith 1

Caliphate 251–52
Campaign for Nuclear Disarmament (CND) 150
Carpenter, Edward 32
Carter, April 151
castes 255
celibacy 6, 56–57, 86, 92, 123
Chakravarti, Nalini Ranjan 165, 169
Chamberlain, Joseph 103, 111
Chandra, Sudhir 224
Chandulal, B.D., 66
charkha 233–35, 237
Churchill, Winston 177
civil disobedience 9, 100, 112–13, 141, 144, 150–51; and Gandhi 8, 20, 85, 113, 217, 254; see black civil disobedience
Civil Disobedience Movement 83
civil rights 8, 11, 188, 256
Civil Rights Act of 1964 190
civil rights activists and groups 11, 141, 184, 186–87, 190–92
Cobbe, Frances Power 27–28
colonial medicine 38
colonial South Africa 7, 47, 55, 216, 251, 253
Comfort, Alex 147
Congress of Racial Equality (CORE) 186–88, 190, 194
constructive work 7–8, 84–85, 94
corporeal realm 50
cosmopolitan 2, 4, 29, 166, 207, 209
cosmopolitanism 33, 120; non-european 13, 247; *see* radical cosmopolitanism, vernacular cosmopolitanism
cosmopolitical sensibility 247, 255
cottage industry 225, 228
Craddock, Richard 168
Crossby, Ernest 32

curative practice 39
cyborg economy 27
cyborgs 24

Dalit 13, 130, 245–46, 255–56, 258
Dalpatbhai, Jagabhai 66
Dandi march 91
Darwin, Charles 27, 29–32
Darwinian evolutionism 5, 29, 31
Dayal, Lala Har 256
Dealers' Licenses Act (DLA) 102, 104–5, 109, 111–12
Delhi 163, 174–75
democracy 12, 174, 248, 250, 255, 257; see representative democracy, American democracy, parliamentary democracy
democracy movement 173, 176–77
Derrida, Jacques 5, 32, 41, 52, 56
Desai, Mahadev 84–85, 96
Desai, Narayan 84–85
developmentalism 12; developmental 224, 228, 231
Devji, Faisal Fatehali 252–53
Dewey, John 256
dhamma 258, 260
dhani 123–26
Dhruv, Anandshankar 71–72
diaspora 177, 206, 213–14: see Indian diaspora
diasporic writer 212
dietetic 18, 39–40, 45–46, 51–52, 90
dietetic asceticism 39–40, 45–46
diffusion 10–12, 141–42, 152
Direct Action Committee Against Nuclear War (DAC) 149
Dobama movement 172–73
Doniger, Wendy 49
Du Bois, W.E.B. 185, 187, 258
Dundee 104
Durban 87–88, 100, 104, 107–8, 110–12, 166, 256

East India Company 24
ecology and ecological 31, 223, 233
embodiment 4, 92, 224
Empire 19, 57, 209, 246–52, 255, 258–60; modern American Empire 12; see British Empire, Roman Empire
Escombe, Harry 101
ethical self-cultivation 5, 38, 61
experimental ethical living 46
experimentation 10, 19, 40, 48, 97; with diet 88, 90

Fanon, Frantz 5, 38, 258
Farmer, James 186, 188
fasting 4, 6, 43–46, 66, 69–77, 88, 170–72
fin de siècle vegetarianism 4, 18
fin de siècle zoophilia and animal welfare 19–20, 24, 27–29, 31–33
Fischer, Louis 83, 253
Foucault, Michel 22, 25
Fox, Richard 143
Freud, Sigmund 212
Friends of the Western Buddhist Order (FWBO) 258
friendship 4, 7–8, 42, 86, 89–90, 212, 252

Gandhi as Christ 143
Gandhi Memorial Hall 11, 174, 176, 178
Gandhi Reception Committee 169
Gandhi, Kasturba 48, 50, 89
Gandhi, Maganlal 8, 85–86, 91–97
Gandhi, Manilal 48–50, 92
Gandhi, Manu 123
Gandhi, Ramdas 48
Gandhism 9–10, 141–45, 148–49, 151–52
Garvey, Marcus 185
gastrointestinal disturbances 45
Gates, Bill 223, 230
gender 11–12, 20, 31, 120, 190, 195; and Boyarin 206, 212–15
General Council of Buddhist Associations (GCBA) 167, 170
Germany 207, 251, 254
Ghosh, Amitav 10, 164
Gita Rahasya 165
The Glass Palace 165
global benchmarking 229–30
global democracy 13, 248, 250, 255, 261
global democratization 13
global diffusion 12, 141, 152, 164
global politics 3, 152, 142, 248
globalisation 1–2, 10–11, 141, 152, 247–48
globalise 9–10, 141, 152, 230, 252–53, 260
grand structure of the law 113
Gravers, Michael 171
Great Depression 247
Green, Martin 87–88
Gregg, Richard 148
grief 1, 13, 93
Guha, B.C. 169
Gujarat 69, 95, 124, 167, 249
Gujarati thalassocracy 250, 253

Index

Habib, Haji 67
Haldar, B. K. 170
hand-spinning 171
Haraway, Donna 27, 31
Hardt, Michael 255
Harijan 59, 143, 254
Harijan peoples 185
Hathorn, Kenneth 105
himsa 46, 60
Hind Swaraj 3, 7, 9–10, 68, 78, 90; and medical profession 38–39, 44–45; and *swa* 115, 121, 123, 125–26, 129–31, 133; juxtaposed with Sarker Committee Report 13, 223, 225–28, 230, 232
Hindu *shastric* literature 47
Hindustan 33, 127–30, 132–33
Hitler, Adolf 207
Hlaing, U Chit 167–69, 176
Hobsbawm, Eric 1, 247–48
House of Commons 146, 148
Houtman, Gustaaav 175
humanism 27
humanitarian 41, 43–44, 53–56, 60
Huxley, T.H. 226

IIT Kharagpur 223, 234–35
The Iliad 212
illness 5, 38–40, 43–44, 46, 48–52, 61
imperial masculinity 4, 259
indentured Indian labourer 54
India League of America 187
India Office records 142
Indian diaspora 4, 10, 164–65, 167, 174, 248
Indian Gadar Party 256
Indian Home Rule 113, 116 *see Hind Swaraj*
Indian Institutes of Technology (IITs) 13, 223–24, 226, 228–38
Indian National Congress 167–68, 173, 185, 254
Indian Opinion 59, 87–88, 259
Indian sepoys 165, 177
Indic 40, 43, 45–46
industrial development 225, 227–28
intentional community 83, 88
intimate caring 38, 61
Ipswich pacifists 149

Jain soteriology 43
Japanese invasion 254–55
Jequier, N. 234–35
Jerusalem 12, 205–6, 208–9, 211–16

Jewish identity 12
The Jewish War 12, 205–8, 210, 212–14, 216
Jews 104, 205–8, 210–14, 216–17, 254
Jews and Palestine 208
Johannesburg 47, 67, 90
Johnson, Mordecai 186
Jones, Mervyn 150
Josephus 12, 205–8, 215–17; and Boyarin and gender 212–15; defending Josephus 208–12
justice 9, 68, 72, 76, 84, 251; and Buddha 260; and nonviolence 177; and Polak 87; for animals 21; in medicine 60–61; *see* social justice

Kalelkar, Kaka 93
Kallenbach, Hermann 8, 86, 88–91, 94, 207
Kamauk 11, 171, 174, 176–77
Kaur, Rajkumari Amrit 253
Keer, Dhananjay 245–46, 256
Key to Health 38, 46
khadi 96, 174, 234, 246
kharu sudhaara 116
Kheda 66
Khilafat Movement 251–53
King, Martin Luther, Jr. 2, 11, 179, 184, 186, 193
Kingsford, Anna 28
Kipling, John 26
Krell, David 44, 50
Kreophagy 4, 18, 29
Kropotkin, Peter 31–32
Kumbh Mela 92

Labour Party 145
Lal, Vinay 248–49
Laski, Harold 256
late-Victorian 4, 18, 20, 30, 32–33
late-Victorian radicalism 18
Laughton, Frederick 105–7, 109, 112
Law 1–3, 25–26, 32, 124, 178, 256; and American civil rights 190, 193–94; and animal welfare 21–23, 31–33; and Gandhi 8–9, 100, 112, 113; and Indians in South Africa 8, 43, 57–58, 67–68, 100–109; and Josephus 209, 211; imperial and colonial law 8, 51, 58, 167, 171; Salt Law 233; 'subjects in law' 55–58
lawlessness 1

'law of unconditional hospitality' 5, 41–42, 56, 60
lawyer: Gandhi as 7, 9, 53, 59, 86, 90, 185
legal experience 100
leper incident 5, 41–42, 52–55, 58–59
Levinas, Emmanuel 52, 58
Lewis, Ethel A. 145
life 5–6, 29, 38–39, 43–49, 59–61; sentient life 30–31; life unlimited 5, 38, 48
Light, Henry 28
Lingwood, Denis (Sangharakshita) 257
litigation 100, 103, 107–8, 113, 184
Lively, Walter 192
Lloyd, Susanne and Rudolph 51
Longyi 176
love 6, 13, 59, 71, 77, 89, 96; and animals 27–29, 32; and motherhood 123; and truth 3, 73, 260; of medicine 39, 41–42, 52

machine 227–28, 233, 235–37
Madanjit, Pundit 167
Mahadevbhai D, 70
Maharaj, Somnath 107–9
Maharaj, Tilak 74, 75
Mahatma 12, 18, 83–87, 89–97, 141–44, 245
Mahatma Gandhi Memorial Association 174
Mahatma Satyagraha Movement 170
Malaviya, Madan Mohan 74–75
Malcolm X 184–85, 189, 192
Manchester 229–30
Manusmriti 49–50
Maritzburg 105, 109
Martin, Richard 20–21
Martin, Rudell 183–84
Marxism 257, 260
Masada 12, 206, 212–14, 217
Mason, Justice 106–7, 109
Massachusetts Institute of Technology 229
McCarty, Margaret 193–94
medicine 4–5, 38–48, 50, 55–61, 88, 208
Mehta, P.J. 166–67, 169
Mehta, Uday 252, 258
military junta 173
Mill, James 24
Mill, John Stuart 5, 23–24, 26
Minault, Gail 251
minimalism regarding food 45
mitrata 42
modern liberal discourses 55

modernization 42, 224–25, 227, 231
Moksha 85
Moore, Howard 31
moral jujitsu 148
Mother Rescuers of Poverty 183–85, 191–94
multitude 54, 216, 255
Muzumdar, Haridas T. 187
My Experiments with Truth 18, 84

Nageinda, U 169, 171
Nanda, B.R. 83
Nandy, Ashis 3, 224
Natal 56, 58, 90, 100–108, 110, 112–13
Natal Indian Congress 103, 107, 110
Nation 33, 74–75, 128–29, 215–17; Burmese 175; Indian 84, 166, 225, 246; Jewish 206, 212–13; 'father of the nation' 84, 223, 238
National Association for the Advancement of Colored People (NAACP) 185–86
nation-building/nation-making 4, 12, 175, 223, 227, 230–32, 256–57
nation-state 216–17
Nazi Germany 254
Negri, Antonio 255
Nehru, Jawaharlal 84, 163, 173–74, 187, 223–31, 254–55
Nehruvian 13, 223–25, 230–31
neighbourliness 57, 86
neo-Buddhist dalits 258
Nero 209
New Ager 88
New Jewish Cultural Studies 213
'New Left' 141, 150, 152, 190
Newcastle 105–6
Nine Troubled Years 246
nitishastra 226
non-cooperation 19, 185–86, 188
Non-Cooperation Movement 83
non-European 13, 247, 253, 258
non-governmental sociality 24, 32
non-indigenous 18, 229
nonviolence 9, 12–13, 45, 47–48; and Gandhi 4,100–101, 141, 170, 177, 208, 254; Gandhi as apostle of 4, 163; Gandhi modalities of 9–10, 12, 19, 58, 142, 148, 151–52, 184; and Hindu life-practice 247, 250 *see* ahimsa, thekaana, satyagraha, sarvodaya, Peace Pledge Union
Nonviolence Commission 144
nonviolent dietetics 47

nonviolent protests and activism 8, 11, 144–52, 167, 171, 186–90, 195; *see* Mother Rescuers of Poverty
nursing 5, 8, 38–44, 47–49, 51–61

Operation Gandhi 146–52
Orientalist hyper-difference 10, 143
The Origin of German Tragic Drama 206
The Origin of Species 30
Orwell, George 165
Osman, Dada 110–12
Ottama, U. 11, 167–69, 173, 176, 178
Ottoman Empire 216, 251, 252
over-consumption 44

The Panchtantra 226
Pandit, Lalita 224
panopticon 25
parasite 45
parasitical medical profession 45
Parel, Anthony 115
parliamentary democracy 9, 126
passive aggression 145
Patel, Vallabhbhai 68, 84–85, 95
peace movement and peace activism 2–3, 11, 141, 145, 149–50
peace movements 9, 145
Peace News 143, 146
Peace Pledge Union (PPU) 143
Peace 75–76, 125, 252; and nonviolence 1, 186, 212; *see* Gandhi Memorial Hall, *satyagraha*
peaceful protests 2–3, 8, 67, 141–42, 145–47, 149, 184–86; *see* Black Women's movement, nonviolent protest
Peloponnesian War 206
Perlmutter, Howard 224
Phoenix Settlement 7, 83, 86, 92, 97
Plato 21, 209, 216
Polak, Henry 7–8, 86–89, 94, 144, 207
Pollock, Sheldon 249
postcolonial theory 38
Prakash, Gyan 224
Prince of Wales 167
The Problem of the Rupee 256
public housing 11, 192
Pultney, William 23
Pyarelal 93
Pythagoras 209

quack 5, 38–39, 43, 47–48, 51
quackery 5, 39–40, 42–44, 46–47, 49–51, 58–61
the Quarantine Act 101–2, 104

radical cosmopolitanism 4, 19, 31
Rai, Lala Lajpat 187, 256
Rajak, Tessa 206, 216
Ramrajya 84
Randolph, A. Phillip 186
Rangoon 10–11, 164–73, 178, 257
Rawlins, Kathleen 144–48
Raychand 8
Reclus, Elisee 32
relationality 3, 5–7, 20, 25–27, 30–32, 259
representative democracy 118, 120–22, 124, 257
Richardson, Gloria 190
Ripon, Lord 103
Roman Empire 12, 206, 209, 212–16
Roth, Cecil 208, 252
Round Table conference 246
Rowlatt Bills 51
RSPCA 22
Rushdian 13
Rushdie, Ahmed Salman 13
Ruskin, John 8, 83, 86–88, 259
Russell, Bertrand 226
Rustin, Bayard 11, 186, 188, 190

Sabarmati 7–8, 71, 83, 91–97
Sabarmati Ashram 71, 84, 91, 93, 96
Salt March in 1930 91, 172, 174, 185, 187
Salt, Henry 4, 17–19, 27, 31, 33
samabhava 44
Samaj, Arya 187
San, Aung 163, 173–74, 178–79
Sankaing, Han Tin 171
the Sanskrit Cosmopolis 249
Sarabhai, Ambalal 66, 69, 71, 72
Sarabhai, Anasuyaben 66, 68
Sarker Committee Report 13, 223–28, 230–31, 233
sarvodaya 1, 85, 97, 259
satyagraha 1, 118, 125, 130; formation of 56–58, 68–69, 92; and Gandhi 10, 42, 51–52, 84–86, 90, 254, 259; and Burma 164, 166–68, 174–75, 178; Gandhian *satyagraha* 4, 186–87
Saunders, Resident Magistrate 105
Schlesin, Sonya 207
Schumacher, E.F. 232, 236
Scott King, Coretta 186, 191–92
Second Anglo-Burmese War of 1852 165
secular 43, 169, 213, 227, 257; secular leaders 11, 167, 251

segregationist 149, 186, 188
self-abnegation 6
Seligman, Edwin 256
Sethi, J.D. 227, 236
seva 54, 61
Sevagram 54, 83, 91, 94, 97, 207
Shabha, Maha 169
Shastri, Parchure 43, 52, 54
Shwedagon 164, 166, 169, 172, 174–75
Silicon Valley 230
Singh, J.J. 187
Skaria, Ajay 9–10, 42, 57, 115
Skidmore, Monique 178
social justice 178, 184, 186
socialist 5, 24, 29, 150, 173, 247
socialist-anarchist 20
soul-depressing orality 45
South Africa 8, 52–53, 56, 96–97, 149; and rural farms 7, 52; Gandhi as a lawyer in 8, 53, 59, 92, 100–101; Indians in 57–58, 83, 89, 102, 185, 254; *see* colonial South Africa, Zulu Rebellion, Phoenix Settlement, Natal Colony
South African legal system 8–9, 43
South African society 42, 48, 55, 57–59, 87, 89
Sparsha 236
spinning wheel 170–71, 174, 233
spiritual 77, 85–86, 163: and Ambedkar 257, 258; and Aung San Suu Kyi and Burma 164, 169, 172, 175–79; and relationships 7–8, 90, 94; and the body 6, 45; and Tilak Maharaj's imprisonment 74–75; and technology 224, 230; and Tolstoy Farm 88–89, 91, 97
spiritual suffering 75–77
Steele, Harold 149
Stokes, Eric 24
subaltern 42, 52, 54, 58, 118, 165
subaltern responsibility 127, 129–31, 133–34
'a subject in law' 55
submerged network 145
suffering 30, 54, 68, 70, 113, 148; and the body 5–6, 40, 43, 47, 50–51, 55–61; see spiritual suffering
Suu Kyi, Aung San 163–64, 168, 171, 173–79
swa 9, 116–21, 125, 127, 129–34
swadeshi 11, 86, 116, 168, 170–72, 174, 177
swaraj 11, 52, 77, 91, 166–70, 251; in *Hind Swaraj* 9, 115–20, 130
'the systems of the mouth' 44, 46

Tagore, Ribindranath 164, 175–76, 224
Taylor, Daniel 108, 110, 112
Taylor, Thomas 21
Templewood, Viscount 246
Terrell, Mary Church 185
Thakin 167–68, 171, 173
Thant, U 174
thekaana 119–27, 129–34
therapeutics 38–40, 48–51, 59, 61
Thompson, David 248
Thormann, P. 232
Thucydides 206, 208, 216
Thurman, Howard 186, 188
Tilak, Lokmanya Bal Gandadhar 165, 170, 173, 175
Tobias, Channing 186
Tolstoy Farm 7–8, 83, 88–91, 97
Tolstoy, Leo 8, 29, 32, 87–88, 259
Torah 215
translation 141–45, 258–60; of *Hind Swaraj* 7, 9–10, 12, 90–91, 115, 119–29
transnational 4, 18, 141
Transvaal 67, 90, 101, 104, 113
Treaty of Versailles 251
Trist, Eric 224
Tulsidas, Gosvāmī 77

UN Conference on Racism in Durban, 2001 256
Unto This Last 87
Untouchables 185, 187, 207, 246, 256–57
utilitarian philosophy 21, 23
utilitarianism 5, 20–24, 26

vaids 5, 49
Vaishnava 69
Vanda v. Newcastle 106
veda 47
The Vegetarian 18–19
vegetarianism 4–5, 8, 17–20, 29, 32, 86–90, 259; and medicine 45, 47, 49–50
vernacular 1, 224, 245, 250, 257–60
vernacular cosmopolitanism 245, 250, 258–59
veshya 9, 115, 117, 121–27, 133, 134
village economy 228
violence 13, 130, 151, 117–19, 122, 131–32; and animals 20, 28; and Burma 168, 172, 175, 179; and Gandhi 40, 101, 115, 208, 215, 217, 259; and racial exclusion in the United States 189, 190–92; and rebellion of 66 12, 206, 211, 213, 215; and *thekaana* 124,

126, 129; and *veshya* 133–34; of consumption 44–48;
Vision 2020 231
Vissara, U 168, 171–72, 176, 178
volunteer ambulance work 42, 56, 60
Vossara, U 168
Voting Rights Act of 1965 190

Walker, Derek 150–51
war 1–2; and colonialism 27, 56; and Gandhi 13, 41–42, 58, 60, 149; and medicine 58–61; second Anglo-Burmese War 165; *see* Boer War, Josephus, War Office, World War One, World War Two, Zulu Rebellion
War Office 148–49
Wardha 7–8, 83, 91, 94–97
Washington, Booker T. 256
We Burma Association (*Do-bama Asaiyone*) 171
weavers 171
welfare rights activism 11, 183–84, 187–95
Wells, Ida B. 189
Wendt, Simon 189

Western over-likeness 10, 143
Whyte, Frederick 167
Wiley, George 187, 194
Win, Ne 174–75
Windham, William 23
Woolf, Brigadier 228
World Buddhist Conference 257, 260
World War One 166, 251, 255
World War Two 143–45, 186, 207, 225, 229, 247–49, 253–54
world-historical 246
wunthanu era 168

xenophilia 18, 31

yarn 171
Young India 177, 252
Young Men's Buddhist Association 166

Zimmerman, Francis 47
Zionism and Anti-Semitism 207–8
Zionist movement and Zionism 12, 206–8, 212–15, 217, 252
zoophilia 4, 18–19, 27–29, 31, 33
Zulu Rebellion 5, 41–42, 52, 56–61

eBooks – at www.eBookstore.tandf.co.uk

A library at your fingertips!

eBooks are electronic versions of printed books. You can store them on your PC/laptop or browse them online.

They have advantages for anyone needing rapid access to a wide variety of published, copyright information.

eBooks can help your research by enabling you to bookmark chapters, annotate text and use instant searches to find specific words or phrases. Several eBook files would fit on even a small laptop or PDA.

NEW: Save money by eSubscribing: cheap, online access to any eBook for as long as you need it.

Annual subscription packages

We now offer special low-cost bulk subscriptions to packages of eBooks in certain subject areas. These are available to libraries or to individuals.

For more information please contact webmaster.ebooks@tandf.co.uk

We're continually developing the eBook concept, so keep up to date by visiting the website.

www.eBookstore.tandf.co.uk